THE PSYCHOANALYTIC STUDY
OF SOCIETY

Volume 10

THE PSYCHOANALYTIC STUDY
OF SOCIETY

Volume 10

Edited by

WERNER MUENSTERBERGER
L. BRYCE BOYER
SIMON A. GROLNICK

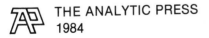 THE ANALYTIC PRESS
1984

Distributed by
LAWRENCE ERLBAUM ASSOCIATES, PUBLISHERS
Hillsdale, New Jersey   London

The Analytic Press

Distributed solely by

Lawrence Erlbaum Associates, Inc., Publishers
365 Broadway
Hillsdale, New Jersey 07642

Library of Congress Catalog Card Number: 61-486
ISBN: 0-88163-004-7

Printed in the United States of America
10   9   8   7   6   5   4   3   2   1

Editors

Contributors

Karl Beckson, Ph.D. Professor of English, Brooklyn College, CUNY; Lecturer of English in Psychiatry, Cornell University Medical College.

Daniel P. Brown, Ph.D. Associate Director of Psychology and Director of Hypnotherapy Service and Training, The Cambridge Hospital, Cambridge, MA; Clinical Instructor, Harvard Medical School.

Laurie Adams, Ph.D. Professor of Art History, John Jay College, CUNY; Member, New York Society for Psychoanalytic Training.

Stanley J. Coen, M.D. Faculty, Columbia University Psychoanalytic Center; Associate Clinical Professor of Psychiatry, Columbia University, College of Physicians and Surgeons.

Charles Ducey, Ph.D. Director of Psychological Training, Department of Psychiatry, The Cambridge Hospital, Harvard Medical School, Cambridge, MA.

Jack Engler, Ph.D. Clinical Fellow in Psychology, Department of Psychiatry, Harvard Medical School at the McLean Hospital, Belmont, MA

Stuart Feder, M.D. Faculty, The New York Psychoanalytic Institute.

Arthur E. Hippler, Ph.D. Associate Professor of Anthropology, University of Alaska, Anchorage.

W. W. Meissner, S. J., M.D. Associate Clinical Professor of Psychiatry, Harvard Medical School.

Paul Parin, M.D. Zurich, Switzerland.

Gilbert Rose, M.D., Lecturer in Psychiatry, Yale University Medical School; Member of the Editorial Board, *International Forum for Psychoanalysis.*

Edwin R. Wallace, IV, M.D. Associate Professor of Psychiatry and Director of Psychotherapy Education, Medical College of Georgia, Augusta, GA; Member, Editorial Board of *Bulletin of the History of Medicine.*

Contents

PART I

ANTHROPOLOGY

1

A Case of "Brain-Fag" Syndrome: Psychotherapy of the Patient Adou A. in the Village of Yosso, Ivory Coast Republic

PAUL PARIN

Translated by Patricia Klamerth

During the course of our ethnopsychoanalytical field research among the Anyi of the Ivory Coast Republic, a young man named Adou A. made an appointment to talk with me. My interviews with him, begun in the interests of our study, developed into effective, psychoanalytically oriented psychotherapy. The case report has been published in German (Parin, Morgenthaler, Parin-Matthèy, 1971), but was not included in the American edition of our book (id., 1980).

The disturbances from which Adou A. suffered are typical of many students of high-school and college age in West Africa and frequently compel their victims to give up their studies entirely. The course of psychotherapy sheds light on the genesis and the internal dynamics of the disturbances involved against the background of the culture-specific psychical development of a young man living in an Anyi coffee-growing village located in the rain forest belt of the eastern Ivory Coast. Insofar as possible, the method and the technique of resistance analysis followed the pattern established in Freudian psychoanalysis. No remuneration was requested or offered. The interviews were conducted in French and took place in an open-air tent, furnished with a table, two chairs, and a cot, which I had set up in the shade of a tree on the outskirts of the village of Yosso (approximately 300 inhabitants).

PRELIMINARY INTERVIEW (1 FEBRUARY 1966)

In a courtyard in Yosso a young man in European dress advances to greet me. He is the grand-nephew of Madame Akouassi, whom I regularly supply with medicines, and whom he addresses as "maman" (mother).

With great politeness he delivers his "first news," explaining that he has come from Abidjan with the village chief of Yosso, Monsieur N., to work for him, and that he will be going out into the rain forest with the foreman, whose job it is to mark the trees to be felled for their precious wood.

He also tells me that he is sick. He has lost his memory and thus has had to abandon his studies. He informs me that two psychiatrists (Dr. Abeh in Bingerville and Dr. Duplessis in Abidjan) had examined him thoroughly because of his complaint—his head, his eyes, blood tests, and EEG—and had found nothing organically wrong. Nevertheless, he insists, there *is* something the matter with him. His mind no longer functions properly, and he is bothered by an itching under the skin (he shows me the inner side of his lower arm).

When I suggest that he come to my medical consultation hour, he replies that today he has to go out into the rain forest, but that he will come without fail tomorrow at nine o'clock.

(Much later, in one of our therapy interviews, Adou asks me what this treatment is called. At my reply, "psychoanalysis," he recalls that one of the two psychiatrists had mentioned that he might be cured by this method, but that there was no one in the Ivory Coast Republic who was able to apply it. He adds: "It's a good thing that I have finally found someone here in Yosso.")

FIRST INTERVIEW (2 FEBRUARY 1966)

I arrive in the village at eight o'clock and, with the help of some children, unlace the tent. Then I go down to the road where I meet Adou.

Adou chats with me on our way to the tent, and as soon as he is seated opposite me, he continues the conversation. We are "two intellectuals in a Negro village"; on this basis he is able to identify with me. At the beginning of the hour we are disturbed several times by villagers who want me to treat them. I greet them briefly and ask Adou to interpret for me and explain to them that I will examine them later. Soon he begins to do this independently, calling out to them before they reach the tent and telling them to go back to the village and make appointments with my "assistant" (our interpreter, François) to be examined.

Later on he often comes back to this identificatory response, remarking about how dreadful it is that the people here in the village have no medical care and how sorry he is for them. Things were better in the village in which he grew up; there, at least, they had a medical orderly, and the hospital in Abengourou was only twenty kilometers away. In Yosso, though, when a child gets sick, it simply dies. And this, he feels, is very wrong.

It becomes clear to me later that Adou himself feels like a child who has no one to take care of him and who might simply die. His self-pity is expressed in various forms, such as when he wonders just how I happened to come to Yosso, and pretends to himself that I am being paid by the government as a doctor to help the people here. Actually, the village means little to him; he is not one of its inhabitants. He is a stranger here. And despite the fact that he is in the process of consulting me, this means that I am only here for the villagers and have no intention of helping *him*.

Without any prompting on my part, Adou describes his illness. He has two groups of symptoms which are closely related, one group in his head, and the other in his body. When he speaks of the latter group, he usually points vaguely to the inner side of his arm or occasionally to his chest.

Adou feels a pain in his head, between his spine and the back of his head, and this pain is constant, except when he is asleep. This is the consequence, or perhaps an accompanying phenomenon, or perhaps the reason for his inability to remember anything. Prior to his illness he had only to listen attentively in class and he would remember what the teacher had said. He was good in examinations and was always able to repeat what he had learned, not always by heart, but at least the sense. He had only to read a thing through once to be able to remember it. But since his illness began, he has found it impossible to remember anything, no matter how hard he tries, even when he goes over the lesson several times. And it's not only his lessons—he can't remember "anything at all." He forgets everything people tell him to do, everything he sees, reads, or hears. His head is very sick.

The second group of symptoms, the physical ones, are either the cause of his forgetfulness, or are the result of it, or are connected with it. He can feel something moving around in his body, worms underneath his skin; they leave him no peace, he is already weak and has lost weight, as anyone can see. People can tell from his face, especially from his eyes, that he is sick. (Adou is powerfully built and is obviously well-nourished. His eyes and face are perfectly normal; his expression is somewhat depressive.)

Adou describes his ailment as suddenly appearing "two years ago" when he was attending school in Bassam, and as a result of it was forced to repeat the same class twice without passing. Since that time the ailment has continued unabated, with no sign of remission, let alone improvement. Later on we shall have to reassess and correct all this information.

Adou describes his symptoms in somewhat the same fashion that gravely depressed European patients usually speak of their ailments, though it must be admitted that his mood is far less depressive. Sometimes he seems fearful, like a typical hypochondriac, sometimes resigned and hopeless; sometimes he bemoans his fate and blames others for it; and sometimes—when he speaks of the worms in his body—one has the impression that he is the victim of physical hallucinations. All in all, his laments are more resigned, more stereotyped, more matter-of-fact, and less demonstrative than those of hysterical European patients.

So far, Adou has been speaking spontaneously, interrupted only by occasional questions from me. Now he begins to repeat himself, telling me again about the two psychiatrists who had examined him and giving me to understand that they had deliberately withheld the proper medicine. Once again he intimates that there is no one who is willing to help him.

When I make no reply to this, he repeats the account of his illness, especially his inability to remember things. At this point I venture my first interpretation, explaining to him that he has experienced some very bad things and that this is why his head refuses to remember anything. At first he accepts my interpretation; he laughs, but then comes right back to the stereotype account of his symptoms.

I interrupt him after a moment and explain to him the basic rules of psychoanalysis, emphasizing that he must talk with me for one hour every day and tell me whatever comes to his mind.[1] I point out that this is the only proper treatment for his illness. He would lie on the cot, completely relaxed, I would sit behind him, and he would tell me his thoughts, just as they came to him. Again, to begin with he is delighted and agrees. But then an objection occurs to him, and he informs me that he will be in Yosso only until Friday. I reply that we can't possibly get very far by Friday, that treatment of this kind requires much longer. Hereupon he says that he could come back to the village after his trip and continue the treatment. He adds: "It would be better, though, if you would give me some medicine. That would be quicker and simpler." My response to his request for medicine is to assure him that I will tell no one anything about what we discuss together and that this discretion is necessary so that he can tell me everything. I promise him that I will always interrupt our conversation if we should be disturbed by visitors.

This confirmation of my willingness to concern myself with him and to keep his secret has an immediate and extraordinary effect. It appears—not only at this moment, but also during the later course of treatment—that Adou is capable of accepting friendly interest in exchange for the "object withheld," but that his feeling that he is somehow being taken advantage of is not so easy to dispel.

---

1. To choose interviews of one hour a day, as with European patients, may or may not be appropriate to other cultural settings. All three members of our team felt this suited our Anyi partner. I would not advise maintaining this setting in other cultures if it seems to provoke resistance or acting out.

Adou starts to relate the story of his life, beginning with the period of poverty and loneliness in Bassam and going on to his childhood, then the later years, with their setbacks and disappointments. The episodes he narrates are not chronologically ordered, but related in keeping with the contrast between the time before his illness—when everything was good—and the period after his illness began—when everything became bad. This turn for the worse is now attributed to the evil machinations of his teachers or of Monsieur N., who favor others over him or withdraw their patronage for selfish reasons and discriminate against him, and now to his poor physical condition. It is significant that Adou's complaints of pains in his head and of his weakened body with its peculiar internal upheavals appear consistently when he is forced to recall sad, lonely periods of his life. His accounts of occasions on which he played a more energetic role, presumably during periods when he did not feel so alone, generally end in a repetition of his suspicions of evil-intentioned persons, suspicions that I would immediately regard as paranoid distortions of memory if they occurred in a European.

The most important events in Adou's life are outlined chronologically below. He contradicted himself several times in his account of his most recent years. His conscious belief that his sickness began while he was attending school in Bassam and that it resulted in the unfortunate dependence on his uncle, Monsieur N., which began immediately thereafter, could not be substantiated. The onset of this illness is the only significant episode in his life which—later on during the course of treatment—I shall have to place at a different point of time. Though all his other memories were subsequently embroidered in great detail, it was possible to confirm them during treatment.

Adou has no idea how old he is—and in this he resembles most Anyi who were born in a village. He gives his age as 19 or 20. The reconstruction of his life story makes it seem more likely that he was about 23 at the time he came to me for treatment.

He was born and raised in a village located some twenty kilometers from Abengourou along the road leading to Agnibilekrou. He is his mother's only child. He reports that from early childhood he was always alone; not only did he have no brothers and sisters, but he was also without playmates. His parents are planters. He makes no mention of whether his mother or father ever had other marriage partners, either before or after his birth. He describes them as simple people who were never very successful in life because neither had important relations of any kind who might have helped them along. They worked their plantations separately, but together they managed to save enough money to be able to send their son (then about 9 or 10 years of age) to a foster father in Agnibilekrou so that he could attend school there. Adou proved to be such an apt pupil that he was able to pass the examination admitting him to a secondary school ("collège"). He tells me nothing about this foster father, but does mention that he had no friends or playmates during that period and was often alone.

After passing his examinations, he enrolled in the secondary school in Bassam. There he did not live with a foster family, but rented a room of his own, bought food at the market, and cooked for himself. His father had given him 2000 or 3000 francs*. When his money ran out, he wrote to his father. He often had to go hungry because it took such a long time for his parents to send him money. During the school vacations he was unable to return home (as he had been able to do when he was still in Agnibilekrou).

Apparently he was unable to make any friends in Bassam. He was different from the other young people, he explains, and his clothes were different. When he sees that I do not understand what he means, he says: "Just look, my shirt is all ragged." (And in fact Adou does have on a brightly-colored, extremely tattered shirt of European cut with a pair of blue jeans that are rather the worse for wear.) He complains that his schoolmates, like the people here in Yosso, were unable to understand why he wore a ragged shirt. But he didn't want any other shirt, and in fact he didn't have any others; he was what he was—different from the others.

Apparently Adou was one of the poorest pupils in Bassam and—either at the time or later—had made a virtue out of necessity. He deliberately dissociated himself from his school fellows and voluntarily renounced the prestige that better clothing would have conferred (this presumably made it possible for him to avoid having to reproach his parents, who were unable to do any better for him). On the other hand, Adou developed the fantasy (or formed the opinion) that the teachers in Bassam had been bribed by the parents of other pupils, who were richer than his own parents, to have him removed from school in order to give his place to a wealthier boy. In his mind this unjust discrimination goes hand in hand with the other reason, namely that his sickness prevented him from learning his lessons properly.

Adou's later attempts to complete his secondary education were apparently interrupted by intervals lasting months, or even years, during which he lived in the household of his "uncle," Monsieur N., in Abidjan. His first attempt took him to the vocational high school, which he attended only a few months; later he enrolled in the Naval School in Grand Bassam, where he stayed for nine months. According to one ver-

---

*In 1966 1000 CFA francs was equivalent to U.S. $4.50.

sion, he did well in this school and passed his examinations at the end of the trial period, but then was dismissed for the same reason as in Bassam; the instructors, all of them whites, were corrupt and sent him away so that they could give his place to a child of wealthy parents. According to a second version, he enjoyed the months at the Naval School, where he did well and never contradicted his teachers, but—again for the reasons already mentioned—failed to graduate. In still a third version, he speaks of his illness—it was the Naval School that referred him to the two psychiatrists—as the reason why he had to give up his studies there.

He tells me that if he could have followed his own inclinations, he would have become a mechanic or a medical orderly. Even now, he says, he could enroll in a two-year course for medical personnel, but he does not intend to do so because he would be handicapped by his illness and only fail again. He would like to have a real profession and earn money so that he could send something to his parents.

Adou's accounts of his various failures create the impression that, presumably for years, he has been so lonely and so depressively inclined that he is no longer capable of studying with any prospect of success. He does not blame his parents for this, but rather his illness, his teachers, and the doctors. This is a conspicuous deviation from the norm, because other Anyi who have failed in school in similar fashion invariably tend to blame their parents; also because we have regularly observed that in other Anyi young people the active renunciation of attractive clothing and of association with comrades is never a permanent character attitude, but at most a temporary form of behavior that can be traced back to an acute affront. In Adou's case (he is capable of actively renouncing things which he passively wishes to obtain), the fact that he seems less depressive than many other Yosso or Bébou young people who are better off than he is may be connected with this achievement of his ego.

For some time now, probably even prior to his attendance at the Naval School, Adou has been living in the household of Monsieur N., for whom he voluntarily performs odd jobs without payment. Adou has frequently accompanied him on business trips as his interpreter, for Monsieur N. has never learned more than a few words of Adou's language. Monsieur N.'s obligations towards his assistant are just as vaguely defined as Adou's tasks. When Monsieur N. needs him, he has him summoned and issues his orders. Adou receives no salary and demands nothing of him, though he does expect Monsieur N.'s mother to look after his needs, at least to see that he is given his meals.

Even in the simplest assignments, says Adou, who has now come to the end of his life story, his forgetfulness is such a handicap that he is not good for anything. He relates that Monsieur N. sent him twice from Abidjan to some village (to Yosso perhaps?) to collect a few cans of paint. Each time Adou made the trip for nothing because on both occasions he had forgotten his purpose.

Here I present my second interpretation: this kind of forgetfulness is a sign that Adou has something against his employer. Perhaps he does not want to do anything for Monsieur N. because Monsieur N. does not provide for him properly. At first Adou laughs and admits that this is quite possible, but then he adds that it's not exactly the same thing as when one goes into a shop for something and then cannot remember what it was. His mind is simply unable to retain anything at all, it goes completely blank, and there are animals underneath his skin—he looks worriedly at his forearms, as if he expected to see them there—and he can feel the animals all through his body.

My interpretation was evidently premature. I declare today's interview at an end, while Adou, still thinking of his bodily sensations, begins to speak admiringly of how, by treating its inhabitants, I am contributing to the health of Yosso.

The course of this interview was similar to what one can experience with rather lonely, timorous, youthful patients in Europe. Adou's mood fluctuated between a childlike expectation (occasionally developing into a depressive wish fantasy), that the doctor finally was going to find out what was wrong with him and would help him, and a disappointing conviction that nothing could be done for him, that all was hopeless. Sometimes his trouble is other people (his teachers and instructors), and sometimes the sensations he feels in his body. His suspicions are directed only briefly and very vaguely towards me and—consciously at any rate—not at all towards his parents or Monsieur N. Although his attitude towards his illness has paranoid overtones, and although the description of his symptoms is more consistent with a grave disturbance of his body feeling than with hysterical disturbances, he does not go so far as to assert that his mind has been bewitched. His loneliness, his poverty, and his lack of contact with his fellows seem to bother him very little; he sees nothing abnormal or pathological in these conditions, but rather accepts them as a part of his personality.

Adou speaks excellent French. During our talks his emotional involvement is good. What he has to say is expressed much more coherently and clearly than is the case with other Anyi young people. Nevertheless, a good deal of his life story remains obscure, incomprehensible.

At this point, it should be emphasized that during psychoanalytical exploration we deliberately accept the disadvantage of certain gaps so as to not disrupt with our questions the order of narration selected by the patient. For example, throughout the entire course of treatment we learned nothing about the relationship between Adou and the foster-father in Agnibilekrou with whom he lived during the five or six years of his schooling there and in whose home, as we discovered later, the first symptoms of the boy's illness appeared. On the other hand, by the time the treatment was nearing its end, it had become clear to us that while Adou accepts orders from some authority figures (such as Monsieur N.) without resistance, an over emphasis of his submissive role hems him in and makes him ill. He has no expectations of positive wish fulfillment (care, attention, affection) from such figures. When he is confronted with failure, he feels more persecuted by others than disappointed in himself. There are other authority figures to whom he submits, his parents for example; in this case there *are* wishes involved, some of which he fulfills by means of identification. Conversely, he feels the wish to care for them. Disappointments and other conflicts are warded off primarily through identification. Finally, there is a third type of authority figure from whom Adou expects a great deal. As long as he is able to identify with these authorities, his mood is slightly manic. Originally, these figures were gratifying, good objects, capable of being projected in any direction, as required. These are figures one strives to emulate, not figures to whom one must submit. When they emerge from Adou's fantasy into his real environment, they, too, are often disappointing. Such persons probably partake of the idealized parent images of early childhood. Disappointment in them leads either to a feeling of sadness, to the oral wish to be given something, or as is the case with the first group of figures—to paranoid anxiety.

Second Interview (3 February 1966)

When I arrive in Madame Akouassi's courtyard to bring her the promised medicine and to pick up Adou, I find him rocking an infant in his arms. Three small children are dancing around him in delight and playing with him. Madame Akouassi's is standing nearby, watching the scene. Politely, Adou places the infant in his aunt's arms.

On our way to the tent, Adou tells me that he gets along best with children "until they are so big" (he indicates the height of a 10- to 12-year old child). "Children of this age like me and I like them; but when they get old enough that they could be my friends, something always goes wrong." During the session that follows, he interrupts his account of his unhappy fate with a repetition of his remark about how well he understands small children. This leads me to assume that up to that age he enjoyed a happy childhood. It was only after he left his parents and after the onset of puberty that things began to go wrong for him.

Spontaneously, Adou begins to tell me about an affair that had the whole village holding its breath yesterday. A young man, a stranger from Korhogo, had made use of a sly subterfuge to sneak into the bed of a married woman. The woman's husband heard of what was going on, returned home unexpectedly with some of his friends, and caught the adulterer in flagranti. They gave him a good thrashing and he had to flee to the forest. Adou finds the whole business amusing; he is quite clearly on the side of the husband and morality.

Despite the relaxed, matter-of-fact fashion in which he relates this story, it contains the most important theme of our second session, a matter which is apparently a serious personal problem for Adou himself. He cannot permit himself to be like that young man who wants to sleep with a married woman, the mother; by avoiding aggressive rivalry, by submitting, and by renouncing his own wishes, he stands safely on the side of morality, but is as helpless as a child when it comes to coping with his life.

He continues, assuring me that he does without attractive clothing and thus renounces the society of companions; he is content when he has enough to eat and drink. The only reason he wants to earn money is to be able to build his parents a better house. When I suggest that his renunciation also gives him a feeling of greater independence, he does not understand what I mean. Getting along without attractive clothes, companions of his own age, and girls does not seem to be easy for him, nor can he conceive of wanting to be more independent. All he needs is good health —and he begins once more, as in our first interview, to enumerate his symptoms, asking: "Isn't there some medicine to cure this itching under my skin? Can't they operate on my head?"

These hypochondriacal, imploring pleas are in striking contrast to the energetic and ruthless manner in which Adou chases away village patients who come to consult me during "his" hour.

I explain to him that if he is so ill, he is neither able, nor expected, to assume responsibility for his own life, that it is up to others to care for him as if he were a child, but that these others, myself included, would disappoint him, too, just as he had been disappointed as a child. But all this has no effect on his stereotyped laments, and he goes on to describe a terrible cough from which he suffers. I point out that I have a white colleague in Bébou who also coughs the whole night. Since Adou identifies with me in keeping our interview sessions free of outside interruptions, I expect him to identify as well with my attitude towards illness.

My remark fulfills at least half its intended purpose. He continues to speak of the "misfortunes" that befall him continually, but there is hardly any further mention of his physical ills and none at all of his cough. I interpret for him, saying that all these misfortunes caused by other people—his parents' poverty, the fact that he was unable to find work in Abidjan, that his teachers discriminated against him in school, that Monsieur N. never pays him for his work, that the young men in Yosso never talk to him but spend their time running after girls—simply mean that there is no point in his even trying to better his lot, since it is always the others who are to blame for his difficulties.

This interpretation elicits an unexpected response. Adou sits up, suddenly pulls off his shirt, kneels beside my chair, and leans over backwards across my knees, so that I am confronted with his bare chest. He places his hand over a thickened cheloidal scar about six centimeters long over the sternum, then seizes my hand and guides it to the scare so that I can feel it. I remain silent. Adou straightens up slowly. "It would be good," he says, "if that scar could be operated on. It's too bad it's not a tropical ulcer, because then a shot of penicillin in the buttocks would cure it. I've shown it to doctors and orderlies several times, but they all say there's nothing they can do. I always do just what they tell me to, buy all the medicines, but I'm still sick. I can't learn anything and that's why I can't go back to school."

Obviously my exhortation to him to be more active has enhanced the transference of passive-homosexual desires, by means of which he hopes to ward off the danger (castration anxiety) inherent in a phallic-competitive attitude. The acting out I have described came impulsively, suddenly; the cheloidal scar had never figured previously in his complaints. I merely assure him that he is a fine fellow, that the scar won't kill him, and that he doesn't need an operation.

Adou resumes his position on the cot. He has overcome his anxiety; I have neither assaulted him sexually nor operated on him. He has become "a fine fellow" and is busy identifying with what I expect of him as such. Admittedly, the term has a meaning for him that is specific to himself and to his milieu. He criticizes the young people of Yosso. They are lazy, he asserts, and have no respect for their elders. When their fathers reprove them, they answer back and call them assholes ("con"), and if the fathers try to beat them, they strike back. They are good for nothing and will never succeed in life. On the other hand, he reveres his parents and has always obeyed them; it is only that they are poor. This is not his father's fault, for he had no uncle. This is one of the disadvantages of the matrilineal inheritance laws, and it is these laws, the system, and fate in general that he criticizes, not his father.

Now that his castration anxiety has been overcome, for the moment anyway, and he has been able to identify with me—in order to ward off a passive-homosexual impulse, he is in a position to adopt independently the "normal" behavior pattern of the Anyi, to submit to authority and to criticize intelligently.

On the other hand, his passive dependency (or its pathological component) has not been overcome by any means.[2] He realizes that he finally
ought to learn some trade, or at least complete his treatment with me, but
Monsieur N. would never permit him to take up an occupation—out of
pure selfishness, so that he can continue to exploit his nephew—and he
will surely send him away from Yosso, and that will be the end of the
treatment. Today, to be sure, Adou no longer speaks of his employer in
such glowing terms as yesterday.

I am tempted to give Adou a letter for Monsieur N., asking him to let
his nephew stay in Yosso for a while; this (i.e. the counter-transference it
reflects) makes it clear to me just how intensely my patient is appealing to
me. On the other hand there would be nothing gained if my interference
only served to subject Adou to my authority rather than to that of his
uncle. I would simply be helping him to transfer to me the dependency
strivings that make him so helpless and unsure of himself.

In the absence of any reaction to his fears on my part, Adou resumes
his tirade against the young people of Yosso. "Not one of them is willing
to talk with you. I'll be back tomorrow at eight o'clock." With these
words, he himself for the first time takes the initiative in arranging for
continuation of the treatment.

The course of the second interview suggests that the patient's complaints, though still hypochondriacal and anxious, are hysterical rather
than depressive-psychotic. The fear of adopting an active, masculine-
competitive attitude seems to correspond to castration anxiety, which is
warded off partly by a turning to (anal) passivity and homosexual object
choice (in keeping with the negative outcome of the oedipal conflict), and
partly by conversion. The peculiar overtones coloring his physical complaints as well as their paranoiac character (less pronounced today) suggest that Adou's anxiety has its origin in pre-oedipal fears. Occasionally
he is able to overcome both his passivity and his anxiety through identification. It seems clear that his childlike attitude towards me and

---

2. The culture-specific passive dependent attitude of the male Anyi is further discussed
    subsequently.
        I am convinced that the best, or even the only, way to further the art of psychoanaly-
    tically oriented interviews with people of non-western cultures (as well as with lower
    class Euopeans) is to make early interpretations of resistance. This way the deepening
    transference prevents interruption of the sessions with partners who have no (e.g.
    "research-patients") or little motivation to continue (as Adou). Of course in this sec-
    ond session I could not be sure how much of Adou's passive dependency was culture-
    specific and how much was not. At least I knew that when the scar was exposed his
    acting out was intense as was my feeling that I should help him against his uncle. To
    interpret attitudes which are culture-specific does no harm at all, no more than inter-
    pretation of normal behavior in our culture. Rather, it facilitates subsequent steps
    aiming to distinguish idiosyncratic from ordinary traits.

towards his parents, even though it, too, is passive-dependent and masochistic in character, cannot be regarded as truly pathological, primarily because it is accompanied by better ego performance, a reasonable way of looking at things, and a keen intelligence. Adou's comments on the deplorable social and hygienic conditions in Yosso, on his parents, and on the consequences of the (now superseded) traditional law of inheritance through the maternal lineage are alert, well organized, and reflect intelligent interest on his part. When he is confronted with his illness, his unhappy situation, and especially with the problem of whether or not Monsieur N. may make it impossible for him to continue his treatment, he is as helpless as a toddler; even his use of language becomes childlish and faltering.

THIRD INTERVIEW (4 FEBRUARY 1966)

Adou: "There is a certain sickness here, which makes children have fits, once a week or once a month. They act as if they were crazy, but not quite. They're not crazy and they're not normal; they just do whatever they please." (A little boy of about ten, who looks erethistic and somewhat feeble-minded, refuses to be chased away like the other children; he remains standing about ten meters away from the tent, sometimes pulling faces and sometimes smiling slyly.)

Adou: (continuing) "These children can't be brought to their senses. It's all the same whether you say something nice to them or threaten them . . . They don't act like normal children. They refuse to obey. They have to be spanked, to feel it on their own skins, then they'll obey. By the next time they've forgotten everything and refuse to obey all over again."

A few moments later he jumps up, grabs a stick, and chases after the feeble-minded boy, but does not strike him. Apparently he wants to show me that this is the proper way to deal with them.

I interpret this as an appeal to me; this is the way Adou would like me to deal with him, then he would be satisfied. He himself is not crazy, of course, but not normal either, because he forgets everything. Yet Adou is utterly frank and confiding with me. I have the impression that he has not warded off the passive-homosexual transference to me. The idea of being beaten serves on the one hand to gratify a desire for punishment; at the same time it emphasizes the distinction—those little boys need a thrashing; I don't, I'll obey when I'm told to. During the course of this

interview I offer a number of interpretations: "You want to keep on being a little boy"; "You don't want to grow up because then you feel
alone"; "You think like an adult, but your character is like a small
boy's—as long as you were a little boy, you were happy at home. And
you were an intelligent little boy, that's why you still want to go back to
school, just as you did then."

Adou's reply to the last interpretation is rather surprising: "You can
waste a lot of time with girls. The other boys run after them, but I don't
even talk to them any more." And this, he says, is the reason why he is
never able to get along with boys of his own age, why they refuse to accept him. And he concludes his lengthy speech with the words: "I can't
just make up my mind to lead my own life. First I have to get rich and
take care of my parents, and then, maybe, I'll be able to think of girls."

I interpret: "You're afraid of girls and you're afraid of male companions of your own age. You want to give up both and continue your
schooling. That way you may be able to help your parents. And that's
something you're not afraid of."

My patient lies on the cot, completely relaxed. He replies to my interpretation as follows:

Adou: "I want to go on working with you, to get to know myself
better, and to get well at last. But I don't dare ask Monsieur N. to let me stay here in the village. If you could give
me a letter for him, then surely my uncle would allow me
to stay here. But I don't know whether that would be good
or not."

Parin: "I don't believe that would be good. It would make you
just as dependent on me as you are now on Monsieur N.
and as you used to be on your parents."

Adou looks around at me in horror, sits up on the cot, and then cannot help laughing. On the whole he seems much more relaxed. He has
spoken of his illness three times, very briefly—once when he was talking
about his school, once in connection with his mention of girls, and now,
in response to my last interpretation. He unbuttons his shirt and asks me
whether it might not be possible after all to have the scar removed by
surgery. This time I reply: "So far you've always gone to see the medical
orderly. If you now turn yourself over to me and I cut something out of
your body, you hope that it will make you well again. Then you would
have submitted to me completely."

He makes no reply to this, but his mood undergoes a change. He sits
up on his cot and inquires very objectively about the training of medical
orderlies in Switzerland. After a fairly long interval he comes back to his
scar and tells me that the orderlies had once removed such a scar from his
back. He adds that the result was not at all satisfactory.

Adou continues to relax on his cot till the end of the hour. He talks about how much he enjoys going out into the rain forest alone. He goes fishing and watches the animals. Many human diseases are transmitted by animals that are sick. Once he had even written a letter to the Ministry of Health, suggesting that they set up a veterinary service to deal with this problem, but naturally he had never received any reply. It was always that way whenever anyone suggested something sensible. Towards the end of the hour, a few children appear outside the tent, but—as is usual whenever Adou and I are deeply engaged in conversation—it is no problem to get them to leave. Adou tells me once again that the villagers do not like him, "because he is a stranger" (thus no longer because he is poor or because he dresses differently . . .).

My interpretation of his wish to be a small child again brings us to his rejection of the opposite sex. And here he expresses his desire for dependency more directly. I am to protect him from Monsieur N. At the conclusion of our interview I interpret for him the passive desires he projects to me, as evidenced by his wish to have me operate on him. As in the previous interview, this results in his identifying with me and at the same time in an enhancement of his self-esteem and in an improved functioning of the self as a whole. I make the following entry in my records: good therapeutic success through interpretation of passive-homosexual desires; reinforced identificatory transference.

FOURTH INTERVIEW (10 FEBRUARY 1966)

Adou has gone to Abidjan with his employer, leaving me a message to the effect that he would be back in a few days. This was six days ago. When Adou returned after three days' absence, I happened to be away. Yesterday he drove to Bébou to look for me with the white foreman hired by Monsieur N.

In other respects as well, Adou is now taking a more active part than before our interviews were interrupted. It is possible that my interpretation of his passive submissiveness may have had some effect, or perhaps, now that he has been "compelled" to submit to Monsieur N., he feels surer of himself in his relationship with me. N. is a violating, evil figure, a split off father-imago, while I represent the good, nurturing aspect of the father-imago. The latter assumption is substantiated by Adou's passiveness in allowing me to lead him to the tent, despite the fact that he had been looking forward to our interview and had been waiting for me. Back on his cot, he complains about the people in the village, saying that they wouldn't even give him a place to sleep. He had had to spend the entire night in a deck chair. He also complains about his employer—if Monsieur N. refuses to pay him for his work with the lumber crew, then he'll look for another job. N. is not the only employer in the world. He brusquely sends his great-aunt away when she comes into the tent to consult me.

When Adou once more adopts his "altruistic" pose, when he begins to stress his own modest way of living and to emphasize how sorry he is for the poor, suffering, ignorant people of Yosso, I make it clear to him that he is trying to think in the way he believes I think, and that he is thinking for others in order to avoid having to think about his own problems.

And—predictably—he starts to speak of the problems connected with his schooling. His memory is simply too poor, he complains. I assure him that I have never noticed it, and he admits that his head no longer bothers him quite so much as it used to. But it's not just because of his memory, he continues, he ought to look for a better job. He'll never get anywhere with the few thousand francs that Monsieur N. pays him (so N. does pay him for his work; apparently his feeling that N. is exploiting him is somewhat exaggerated). "I've got to have a profession and earn some money. The entire village is living on Monsieur N.'s eternal promises, which he never keeps. I'm going to look for another job."

Adou is no longer bothered by his inability to finish his schooling or by his mental trouble. Nor does he ever mention the other, physical symptoms any more. He has achieved identification with me and, once I have made this clear to him, is able to make use of some of the activity potential and aggression inherent in him. The "evil" Monsieur N., who had forced him to interrupt his treatment, is no longer an omnipotent pursuer, but merely an unsatisfactory employer. The difficulties now lie outside, no longer inside Adou himself.

Girls and women are mentioned only briefly. Adou feels that the ones here in the village tend to marry men who are too young and not yet able to provide for their children. In fact, he says, when a child gets sick, the only hope is that kind-hearted whites may turn up on the scene and treat it free of charge; otherwise it would be doomed to a sorry death. Adou himself is the poor abandoned child who is brought to me to be cured; he imagines himself at my side as I treat my patients, and he links this positive and identificatory transference with his own personal problem, namely that he is unwilling or—as I suspect—unable to develop any relationship with a woman.

FIFTH INTERVIEW (11 FEBRUARY 1966)

Adou is in a cheerful and friendly mood. He finds ample opportunity to identify with me when he speaks about the dreadful conditions in the village. He has no job at the moment, and goes fishing a lot; he intends to go today, too, though it is so hot that the fish certainly won't be biting. He speaks with great interest of my car. He seems much healthier now, like a rather childish young man.

About halfway through the hour, I decide to seize the initiative; I say that he is talking about "the general interest" when he means only his own. When he fails to respond, I interrupt him several times, pointing out that he is talking only about things we have in common, never about things we do not share.

He begins immediately to rail at Monsieur N., accusing him of being not only a halfbreed, but also a skirt-chaser. Right after he arrived in the village, he forced a young woman to sleep with him and got her pregnant, and now the same thing has happened again. He's constantly deceiving his wife in Abidjan. He lets his aged mother do all the work. Even in the capital he had treated her like a common servant, so that she finally decided to move back to the village in spite of the lack of conveniences here. And here in Yosso, Monsieur N. goes right on being inconsiderate and fathering children right and left. His old mother is expected to cook for his concubines. The villagers are sadly mistaken if they believe that a halfbreed like him, interested only in his own profit and pleasure, will bring them work.

When he senses that the hour is coming to an end, Adou resumes his gentle mood and once again becomes the "good little boy" whose only aim is to take care of his parents and—he mentions this in passing, as it were—perhaps to go back to school again after all.

Adou's tirade against Monsieur N. reveals envy, homosexual admiration, and submissiveness. His interest in chemistry, medicine, and disease—an interest shared with me—probably also represents an attempt to cope with his hypochondriacal anxieties.

SIXTH INTERVIEW (12 FEBRUARY 1966)

I have the impression that Adou, who seems even more childlike and more gentle than during the previous interview, is struggling to maintain his precarious psychological balance. A plump, healthy-looking little boy dressed in an extremely skimpy shirt who dares to approach our tent all by himself fills Adou with delight. "He's so sweet and round, so nice and strong, really more like a baby, even though he's older. What I like most about little children is that they're still so awkward." He identifies himself with the little boy, who is awkward and alone, and also with the mother who cares for him. Abruptly he informs me that he has to leave Yosso. He cannot ask anyone to give him a place to sleep, and he expresses his pity, not for himself (at least not in so many words), but—altruistically—for the other poor inhabitants of the village.

When I explain that what he really wants is to be taken care of himself, he comes back to his inability to remember anything.

Adou: "For instance, I can never remember the number of our mailbox or the license number of Monsieur N.'s car, though I've seen them both often enough."

Parin: "You're mad at him, that's all."

Adou: "That's right, I am. I'm going to look for another job. I'll stay here a few days more and then go fishing along the Comoë (River). And then I'll go to Abidjan and try to find a real job, so that I'll have something to fall back on when I finish my treatment here. But my memory is still not so good as it should be."

Parin: "People are very likely to forget things they find unpleasant, especially things from childhood."

Adou: "I was very happy as a child . . . Our village was not so backward as Yosso. But those people who have forgotten things just don't want to admit to the doctor that they have venereal disease; then the doctor makes a wrong diagnosis and can't cure them. It's impossible for a European to know about all the diseases that occur in Africa. My own mother has venereal disease. She can't have any more children. Two days before her period is due, she has pains down there. If I had enough money, I would take her to a specialist in Abidjan. She ought to have an examination. She's still young, and she could easily have more children. That would be the best thing for her."

Parin: "You're ashamed to talk about your own sexual difficulties. That's why you want to help your mother."

Adou: "There are people who go out into the rain forest, suddenly keel over and are dead. Sometimes it's their own fault."[3] (Because they go into the forest on a day when it is forbidden.)

---

3. A reader of this paper objected that id-analysis would be in place here; e.g. one should have interpreted the dangerous rain forest as a wet vagina. I may add that id-analysis could have been easily justified with Adou as with other Anyi informants. It certainly would provide data about sexual practices within the cultural context. However, we felt that a more or less strict adherence to ego-analysis provides a better understanding and a less confused picture of psychic structure, while the provoked irruption of sexual

Adou relaxes on the cot and, undeterred by my questions, discourses fluently on deadly enchantments until the end of the hour. He himself has witnessed cases in his own village. A young girl, for example, had met sudden death in this fashion. Sometimes it happens to old people, then again to young persons. Despite my attempt to link these tales with his recently expressed fear of venereal disease, he continues to speak in general terms: "You have to ask the shamans; if the reason was not sickness, they just know. I know nothing about it myself."

Before he leaves, Adou informs me that he wants to interrupt his treatment for two days. Tomorrow he intends to go fishing, even though the fish aren't biting right now, and the day after tomorrow is Sunday.

Even though the positive relationship with me and the identification with me as a European, a doctor, and a stranger in the village have brought about some improvement, Adou still does not dare to speak of his sexual anxieties. It is striking that he speaks so frankly about his mother's venereal disease. This is certainly not due to any uninhibited sexual interest in his mother, such as a non-repressed oedipal passion or anything of that kind. In the first place, the Anyi see nothing shameful in speaking openly about the sexual functions of the female, and in the second place, as a result of Adou's renunciation of the male role, that is, his desire to remain the "good little boy" (negative outcome of the oedipal conflict), his relationship to his mother has been desexualized and remains relatively accessible. In terms of transference: I am not supposed to heal his own sexuality, for that would give rise to anxiety (castration anxiety) in him. Instead, I am to heal his mother so that she can have more children. I am even to help her become pregnant so that he will no longer have to fear her, but can remain a child himself and can gratify (with me) his passive and (with his siblings) his active female-maternal desires.

My assumption (confirmed by later interviews) that Adou feels himself sexually disturbed might well imply that it was his shame at the inadequacy of his maleness, and not his anxiety, that prevented him from talking about his own sexuality. Yet neither his gestures nor his behavior indicated any feeling of shame whatsoever, and he was always able (prior to this time and afterwards) to speak about sexual matters without the least embarrassment. The renunciation of male sexuality is a matter of personal pride for him, for it brings him into harmony with the ego ideal of the "good little boy." The assumption that my treatment had mobilized not shame, but castration anxiety, can be regarded as confirmed. Initially this castration anxiety is warded off by repression and by the

---

strivings tends to obsure the whole relationship unless a longer series of interviews is feasable (see "Jean-Pierre" in Parin et al., 1980; pp. 248–305). About Adou's sexual life, see pages 192–204.

cathexis of a displacement substitute (I am not the one who is sick; my mother is). When I expose this defense by interpreting it, it is replaced by another one.

Adou is no longer afraid. His thinking is coherent, and his behavior towards me is characterized by self-confidence. He is talking about the deadly influence exerted by witches and shamans. Judging from the content of the dangers he mentions, a regression from the phallic to the oral phase seems to have taken place; he speaks of being poisoned, devoured, annihilated instead of being sexually injured. His defense mechanism is now projection instead of the previous repression and displacement to a different object. Accordingly, we can assume a regression to a more primitive form of defense. Inasmuch as he shows a general improved functioning, that is, there has been a trend towards the restitution of various ego functions, we can surmise that the regression described above took place "in the service of the ego." Oral (aggressive and libidinal) desires evoke less anxiety in Adou than phallic (and anal) ones. The projection to witches and shamans is in keeping with the animistic beliefs of his people. This means that the discrepancy between the ego ideal (whose individual shaping conforms to the ideals of the subject's environment) and the ego itself becomes smaller. The objects to which aggressive and dangerous libidinal tendencies are attributed have not merely been projected outside; they have been conjured away in the form of definable spirits and shamans. (The animistic religion espoused by the Anyi can be viewed as a successful attempt to localize threatening objects outside instead of inside, in the self.) And finally, this form of defense permits its user to cope better with reality. For spirits can be conjured away, and shamans can be bribed; it is possible to evade these "external" dangers by resorting to a form of behavior similar to that of our phobic patients. The process of consulting the magicians had taken the place of the anxiety-filled thoughts of sexual injury that the individual is unable to banish; for it is the function of the magicians to provide the means with which danger can be met.

We have given detailed consideration to an example of "normal" behavior on Adou's part because it offers a chance to derive the functioning of a defense mechanism from the event (warding off castration anxiety) that gave rise to it and then to describe the psychology of the resultant behavior with some degree of exactness. The projective-animistic attitude is typical of all our Anyi subjects. The situations in which such behavior is appropriate are many and varied; the need to ward off castration anxiety is only one of them.

Identification with me has not given Adou adequate protection against his castration anxiety. He has to interrupt the treatment a second time, thus, in effect, abandoning me. There is a good deal of passive defiance in this, as there is in his illness as well, and also a certain anticipatory defense—it is he who abandons me, so that I cannot abandon him, which would be tantamount to a punishment of sorts. For he also loves me, and is not only passively submissive to me as he is to Monsieur N. As long as he identifies with me, he can take part in the most satisfying conversations, his thinking is logical and ordered, and he enjoys a high degree of self-esteem.

In a European youth as well, the narcissistic gain to be derived from such an "ideal" relationship would be a predictable development and a useful aid in the process of treatment. It seems to me, however, that Anyi men *must* have an identificatory relationship to a phallic-active or even aggressive authority figure if they are to function well. For one thing, they cannot overcome their castration anxiety any other way, and for another, their own identification with the female is so strong that this is the only way they are able to acquire masculine character traits, not to mention a phallic-oriented behavior pattern.

SEVENTH INTERVIEW (25 FEBRUARY 1966)

(Resumption of the Talks Interrupted 13 Days Before)

Yesterday (on the 24th) I happened to meet Adou on the street. He greeted me in friendly fashion, but his expression was rather sad. He told me that he had been back for several days, but that now he was leaving for good, for Abidjan—tomorrow or the day after—in order to look for a decent job. He says that he is fed up with Monsieur N. and that there is no point in wasting his time here any longer. And he says goodbye to me. (I know that there is a car leaving for Abidjan tomorrow.)

I suspect that Adou is disappointed in me because I had to be away for two days just when he returned. But he seems so determined to leave that I have no opportunity to test this hypothesis. I can only request him to go to Goldy (Parin), who is in Yosso this morning, to take a Rohrschach test. He offers a number of rather lame excuses, which I refuse to accept, saying: "No. You have to take the test in any case, and it might just as well be right now." Whereupon he agrees.

(No interpreter is needed for Adou during the test. He gives numerous answers, some of them highly original, enters into the spirit of the game, and—in the end—is well satisfied with his own performance. He experiences the request to interpret the shapes as a kind of school examination, which he passes with flying colors.)

Following the test, Adou's attitude undergoes a complete change. He told Goldy that he intended to remain here for a long time and to con-

tinue his treatment with me. In reply to my query whether we should
schedule more interview sessions, he answers, by all means, whenever I
like. He gives me precise instructions as to where I am to pick him
up—smiling broadly the while.

It is conceivable that the transference significance of the test may have
calmed his castration anxiety—the father had sent him to the mother, he
had been permitted to impress the mother as an intelligent son, and the
father had no objections. In other words, I had made up for his disappointment at my not being available when he first came by undertaking
something on his behalf. Quite probably it was my firmness in insisting
that he had to take the test that brought about the change in his mood.
His passive defiance, his spoilsport mood, and his intention of fleeing
(akin to his earlier flight into illness) were overcome by the "gratifying"
compulsion exerted by loving parents and gave way to joyful compliance.

During this interview, Adou makes no mention of his "illness" or of
his schooling. He is now supervising—without pay, he says—the work
going on at the house Monsieur N. is having built in Yosso.

Without any preamble, he suddenly asks me whether I have a remedy
for "clap," adding that he has suffered from it ever since he was five
years old. I encourage him to give me more details about his sickness. It
turns out that since his fifth or sixth year he has had the feeling that there
is something wrong with his genitals. He has noticed hardly any physical
symptoms, except that about once a year he feels a slight burning sensation in his urethra for a few minutes after urinating. He is convinced that
this must be a very grave illness.

I explain that this sickness, like the sickness in his head, is caused by
his anxiety, and that this anxiety must be connected somehow with his
sex life. Right away Adou loses interest in his own illness. He starts to tell
me of his desire to become a doctor and says he would like to come to
Switzerland with me for this purpose. He wants to be able to help people,
as I do, etc., etc. I try to make it clear to him that the reason he wants to
come with me and learn how to help people is that he himself needs help
in connection with his sexual anxieties and does not dare to speak about
them.

EIGHTH AND NINTH INTERVIEWS
(26 AND 27 FEBRUARY 1966)

Once Adou happens to make mention of his "sexual disease," he takes
refuge in a relaxed identification with me. He would like to be like me. In
addition he would like to be with me and stay with me. He experiences

my interpretations as rejections. Nevertheless he is not offended; in fact he takes pleasure in the fact that I correct him, and shows intelligence and eagerness in his efforts to become more like me and to learn from me. At this stage I probably represent the "good father," who also has maternal qualities and who takes an active interest in his son. The women have been eliminated; there is no longer any motivation for aggressions, and anxiety is evaded.

Adou would like to have my address, he would like to be as I am. When I try to show him that he is making an ideal figure out of me and that he would like to become what he imagines me to be, he visualizes himself in the role of a learned man, a scholar whose mission is to live and work for all mankind and not just for his own family.

During the next hour he asks me whether I wouldn't like to go fishing with him. He tells me that there are prehistoric settlements in the rain forest that he would like to show me—I could do some research there, or collect insects, like a professor from America whom he once assisted.

Since his speech is becoming more and more perfunctory and beginning to falter, I try repeatedly to make it clear to him that he is simply attempting to evade his personal problems and his anxiety. This only serves to make him more "European"; he speaks disapprovingly of the African "evolués" who migrate to the cities and let their villages go to rack and ruin because they are afraid of the devils out in the bush. Next, he takes up the topic of diseases, even including those that afflict European children, leaving them mentally deficient so that they fail in school because they are unable to remember anything. It is obvious that he wants me to correct him, to instruct him. Finally he is completely relaxed. He gives me his views on the conflict between the Russians and the Americans and then talks about my car. I make a note to show him during the next interview that the more alien, and thus uncanny, I seem to him, the more he must try to adjust.

TENTH INTERVIEW (1 MARCH 1966)

Adou opens the conversation with the topic of money, declaring that one ought to work and earn money as long as one is still young. Then, in the manner of an agent from one of the development aid organizations, he outlines a number of proposals for ways to help the young people in Yosso to earn more. I try to show him how alien I am to him, and suggest that this is the reason why he feels it necessary to act so "European." I tell him that he is afraid of me and that when he is here talking with me, he is no longer sure just where he belongs—with his family or with me.

This inspires him to relate a story he has heard recently. A Djoula had kidnapped two small children and had sold them for 200,000 CFA francs. The children were old enough that they could talk, and they insisted that they came from here, from Yosso. But the village had not reported any children missing. Finally, everyone accepted the explanation that these must be children from Yosso who had died long ago and now wanted to come back. Adou becomes thoughtful, and says: "I don't know whether this is a true story or one that people have made up. It's the children I'm thinking of. The whole business is strange. In a village the size of Yosso, the people must know whether or not a child is missing."

Adou's tale proves that my assumption is correct; he really does not know where he belongs. He has transferred his "family romance" to me. But he has come to realize more clearly where *I* belong.

My patient's eyes follow the flight of a pretty butterfly that has found its way into the tent as he muses: "The blacks say that when the butterflies gather in large flocks and rise from the grass like a blue cloud, it is time to get out the 'dabas' (picks) and go out into the bush to plant the cassava. That's what they say, and they do it, too. The plants that grow here are so different from the ones that grow where you live. You have no way of knowing how things are here."

Outside the tent a woman goes by, carrying a baby on her back. She stops and points at me, obviously trying to frighten the child. She is probably saying something like "Look, that's the evil white man," or "If you don't obey, the white man will get you!" She laughs as she speaks, and the baby laughs, too.

> **Adou:** "The children are afraid. As long as they don't see anything bad, they have no reason to be frightened. But their mothers show them bad things deliberately." (He sits up and changes the subject.) "Here they don't have any marketplaces; the people sell their wares along the edge of the road. You should see the marketplace in Katiola, every Friday—you should see the pottery they sell, spread out over hundreds of meters. You'd like that. If you ever come back to Africa, you ought to make Katiola your headquarters."

Before I have a chance to reply, we are interrupted by Benoit, a Mossi whom I have treated and who has just recovered from a bout with pneumonia. He enters the tent thoroughly inebriated, sits down on the cot beside Adou, and stammers something totally incomprehensible in French. I stand up, shake hands with him, and maneuver him gently out of the tent. He departs with a friendly farewell. Presumably this was a thank you visit to show his appreciation for my having treated him successfully.

Adou: "He's completely drunk. People start drinking early in the morning, and then they don't know what they're saying. There's no way to stop them. Benoit goes out to get palmwine before he even has breakfast. By midday he's drunk as a lord and has no idea what he's talking about."

Parin: "Maybe you, too, are afraid of not knowing what you are talking about—like the woman who tells lies, or like Benoit. You were just telling me that I ought to go to Katiola. But right now I'm here, and there's nothing you can do to get rid of me."

Adou: (laughs, pauses for a moment, then goes on): "When I sleep well, I don't have any dreams. It's the dreams that always deceive me. In my dreams I see myself living in luxury. I am in a beautiful house, where there's everything I could possibly wish for. Yes, that's the truth—when I dream, I deceive myself."

Parin: "Have you had any dreams lately?"

Adou: "Yes, I have. The day before yesterday. I dreamed about a huge shop—like the ones the Syrians have in the downtown section of Abidjan. It had all sorts of things for sale. It was beautiful to look at.

Sometimes I dream that I am in a car. I'm steering it— I know how to drive. Either I'm driving the car first, or I'm repairing it. Something is wrong with it and it won't go. I fix it and drive off again."

Parin: "These dreams of yours fulfill wishes."

Adou: "Exactly. But whenever I dream of a young girl, even when she's extremely young, it brings me bad luck. And that's not good at all. A dream of that kind lasts all night. All I do is talk with the girl, and it goes on and on. It's nice, and the girl is sweet, and I keep on talking with her. But it brings bad luck. I've learned that from experience."

Because these dreams upset him, Adou had bought a book on the interpretation of dreams, and the book also said that dreams like his brought bad luck.

    Adou: "The day I was sent away from school I had a dream like that."

He tells me that he dreamed of the young girl three times, and that was a sign that something bad would happen to him at school.

    Adou: "When I dream that I am driving a car, or that I'm sitting in a pirogue, that's good. Then I can do anything I want; when I'm talking with girls, I can't."

    Parin: "You're afraid that something bad is going to happen, that you're going to be dismissed from school. Then you dream of something pleasant, something you want to happen—like talking with a pretty girl, for example. But that's something you're not allowed to do. You mustn't even do it when you're awake, you're afraid to. What happens at school is your punishment for having dared to talk with the girl."

    Adou: "Exactly the same thing happened in Agnibilekrou. I saw a young girl who was all alone. She was very young, and we spent the whole night together, talking. And the next day I got a failing mark on my essay. Before I knew it, I was two months behind in school, and I got further and further behind, and they told me I wouldn't be allowed to continue. That all happened because of those dreams."

    Parin: "What can you tell me about this girl?"

    Adou: "I just imagined her. I didn't know her. She was very young, younger than I was at the time. But it brought me bad luck. I got a failing grade and was expelled from school. That dream went on the whole night, and the next day I failed on my essay."

    Parin: "It could easily be that your desire to have a girlfriend interfered with your schoolwork."

    Adou: "Swiss watches are very good. There are very thin ones—I've seen them in the shops. Yours is not so thin."

Parin: "I understand. The conversation is beginning to embar-
rass you, and you think that since I am fortunate
enough to possess such a good watch, I ought to take a
look at it and stop talking. As a matter of fact, we've
been at it for 55 minutes. Let's stop."

Adou (laughs): "See you tomorrow!"

Once I have finally succeeded in interpreting Adou's "European"
identification, now clearly recognizable as a form of resistance, he shows
me—with his tale about the children who were sold by their kidnap-
pers—how alone and abandoned he himself feels. He is afraid of losing
his self-control here with me (like that woman, or like the drunkard,
Benoit) and is able to admit that I, as a white man, am incapable of
understanding him, and that, since no understanding is possible, he
wishes I would go away. Here it is impossible to decide whether it is my
alien status—as a white—or the fears Adou has transferred to me that
have contributed more to the development of his resistance.

Once he is able to express with impunity the "aggressive" wish that I
should go away, he confides his dreams to me, i.e., a part of his life over
which he has no control. He begins with the wish-fulfillment dreams
(corresponding to the Freudian "childhood dreams") that compensate
for his sad lot in life, and recognizes them for what they are. Probably he
interprets my comment to the effect that these dreams express his wishes
as permission to confide in me even more. Anxieties that are latent in his
dreams can be overcome by means of dream-work; for example he is able
to repair the car.

The dreams about "talking with a girl" which he tells me subsequently
are clearly subject to a number of distortions. I restrict my interpretation
to only one distortion—the fact that he views the dreams as portents and
the misfortune that follows, i.e. his failure in school, as a magical consequence of the ill-omened dreams; I define the conflict that exists between
his sexual desires and his duty to do well in his studies, and explain to
him that his academic failure is a self-inflicted punishment for his forbidden desires.

The latent content of "we spent the whole night together, talking"
may well be sexual. The "very young girls," whom he "does not know"
could very well represent an older woman of his acquaintance, his
mother, for instance, whom he longs for and whose sexual disturbances
(with which he identifies) preoccupy his mind. But what I have learned
thus far about Adou's personality makes it seem more likely that the
"very young girl whom he does not know" stands for a "young boy
whom he knows very well," and that "talking together" represents a

compromise between his fondness for younger children, his desire for companions of his own sex, and the anxiety-evoking homosexual desires that he has defended against.

It is impossible to decide which of these desires are reflected in his dreams. The fact that Adou takes the initiative to end the interview tells me that his resistance is increasing again.

During the interview reported here Adou has revealed something more—or rather corrected previous statements—of the story of his life and his illness. His academic failure did not begin in Bassam, where he probably did not attend a secondary school ("collège") at all, but much earlier, in Agnibilekrou, when he was living with his foster father and failed to pass the final examination in the primary school. In fact, in Bassam he was presumably trying to complete his primary education. I assume that the fact that he first told me that he had graduated from primary school and had encountered his first difficulties at the "collège" in Bassam—in other words, that he had lied to me—reinforced his fear and thus contributed to the development of his resistance. Thus his failure in school and the onset of his illness (at the same time or later) took place at a time when he was not yet living far away from home and could still visit his parents. Since he attended school in Agnibilekrou until he was about fifteen or sixteen, his academic difficulties may have begun with puberty. It is not improbable that his foster father, parents, or teachers may have warned him against going with girls because it might interfere with his studies.

Eleventh Interview (2 March 1966)

At the beginning of the hour, for the first time, Adou is in a state of confusion, something which happens repeatedly to other subjects (Jean-Pierre and Elisa, for example) when they talk with us. Though he articulates normally, his speech is incomprehensible, exhibiting the total disregard for grammar and syntax characteristic of "word salad." His ability to comprehend is presumably reduced as well. He mentions that he has just come from Monsieur N.'s house. I do not understand which house he means, the one that is now under construction, or the house of Monsieur N.'s mother. He becomes confused and begins to stammer, like someone who has been caught in a lie. He mutters something about meals. As if to calm him, I inquire whether he does his own cooking or whether he has someone to cook for him. He replies: "That depends on you."

After a few minutes Adou's confusion subsides and he is able to speak normally once more. He remains tense, however, more nervous than I have ever known him to be before.

There is a good deal of excitement in the village today—the female shamans are going to dance. While we are talking in the tent, we can hear the sound of drums and excited conversation. A woman passes by, on her way out to the bush. Adou calls out to her: "You're going out to the bush today?" (It is a Wednesday, the day the spirits forbid people to work out in the bush.) She replies: "I couldn't care less. I'm a Christian." Adou turns to me: "The Attié," (normally Adou finds this neighboring people anything but congenial) ". . . they have no magicians. They pay no attention to that sort of thing. They're better off than we are." He pauses, then goes on: "Yesterday it almost rained. We get some very bad thunderstorms here. One time the wind blew off the tin roof of a house. The wind often comes during the night, and then it kills people; the houses are no protection . . . And what people eat here is not good, either; it can kill you . . ." In sentences that are barely coherent, he describes the uncanny and dangerous things that one is exposed to in Yosso.

On our way to the tent, Adou felt the urge to hug and kiss a child about one and a half years old. He explains: "Its mother neglected it. It was still crawling on its hands and knees. I taught it to walk."

The other, older children are getting on his nerves today. The feeble-minded boy is there; there is also a saucy five-year-old girl, and three other children. They tease him and he threatens them, rushing out of the tent as if to grab them. The children act as if they thought he was playing tag with them. He picks up a stick and shakes it at them, takes off his sandals, and pretends to throw them at them. The children scream: "You can't catch us! You can't run because you have feet that point backwards, like the spirits in the forest!"

Obviously it is Adou himself, with his nervousness and his anger, who is making the children so excited that they refuse to go away. The feeble-minded boy stands balancing on one leg; he has wound his scarf around his throat and masturbates, grinning fixedly at Adou.

Some 40 minutes later, we have still not succeeded in getting a sensible conversation started. I tell Adou that he is responsible for provoking the children and that he is using his anger to keep them here because he doesn't feel like talking with me—all to no effect. Suddenly he leaps to his feet and holds out a coin to the feeble-minded boy. The boy approaches and is about to take the money when Adou grabs him by the arm and drags him into the tent. He lays him across his knees and spanks him as hard as he can. He releases the little boy, who holds his smarting rear and asks me for some medicine for it, then departs. Adou, now calm and relaxed, lies down comfortably on the cot. He is silent.

Finally, I ask him what he is thinking about. He replies that he had gone fishing the day before with a small friend, evidently a boy of about five or six. They didnt't go fishing on the Manzan River, or on the even broader Comoë, but along a tiny brook. Adou caught five fish, the other boy only one. It's ridiculous, he adds, how small the fish in this brook are, but he enjoyed it anyway.

Adou turns the conversation to food, asking me whether we eat frogs in Switzerland, too. The French eat them, he assures me. Here people prefer snails. The Mossi are not too fond of snails, but they love snakes. He speculates on what might be regarded as the best food for human beings . . .

Towards the end of the hour, he reverts to the Americans and the Russians. This is a "neutral" topic; both nations are far away, and we can discuss them together. The subject is a particularly good one for Adou, since it helps him to identify with me. In reply to his question earlier, I had told him that I had been in the Soviet Union and that, like him, I would like to visit America some day.

Adou's confused state at the beginning of the hour, the tension in the atmosphere, and also his moodiness and the events leading up to the spanking of the feeble-minded boy can be regarded as a consequence of what he had experienced during the previous interview session.[4] There is no doubt that Adou, fearful of being punished for his sexual desires, has developed a resistance that takes the form of reversible ego regression. He is confused, even his communicative competence is temporarily disturbed; his relationship to me is less close, and he is exposed to tensions which he is unable to verbalize and which drive him to aggressive behavior (acting out).

It can be assumed that my interpretation, namely that Adou's failure in school was either a consequence of or a punishment for his forbidden desires, was perceived not as a mitigating explanation, but rather as a threat. It is impossible to state with certainty whether or not we are dealing here with oedipal wishes, with phallic tendencies directed to the mother. They could also be passive desires to be violated, desires whose object (after the termination of the oedipal conflict) was the father. Adou has less fear of the latter type of sexual urges. His castration anxiety is warded off through identification and is replaced by the permissible

---

4. A European patient could display a state of confusion and disturbed "word salad" speech to show to his partner how crazy he is, or to let him known: "Certainly you think I am crazy (for instance because I fear the shamans)." Among the Anyi, similar confused states are considered as inevitable normal events; they have no connotation of craziness. Incidentally, not even kings can avoid stammering this way (see Parin et al., 1980; pp. 306–308).

   At other times, Adou has an attitude of detachment and contempt, sometimes he alludes to his involvement with and respect for shamans and other "magical" beliefs without disturbing our relationship. Perhaps this time he was afraid I could but would not protect him and felt helplessly exposed to these culture-specific agents of unconcious-aggressive and omnipotent phantasies.

masochistic desire to be operated upon (the business of the scar in the second interview) or otherwise medically treated.

It goes without saying that Adou's perception of my intepretation as a threat is based on a number of premises. Projection to physical symptoms typical of the "hypochondriac" and to the "paranoiac" persecutions practiced by his teachers has been superseded by a more conscious processing and internalization of the conflict.

In order to understand just what Adou is experiencing; we must think back to similar situations with European patients whose ego formation has been disturbed by a particularly intense constellation of problems at the pre-oedipal stage and who suffer from neuroses characterized by pregenital fixation. Then we must review carefuly the course of this particular interview.

An *uncontrollable development of anxiety* is responsible for the regression (including linguistic deterioration). The aggressor (unconsciously) is first of all the patient himself (phallic desires directed to the mother), while the *counter-aggression* stems from the partner (the avenging father or a violating figure, the father or the phallic mother). Once the regression has taken place, oral anxieties have been mobilized to replace the castration anxiety, or, more precisely, the castration anxiety is now expressed in oral form (uncanny fantasies, spirits, a deadly flash of lightning, poisonings). Adou is able to ward off oral anxieties by means of projection. Object cathexis is withdrawn from the analyst and is assigned to the women who pass by the tent, the female shamans, and above all the children. And this *shift of object* in itself represents a restitutive process—the oedipal objects, with whom the patient has conflicts he is unable to resolve for the moment, are replaced by other, preoedipal ones. Conflicts with the last-named group of figures can be resolved by projection (the female shamans, for example) and, above all, by identification. These identifications have special significance—not only for the interview described above, but also for the ego formation of our patient and, very probably, for the character development of a great many Anyi. For this reason we shall describe them in some detail.

The first group of identifications has to do with Adou's mother. This means that his behavior towards children reflects his experience of how his mother behaved towards him when he was a child. He takes care of infants, fondles them, and shows a motherly concern for their well-being; at the same time he chases older children away, lets himself be annoyed by them, threatens to hit them, and in the end carries out his threat. In these indentifications with the mother, self and object are not clearly delineated. Sometimes the patient is the mother, and sometimes the child, the baby who wants to be cared for and petted, and also the toddler, who clings to his mother and provokes her with his defiance, who desires punishment to take the place of the tenderness that is no longer forthcoming. The fact that all the Anyi mothers we were able to observe demonstrated the behavior that we attribute to Adou's mother, serves to substantiate this reconstruction.

There is a second group of identifications far more specific to the course of Adou's life—for example, the identification with the maternal aspects of the father (in contradistinction of the rival father and his aspect as an aggressor). It manifests itself in defiant, provocative behavior towards the father and in ultimate passive submission to him. One facet of Adou's identification with his father was quite incomprehensible in the beginning and was not clarified until the fifteenth interview, when Adou related a childhood memory. I refer here to his oddly sadistic behavior towards the feeble-minded boy—first enticing him with money to approach, then seizing him and beating him—which did not seem at all consistent with Adou's character.

Even earlier (in the third interview) I had suspected that Adou was trying to show me something by his treatment of the feeble-minded child—this is the way you should treat me; he has to feel it on his own skin. Unconsciously he was acting out what I, as a father, should do with him. At the same time he himself is the little boy who is spanked. The feeble-minded boy cooperates and demands some medicine for his smarting buttocks, just as Adou had asked me for medicine. That Adou has not simply worked off his aggressions and feels calmer for this reason, but that he has acted out and experienced the blows as if he had received them himself, is clear from what he tells me afterwards: he is a very good little boy, he goes fishing for little fish with another little boy, and is interested in food. Using this as a point of departure, he is now able to reestablish the more mature form of his identification with the aggressor, with me, the European, which he had been forced to abandon during the previous hour.

TWELFTH INTERVIEW (3 MARCH 1966)

My patient arrives in an ebullient mood. He announces that Monsieur N. will be coming to Yosso sometime during the next few days. Casually, he remarks that he no longer intends to let himself be exploited by his employer. For example, when Monsieur N. sends him away on a trip he is going to demand money from him, instead of having to beg or borrow the necessary funds and then wait patiently until Monsieur N. sees fit to reimburse him for his expenses. The impression he makes is not exactly that of a clerical employee in Europe; he is more like a European teenager who does odd jobs for his father and has now reached the stage where he feels grown-up enough to be paid for them.

Then he drifts into his altruistic "European" manner of speaking. His posture is tense; he begins to talk about medical matters and asks me a great many questions. He wants to know, for instance, whether there are many insects where I come from. When I decline to be drawn into this sort of conversation, he comes back to the Americans and the Russians. What interests him most is which of the two will be the first to send a manned satellite to the moon.

I remark: "Actually you're only interested in where there's a contest, a controversy—where one side can beat the other. All this friendly helpfulness of yours is just a substitute."

Adou: "If the Russians conquer the moon, they'll be at a tremendous advantage." (This reminds him of some of the races in Africa, the Bété, for example.) "It's easy to tell them from the others, they're always quarreling with one another."

Parin: "There's even more difference between blacks and whites. You're living in a permanent conflict with me, but you refuse to admit it."

Adou does not respond directly to my comment. His statement that the Mossi and the Anyi, different as they are from one another, both observe the custom of taking enemas, except that the Anyi use a rubber syringe and the Mossi a bamboo pipe, is actually intended as a protest. (It is as if he knew the answer to the question of why he cannot tolerate competition—because, like all Anyi, trained to passive submission by the daily enemas, he has been violated by the phallic mother.) He himself has stopped taking enemas since his mother no longer administers them. "I'm too modern. I use suppositories instead. That's all."

I interpret his submissive acceptance of me, whom he always feels constrained to place on a pedestal, and his passive, defiant obedience towards Monsieur N. as the consequence of a character attitude he had acquired at the time his mother was giving him enemas every day against his will and he still had to obey her in everything.

Adou points out how unhygienic enemas are; laxatives are much better; he takes them, too, now and then. He can hardly have misunderstood my meaning, but he cannot bring himself to accept it. He adopts his "European" pose in order to deny the content of my interpretation.

I repeat: "It's not your belly that suffers, it's your character. A person turns into an asshole ("con") when he always does what he is told and is scared to speak his mind if he thinks it may lead to a quarrel or to rivalry."

Adou's response comes like a shot from a pistol: "Do you have any children, Monsieur?" Though he has often asked me questions about

things in Europe, this is the first time he has ever asked me anything really personal.

In the course of a rambling speech, it gradually becomes clear how
much Adou would like to be my child. He goes on to say how absolutely
necessary it is to have children, and that he, too, will have to think of
having some some day, so that they can take his place when he grows old
and dies.

Adou is capable of pursuing adult, masculine goals. The passive-sub-
missive behavior acted out during the previous hour could now be interpreted. His question "do you have any children?" shows that the
transference to me has become firmer, is less impaired by anxiety and aggressive tendencies, and that he has managed to regain, perhaps only
temporarily, a part of his active role as a male.[5]

I have to cancel our interviews for the next three days because of a trip
to Abidjan. On the fourth day, I receive a short letter from Adou, very
neatly and correctly written, explaining the reasons why he will not be
able to resume his treatment for another two days. He now has a real
job, and no longer feels "compelled" by Monsieur N.

And then Adou disappears from Yosso. On March 17th, two weeks
after our last interview, I run into him on the street. He comes up to me
with a broad smile and apologizes very politely for his absence, clearly
annoyed with his employer because he had to accompany him to Abidjan
and had had to leave so suddenly that he did not even have time to pack
his razor.

He would like to come to talk with me the following day, but not until
after the medical consultation hour, because he has some work to do first
at the building site.

When I open the consultation hour down in the village, Adou comes in
and says with some embarrassment: "Today I'm your first patient." For
several days now he has noticed mucus in his stool, a symptom of the
amoebic dysentery he used to suffer from. I give him the appropriate
medicine, and he thanks me, stopping a moment before returning to
work to play with a baby on its sister's back, waiting its turn to be
examined.

THIRTEENTH INTERVIEW (18 MARCH 1966)

When Adou once again begins to speak of sickness during the course
of the hour, I suspect that the fact that I gave him medicine yesterday has
reinforced his neurotic desire to have me treat him.

---

5. The drift of his associations and his mood support the view that either he did not want
    to attack the therapist or he could successfully ward off such hostile feelings.

I comment: "You're still afraid of diseases." To which he replies: "Naturally. If a person gets bitten by a snake, there's nothing he can do about it. But for diseases that don't kill you right away, you can at least go to the hospital in Abengourou or Adzopé . . ." Adou is now more realistic in his attitude towards sickness. There is no longer any trace of his earlier irrational longing to be cured of his mental sufferings by having his body treated.

Adou has divided the paternal figures upon whom he depends into two groups, the good ones and the bad ones. I am among the former. When I leave, he will still have his father to turn to. He can go home to his village any time he likes; if he should become ill, his father would take care of him.

Adou complains about the bad authorities, primarily Monsieur N., and he tells me something about his experiences in Monsieur N.'s household. In the summer of last year, one of the schools to which Adou wanted to apply for admission required that Monsieur N. wrote a letter of recommendation for his foster son. "I didn't write anything good about you", Monsieur N. told Adou, "there's no reason why you should be able to do in two years what it has taken me forty to accomplish."

In Adou's eyes, Monsieur N. is a bad fellow because he is halfbreed. If he acted in any other village, as he does in Yosso, the people wouldn't stand for it. The people of Yosso had decided never to keep pigs again, because they made the village so dirty. Monsieur N., in his capacity as chief, gave orders that all the pigs were to be slaughtered. Then he himself went ahead and brought some more pigs into the village, and they run around everywhere and make the whole village filthy. Nobody protests. Nobody likes Monsieur N.; everyone is afraid of him because he is successful and powerful. If a thing like that happened in Adou's home village, the inhabitants would simply kill the chief's pigs, and keep on killing them until he realized that he couldn't get away with everything. But here nobody does anything.

Adou is speaking in free association, completely uninhibited. The village children no longer bother us. When they do come to the tent out of curiosity, they soon get bored and go away again.

In his social and political views, Adou is less altruistic than he used to be, more like other Anyi. If Kwame N'krumah (who has just been granted asylum in Guinea after the army's coup d'etat) should try to return to Ghana, he would be killed. The Ghanaians, according to Adou, have always been the most savage of all. The peoples here along the Ivory Coast are not so cruel, except perhaps the Attié. When the whites first came here, the Attié killed them. He refuses to consider my objection that at that time the whites came as conquerors and enemies. Other Africans, he points out, soon discovered that they could get along very well with the whites. He himself was once in the land of the Attié, on foot. He was thirsty and asked for a drink of water in a village. They refused to give him any. That's the sort of people the Attié are.

The Attié are traditionally the "bad neighbors" of the Anyi. They put a stop to the conquests of the Anyi in the 18th century and drove them back into their present territory east of the Comoë River. The fact that Adou now shares the prejudices of his environment is a sign that his attitudes have become sounder, more normal. Many of the stories he tells me today reflect the slightly malicious satisfaction at aggressive actions that is characteristic of so many Anyi. The narrator takes pleasure in relating these aggressive events, but in the end dissociates himself from them—not for reasons of morality, but with an odd turning to the dictates of common sense. It is as if they were saying: "It must be nice to be able to fight so ruthlessly; unfortunately, I can't, so I have to try to gain my advantage some other way."

While he was in Abidjan, Adou went to two movies whose heroes impressed him tremendously—*Hannibal* and *Ben Hur*. Both heroes defeat their enemies, but refrain from killing them. My patient explains that they probably think it may be to their advantage some day if they spare their foes—after all, people have to depend on one another. This is the way he would like to be, too.

In the oedipal situation, the desire to kill the father is evaded. The sado-anal fixations lead to aggressions directed to rivals, and if these aggressions cannot be warded off by a turning to passivity, oral regression takes place. The more mature form of the latter is identification with the father in a form which partakes to a considerable extent of the earlier "oral-incorporating" modality of the identification process. Still another form of regressive defense against sadistic aggressions is the wish to obtain an advantage of some kind from the enemy. We shall deal elsewhere with the change of object that takes place, from the rival-father to the mother, in this type of regression.

In the foregoing discussion, I have stressed a number of healthy, "normal" aspects of Adou's character, aspects which would strike the observer as peculiar or even pathological in a European. On the other hand, Adou has acquired insights comparable to those we try to bring about when we treat Europeans as well. During this interview he confesses: "I'm very easily discouraged. When I want something, and I run into difficulty getting it, I'm completely paralyzed. I'm incapable of taking any action at all, and I can't even think any more. I could resign myself to this state of affairs, because I really need very little in life. But I have other goals as well. I want to be able to help my parents some day, to have plantations myself at home, and to introduce new crops. The only reason why there's any point in staying with Monsieur N. is that I can learn something from him. Now, for instance, I have learned how a house is built. When there's nothing more he can teach me, I'll leave him."

FOURTEENTH INTERVIEW (19 MARCH 1966)

For a short time at the beginning of the hour, my patient is in a state of confusion, muttering that he had expected me earlier—or later, that he had missed me because he had confused the trucks transporting the first loads of lumber (huge vehicles, with a loading capacity of some 20 tons or so) with my Landrover.

As soon as he pauses for breath and leans back on the cot, his confusion vanishes. He asks me a question: "What is your little assistant (François, our interpreter) going to do when you leave?"

Adou has obviously been thinking of my departure, of the separation that lies before us. This is more realistic than his earlier wish to accompany me. His grief had led to bewilderment and regression for a short while (as during the eleventh interview).

I assure him that I can understand his worrying about the future and that I realize that he has good reason to be afraid of sickness.

Calmly, Adou goes on speaking and comes to the problem of "blacks and whites in Africa." For the first time in talking with me, he emphasizes the legitimate interests of the black Africans, without self-abnegation, but also without resentment. After exactly 60 minutes he suggests that we terminate our conversation. Adou has no watch, and from where he is sitting is unable to see mine, either. It is extremely rare to find such a precise feeling for time in an Anyi. In reply to my inquiry as to when our next interview should take place, Adou says: "Tomorrow is Sunday; I'm going fishing. I'd like to come again on Monday."

On Sunday afternoon (March 20th), I drive some women who have been visiting in Bébou back to Yosso, and we pick up a few young people on the way. There's a football game going on in Yosso today, and a dance in the evening. I run into Adou, dressed in the old, patched clothes he wears out in the bush and accompanied by several children, as he is just returning from his fishing expedition. He is in a happy mood and starts a conversation with me, in which he soon includes my passengers, but only after having stopped to pick up a baby, whom he rocks on his hip as the women do. He says that he has had a good day. The conversation turns to a minor accident that has just occurred—without my noticing it, a 19-year-old youth had hopped a ride by clinging to the rear of my car and had lost his hold and fallen onto the road, without, however, suffering any serious injury. Adou reacts like a true Anyi: "Good! That will teach him a lesson; if he ever tries such a silly thing again, he'll break his arms and legs."

Adou takes no part in the activities going on at the football field, where the young people are strolling back and forth, calling out to each other as they pass. They all seem nervous and uneasy, and the remarks they make are usually malicious.

FIFTEENTH INTERVIEW (21 MARCH 1966)

Adou resumes his laments about how awful it will be for Yosso when I am gone. I point out that I am leaving because I came here originally to carry out certain investigations that interested me, not to treat the villagers. Hereupon Adou begins to talk, quite sensibly, about his own future. If he cannot become a medical orderly, which he would like most of all, then he intends to take a course as a mechanic. Referring back to yesterday, he explains that there are two reasons why he does not like the young people in the village: first, because all they are interested in is spending money and buying attractive clothes, and second, because they have no respect for their parents. "Right now, my father is still supporting me; later on I'll have to think about earning money myself. Now I'm still learning." It strikes me that this time he does not mention his desire to take care of his father.

Enthusiastically, Adou describes the wonderful days he has spent fishing and roaming about in the rain forest. It is there that he feels happiest.

"Even when I was a little boy, I always loved going out into the forest with my parents. In fact it was one of those times that my father beat me, the only time he ever did. I wanted to go out to the forest with him, and he didn't want to take me along. He gave me a five-franc bill to get me to stay home. That was before coins were introduced. I took the bill and tore it up. And that's why my father beat me. He kept the torn bill; later on they always used to show it to me as a reminder when I refused to obey."

It is the childhood memory of Adou's that explains his odd behavior during the eleventh interview, when he gave the feeble-minded boy a spanking. At that time he was trying to show me how he wanted me to treat him. He played the role of the father, roughly pushing away the little boy clinging to his legs, and giving him money to get rid of him, money that the little boy defiantly tears up. In the end, he finds masochistic enjoyment in his father's attentions, which take the form of a beating. This experience is repeated during treatment, when Adou is confronted with the prohibition of his sexual desires. As a "screen memory," his relation of this incident from his childhood helps me to understand the genesis of certain character traits which later impeded his development in the direction of male independence.

The wish to stay with his parents like a "good little boy" was in keeping with the affectionate, passive desires which Adou had probably transferred from his mother to his father. Since he was not permitted to remain at home (and in reality did not want to), his thoughts often revolve around the idea of returning home at some time in the future and taking care of his parents. And he is able to experience this happy, desired, and—for him—normal state when he goes fishing in the forest (for his father took him along after all) together with a few children (for his behavior towards the children is what he wanted his parents' behavior towards him to be). By renouncing his own phallic goals he has remained an obedient son, but at the same time childlike, ineffectual, and in fact, sick; he is unable to assert himself aggressively, or even actively. If he were successful in school, it would make him superior to his parents; if he were to go with girls, he would be acting contrary to his parents' admonitions; if he possessed attractive clothing and enjoyed wearing it, he would be doing an injustice to his parents, who could not afford to buy it for him, and this would be a type of phallic exhibitionism. There can be no doubt that Adou's renunciation of money and success embodies a good deal of passive defiance, as if he were still tearing up the money his father gives him and defying his father to beat him. His father's money cannot tempt him to give up his passive, childlike wishes.

SIXTEENTH INTERVIEW (22 MARCH 1966)

Adou starts off the hour with a tirade against Monsieur N., insisting that he is not dependent on the latter's money. Referring back to yesterday's interview, I explain that his rejection of money is not due to the fact that his needs are so modest, but goes back to his defiant rejection of the money his father offered to him. Even today, I add, he is still trying to show people that if they don't like him, he wants nothing to do with their money.

Adou half turns to smile at me and concedes: "That's so, I never want money just for myself." But the people of Yosso are poor—"They have no doctor to take care of them. Everybody's forgotten them."

Parin: "What you mean is that I'll go away and forget all about you."

Adou shakes his head, then agrees: "Yes, that *is* what I mean." Then, for no apparent reason, he launches into a paean of praise for the Attié. When they have a child in school, the whole family gets together to contribute to its support, while Anyi children only turn to their immediate parents.

> **Parin:** "You are dissatisfied because your parents didn't contribute more towards your support, and because I'm not contributing as much as you think I should."
>
> **Adou:** "I don't ever let anyone give me an injection. I'm against them. Not like the conceited people here in the village. When I need something, I take pills, but not so often that there's any danger of my getting used to them."

I try to make him see that he has become dependent in a different way than other Anyi. He does not wait impatiently for an injection, as the children do for their enemas. He renounces money and waits for someone to take care of him. When he sees that nobody is willing to, he becomes sad and has to treat his body with pills.

This time Adou accepts my interpretation. "That's true," he says, "but right now I feel fine and I don't need any pills."

He mentions my coming departure, and says that he would like to give me a present. He has been out in the rain forest looking for tools from the Stone Age, but he is not very well acquainted with this part of the country and has not been able to find any. But he does tell me that the people who used to live here in prehistoric times left a monument in the Comoë River; they carved a rock that protrudes from the surface of the water during the dry period to resemble a girl's breasts, so that they appear to be floating on the water. If you walk past the rock and sprinkle it with water, there will be rain. This is one way to make it rain.

Adou falls silent. He yawns. He sleeps very poorly here, he complains, and has no dreams. If he could see his parents in a dream and talk with them, then he would go home to his village and visit them. He loses himself in the contemplation of plans for helping his village some day by introducing new crops on his plantations. After a lengthy discussion of such plans, he concludes:

> **Adou:** "Yes, in most families there are quarrels. When a stranger happens to be present, they're polite and friendly to one another. As soon as he's gone, they start fighting again."

Parin: "I imagine there's some quarreling in your family, too. If your father were really such a good man as you say, you'd probably be working with him on his plantations."

Adou: "But he *is*! He has a very strong character. He doesn't drink. Only once, during the funeral festivities for his own father, then he drank a lot, but it didn't last long. He's not so fond of the rain forest as I am, though. He doesn't enjoy going out there. Even on Wednesdays I always used to go out. My father stayed in the village. But you're right, there *is* something my family fights about—my father and mother, that is—and they have for years. They can't agree on how the work should be done; that's why they don't work together. My mother always wants to use the bushwhacker herself, she says she doesn't really feel alive otherwise. But my father says that's not right; you have to hire workers for that job. He won't touch a bushwhacker himself. He doesn't enjoy working in the forest."

Parin: "Which one do you help when your mother and father disagree?"

Adou: "I work with my mother, because my father has money enough to hire helpers. My mother has no money, and I prefer helping her because we both work the same way."

And enthusiastically he describes his mother's enterprise and efficiency in baking and selling a special kind of small round pastry; this brings her enough money so that she can manage on her own. His father has no say in what she does with this money, and she has used it to enlarge her plantations.

Parin: "Your parents are probably very glad to see you when you come for a visit."

Adou: "Oh, yes . . . They are—but they always want me to sit around in the village while they're out working. They say it tires me too much to go out in the forest, and that if I get tired, I'm liable to be sick. Sometimes I try to sneak out early in the morning, but they always wake up and tell me not to go. But I go anyway."

I establish a link between his parents' fears for his health and his own anxieties in this regard.

Adou: "Yes, you're right. When I feel tired I always start thinking about what my parents say. Especially what my father says—you get tired and then you begin to be aware of your own body."

Parin: "Well, at least in this respect you are like your parents."

Adou (laughing): "No, I'm not like them. There are two things I don't like—affairs with women, and quarreling. I can't stand them."

Parin: "Then you think it's the same thing—to take a wife and to quarrel. That's why you're afraid to have anything to do with women. Because you're afraid of getting into a quarrel. And if there's no conflict with the wife, then you think there is bound to be one with her father, or with another lover."

Adou: "No, that's not it. It's just that I haven't reached that point yet. If I have a wife to take care of, I can't concentrate on making a success of my life. Supporting a wife requires all your energy. You have to take care of your family, and that's the end of your career."

Adou returns to the subject of his parents, assuring me that their quarrels are not really so serious. He himself could easily find a girl with whom he could get along, but this would interfere with his career all the same. Once again he loses himself in fantasies of the future—how wonderful it would be if he could attend the school in Bobo Dioulasso and become a real, trained medical orderly. But that school will not admit him because he has no high school diploma. Last year the school accepted only applicants with diplomas. Adou falls silent.

Parin: "You want to become a doctor, like me, or at least a medical orderly. That way you would have something from me. You have your fear of sickness from your parents. You would like at least what you want to become to come from me."

Adou: (after a lengthy pause) "Yes, I admit that. I'm thinking of your return home. What route do you plan to take? Are you going via Mali? Or is that too far?"

Parin: "Yes, by way of Mali."

There is a long pause. Adou's cheeks are wet with tears.

Parin: "You are sad because I am leaving, and you can't even become a medical orderly."

Adou: (laughing through his tears, wiping them away) "No. I'm not sad. I'm just thinking about how dangerous it is in those countries you're going to be traveling through. Won't you be constantly being searched by the police? The people there are very strict with travelers. What will you take along in the way of provisions? There's nothing to eat in those places—nothing at all in Guinea, and very little in Mali."

I do my best to reassure him, and his mood becomes more cheerful. Now he is speculating about the adventures one can have on such a trip. He concludes with the words:

Adou: "I'll certainly never be able to take a trip like that. The most I can hope for is that someday I'll earn enough to buy the food and clothing I need. But trips like that—I'll just have to get along without them. How often will we meet again before you leave?"

Parin: "Once, or perhaps twice more."

During this hour I make use of the insights Adou has gained into the conflict with his parents to show him that he has reached a deadlock in his passive, self defeating waiting for his parents to provide—in the last analysis, inadequately—for his welfare. He responds by describing his parents more realistically, telling me about the quarreling that has been going on between them for years, and—inadvertently—making it clear to me why he cannot stand to live at home. Even his identification with his father's exaggerated, hypochondriacally colored fears for his health seems open to question. The "more mature" identification with me is untenable. He is sad because I am leaving him, and is able to cope with his grief.

SEVENTEENTH INTERVIEW (23 MARCH 1966)

It is obvious that my patient is reluctant to involve himself with me more deeply in the time we have left. Soon after the beginning of the hour, an ant crawls over his forehead. He removes it calmly with the words: "When they're very young, they don't bite. The older ones do, of course. Sometimes even the young ones bite in self-defense if you knock over their hills."

Adou discourses on the problems faced by his people. He is skeptical of the abilities of the Africans, and does not believe that they will ever learn to study their land, their diseases, their habits and customs systematically and scientifically. If they were ever given grants for such research projects, the money would all be spent on food before the projects even got started. Still, he no longer views the future so pessimistically as before. The 1964 law replacing matrilineal inheritance by inheritance through the paternal line was at least a step in the right direction.

Parin: "But you yourself have neither a father nor an uncle from whom you can expect to inherit anything."

Adou: "I don't need any inheritance. I can make my own way."

Adou asks me a number of questions, and I answer him more fully than I usually do.[6] Then I ask him, in return, to answer some questions for me, too. I ask him about his sex life. Since he replies without embarrassment, and since his answers are detailed and contain no contradictions, I assume that the information he gives me corresponds to the facts. He informs me that he did witness sexual acts on occasion while he was living at home, but hardly ever spoke about them with his parents or his friends. He masturbated only as a child. At puberty he began to have nocturnal emissions; at this time he found it easy to get along with girls, and had intercourse with various partners on a number of occasions. He never experienced any difficulty in this respect. Many of his friends had trouble with delayed ejaculation as long as they were not well acquainted with their partners, but this was never a problem for Adou. Here in Yosso, he mentions, there are only two girls who are still unattached, and he would probably have no difficulty getting one of them. But neither one appeals to him. But because he has no girl here, he is having nocturnal emissions again, sometimes accompanied by dreams, and sometimes not. He is unable to recall the dreams. No, his "clap" has never bothered him during intercourse with girls; in fact it has never occurred to him in this connection that he might have a disease.

Adou amplifies this clear and simple account with some remarks that appear to be much more problematical, concerning just how a young

---

6. My attitude was geared to transferring the interviews to a more superficial level as our departure from Anyiland was imminent.

man goes about finding a girl to marry. The customs are no longer the same everywhere. To Adou the best system seems to be the one followed in his home village. The young man simply asks his parents to suggest a girl. Once permission to marry has been received, the young man must then see how he gets along with his prospective wife. This includes sleeping together in order to make certain that the sexual aspect is also satisfactory. If it is not, he asks his parents to suggest some other girl. Any other system, Adou assures me, would be bound to have disadvantages. Here in Yosso, for example, a young man simply picks out a girl and declares her his wife—all without any ceremony, without any exchange of drinks or marriage gifts, and even though the families may not agree with the match. This only gives rise to dissatisfaction and usually leads to divorce. But even when a young man requests an older woman to act as intermediary, or perhaps one of his friends, or a girlfriend of the girl he is interested in, or—even worse—when the two families decide on a marriage without consulting the young people involved, as the custom used to be, the result is only trouble and unhappiness.

It can probably be concluded that Adou is not suffering from a disturbance in sexual functioning; this does not contradict in any way the assumption that the phallic-oedipal phase of libido development in his case was such that he lacks the ability to feel and act like an independent male. Many European patients in whom a fixation to pre-oedipal experience modalities predominates are sexually potent precisely because they arrange their love lives in such a way that no oedipal rivalry can emerge. Adou's psychical development during childhood was such that he was later unable to tolerate the separation from his parents, his disappointment in them, and the exacting demands made upon him in school.

The symptoms of his illness, "brain-fag" syndrome with accompanying signs of hypochrondia and paranoia, disappeared when he succeeded in mastering his anxieties, which had been transferred to me. It is possible, of course, that the same symptoms may reappear if he is subjected to similar stress at some time in the future. The acquired insights have not yet been worked through adequately. At the moment, however, the patient's predisposition to anxiety is less than in the past. There has been no serious regression, and above all the more disturbing impairments of body feeling have disappeared. The tendency towards repression is greatly reduced. Paranoiac projections have given way to more realistic attitudes. Passive-homosexual tendencies and instances of passive-masochistic defiant behavior have decreased, and that latter are no longer transferred indiscriminately to every authority figure.

Adou's character formation should not be viewed as pathological merely because it has failed to protect him against developing certain serious symtoms. At the present time he is in a very difficult situation, one which offers very little hope for his future prospects in life; yet his mood is normal and his mental processes satisfactory. He is capable of making plans that seem as reasonable as possible under the circumstances, and his relationship to his family and to his fellows is characterized by a lack of any special feeling of hatred and by wishes that he can reasonably expect to see fulfilled. That there has been no fundamental change in Adou's character is demonstrated by the course of our final interview.

EIGHTEENTH INTERVIEW (24 MARCH 1966)

Together with a group of workers, Adou comes into the village from the lumber camp in the rain forest. He makes a self-confident impression, just like a real foreman. The only incongruity is the high-school textbook on Greek history that he carries along with his bushwhacker and that contrasts oddly with his work-clothes. Later he shows me the well-thumbed, ink-spotted book. He has actually read it, and knows what is in it.

In the village, he complains, he is still being treated as a stranger. This is not directed against him personally; no stranger ever feels entirely at home in a village like this. His next words seem to contradict his statement that he feels like a stranger. He relates the legend of how Yosso was first founded. The ancient breadfruit tree, towering over all the others, sprouted from a twig stuck into the earth by the first inhabitant of Yosso to mark the place where he was accustomed to bathe.

In reply to my question about the sickness in his head, Adou says that he has no way of knowing whether or not he is cured. At the moment it no longer bothers him. And he thinks that, if he should return to school, he would not let himself be so easily discouraged the next time. But whether his mind would function properly, whether he would encounter corrupt instructors or good ones—these are things he is not sure of. On the whole, he says, whether or not he succeeds in achieving a position in life will depend mostly on himself. But one thing is certain—before he dies, he wants to have a son.

Looking back on his illness, Adou mentions that in April 1965 he had spent a month with Master Edjro Josué in Akrodjo in the hope of being cured of his forgetfulness (Parin & Parin-Matthèy, 1980). But Edjro had not helped him at all. Obviously the Master's powers had been diminished by his sojourn in the forest. People said that he was still able to cure the blind, but Adou's memory had remained just as poor as before. Naturally he had made the usual confession, drunk the holy water, and—for a time anyway—observed the taboos connected with it. It was like going to a doctor, and doctors also don't want their patients to take any medicines they haven't prescribed. But there was no power behind it all. According to Adou, all Edjro does is to try to train people's characters; otherwise he accomplishes nothing. The best part is that he refuses to accept money from people. And Adou liked him better as long as he wore only a pair of shorts while he was working; now that he has started all that nonsense with robes, like a Catholic priest, he doesn't like him any more.

I call Adou's attention to the fact that Edjro's rejection of money and beautiful clothing reminds me of his own attitude, and he admits with a laugh that I am right. In Adou's case it is the renunciation of phallic-exhibitionist attitudes that opens the way to greater independence. Only when one has submitted to a constraint can one become active and strong. What, for our ego, stems from phallic activity is in his case the product of sado-anal submission. Once he has internalized the anal phallus of the mother, he is able to live with it "like a man."

To my surprise Adou continues this line of thought and—with the following comment—summarizes what he hopes to gain from a genuine cure and a feeling of well-being:

Adou: "My father told me this. There is another healer who lives in Ferkessedougou. If you drink *his* holy water and then break his commandments, he really kills you. That's the secret of his success. When someone has the power to kill, you have to obey him. And that way you are cured."

(25 March 1966)

Adou helps me to dismantle our tent. I make him a present of medicines for amoebic dysentery and malaria as well as some antibiotics. He is surprised at the quantity and says that he had not expected so much. He writes down his address—c/o Monsieur N., Abidjan—on a slip of paper for me so that I can send him a copy of the photograph I took of him while he was helping with the tent.

Two years later I receive a long letter from my patient from which I am able to deduce that he has not resumed his studies and that his illness has not reappeared. With gratitude and with a feeling of melancholy, he cherishes the memory of our friendship.

Adou differs from the other Anyi with whom we had daily interviews in that he does not feel that I am forcing him to come to me for treatment, but sincerely hopes that psychoanalysis may provide a cure for his illness.

Yet he, too, is unable to avoid entirely the feeling that some sort of compulsion has been exerted on him. He is exposed repeatedly to compulsion on the part of Monsieur N., who orders him to go away, to stay here, to work for him. During the early stages of treatment I had the impression that he was gradually succeeding in asserting himself in the face of Monsiuer N.'s repressive authority, and that his health was improving as as a result. In the end, however, he seems to have retained his basic, passive-masochistic attitude after all.

The therapeutic success of our interviews can probably be attributed to the fact that the "negative outcome of the oedipal conflict" was transferred, made a part of Adou's conscious awareness through my interpretations, and successfully processed by his ego through an act of internalization and detachment from the father whom he loves and to whom he had submitted. He had transferred to me the compulsion exerted by his father. The corresponding screen memory from childhood is the scene in which his father beat him after first having rejected the boy's love, which led to Adou's gesture of defiance in tearing up the money. In Adou's case the "negative outcome" of the oedipal conflict is a pathological construct of the type found in male European patients in whom it has led to the development of a strong, unconscious homosexuality. Introjection of the father's authority as the outcome of the oedipal conflict and the resultant formation of the "paternal" super-ego—a normal process for Europeans—seems to have played no decisive role in Adou's case.

The wish to be compelled by an omnipotent figure, however, is still present. During our final interview Adou expresses his admiration for the healer who kills the patients who do not obey him and thereby is able to effect real cures. Submission to the will of the omnipotent, compelling mother has also contributed to the formation of Adou's character; this pre-oedipal fixation is reflected in his tendency to submit to a hierarchic-authoritarian power (despite his conscious identity as an outsider) and in his attitudes towards his own body. I could safely assume that Adou, like most Anyi children, had been treated by his mother with forcibly administered chilli-pepper enemas and with harsh commands. An introjection of this aspect of the mother leads, first, to a form of behavior which—in a European—could only be described as an altruistic, submissive, and masochistic spectrum, and, second, to a preoccupation with the functioning of one's own body which—to us—seems hypochondriacal in the extreme. The first may have formed a component of Adou's super-ego in relation to the social group; this super-ego, of course, can fulfill its function only when the environment responds "appropriately." The second enables Adou to deal independently with his body, which had been violently manipulated and anally stimulated by his mother until he reached the end of the toddler stage. The fact that he alone, and no one else, controls his body and what it contains confers a measure of secondary autonomy of his ego.

In European males, the syndrome of identification with a pre-oedipal mother who stimulates the child's body and violates him anally, combined with a negative outcome of the oedipal conflict may lead to homosexuality. And the same *can* be true of an Anyi as well. Adou, though, seems to have internalized the pre-oedipal mother image more completely and to have assimilated it better than is usually the case with European homosexuals. His castration anxiety and his submission to his father have led to a clearly recognizable, but by no means decisive, homosexual turning.

Adou's identification with the maternal-nurturing aspects of my person enabled him to see in me the "good," weak mother instead of the strong, cruel, compelling one, to whom one has no alternative but to submit. When he is feeling sad because of our coming separation, he immediately imagines that I, too, am weak, hungry, and helpless in the hands of the police, who search my person and beat me mercilessly.

One of the ways that would make it possible for an Anyi to be healthy and to function normally would be for his submission to the compulsion exerted by the mother to be transferred to a male-paternal authority from whom he would receive commands to achieve and, at the same time, affection, security, and food (as he had from the mother during the nursing period), but who would remain exempt from passive wishes originating in the oedipal conflict (negative outcome). Good chiefs can fulfill this function for their subjects.

As regards these needs at the adult level, the matrilineal family structure offers the advantage that the male authority figure is not a member of the individual's immediate family, but rather a relative or a chief, someone who does not live in the same household and whose person is not cathected with the legacy of oedipal rivalry. In addition, an oedipal father seems to be indispensible, with whom the subject carries out the rivalry conflict and experiences castration anxiety, and who ultimately serves as an identification ideal. From the point of view of the functioning of society, the disadvantages of this psychical development lie in the fact that there are too few chiefs who are sufficiently authoritarian and at the same time possess the maternal-nurturing quality, that the office of chief has been stripped of its political power, that the need to organize for military actions has long since become superfluous, and that the patrilocal family has become extremely rare. Men whose wives and courts have been bestowed upon them by a chief are entitled to head a family outside the lineage of their wives and can be experienced as oedipal fathers. The rest, materially dependent on their wives and their wives' families, are incapable of serving as sufficiently stable father images because of their weaker position in comparison with their wives, and the resultant instability of their marriages. Children who are given away

to other families, or who have to follow their mothers from one husband
to the next, are especially disadvantaged as regards ideal paternal figures.
All male Anyi, however, have a tendency to act "independently" only
when they are able to convince themselves that they are being compelled
to do so.

THE "BRAIN-FAG" SYNDROME

The disturbance from which Adou suffered was described by Prince
(1960) as "a very widespread syndrome among students in southern
Nigeria" (most of them Yoruba). A later study revealed that of 844
students enrolled in secondary schools and colleges, 54% suffered to
some extent from this "brain-fag" syndrome (in other words, "a brain
that has had too much crammed into it").

The fact that the syndrome is found among students coming from different cultural areas in Africa, and that their complaints (and other
symptoms) are invariably related with their inability to continue their
studies, suggest that it may be a consequence of Europeanization, of the
stress caused by cultural change. For where there are no higher-level
schools, there are no mental breakdowns among students.

The attempts made so far to explain this ailment and to classify it in
diagnostic terms have been characteristic of the difficulties encountered
by European psychiatry when it is applied to patients from such a totally
different culture. Designation of the brain-fag syndrome as a consequence of acculturation is hardly more illuminating than the opinion
held by the Anyi—that it is a disturbance in the spiritual equilibrium of
the individual concerned (which does at least imply consideration of the
constellation of material and magical influences to which the patient has
been subjected).

Taking Adou's "case" as a basis, we would like to attempt to establish
a correlation between this and other criteria, no one of which is actually
false, but each one of which—taken alone—is inadequate. In Adou's
case Europeanization intensified an already present disturbance in the
development of his feeling of identity, influenced the manifest content of
some (though not all) of his symptoms, and ultimately provided his ego,
super-ego, and ideal self with new possibilities for the gratification of
identificatory needs.

In the beginning we assumed (Boroffka and Marinho, 1963; Prince,
1960; Savage and Prince, 1967) that we were dealing with a psycho-
neurosis, and tentatively diagnosed either hysteria coupled with disturbances in ego formation going back to childhood or a borderline condition characterized by hysteriform symptoms. Later we realized that there
are specific aspects in the normal course of ego development among the

Anyi which account for the fact that the moderately serious neurotic disturbances we observed in them may resemble European borderline hysteria in their manifestations, though not as regards their prognosis or course. Depression, which has been suggested as a possible diagnosis for brain-fag syndrome (Neki and Marinho, 1968) can be regarded as an accompanying symptom of the neurosis. An early dynamic explanation (Prince, 1960) was based on the hypothesis that the European approach to higher education requires of the Anyi that they work alone, responsible only to themselves, and according to a systematic plan, whereas they have been brought up in a collectivist society, whose greater "orality" and emphasis on drive gratification cannot possibly prepare them for such a task. And in fact many Anyi *are* ill-suited to tasks that require independent, isolated activity and individual responsibility. Whether or not they are able to perform such tasks satisfactorily has nothing to do with their having grown up in a collectivist society, but depends upon whether or not they have learned to work through their conflicts adequately within that society. It is above all the "negative" outcome of the oedipal conflict, which often makes itself felt as a neurotic disturbance even in our "individualistic" society, that makes Adou vulnerable to an outbreak of his neurotic symptoms. Thus, his illness is not the result of a conflict with the group or with the will of his ancestors as embodied in the traditions of his society (Savage and Prince, 1967). He possesses an internalized super-ego of his own, which has come into conflict with his desires, giving rise to guilt feelings which immobilize him. On the other hand, one can imagine that the "clan conscience" might have made it possible for him to work through his conflicts in another fashion if he had lived in a smoothly functioning Anyi environment, and that his ego might also have remained better able to function if he had not been deprived of, and—as it were—isolated from certain functions of the "group ego" by his choice of profession and his neurosis.

The purpose of the foregoing speculations is not merely to demonstrate once again the inadequacy of Western psychiatry in a non-Western society. We have tried to show that there is much to be gained by treating psychical ailments according to the established psychoanalytic model. Under these circumstances, it is not difficult to equate African with European psychopathology, and to trace back seemingly irreconcilable discrepancies to specific differences in ego formation, the organization of defenses, and libidinal fixation.

BIBLIOGRAPHY

BOROFFKA, A. & MARINHO, A. (1963). Psychoneurotic syndromes in urbanized Nigerians. Quoted from *Transcultural Psychiatric Research: Review and Newsletter*, 15:44–46.

NEKI, J. & MARINHO, A. (1968). A reappraisal of the "brain-fag" syndrome. *Report on the 2nd Pan-African Psychiatric Conference,* Dakar.

PARIN, P., MORGENTHALER, F. und PARIN-MATTHÈY, GOLDY (1971). *Fürchte deinen Nächsten wie dich selbst.* Frankfurt/M.: Suhrkamp and S.T.

_____ 1980). *Fear Thy Neighbor as Yourself: Psychoanalysis and Society among the Anyi of West Africa.* Chicago and London: The University of Chicago Press.

PARIN, P. & PARIN-MATTHÈY, GOLDY (1980). The Prophet and The Psychiatrist. *The Journal of Psychological Anthropology,* 3:87–11.

PRINCE, R. (1960). The "brain-fag" syndrome in Nigerian Students. *Journal for Mental Science,* 106:.

SAVAGE, CH. & PRINCE, R. (1967). Depression among the Yoruba In *The Psychoanalytic Study of Society,* vol. 4. New York: International Universities Press, Inc., pp. 83–98.

2

Eskimo Social Control as a Function of Personality: A Study of Change and Persistence

ARTHUR E. HIPPLER

INTRODUCTION

This paper stems from continuing research by the author for the Alaska Supreme Court into Alaska native approaches to conflict resolution and their bearing upon the rural (bush) justice system in village Alaska. I propose that attitudes toward social control (law) reflect personality dynamics in both general and specific forms, that responses to changes in social control systems will reflect personality dynamics in both general and specific forms, and that responses to change in social control systems will reflect unconscious shared dynamics of the members of the changing group.

A pattern of significant continuity in Eskimo approaches to dispute resolution, at least in Alaska, is discernible during the period of recorded and intensive contact with Euro-American society and its laws. This continuity appears to relate in part to the seeming paradoxical behavior of Eskimos described by scholars and others who have observed Eskimo attitudes that shape group behavior and group life. The hallmark of this continuity in the realm of law is the Eskimo attitude concerning the appropriate style of dispute resolution, i.e., the need to avoid conflict paradoxically resulting in no organized method of controlling conflict. This attitude and especially its elaboration in Eskimo practices of conflict avoidance may, we believe, be usefully approached by addressing Eskimo behavior in terms of a "cultural personality" which we have

This paper is based on research supported by grants from National Science Foundations (NSFGS 3026), National Institute of Mental Health (NIMH DERP NH 16338-01-1 RO3MSM) and Department of Health, Education, and Welfare Title I FY 72-001-005 and N.S.F. GS 38284. Institutional support was provided by the Institute of Social and Economic Research, University of Alaska, Fairbanks, Alaska.

reason to believe has retained substantial continuity during this period of contact with Euro-American society.

Briefly, I suggest that attitudes toward law which entail fundamental notions about appropriate and inappropriate interpersonal behavior, particularly approaches toward the resolution of disputes, are grounded in large part in unconsciously held beliefs and personality structure, which change much more slowly than such overt aspects of culture as clothing, weaponry, etc. Therefore, adaptations to changes in overt legal process imposed by outsiders will often be guided by unconsciously shared expectations which are not easily amenable to rapid change.

To present this idea I will first discuss briefly the habitat and culture of precontact and early postcontact Eskimos, the specific cultural traits generally agreed upon as existing in Eskimos by early observers, and then a reconstructed aboriginal Eskimo cultural personality.

These cultural and personality attributes have significant bearing upon salient Eskimo attitudes toward conflict avoidance and resolution. While these attitudes in aboriginal times cannot technically be called "law ways," their imprint upon a legal system that did emerge through the village council in territorial days was profound. Equally important are the more negative implications for successful delivery of legal services to Eskimo people by Eskimo judges and village public safety officers who have shown continuing difficulty in adapting the adversary system to Eskimo needs and expectations. I shall show how apparent changes in "law ways" have, in fact, obscured a fundamental continuity of unconscious attitudes and, in fact, behaviors and outcomes.

The working hypothesis of this paper is that approaches to conflict resolution, or the absence of such approaches, relates to something more profound than some changed cultural trait. Education, or the introduction of new ideas and social mechanisms, does not appear to be sufficient to supplant or replace attitudes toward the resolution of disputes when such attitudes emerge from longstanding personality patterns.

The statements in this study concerning Eskimo culture are based upon our field work over a six-year period and an analysis of the ethnographic record (cited where relevant). Specific law ways information was derived from field work (much of which was carried out with Stephen Conn) with the oldest Eskimo informants from all present North Alaska Eskimo communities except one, from several villages no longer in existence, and from the ethnographic record. Personality information was derived primarily from an analysis of the extant ethnographic record and secondarily from our own observations of Eskimos (especially of their socialization practices) in many communities during a six-year period, as well as discussions with scholars who have studied Eskimos in Canada and Greenland. In addition, we have made use of Thematic Apperception Test results from 30 young Eskimos in their early twenties who came from several villages, and 118 Rorschach protocols from a Yukon Eskimo village (Boyer et al., 1978). We have also relied upon the observations of psychoanalysts and psychiatrists who have worked with this population, as well as others who have analyzed the results of projective test results for Eskimos. These are cited when they are relevant.

Finally, but not of least importance, our analysis of Eskimo law ways is also based upon available written village records of village council meetings, communications with early Eskimo commissioners of law, with law enforcement personnel in Alaska, as well as with Eskimo magistrates, judges, and villagers informed about contemporary village processes of justice.

ALASKA ESKIMO CULTURE: A BRIEF OVERVIEW[1]

While there are differences between the Inupiat of North Alaska and the Yupiat of South Western Alaska, most of what we have to say has significance for all Alaska Eskimos since Eskimo cultural affinities are relatively strong from the lower Kuskokwim River in Alaska to Northern Hudson's Bay in Canada. We have not hesitated to use supportive materials (as well as those which disagree with our hypotheses) from Alaskan and Canadian Eskimos (identified as such) due to a belief generally shared by anthropologists that there are unusually strong affinities between Eskimo groups across the Alaskan and Canadian North.

Aboriginal Eskimos were a people who lacked a system of law and formal social organization beyond kin groupings. By law, we mean (1) a clearly discernible normative system of rights and wrongs, duties and obligations with (2) the intent of universal application in case disposition and a (3) prescribed method of enforcement with (4) procedures for adjudicators of disputes and conflicts. Eskimo society lacked these elements.[2] "Law ways," such as they were, and described below, were so integral a part of all other aspects of life in Eskimo society that, in an Anglo-American sense, they may not be considered autonomous.

Not only was there very little in the way of "law" in Eskimo society,

---

1. Apart from sources noted elsewhere, additional information is derived from Hippler (1968, 1969, 1970a, 1970b, 1974); Hrdlicka (1936); Jenness (1953); Lantis (1938, 1947, 1959); Lucier (1954, 1958); Parker (1962); Preston (1964); Rodahl (1963); and Rasmussen (1952).

2. This characteristic of Eskimo life has been commented on by Hoebel (1940-1941, 1954); Van den Steenhoven (1959); Grayburn (1968, 1969); R. Spencer (1959); though Pospisl (1964, 1971) disagrees. We have discussed Pospisl's position elsewhere (Hippler and Conn, 1973).

there was also little formal social organization beyond kinship group-ings. That is, no clearly defined chieftains or councils, as such, and no established legal procedures apparently existed in precontact times. The basis of the existing social organization was the nuclear family, extended through bilateral and fictive kinship ties to an ever-widening range of people. As Heinrich (1955, 1960) noted, each individual was surrounded by a close network of kinfolk with whom he had clearly defined, as well as unavoidable relationships. Outside of this narrow range, the Eskimo had a circle of known distant relatives from whom he could arbitrarily select desired relationships. Beyond that was the "other" group which included everyone else. But even with this "other" group, one could establish fictive kinship ties through wife exchange or other practices.

Instead of creating many useful and intense ties with many people (which could lead to the development of corporate structures), Eskimos tended to use this form of kinship organization to create a series of mutually exclusive circles inhabited by a nuclear family and, ultimately, by the individual. In effect, though, he was related to nearly everyone nearby; he tended to act in some ways as though he were related to no one and, in fact, tended to stand alone. This occurred in the face of strong feelings concerning others' opinions of him (Heinrich, 1955, 1960). Briggs (1978) notes similar phenomena in the Canadian Eskimos.

While it is true that the more ramified kin ties are, the more diffuse their importance can be, this lack of close affect was not simply a func-tion of the kinship system per se, but rather of basic Eskimo attitudes. That is, while a bilateral kinship system does not prescribe relations so minutely as a unilateral one, Eskimo cultural personality predisposed the individual toward a diffuseness of ties.

Eskimo kinship structure as well as Eskimo attitudes toward other per-sons created a social milieu in which the context of one's person-to-person relationship, rather than abstract prescriptions about behavior, determined one's interaction with others. Eskimos did not subscribe to the idea of a majority rule. Most of the time, a man went his own way without censure or interference from others. (There were notable excep-tions, as we shall point out.) Nor would he be expected to interfere with others. Though individuals tended to be conscious of others' subtly ex-pressed ideas, no one had overall control in Eskimo society. There were no formally designated leaders who could legitimately sanction or define obligations and articulate conflicts. This is the most critical fact for an understanding of Eskimo methods of social control.

While Eskimos lived in villages of several hundred people, and while some communal cooperative activity is necessary to hunt large sea mam-mals, there was little in the way of formal social organization or law. This is only one of a number of apparent contradictions in Eskimo society.

Other aspects of Eskimo life have an equally contradictory flavor. (Ferguson, 1960 and Briggs, 1975 have documented this for Canadian Eskimos as well.) Eskimos tended to be generally friendly and cooperative, believing that they should never interfere in the life of another. This belief extended even putatively to children, who were not punished or overtly commanded, and was supported by a cosmology in which all men and animals, and indeed the entire universe, were systematically bound to each other and, in fact, part of each other. In seeming paradox, individual murder was common, as was suicide; and intergroup violence, though less common, was not rare (Hippler, 1975).

Eskimos apparently willingly shared the proceeds of the chase; in some cases, for example, the sharing of sea mammals, the procedure was ritualized though sharing often seemed to follow kinship lines (Burch, 1978). At times, men even shared wives. Above all was an intense concern in all aspects of life with honesty and reality testing. Nonetheless, at times people became irritable when forced to share; much of the jealousy between individuals was based on the supposed permissive sexual sharing which in some cases was, in fact, a response to fears of wife stealing. Shamanism and witchcraft were common. Much of the misfortune of life was attributed to taboo breaking and shamanistic intervention, even though the shaman was necessary to bring game and to heal the sick (who were often themselves believed ill due to taboo breaking or the actions of another shaman).

People tended to fear the supernatural world which often was not distinguished clearly from the natural, and almost all life activities were circumscribed by a complex set of taboos, which were nearly impossible to avoid breaking. Their abrogation inevitably seemed to result in personal misfortune.

Putatively leaderless and egalitarian, Eskimos suffered periodically from local "bullies" who would dominate them, and take goods and wives for themselves. While openly friendly and smiling to visitors, some stole from visiting whaling ships (see Cook and King, 1785; Franklin, 1828; Jarvis, 1899; and Simmonds, 1852) and were always unsure how to interpret each others' behavior if it strayed from acceptable norms. This is still true in many communities (Bogojavlensky, 1973).

These apparently disparate behaviors become explicable as part of one network of interconnected attitudes and ideas related to the Eskimo cultural personality, which had its origins in the socialization experience.

CULTURAL PERSONALITY

Cultural personality is a construct similar to Devereux's "areal personality" and "ethnic consciousness" (1956) and includes the whole of the unconscious concerns and interests, defenses and coping mechanisms which characterize the members of a cultural group. The concept also includes those institutionalized expressive behaviors that reflect defensively or creatively these fundamental concerns, and which are part of the shared heritage of the group. The definition does not demand that all individuals in the group have identical unconscious structures and defenses. Variance is a fact in all societies. The concept does suggest why diversity that exists is overridden to some degree by the internalized pressure and molding potential of that which is shared.

This concept is meant to provide a dynamic explanation for intercultural similarity, through the assumption that the processes of similar socialization and identification with ego ideals can press the individual toward central tendencies not only of behavior but, to some extent, of unconscious organizations. Though a theoretical device, there is some evidence through the findings of Boyer et al., (1978), for its validity as applied to the Eskimos.

ESKIMO PERSONALITY AND ITS ROOTS

Cultural personality and observed adult behaviors and values can be substantially attributed to socialization. I caution, however, that while it is reasonably certain that the behaviors described here are generally true to life, the connections to antecedent socialization can only be inferred. I try to do so primarily within the framework of my understanding of the present state of psychoanalytic developmental psychology. Ultimately, these analyses do not have the benefit of being related to findings directly derivable from the psychoanalysis of Eskimo patients, and are also limited by my own capacities. They bear the additional burden of attempting to understand earlier and present behaviors in light of contemporary observations of socialization and of earlier observations made by psychoanalytically unsophisticated observers.

I have not observed these behaviors so systematically as I believe would be optimal and my generalizations must be, to some extent, hedged and guarded. Nonetheless, a careful review of all the anthropological and related literature on Alaska Eskimos and a substantial familiarity with Canadian work, as well as reliance upon the observations of social service workers, psychiatrists, and others familiar with Eskimos, lead me to believe that the suggested relationships I shall outline are reasonable "best estimates" at this time.

The Eskimo infant generally received intense, continuous, warm, early maternal care. The quality of care which the infant Eskimo under one year of age received was apparently generally more nurturant and supportive than nearly any other reported in the literature on cross-cultural socialization with the possible exception of the Baganda of Uganda (Geber, 1958). Eskimo children traditionally carried in a parka on mother's back were, aboriginally, in virtual continuous skin-to-skin contact much of the time and were rarely separated from the mother even for short periods.[3]

It is postulated that this intense closeness and nurturance had at least one beneficent effect on Eskimo personality. A sense of security about the universe tends to be generated and feelings of trust and competence are enhanced by this closeness (Erikson, 1950). I have noted some unusual cognitive capacities of Eskimos, such as the ability to write one's name upside down, backward, forward, and in a mirror image with equal facility; an ability to observe and feel comfortable with pictures whether they are upside down or not; and the ability to repair internal combustion engines, take them apart, and put them back together again after allegedly seeing them for the first time, or make mechanical repairs with very limited materials. It is difficult to say how widespread such capacities are. At least one investigator (Kleinfeld, 1970, 1971) has systematically tested for these unusual cognitive and perceptual abilities and has established some proof of their existence through psychological tests.[4]

It is this intense and early nurturance that assists both the physical maturation and the psychological development of Eskimo infants, probably providing one of the basic cores of the adult personality.[5]

Eskimo children, in fact, are so intensely close to their mothers at this early stage that from the infant's perspective, psychological fusion was probably easily maintained; but the nature of the closeness may have marred the child's capacity to grow away from the fusion, contrary to what might be expected. Though the infant was and is still often fed on demand, the mother tends to use the breast to pacify him. Eskimo mothers, as Briggs (1970b) has pointed out occurring in the Canadian North (and our own observations support this), are not very tolerant of a crying or fussy child. By stiffening her body, against which the child is

---

3. A number of authors have commented on the remarkably permissive nature of Eskimo childhood (Pettit, 1956; Simpson, 1875; Fejes, 1966; Heinrich, 1955; Gubser, 1965; M. Spencer, 1954, are only a representative sampling.)

4. Kleinfeld (personal communication) has noted, however, that these capacities seem to lie primarily in the area of concrete cognition.

5. Giovacchini (personal communication) suggests that the earliest developmental progress of the child (prior to the development of the child's capacity to fantasize) is always enhanced by nonfrustration and indulgence since this permits full development to occur. Of course, the use of judicious frustration at later, more mature levels of development also acts as a spur to further development. Of course this depends upon the child's capacity for symbolism and fantasy.

almost always held, she communicates this distaste. She then tends to use her breast to pacify, but usually only after the child has begun to quiet down. Thus, we believe, the mother sometimes uses the infant's fusion needs to control him.[6]

One interpretation of this early signal—and it is one which is reinforced again and again—strongly suggests to the child that his well-being is dependent upon pleasing his mother. In later years, this attitude is applied to society at large while it is repeatedly inculcated in the child. In a general sense, of course, all human beings probably extend their relationships with parents to others. Here, I only suggest that the Eskimo tendency toward concern with others' attitudes tends to be stronger than is common in Euro-American society, and the specific method of control is through shame.

This general, but controlled, indulgence of Eskimo children continued for many years, but I believe one critical period to have occurred at approximately the seven-to-ten-month period of life when the infant is first learning self-other distinctions. During this period when the "normal" infant is ordinarily beginning to respond to the "good" (present-feeding mother) and perceived "bad" (absent-nonfeeding mother) (Lewin, 1950; Klein, 1932, 1957; Mahler et al., 1975), it would seem that such a distinction is slowed down for the Eskimo infant, in part because the mother's needs do not ease the way for separation-individuation. One possibility exists that it is this retardation of self-other recognition which forms part of the core of (partly defensive) egocentrism of Eskimo character and is the cornerstone upon which further character development is laid, particularly the tendency to avoid violence and express overt friendliness with everyone.

Specifically, the infant, massively indulged during the period when most infants come to view the self and the mother, (and consequently the self and the universe) as coterminous, is offered an essentially benign but controlling view of the universe. Perhaps because of this, the maturing Eskimo seems to have retained feelings of oceanic involvement with all of life, the interconnectedness of all things, and the powerful boost of a secure, optimistic, and nearly omnipotent self, which reflects itself perhaps in the mythological interconnectedness of all life.

Finding its wishes anticipated and gratified at nearly every turn, and experiencing minimal frustration, it seems the infant could not help but believe that the universe (with which it was unconsciously coterminous)

---

6. Some Eskimos who have read earlier works of mine (Hippler, 1974) have suggested that this is an overly romantic view of child socialization as they experienced it. Their recollections may refer to later age socialization and probably reflect the Boyer et al. findings we quote below. Nonetheless, I am not certain how this communication actually works, in spite of its apparent effectiveness.

was essentially benign. Unlike Athapascans, who, it is suggested (Hippler, 1973; Hippler, Boyer, and Boyer, 1975), tended to internalize feelings of interior "badness," for the Eskimo child the major introject at this stage was a feeling of supremely confident, nearly omnipotent "goodness." But this "goodness," nonetheless, was and still is, I believe, tinged with some degree of fearfulness. The mother's indulgence in the child appears to have narcissistic elements which set up barriers against full individuation. That is, the mother does not strive to create a basis for secure, independent identity for the child but tends to relate to him* projectively, subtly thwarting independent moves in favor of using the child to gratify herself. The child remains confident only when he is with the mother. With a small infant this is not a problem; mother is usually there.[7]

This situation seems to be marred for the infant when, with the onset of the second year of life (or earlier), he begins to be the object of occasional, unpredictable, and sometimes harsh teasing by other relatives. The teasing often took (and takes) the form of jibes about his wanting the breast and threats of withholding it from him. His infantile dependency needs, therefore, were flaunted at him even though these needs are not unreasonable for an infant.

Further, the infant was often teased and shamed at this age for inappropriate defecation and urination (though it appears to us that no attempt prior to this was made to inculcate "proper" behavior) which often sent the child into rages of frustration and attempts to rush back to the mother for support. The mother would offer little comfort to the toddler.[8] Henceforth this pattern of response tends to become the dominant one for the Eskimo child. Overt frustration, for which he has minimal expectation and tolerance since he has received so little of it as an infant, is met expectably with rage or sometimes with confusion and fear. This rage is socially disapproved, and the child then feels isolated and fearful.

---

*The terms him and he are used only to enhance the flow of writing.

7. I am not suggesting here that this massive early indulgence is "bad" per se. Quite the contrary is true. Occurring, however, as it did in conjunction with the development of a maternal style which manipulated closeness for the mother's own self-interest, it tinged the growing security of the child with an inability to break from the mother and consequently left it with a residue of continued need for the dependent, oceanic feeling and a concomitant need for external approbation. Alternatively, Giovacchini (personal communication) suggests that such early socialization could *not* result in a fearful adult unless it were either *not* so indulgent as assumed or, perhaps, followed by a substantially less supportive system. It is the latter which we suspect.

8. Jean Briggs (1978) suggests that while she sees among Canadian Eskimos a continual effort to elicit reason from the growing child she also notes the "teasing games," though she finds them more complex and related to more issues than are referred to here.

He then turns to his previous reliable source of comfort, his mother. Alternatively, one might also suggest that the frustrations are actually more intense manifestations of the earlier controlling aspects of maternal behavior. In any event, their message seems to be one of frustration which is not easily solved without resorting to withdrawal.

The teasing, in which the mother sometimes took part, was sporadic, and unpredictable. In addition, it ended as abruptly as it began; circumstances then tended to return to "normal." One possible effect upon the enraged child, was that it impressed upon him that the universe, no matter how nurturant, was often unpredictable but could be tolerated by disengagement or by defensive ego aggrandizement (an insecure boastfulness covering feelings of inadequacy) at a later stage.

In addition, the often teasing mother, did not permit the child's emotional response to achieve fruition. When the teasing caused the child to be enraged, mother clucked disapproval, smiled at him, nuzzled him, and quieted him down much more quickly than he apparently would have wished. Freeman, Foulks, and Freeman (1972), observing this kind of response, felt that this sequence represented the mother's attempts to control the infant's hostility by moving herself from a passive to an active position. The child learns to control himself "in order to elicit the desired response from the *external* object, his mother" (Freeman et al., 1972).

Ordinarily the infant would have passed the maturational stage at which he would normally begin to distinguish self and other and acquire a residue of ego which could not support a belief that the universe (or the self) was essentially bad. Thus, it was not his "evil" which he experienced but the demands of the unpredictable but controlling, external human environment. Under such circumstances, the child may find difficulty in integrating remnants of "ego islands" or in comfortably integrating good and bad maternal images or creating an integrated nonsplitting personality. These are issues demanding additional research, and I am unsure of them at this point. On the other hand, Briggs (1978) suggests that in Canada she has seen evidence that such practices cause feelings of personal "badness" among children, which may suggest a problem in their ego integration.

Characteristically, the infant's strategy in response to failure of his rage to end his persecution tended to be a sulky withdrawal. Finally, he refused to show affect. Since this usually ended the teasing, it had the effect of encouraging withdrawal as the appropriate technique to avoid interpersonal unpleasantness in later life. The residue of rage, however, seems to have resulted in a somewhat different but coterminous set of attitudes. The infant learned that the moral of the behaviors he observed was that if one could get away with persecution, or indeed, the fulfillment of any desire, one should. In fact, one could only be stayed from this behavior by the threat of danger to the self. Though the child responded in part to a fear of loss of the maternal introject (a residue of which is observable in the continual adult fear of being "left behind"), essentially, the child learned that the only critical elements of control *are outside the self*. Thus, regardless of the overt freedom of action he is permitted, he comes to feel such freedom is finally dependent upon subtle external cues. One possibility, is that he tends to respond by periodic outrage against imposition on his autonomy, and this rage alternates with an anxious dependence upon others' views of his own worth. Kleinfeld (personal communication, 1974) has suggested that on psychological tests Alaska Eskimos seem to score high on field dependence, which is consistent with the presence of externalizing agents of control.

Parenthetically, one of the reasons for the teasing on the part of adults (and other siblings) may have been jealousy of the infant and the indulgence bestowed upon him. Jealous rage was transformed into teasing; the teasing, in turn, was used to train the child in the need to control impulsive responses to powerful beings. But the rage was not always transformed. Many Eskimo families had the custom of designating a "favored" and a "despised" child. Paradoxically, both were treated in nearly the same fashion. After the first two years or so of indulgence, the favored child was often spoken to harshly, given difficult tasks, not praised, given old clothes to wear, etc. Briggs (1978) describes this in the Canadian Eskimo as well. The parents rationale often was that this kept the spirits from taking the child away from them. That is, if the spirits did not know that a child's parents loved him, they would not be tempted to hurt the parents by robbing them of the child.

Among other things, this rationale represents the feelings of an inexplicable universe, that is alternately loving and supporting, and arbitrary, capricious, and cruel, much as parents, relatives, and siblings were on occasion, especially when they would direct jealous rage against the child but explain them as actions in his favor. The rationale itself may provide for the parent a means of avoiding deep emotional involvement which, I believe, is probably more threatening to Eskimos than to some other people.

The least-favored child often received very similar treatment because "we don't like him." This overt statement of angry feelings toward a child tends to support the above-presented analysis. In fact, often there was little benefit to the prepubescent child in being either the most- or least-favored child;[9] one may assume that these identical treatments

---

9. In later childhood, the most-favored status did permit better identification with parents, and the harsh treatment subsided.

stemmed from similar emotions sans rationale. At least one of the emotional difficulties arising from this cultural pattern would be a distrust of warmth, but a simultaneous need for it, and a tendency toward confusion about the overt and covert messages which persons direct toward each other.

This issue is further complicated by the custom of adoption in Eskimo society. As in many difficult, harsh environments, the danger of losing parents was great. Thus many children were unavoidably adopted. While treatment of the adopted child varied, Eskimo tradition and even mythology stressed the poor fate of the orphan, who sometimes paradoxically overachieved (R. Boyer, 1975; Briggs, 1978; Guemple, 1978). It can be surmised that the mythological overachieving orphan may arise from a defensive response by the orphan to actual feelings of helplessness and loneliness.

A more striking cultural pattern is the adoption of a child, both of whose parents are still alive. I have personal knowledge of numerous such adoptions. One form is for grandmothers to adopt the first child of their own oldest daughters. The explanation offered for this is that not only do young married couples make poor parents, but grandmothers feel the right to indulge themselves with a new baby to play with and love. "They [babies] are like plants, or puppies; anyone can water them or play with them," was one grandmother's explanation. Another form adoptions may take is to give a child, named after a recently deceased relative (even now believed in many cases to be the reincarnation of that relative) to the nuclear family or descendants of the deceased. Another form is to give the child as a gift or merely as a gesture of friendship to a barren woman.

When limited to neonates, such adoptions would probably offer no more problems to the adoptee than such adoptions anywhere, although in my experience, Eskimo adoptees do seem to be more at risk for personality disorders and unhappiness in later life. The fact that it is a cultural pattern may militate against some of the worst outcomes; but to know that one has been given up by one's natural parents who often still reside in the community and can be seen by the adoptee to have kept other natural siblings, seems from the comments of adoptees themselves, to have been traumatic and confusing, and to have produced both anger and depression in the child.

The negative outcomes seem to be severely exacerbated by adoptions of toddlers or older children. I have never spoken to one of these children who approved of the adoption or did not harbor resentments. On the other hand, after disagreements with parents, some children voluntarily leave home and seek out a more loving or less oppressive relative. The ubiquity of this familial splitting may reflect the fragile nature of the parent/child tie. Beyond this, the ubiquity of the behavior makes the threat of giving away a child (or conversely the child's threat to leave) credible and become a potential source of greater anxiety. Guemple (1978) suggests that this cultural pattern in the Canadian arctic is so well understood that he does not believe it is severely traumatic. Briggs (1978), however, does not agree.

Two types of psychological tests have shown Eskimo socialization patterns to have produced children and adults the majority of whom lacked a sense of basic trust (Erikson, 1959) and had depressive tendencies. Boyer et al. (1978) analyzed 118 Rorschach protocols taken from lower Yukon Eskimos of both sexes and all ages and found the incidence of "the burnt child reaction" (Klopfer et al., 1954) to be from 60% to 80% in all groups, a figure perhaps twenty times greater than has been found in the general population of the "lower forty eight." Briefly, this syndrome consists of the individual's having been so severely disappointed in his needs for consistent affection and closeness that he became unable to trust the future possibility of dependable love and affection. The need and longing may remain, but the belief that such yearning can be fulfilled is severely damaged.

Thematic Apperception Test findings, based on a random sample of Eskimo college students in Alaska in 1969, suggest that feelings of loneliness, loss of love, and deep longing are the most striking of all the responses. Since these young people were away from home, some loneliness and homesickness responses seem normal; but the quality and depth of these yearnings seem to reflect a deeper psychological malaise, and the ubiquity of the response suggests a culture pattern.

On the other hand, the growing child, two-three-four-years of age, was not specifically toilet trained and, except for the inconsistent teasing, was rarely punished for incontinent behavior. Its exploratory urges were encouraged, and it was assisted in developing a sense of mastery over the physical environment. "Don't touch" is a rarely heard command in Eskimo villages and it is almost never directed at the very young child. Open masturbation or playing with the anus or feces are not necessarily discouraged, and the most stringent prohibition at this age seems to be against violence or interfering with another's life.

Yet, at the same time, I have observed (without being certain of its representativeness) the apparent paradox of children as old as four or five who are quite fearful of straying very far from the mother. There appears to be an "invisible string" between the mother and child; when the child reaches the end of this string, it returns to mother for assurance, frightened of its audacity. Since this appears to occur later than the one and a half year to two and a half year exploration state noted by Mahler et al. (1975), it would seem as though the issue of separation individuation may remain a problem for the Eskimo child beyond a "normal" period.

One way of explaining the seeming paradox between the "encouragement of exploratory behavior" and the actual fearfulness of the child to explore might lie in the fact that the overt and covert messages of the mother are contradictory. At an earlier stage in the second year of life, the mother distracts the child from actions of which she disapproves or which she believes may prove harmful, but she does not do this directly. The child ultimately has to uncover the meaning behind the distractions for himself. Freeman et al. (1972) suggest:

> The Eskimo child here begins to hypercathect and over-idealize the mother in response not only to his doubt about autonomous activity but to several other factors as well. The most important relates to the child's pent-up, frustrated hostility to the mother which threatens the illusion of narcissistic reunion, and is accordingly split off from the mother and projected outside, leaving only the idealized good mother. . .

Freeman et al. also note that the mother tends to encourage this displacement and projection and to foster fears of *tunuks* (white men) and strange monsters of the tundra.

Of course it must be obvious that the socialization against aggression was carried out at the same time that the child observed the teasing of younger siblings. Even though he was occasionally permitted to join the teasing, he was generally discouraged from doing so. Very quickly, the growing child automatically learned to displace his anger and aggression. I have observed small Eskimo children[10] torture young mammals and small birds and, for example, over a period of hours patiently collect enough rocks to stone a tied-down puppy to death. In adult life, Eskimos' dogs are often treated harshly and are routinely kicked more than would be expected in Euro-American society. Grown dogs are supposed to be kept chained at all times as they have a tendency to attack children, and many Eskimo children are indeed attacked by loose dogs or by chained dogs they approach too closely.

The fact that there are always loose dogs, though everyone knows they endanger children, and the fact that people are ambivalent about controlling loose dogs may suggest that both dogs and children are delegates of communal aggressive impulses. Problems about loose dogs and at-

---

10. I have observed this on several occasions. Other observers tend to consider this a
     pattern; I am, nonetheless, uncertain of incidence.

tacks on children are so ubiquitous, and rational responses so sporadic, it would seem that some unconscious problems are being responded to through this dog/child interaction.

This displacement of aggression onto animals may have a positive survival valence. Adult Eskimos are often quite candid about their love, not merely of hunting, but of killing animals. As one older woman said, "We like to slaughter the caribou," in explanation of having killed 90 caribou. She made it clear in context that she meant it literally. We have seen clear cases of the overkilling of game, though motivation, in some cases, may well have been economic (i.e., walrus tusks). But such unmitigated aggression, even displaced, could not be permitted in the past. The killing of animals, whether sea or land mammals, was then and is still often attended by ceremonial attention to the corpse. After killing a caribou, traditionally one slits its throat "to let the spirit out so it won't tell Caribou not to come."

In some ways, all caribou are one, and the spirit of any caribou may communicate with all other caribou, because it is Caribou. This seems to express the tendency toward oceanic feelings and the stated Eskimo belief that all living things are magically part of each other, and more importantly, somehow part of the self and other humans. Perhaps this reflects some diffuseness of ego-boundaries, as well as fear of intruding into another's life (diffuse ego boundaries of the other). Further, the death ritual suggests the need to propitiate after taking a life because of the fear of talion punishment. The talion punishment is stated to be that the caribou (whale, walrus) will not return; i.e., the Eskimo will be denied nurturance. This also suggests the primitive fear of talion punishment from the mother stems from oral devouring urges. While this is probably a human universal, it may be less neutralized or less adequately defended among Eskimos than other groups. The same type of rite applies to the killing of sea mammals. Whale, walrus, *oogruk* (bearded seal) must all be offered a drink of fresh water after they have been killed or they, too, will never come back. The gesture appears to be a kind of statement of "no hard feelings."

The unconscious dynamics leading to such a world view, however, are not solely grounded in the maternal-infant relationship. The tripartite oedipal situation, built upon this unique socialization pattern, creates its own difficulties. The child usually enters the oedipal period in a generally optimistic frame of mind, but with an underlying anxiety concerning maternal separation and autonomy, leading to adaptive hiding of feelings and withdrawal. To some extent, this is modified by the internalization of the good aspects of the maternal object but is complicated by the possibility of forming only a partial introject. The fact, if I am correct, that self-individuation has never been fully achieved and that the mother is hypercathected defensively may act to increase the influences of oedipally based separation-castration destruction fears, which, in turn, rework and organize earlier diffuse ego boundary problems.

For an Eskimo baby, as well as for the oedipal-period child, father is seemingly the only one who can separate mother from child. My own indirect observations, as well as reports from Eskimos and other observers of Eskimos, suggest that male Eskimos at times take their sexual pleasure from their wives with little preliminary affection. Apparently, it is not unusual for the Eskimo father to physically remove the child (or children) lying on or about the mother and to engage in sexual intercourse with little concern for her sexual fulfillment. To the extent that this is so, a constellation of conflict in the father may be implicated. Egocentrism, envy of the child, and vague anger at the maternal (hence any female) object may all be involved. The net result, however, is that the child tends to witness, or at least be aware of, parental sexual activity at very early ages. In the preoedipal phases sexual congress often appears to the child as aggression. Moreover, quite often he is physically displaced for a sexual encounter. The child cannot deal with this directly and must learn to control his own stimulated sexual impulses and become fearful of aggressive impulses which might be aroused by his father's actions. Even the older child who may not be traumatized by anxieties concerning aggression may well observe the lack of tenderness in the sexual encounter. I must stress that such occurrences need not be repeated very often to provide this special (unconscious) view of the world. Further, any such experiences occur in the context of previous experiences which teach a continuity of egocentric behaviors.

The strong socialization against aggression and interpersonal violence is necessary for the child to become an adult Eskimo. He is not only fearful of eliciting his father's rage (which is certainly not unique to Eskimo children, constituting a "normal" fantasy based upon any child's oedipal development), but also builds upon a preoedipal impairment of the development of superego precursors. Briggs (1975) does not support this for the Canadian Eskimo; therefore, I suggest some caution in accepting this postulate and believe more research is necessary in this area.

Such findings may explain the obvious need for physical closeness of Eskimo children including their continual efforts to touch each other and adult objects of affection. More speculatively, this may also explain Eskimo diffuseness and shallowness of affect. There seems to be a capacity on the part of many Eskimos for wide-ranging shallow affect with many people, but the concomitant presence of a difficulty in attaining deep emotional ties. This postulate is offered tentatively, but it does seem consistent with Boyer et al., and with the observations of others. Alternatively, some observers have told me that they do not find this shallowness, but, instead, great warmth. The latter observation does not seem consistent with Boyer et al. but may be explained by a defensive pattern of smiling and avoiding conflict. Of course, this discrepancy may also reflect the perceptual orientation of the observer.

An explanation from a different point of view is that separation by death was aboriginally ubiquitous and that physical separation in the Arctic might well mean death; therefore, this death fear could lead to the need to avoid separation from the group. This seems reasonable, but does not explain the lack of overt communication about so serious a matter as striking one's tent and leaving. It also does not easily explain the Eskimo tendency to give their children away, or their fear of closeness. Regardless of the basis of this phenomenon, it does seem to depict a cultural pattern which itself reflects a psychodynamic trend. Overall, the individual is unsure about his capacity to influence others and is uncomfortable about their capacity to influence him. Emotionally alone, he often seems to be psychologically insecure. In the final analysis, we believe that an Eskimo tends to think that nothing that he does, or is, is finally his own responsibility. Even good luck is not good luck unless someone notices it. However, luck is not attributed *overtly* to negative self-qualities but to the apparent arbitrariness of the universe. In the past, bad luck could be set off by some accidental breakage of a taboo reminiscent of some minor act of the infant to which the mother responds by a momentary withdrawal of her nurturance and symbiotic closeness. Aboriginally, and to a certain extent today, this unpredictability of the universe was expressed by an incredible array of taboos. Their all-inclusiveness made them impossible to avoid, as one couldn't avoid the urgings of mother toward the baby to act in accord with her will and the inexplicable teasing for something one could not help—being a baby. Nonetheless, the taboos provided an ego-syntonic excuse for bad luck in hunting while at the same time reinforcing the communal sense of insecurity. Such taboo breakage could usually be rectified by phobic or counterphobic activity (one could do what the universe desired, even though one could not understand why it so desired anymore than the infant can understand mother's anger at his crying). Eventually, game animals always returned (for the infant, the return of mother's warmth), confirming the hunter's belief in the efficacy of the taboo and countermagic system.

Taboo and counterphobic activities act to neutralize and partially externalize the potential guilt and bad feelings about the self which the child inevitably develops as a result of the kind of mothering described above. Denial, splitting, displacement, and projection all seem evident here, not merely as individual responses, but as *institutionalized,* cultural responses to an expected socialization pattern.

Eskimos did, however, try to master anxiety about the universe. Shamans (*angatqoqs*) were used to "call game" directly and for propitiating offended spirits. Shamans could use damaging magic against those whom they might have helped at other times; thus, they were powerful and omnipotent like the fantasized parents. The shaman made use of his easy access to primary process thinking; and even though a superficial analysis of Eskimo art suggests that many Eskimos were relatively comfortable with primary process thinking, shamans were probably more so and, consequently, more feared (Boyer, 1962; Boyer et al., 1964).

As noted earlier, the principal concerns in Eskimo life seem to have developed around the control of aggression which reflected problems of autonomy and closeness to others. I have suggested this overt concern with aggression was necessary since the expectable adult personality which would emerge from the normal Eskimo child rearing would have difficulties in self-other distinctions complicated by dependency needs and the need to control the aggressive rages resulting from various social frustrations. Since this was so, to some degree the individual would be predisposed, on a primary level, to see all objects in the universe as extensions of the self. But objects would also be seen as external to the self and as controlling the self for their own purposes. Thus, other persons would tend to be viewed instrumentally even for expressive ends. This splitting process probably precluded a full achievement of integrated, emotionally mature development.

As an example, it was not uncommon, though vaguely disreputable, for Eskimo men to copulate with dogs, or to masturbate openly.[11] We postulate that in general narcissistic gratification of sexual urges was his primary interest rather than the development of a deep personal contact with a woman. Alternatively, of course, it is possible that this reflects an ease and openness of sexual expression. There appears to have been greater sexual permissiveness in Eskimo society than in Euro-American society. I suggest, however, that there is a difference between ease of sexual expression and depth of personal commitment. Even more, the tendency to treat women in a domineering fashion may also have expressed a repressed rage against the inconsistent mother and seems more defensive than an expression of sexual freedom. The issue is by no means absolutely clear. Men were quite dependent upon women, while at the same time women were dependent upon men. Such mutual dependence may have eased severe oppression of women by men.

---

11.   Lubart (1976), notes this was taboo for Canadian Eskimos. One would surmise such a peculiar taboo had to be directed against an existing tendency.

Stefansson (1913) shows some striking personal independence on the part of women. On the other hand, my conversations with clinical and other observers suggest there is a fairly strong tendency toward defensive and noninvolved relationships with women by Eskimo men. Joseph Lubart (1976) states that he agrees that the former wife exchange practices may have had a homo-erotic component and that this strongly suggests both ego-boundary and sexual identity problems. This issue requires more careful research.

Eskimo adult men would tend to be intolerant of interpersonal frustration. Aboriginally, men were always careful in hunting and traveling to make sure that their companions did not murder them for some slight or perceived insult. Often men traveled with one hand on their knives. Bogojalensky (1973) notes this as a relatively recent phenomenon in western Alaska. The avoidance of conflict under these and other circumstances was evidenced by the fact that strangers on the trail greeted each other with the comment, "My right hand is empty." Contemporary Eskimos report that even now it is much safer to hunt with brothers or cousins since fewer "accidents" happen that way.

In fact, friendly and smiling appearances were so important that a man who was sulking might be thought to be dangerous; he might even be peremptorily killed by neighbors to preclude his expected murderous rage. A putatively democratic attitude resulted in a kind of social anarchy in which Eskimos acted as almost totally independent agents, constrained only by a pragmatic evaluation of the personal danger which might be attendant upon a given act—which meant, in essence, concern in extreme cases whether others would or could harm him and, ordinarily, whether they would or would not approve (if they knew) of his wishes and acts. This attitude was further colored by an intense need for continual approbation and a covert rage stemming directly from that need, as well as from a lack of approbation.

The effect of this kind of personality structure embedded in the cultural value system of Eskimos created a twofold attitude towards law and social control which can be derived from the statements of informants:

Individuals tended to do what they wanted, to the extent they could without eliciting violent retaliation from others.

Individuals also learned to avoid relationships in which they might be drawn into conflict, unless they could be certain victors in such a conflict.

However, conflict inevitably resulted since the first characteristic predisposed people to egocentric behavior while the second tended to reduce the possibility of important communal activity. Further, the social climate was not conducive to the development of leadership, since people strove to avoid roles in which they had to interfere overtly in others' lives or have others interfere in their's.

ESKIMO "LAW" AND SOCIAL CONTROL

While leaders in many societies act to define the area of conflicts, recreate the balance between disputants, decide cases, or reinforce existing decisions and impose sanctions, Eskimo cultural personality intruded on every aspect of leadership behavior.

Leadership naturally reflects unconscious psychodynamics since norms in any society are the cultural supports for desired behavior which in turn reflect shared psychodynamics.

The unconsciously based message that conflicts were to be avoided at almost any cost meant that even potentially beneficial intrusion into another's affairs was feared and disliked. Eskimo "leaders," therefore, avoided conflict and subtly manipulated behavior without eliciting or defining conflict, imposing decisions or sanctions.

Eskimo norms at their core reflected a belief that one should never interfere in the life of another for fear that such interference would lead to retaliatory violence. One should not kill, steal, commit adultery, tell lies, or in any way intervene in another's life. Yet the corollary to these norms was the implicit statement supported by my informants which derived from the self-concerned personality structure of Eskimos: "unless you can get away with it." One could, in fact, "get away with it" if one were stronger than others. Such a set of attitudes did not predispose Eskimos to initiate formal legal systems.

Yet, a contradictory basic norm existed; men were expected to share and cooperate with each other. Thus, a level of social altruism, or at least enlightened self-interest, coexisted with the self-centeredness I have described—a reality-testing capacity even in the face of otherwise pathological attitudes. This is not surprising given human tendencies toward ambivalence. In this case, moreover, the apparent contradiction is reduced when we realize that the underlying concern motivating "altruism" was conflict avoidance, and much of the sharing was with kin group members with whom conflict was less likely.[12]

---

12. Nonetheless, sharing was by no means equal (and is not now). A family too poor to have power and without a strong adequate adult male to contribute to the sharing system will only grudgingly receive shared food.

These superficially conflicting norms and attitudes meant that only those individuals gifted at subtle techniques of interpersonal manipulation could organize Eskimo group activities.

SANCTIONS AND REDRESS

Sanctions necessary to enforce and make these norms instrumental were not, however, predictably applied and redress was only randomly ensured. Physical sanctions were not "legal" but apparently were almost entirely dependent upon an individual's strength or the strength and support of his allies. Nonphysical sanctions (social attitudes), weak and easily ignored by the antisocial, predictably worked best on those already predisposed toward sociability. Overall then, sanctions in Eskimo society were inconsistently applied, differentially responded to, and almost useless against those offenders who were most dangerous.

Further, redress itself was mild, virtually nonexistent, or at times, extreme, but rarely measured to the offense; hence, redress was hardly corrective and almost useless in remaking the balance between offender and offended. (This limited range of nonmortal sanctions is clearly described by Graburn (1968, 1969) for Eskimos in Eastern Canada as well.)

Since sanctions were very limited, the net effect was that a wide range of wrongs was ignored. Victims had little pacific means of redress and tended to fear further violence if they retaliated. As with the child and its parent in similar circumstances, the adult tended to withdraw in the face of adversity. If the emotional pressure of simply accepting or ignoring abuse became too great, the individual could flee or kill his tormentor; killing was common. Freuchen (1961) and Graburn (1968) describe similar events among eastern Canadian and central Canadian Eskimos. Murder was extremely common; in some communities a quarter of the population was murdered. Informants note that feuds involving vengeance by sons were often interminable. From the ethnographic record, though, this was far more common among Eskimos east of the Alaska groups.

It is clear that Eskimo reluctance to create authoritative structures for dispute resolution and social control relates directly to the Eskimo personality and social structure. In apparent contradistinction to their neighboring Athapaskans, Eskimos vested critical importance in the individual, not in the lineage or the extended family.[13]

---

13. This is a disputed issue. Elsewhere, Hippler and Conn (1972) have argued that Athabascans tried to use more coercive and authoritarian social controls based on a strong chieftainship alternating between matrilineal moieties. This is disputed by other writers; I shall not attempt to continue the debate here (see McKennan, 1959).

On the psychological level, the aboriginal Eskimo's secure competence in dealing with the physical world and his unrealistic optimism, tempered by a fatalistic tolerance of adversity, coexisted with his cautious view of interpersonal relationships. Thus, while he viewed himself as more or less coterminous with the universe, he developed patterns of avoidance, deference, indirection, and circumlocution in a careful attempt to prevent this expansiveness from clashing with identical expansive feelings in his neighbors. It seems understandable in the face of these attitudes that any attempt to create corporate or hierarchical structures with real authority over others would fail. As I shall describe, it was the advent of unassailable outside authority which finally created affective authority structures.

The moral basis of doing right and the primal moral sanction against doing wrong was an assumption *lex talionis* supported by cosmological beliefs and a vast series of taboos containing the idea of immanent justice. Eskimo supernatural beliefs stressed the wholeness and interrelatedness of all things. The living and the dead, the animate and the inanimate were not mutually exclusive categories. This kind of thinking reflects a tendency toward fixation at infantile levels of emotional organization. Bad acts and their punishments were also connected magically as well as pragmatically. This belief system bears a striking resemblance to the kind of thinking prevalent in that stage in the child's emotional and cognitive development in which he assumes that the object he struck has hurt his hand in talion punishment. In parallel fashion, Eskimo religious beliefs assumed that the universe would retaliate for taboo breaking. The child's belief in immanent justice was reinforced in adult life by a belief in supernatural intervention through the shaman, a belief which was reinforced pragmatically by a potential wrongdoer's realistic assessment of the personal damage he would incur either from the *angatqoq* (shaman) or from the would-be victims or his relatives. The shaman, in touch with the powers of the universe, might discover a wrongdoer's evil act and could choose to punish him by magic unless he were dissuaded by gifts.

In addition to normative assumption, a range of more or less adequate sanctions, and the primal psychological bases for proper behavior which I have noted, Eskimos made plentiful use of rationalization. In effect, they often ignored that which could not be handled competently. For example, Eskimos appeared to use each other's goods with impunity. Yet informants have stated clearly that Eskimos did recognize theft and were often upset by someone who would "borrow" something without asking and then fail to return it. To avoid the conflicts that could occur surrounding such incidents, many acts of "theft" were redefined as "borrowing." Even wife theft could be converted into "wife lending" if the offended husband chose not to voice a complaint or pursue the matter aggressively.[14]

Besides this overt nonrecognition of theft, the high social value placed on sharing may also have functioned as a defense mechanism. If someone stole your kayak, it was better to assume he had borrowed it out of need. Such an assumption headed off conflict and made the forced lender a virtuous person. Sharing goods also served a definite survival value, and the sharer gained prestige by his sharing. On the other hand, people remembered those who took advantage of such social amenities and lost respect for them (and, one may assume, tried to hide their possessions when they saw the offenders coming).

Thus, basic Eskimo values concerning avoidance of conflict acted as a social glue. They held together social units which otherwise would have difficulty existing because of other, less useful values such as an individualism which verged on an egocentric disinterest in others. For Eskimos, a man's security depended on his neighbor's unwillingness to interfere in his life. Aside from avoiding relationships that might result in conflict, selectively creating reciprocal obligations with stronger men in one's own or other bands or villages was the best single way to protect one's own life and property. Many men exchanged wives or goods to attain security since these exchanges obligated the receiver and thereby offered a certain degree of protection against violence from him. These arrangements did not always work, however. In some instances among eastern as well as Alaska Eskimos, certain men murdered others for their wives (Freuchen, 1961).

One implication of the pragmatic Eskimo attitudes toward conflict is that violence was quite prevalent in traditional Northern Eskimo society. Another is that extended, if fragile, webs of relationships were woven across hundreds of miles. Both such implications are supported by my own informants and by the research of others. An individual might have a positive trading relationship with a man who was the mortal enemy of another friend and have none of these relationships necessarily impinge on another. All relationships were personally constructed. In fact, some men from one community could be at war with men from another community while others in the two communities traded peacefully. (See Burch and Correll, 1971).

The picture which emerges was a community life marred by sporadic and endemic violence sometimes rising to the level of war, subsiding at other times to the level of feud. This, of course, did not exhaust either

---

14. Wife lending was an act with many social complexities that can be subjected to psychological analysis. For the purpose of this paper, the discussion is limited to those events in which wife lending was actually pre-emptive acquiescence in a potential *fait accompli.*

intra- or intervillage relationships. For example, the Messenger Feast (Spencer, 1959) and the Inviting In Feast (Hawkes, 1913) show more than a nascent sense of the need for alliances between communities; and wife exchange (co-wives as Burch and Correll call it) *did* seem to function to create ties. To the degree that it existed at all, however, social control tended to rest on fear of retaliation by either supernatural or physical sanction. The bully who felt unchallenged by such controls was essentially a free agent.

Eskimos tolerated a bully out of fear until he antagonized enough men to create a body of adversaries. At that point, he usually would be killed. Atangarok, the shaman from Point Hope described by Spencer (1959), is an excellent example. Umealiks, who were boat owner-rich-hunt organizers, at times could get people to do what they wanted but usually not through bullying. The Umealik who attempted to dominate people through physical force would either be killed, which was most likely, or his crew members would simply move too far away from him to be dominated.[15] Contemporary *umealiks* also have no coercive or judicial power, but if they are respected persons, their opinions carry weight.

Faced with these difficulties, Eskimo communities met their needs for cooperative activity and the avoidance of violence by men acting in concert with "no one being boss."[16] If a man wished to initiate activities which demanded the assistance of his peers, he would raise the issue indirectly, never forcing a positive answer and never placing anyone in the difficult position of having to refuse. In so doing, he also protected himself from a disappointing negative response. By a series of subtle and indirect references within a community, all the individuals relevant to a given project could be made aware of the proposed cooperative event. If this were subtle enough, no one would ever have to admit openly that he

---

15. Pospisl argues from his own field work among the small Nunamiut band of Anaktuvuk Pass that the *umealik*, the hunting leader or whaling captain resolved disputes between members of faction or band without being a bully. Pospisl argues that ethnographers have overlooked this leader in dispute resolution for other Eskimo groups because the basis of his leadership is his economic skills and his jurisdiction is limited to persons with whom he has specific familial and economic ties. This does not correlate, he concludes, with the predisposition of ethnographers to seek a single central authority that dispenses justice for the entire society. Gubser (1965) would go even farther, calling the *umealik* (incongruously) a plaintiff. Our field work among the northern Eskimo does not support Pospisl's conclusion concerning the *umealik* and most assuredly does not support Gubser's conclusion.

16. In later years *umealiks* often did sit as members of the village council. However, Milan reports that when the president of one Eskimo village council called himself an *umealik*, other Eskimos scoffed at the analogy. The authority of *umealiks* and councilmen was defined differently (see Milan, 1964, p. 42).

even knew what was being suggested. I have personally witnessed several examples of this subtlety carried out in contemporary communities.

Thus, while social anarchy and relatively low levels of social control might accurately describe aspects of traditional Eskimo life relating to "law," necessary *work* of the social group was accomplished through careful and deliberate subtlety. It seems these two facts of Eskimo life were partly responsible for the contradictory impressions observers have had of Eskimos: on the one hand, smiling and cooperative; on the other, violent, aggressive, and demanding. Both could easily be true, and were.

In sum, the precontact "legal" system supported individualism but opposed coercive judicial authority. This made it nearly impossible for a single leader to initiate predictable mechanisms for social control. When a bully tried to impose his will, he generated antagonism and resistence, and if he persisted, he would finally be put down. The system seems to reflect a positive state of substantial individual liberty. It also seems to reflect anxiety about closeness and intrusion which points to a touchy ego as well as anxiety concerning the intentions of others toward the self. Eskimos have chosen to deal with this complex by avoidance, indirection, and circumlocution.

The structural background to this pattern has changed three times within the last 90 years: first, with the advent of missionaries and "white laws" in the person of the U.S. Commissioner, and more recently with the advent of the Alaska state trooper and local magistrate, and even more recently with the Village Public Safety Officer program. In all cases, the continuities and discontinuities with aboriginal conditions in conjunction with continuity in Eskimo cultural personality seems clear.

Culture Change And The Emergence Of An "Eskimo Court"

While earlier Eskimo society had norms, it distrusted the use of individual power to enforce them. Because retaliation against the powerful was an ever-present reality, socially concerned, powerful individuals in the society did not flaunt their power (hence, rarely imposed normative sanctions). Weaker members of the society who had problems or conflicts also feared asking others for help except in narrowly defined arrangements for short-range advantage. Finally, even the individual who had great social skills had no forum in which he could make those skills universally available.[17]

---

17. While the kashim among Yupik speakers often appeared to provide such a forum, according to our oldest Yupik informants, the procedure was never institutionalized.

American governmental authority involved Eskimos with its agents, literal extensions of American power, and was perceived as such. The missionary and the soldier could, and often did, bring to bear in-sur- mountable force upon criminal Eskimos, thus showing Eskimos the social utility of overwhelming sanctioning power.

Initially, the nature of U.S. intervention and power in Eskimo areas in conjunction with Eskimo cultural personality (1) nearly eliminated the local bullies and recidivist murderers, (2) greatly limited the power of the shaman and the taboo system through missionary influence, and (3) allowed the emergence of a village council system which was encouraged to become the effective agent of social control. This also altered some ex- ternalities of Eskimo life and allowed the play of the Eskimo cultural personality in a new structural situation.

Missionaries (who were the first school teachers as well) brought dramatic changes to Eskimo life as they aggressively challenged the *angatqoq* or shaman. Traditionally, the *angatqoq,* a supernaturally powerful person, was viewed with ambivalence. Capable of manipu- lating the supernatural environment to attract game or drive away evil spirits, he was equally capable of inflicting damage. His actions often seemed arbitrary, and sometimes even gifts would not placate him. There was really no way around him except through another *angatqoq* or, if he became too dangerous, by killing him and risking both magical and physical danger.

To the Eskimos, missionaries not only appeared to control a frequent- ly superior technology but they were unafraid of the shamans,[18] which implied to the Eskimos that missionaries also possessed great magical powers. Furthermore, missionaries offered a peaceful afterlife, always an uncertainty for Eskimos; at the simple price of obeying a few new taboos, authority was provided for abandoning a host of other taboos. Many Eskimos converted to Christianity as the best recourse. In the face of this competition many shamans simply stopped practicing or went "underground," thereby retaining only a limited influence.

The arrival of missionaries was usually attended by agents of U.S. law. American authority, often in the form of a Coast Guard cutter, and U.S. Commissioners provided a means to control endemic murder and feuding. Most importantly, from the Eskimo point of view, this was ac- complished with no individual Eskimo's complicity. Given the oppor- tunity to use outside authority to enforce the Eskimo norm of non-

---

18.   Van Stone (1958, 1962) notes these developments which parallel informants' com- ments from other northern Alaska Eskimo communities.

violence, interpersonal violence was virtually abandoned.[19] Furthermore, the introduction of the village council system allowed Eskimos to institutionalize their own approach to social control.

THE COUNCIL

Village councils date from U.S. contact; whether the council was created by the federal Indian bureaucracy, the U.S. Commissioners, the missionaries, Eskimos themselves, or a combination of these, almost from their inception the councils began to act as quasi-judicial entities in a uniquely Eskimo way. From around 1900 to the early 1960s, which is considered the "golden age" of Eskimo village life, councils attained a capacity for the resolution of local disputes which had been nonexistent before and which has since been virtually destroyed by the expansion of the U.S. justice system and, paradoxically, by attempts to provide more service to Eskimo communities.

As already noted, in traditional communities no one man or formal group acted as the arbiter of social control. By contrast, the council was encouraged by the U.S. marshals, and went on to resolve disputes in a manner that was related to the wrongdoer's character with the goal of reintegrating him into the group. The council could do this for two reasons. First, it acted with full backing of a seemingly omnipotent outside authority. Second, no Eskimo had to take individual responsibility for intervening; thus the system supported a basic Eskimo cultural personality trait. Responsibility was diffused, but the power to sanction was safely in the hands of responsive U.S. marshals. The council provided a forum for those individuals naturally gifted by social manipulation to exercise their talents and indeed to develop techniques of social control which were essentially Eskimo. It also freed the Eskimo community from the continual concern with murder as the primal effective sanction. Violent retaliation against the council would usually mean the removal of the retaliator by the outside authority. Violent retaliation against authority such as police or military forces was impossible, and therefore the council was free to proceed.

First, the councils discovered that by the relatively simple act of informing outside authority, a violent offender could be removed from the

---

19. Until recently, the number of murders in northern Alaska has been extremely low, This situation appears to be changing dramatically since 1970. Burch (personal communication) argues that the decline in warfare actually was a function of a population decimated by disease. This may have been a factor which does not preclude my own explanation.

village. Then, with traditional Eskimo pragmatism, now based on the certainty of outside force which was, nonetheless, not omnipresent in the community, Eskimos could seek methods of social control other than violence. Acting as a kind of society of elders or adjudication board, the council began to receive local complaints.

To initiate these proceedings individuals usually did not present their complaint in open session. Instead, they communicated privately with council members. This reflected the old Eskimo pattern of nonconfrontation and indirection. The council also raised issues in a circuitous fashion. It would state that "there has been talk about such and such a matter that involves A (the alleged wrongdoer) and the property of B (the probable complainant), and we should hear more about it." It then proceeded to call in B alone, other witnesses or people who might have facts, and finally A. It did not encourage confrontation between A and B. Questions to A and A's response were also very circuitous as council members waited for a confession from the accused offender or for others to relate information as it flowed from a more general discussion. The council then reviewed the facts and drew conclusion as a unit.[20]

From aboriginal times, confession has been valued under most conditions.[21] Eskimo confessants did not view their confession as frightening. Their own good opinion of themselves tended to make it difficult for Eskimos to believe that any statement of culpability would be received with shock. Since Eskimo society was noncensorious, confessions functioned to bring news. Confessions also alleviated guilt. Eskimo honesty in confessing to wrongdoing permitted the re-establishment of social harmony and indicated a willingness to accept responsibility for an action. Such notions correspond to the council format.

Only in the most serious cases did council decisions have any immediate effect (e.g., murder, etc.) and then only through contact with outside authority. The councils, however, quickly became gossip forums with the power to coerce the same people who had been moved by gossip in the precontact times, i.e., those who cared what others said more than they valued their privacy and autonomy. However, since this constituted a substantial part of the community and since the old Eskimo anxiety about loneliness, people's opinions, being left behind, etc. still operated,

---

20. Without question, the issue of early Eskimo "police" is one which is worthy of research. An institution so foreign to Eskimo traditions would most likely have developed unique dimensions. My inadequate information in this area, is not sufficient for further comment.

21. Excluded from this discussion are confessions elicited in shamanistic spirit invocation trances.

it seems the councils indirect effects were more substantial than their direct interventions.

Several village councils developed the notion of remuneration for theft and violent acts (those which did not seem to stem from incorrigible attitudes). Most interestingly, the ancient but weak sanction of public opinion became truly powerful when organized by the council. The council imposed such psychological santions as public apology. Lectures were given to malefactors during long meetings in which persons were invited to discuss an accused individual's entire behavior within his family or within the village. Even the baring of facts concerning one's sexual life or mental state was virtually limitless in this forum. For example, female council members questioned young women privately but then reported back to the council to enable the information to be recorded in council records. Predictably, these were powerful sanctions.

Continuities seem evident in the council's activities. The councils used a light touch with malefactors; present day council activities remain concerned with the potential for violence, and they express an unwillingness to impose, but manifest a strong tendency to use, the old Eskimo fear of isolation by village gossip as a means of social control. Discontinuities are evident as well. There are now hints of emerging formalisms and codifications of behavior. In addition there is an apparent increase in intrusiveness into many aspects of life and a willingness to manipulate power, even if it is manifested only in nascent form. While on the surface this looks contrary to the deeply felt opposition to interference, we have a partial explanation for this if we remember that intrusion was feared by the intruder because it could generate violent retaliation, and retaliation was difficult.

The willingness to be more intrusive is perhaps the most striking aspect of the change and requires further explanation. Perhaps intrusive aspects of the council activity may, in fact, be the formalization of gossip. As support for this suggestion, one might note that gossip, with all its aggressive and sometimes overtly hostile aspects, always has been part of the Eskimo social control mechanisms. In fact, the councils may have provided an opportunity to rationalize barbed comment in the guise of needed correction. Barbed comment, clearly construed so that its humor was devastating, was and is a normal Eskimo communication form. Such intrusions do not seem, however, to have been carried very far and were usually associated with very minor matters. Nonetheless, in addition to demanding restitution for antisocial acts, the councils may very well have provided an outlet for unexpressed hostilities, which here could be viewed as proper. It may well be that the actual effect of the village council system was to change the status quo as little as possible and that true reduction in violence actually resulted from the availability of external sanctions.

ESKIMO LAW WAYS IN THE CONTEMPORARY PERIOD: THE MAGISTRATE SYSTEM

A significant departure from the structural evolution of the legal system through the council and its forum occurred when the State of Alaska introduced the Eskimo magistrate and village constable. The magistrate is a statutorily created court that can hear petty misdemeanors and small claims. Judges are usually lay persons who are selected for the part-time position by presiding judges of the superior courts. Consultation with local people varies. Determination where magistrates will sit is a decision of the court system and generally relates to the level of offenses emanating from the village, the influx of population for seasonal employment, and similar factors. Because the position implies a subsidization of at least one village family, magisterial posts are rarely turned down by a village. However, it is not unknown for magistrates to resign because of conflicts with their work, subsistence activities, low pay, and more serious difficulties.

Where the councils acted as bodies and as agents of social control and followed traditional Eskimo lines of behavior in their procedures and expressed Eskimo cultural personality styles, the magistrate system singled out a single resident as judge and interventionist (the person who will *explicate* conflict instead of avoiding it, aggressively redirect another's life, and define and apply sanctions in what seems to be a unilateral fashion). As we might expect, this tends to re-elicit antagonistic attitudes toward authority. Thus a formal legal structure seems to limit the capacity of individual Eskimos to relate their own patterns of socialization to dispute resolution.

The magistrate system itself came about in the context of other significant culture changes. In the post-World War II period, the introduction of massive construction for missile sites, distant early warning sites and airfields, together with increased activity of the Bureau of Indian Affairs in building and expanding schools and the Public Health Service in combatting high levels of pathology and mortality among Eskimos, had significant, direct effects. People began to move more and more rapidly and definitively from isolated camps into increasingly larger villages for wage work, schooling, and medical care. Because the work was episodic, though promising, a boom/bust cycle existed in these communities (see Hippler, 1968, 1969, 1970b). But while the booms attracted people, the bust part of the cycle did not drive them away. Once exposed to better medical and educational services, the Eskimos stayed. Medical services have been very efficient indeed, nearly eliminating tuberculosis and upper respiratory infections as sources of mortality and reducing infant mortality to unheard of levels in this part of the world.

The net result of all these activities was an increasingly sedentary, unemployed population with significant expansion of the number of dependent and nonproductive persons. Social disorder and juvenile delinquency proliferated, especially with the rapidly increasing access to alcohol. At this juncture the magistrate system was introduced. It appears to have been a failure in reducing antisocial activity in a way which was felt to be meaningful by the community. It could not objectively indemnify individuals or the community for offenses, something the council system had accomplished with ease and sophistication. The primary difficulty with the magistrate system seemed to be its lack of "fit" with Eskimo culture and personality.

According to this system, a single member of the village must take up the symbols of outside law to sit in independent judgment of his peers, thus placing the process of dispute resolution within a form difficult for Eskimos to accept. In place of the anonymity of council members, the actions of a single individual are fully exposed, and individual coercive power remains difficult for Eskimos to accept. This feeling against a single authority sometimes creates hostility against the magistrate. In one crowded courtroom in northern Alaska, a man spoke in Eskimo from the rear of the court to the judge, causing the magistrate to dismiss the case immediately. When the state trooper who was present asked in English what had occurred, the magistrate said that the speaker was the defendant's brother and had threatened the magistrate if he proceeded with the case. No such threat would have been made to or acknowledged by the council. Though such a reaction is rare, its implications are important: The magistrate cannot obscure his individuality by submerging it in the group action of a council.

This potential for conflict is met in another more common but more critical way. The usual reaction to the magisterial system is to avoid its formalities. Even magistrates often attempt to avoid their roles, though with little notable success.

Because cases heard by the U.S. Commissioner and, later, the magistrate are almost exclusively criminal in nature, individuals do not consider the magistrate court an appropriate forum for weighing private or civil matters and will not bring them to the magistrate. As noted, no such distinction was made in cases head by the council. For example, whereas one northern Alaska Eskimo village council routinely handled about 100 issues a year, the new magistrate has averaged only three cases per year. The other problems have not disappeared; they are simply not being dealt with since the councils cannot enter the judicial area, and they have rapidly lost confidence in their own capacity to deal with non-judicial matters.

Feeling that they lack the power in their new capacity to ameliorate problems by indirection, magistrates apparently sentence heavily (in some cases) and then suspend sentences to that a balance of nonintervention is maintained . . . *le plus change.* To the extent they are in communities with non-Eskimo police, other magistrates tend to prefer that the police handle minor matters outside the court.

Even though offenses have increased 10-to-20 fold during a 20-year period in one large northern Alaska Eskimo community, the Eskimo magistrate imposes weak penalties (as little as 10% of previous fines) upon now more affluent Eskimos and it is nearly impossible to elicit a jail sentence.

Finally, in recent years, the State of Alaska has instituted a massive program to provide villages with Village Public Safety Officers (VPSOs), trained in police, fire fighting, search and rescue, and emergency medical intervention tactics. Most VPSOs are indigenous people, and the result is expectable. Though the program is still too new to ascertain its effects over time, the immediate results are clear and negative.

Since the rise in criminal activity is severe, perhaps reaching the level of pre-White-contact violence, local citizens, desperate to stem the tide of criminal activity, are usually very happy to secure a VPSO. But where overwhelming U.S. governmental authority once nearly eliminated mortal violence in Eskimo villages, VPSOs seem almost powerless. The same villagers who wanted protection are furious at the first sign of the intrusions necessary to stop the offender. For the Eskimo, contemporary U.S. law fits poorly with Eskimo needs because it is so heavily weighted with arcane tactics which nearly prohibit a rapid and lengthy removal of the violent offenders.

At one time unable to protect themselves, Eskimos again find that, since powerful authority has become distant and local authority is in charge, they cannot protect themselves. Now that almost anyone can "get away with it," the poorly socialized feel free to intrude into anyone's life with near impunity. The more socially responsible are disaffected by the mere presence of a local VPSO (usually young) who claims to have the right to intrude. VPSOs, themselves frequently unable to handle this pressure, quit or become totally ineffective in some districts at a rate reaching 90% in less than a year.

CONCLUSION

Overall, in most villages discontinuities in Eskimo social control are more apparent than real since the occurrence of the first major change, ie: the practice of having murderers removed by outside authority. Behavior and attitudes still appear to be dominated by long-standing culture-specific personality dimensions.

An apparently successful innovation, the introduction of village councils functioned well when nothing serious had to be considered and they could express the traditional cultural personality. From the late 1800s serious matters such as murder were handled by outside authority, reflecting the essential incapacity of Eskimo society to cope with such matters expeditiously. While some minor matters were disposed of by local councils, the councils then functioned as forums for village gossip with its low-level sanctioning power; thus there was no significant alteration of earlier nonintervention norms.

The replacement of councils by Eskimo magistrates has, if anything, enhanced nonintervention as a norm. More formal procedures are brought to bear, more arrests are made, but, except in murder or the most brutal of assaults, disposition of cases remains vague and nonintervening. In these extreme instances, the offender, as was so since 1900, is remanded to outside authority. Finally, the creation of the direct local intervenor, the VPSO, has elicited so much anxiety and anger that the system is nearly a total failure.

If one takes into account basic Eskimo cultural personality attributes, the operations of the council and magistrate become clear: (1) intrusion into another's life is dangerous; (2) it is best to recharacterize wrong doing to avoid conflict; (3) circumlocution and indirection are preferable to direct statement; (4) one is emotionally dependent upon others' opinions and good will; (5) one is not truly responsible for one's own actions; and, (6) rules do not apply if one is in an unassailable position of authority and he can bully others. All of these principles are virtually unaltered since traditional times.

The most parsimonious explanation for this continuity in the face of changing forms seems to lie in the area of cultural personality. While cultural personality changes do occur in populations through time, the conservatism of the basic cultural personality seems to be powerful. The tendency toward violence, affect hunger, and fear of others' opinions as well as an unwillingness to intrude in other lives still fundamentally color social control in Alaska Eskimo communities. Finally, since many of the socialization experiences which create the cultural personality responsible for those outcomes remain unchanged or only slightly altered, it seems reasonable to assume that, regardless of dramatic alterations in the externalities of Alaska Eskimo life, a clearly discernible continuity in social control will remain for another generation.

BIBLIOGRAPHY

BEECHEY, F. S. (1831). *Narrative of a Voyage to the Pacific and Bering Strait.* Vol. I and Vol. II. London: H. Colburn and B. Bentley.

BOAS, F. (1899). Property marks of Alaska Eskimos. *American Anthropologist,* 1, 4:601–613.

BOGAJAVLENSKY, S. (1973). Personal communication.

———— & FULLER, R. W. (1973). Polar bears, walrus hides and social solidarity. *Alaska Journal,* 3, 2:66–76.

BOYER, L. B. (1962). Remarks on the personality of shamans. In *The Psychoanalytic Study of Society,* W. Muensterberger & S. Axelrad (eds.). II. New York: International Universities Press, pp. 233–254.

————, KLOPFER, B., BROWER, F. R., & KAWAI, H. (1964). Comparison of the shamans and pseudoshamans of the Apaches of the Mescalero Indian Reservation: A Rorschach study. *Journal of Projective Techniques and Personality Assessment,* 28, 2:173–180.

————, DEVOS G. A., BORDERS, O., & BORDERS, T. A. (1978). The burnt child reaction among the Yukon-Delta Eskimos. *The Journal of Psychological Anthropology,* 1, 1:7–56.

BOYER, R. (1975). Personal communication.

BRIGGS, J. L. (1970a). Kapluna daughter: Living with Eskimos. *TransAction,* 13–24.

———— (1970b). *Never in Anger.* Cambridge: Harvard University Press.

———— (1975). The origins of nonviolence: Aggression in two Canadian Eskimo groups. *Psychoanalytic Study of Society,* VI. New York: International Universities Press, pp. 134–203.

———— (1978). Personal communication.

BURCH, E. S., Jr. (1978). Personal communication.

———— & CORRELL, T. C. (1971). Alliance and conflict: Inter-regional relations in North Alaska. *Alliance in Eskimo Society.* Proceedings of the American Ethnological Society. L. Guemple (ed.), pp. 17–39.

CHANCE, N. A. (1966). *The Eskimo of North Alaska.* New York: Holt, Rinehart and Winston.

COOK, J. & KING, J. (1785). *A Voyage to the Pacific Ocean Undertaken by the Command of His Majesty for Making Discoveries in the Northern Hemisphere.* London: H. Hughes.

ERIKSON, E. H. (1950). *Childhood and Society.* New York: Norton.

ERIKSON, E. H. (1959). Identity and the life cycle. Monograph, *Psychological Issues,* Vol. 1, No. 1, New York: International Universities Press.

FEJES, C. (1966). *People of the Noatak.* New York: Alfred A. Knopf.

FERGUSON, F. N. (1960). Eskimo personality in the light of nine Rorschachs from the Great Whole River Eskimo. North Carolina University Institute of Research in the Social Sciences. *Research Previews,* 8, 1:8–13.

FRANKLIN, SIR JOHN (1828). *Narrative of a Second Expedition to the Shores of the Polar Sea in the Years 1825, 1826, and 1827.* London: John Murray, (Greenwood Press, N.Y., 1969).

FREEMAN, D. M. A., FOULKS, E., & FREEMAN, P. A. (1972). Eskimo arctic hysteria and superego development. Paper presented to Symposium on the Use of Psychoanalytic Theory in Anthropology. American Psychoanalytic Association Meeting, New York.

FREUCHEN, P. (1961). *Book of the Eskimos.* Greenwich, CT: Fawcett.

GARBER, C. M. (1935). Marriage and sex customs of the Western Eskimos. *Scientific Monthly,* 41:215-227.

GEBER, M. (1958). The psychomotor development of African children in the first year and the influence of maternal behavior. *Journal of Social Psychology,* 47:185-195.

GRABURN, N. (1968). Imcariot: The killings. Paper presented at symposium on Primitive Law, annual meetings, American Anthropological Association, Seattle.

_____ (1969). Eskimo law in the light of self and group interest. *Law and Society Review IV,* 1:45-60.

GUBSER, N. (1965). *The Nunamiut Eskimos, Hunters of Caribou.* New Haven: Yale University Press.

GUEMPLE, L. (1978). Personal communication.

HAWKES, E. W. (1913). The "inviting in" feast of the Alaskan Eskimo. *Memories of the Canadian Department of Mines,* 45:1-20.

HEINRICH, A. (1955). An outline of kinship system of the Bering Straits Eskimos. M.A. thesis, University of Alaska, College.

_____ (1960). Structural features of Northwestern Eskimo kinship. *Southwestern Journal of Anthropology,* 16, 1:110-126.

HIPPLER, A. E. (1968). Some unplanned consequences of planned culture change. In *Higher Latitudes of North America: Socio-Economic Studies in Regional Development.* Boreal Institute, University of Alberta, Occasional Paper *6:11-21.

_____ (1969). Barrow and Kotzebue: An Exploratory Comparison of Acculturation and Education in Two Large Northwestern Alaskan Villages. Training Center for Community Programs, University of Minnesota, Minneapolis.

_____ (1970a). *Eskimo Acculturation.* Institute of Social, Economic and Government Research, *28, University of Alaska, College.

_____ (1970b). *From Village to Town: An Intermediate Step in the Acculturation of Alaskan Eskimos.* University of Minnesota Training Center for Community Programs, Minneapolis.

_____ (1973). The subarctic Athabascans of interior Alaska: A culture and personality perspective. *American Anthropologist,* 75, 56:1529-1541.

_____ (1974). The North Alaska Eskimos: A culture and personality perspective. *American Ethnologist,* 1, 3:449-470.

_____ (1975). Transcultural psychiatric and related research in the North American Arctic and Sub Arctic. *Transcultural Psychiatric Research,* 12:103-115.

_____, BOYER, L. B., & BOYER, R. M. (1975). The psychocultural significance of the Alaska Athabascan Potlatch Ceremony. In *The Psychoanalytic Study of the Child,* VI: 100-133.

_____ & CONN, S. (1972). *Traditional Athabascan Law Ways and Their Relationship to Contemporary Problems of Bush Justice.* Institute of Social, Economic and Government Research, Occasional Paper #7, University of Alaska, College.

_____ _____ (1973). *Northern Eskimo Law Ways and their Relationship to Contemporary Problems of Bush Justice.* ISEGR Occasional Paper #10, Fairbanks, University of Alaska.

HOEBEL, E. A. (1940-1941). Law ways of the primitive Eskimos. *Journal of the American Institute of Criminal Law and Criminology,* 31:663-683.

_____ (1954). *The Law of Primitive Man*. Cambridge, Mass.: Harvard University Press.

_____ (1963). Community organization and patterns of change among North Canadian and Alaskan Indians and Eskimos. *Anthropologica,* 5:3-8.

HRDLICKA, A. (1936). Fecundity of Eskimo women. *Journal of Physical Anthropology,* 22:91-95.

HUGHES, C. C. (1966). From contest to council: Social control among the St. Lawrence Island Eskimos. In *Political Anthropology,* M. J. Swartz, V. W. Turner, & A. Tuden (eds.). Chicago: Aldine, pp. 253-263.

JACQUES, E. (1957). Social systems as a defense against persecutory and depressive anxiety. In *New Directions in Psychoanalysis,* M. Klein, P. Heinmann, & R. E. Money-Kyrle (eds.). New York: Basic Books.

JARVIS, D. H. et al. (1899). (U.S. Revenue Cutter Service) *Report of the Cruise of the U.S. Revenue Cutter "Bear" and the Overland Expedition for the Relief of the Whalers in the Arctic Ocean*. Washington, U.S. Government Printing Office.

JENNESS, D. (1953). Stray notes on the Eskimos of Arctic Alaska. College: *University of Alaska Anthropological Papers,* 1, 2:5-14.

KLEIN, M. (1932). *The Psychoanalysis of Children*. London: Hogarth Press, 1950.

_____ (1957). *New Directions in Psychoanalysis*. New York: Basic Books.

KLEINFELD, J. S. (1970). Cognitive strengths of Eskimo students and implications for education. Institute of Social, Economic and Government Research, Occasional Paper #3, University of Alaska, Fairbanks.

_____ (1971). Visual memory in village Eskimo and urban Caucasian students. *Arctic,* 24, 2:132-138.

KLOPFER, B., AINSWORTH, M. D., KLOPFER, W. G., & HOLT, R. R. (1954). *Developments in the Rorschach Technique. Vol. 1. Technique and Theory,* pp. 275, 293, 362.

LANTIS, M. (1938). The Alaska whale cult and its affinities. *American Anthropologist,* 438-464.

_____ (1946). The social culture of the Nunivak. *The American Philosophical Society,* N.S. XXXV:153-323.

_____ (1947). *Alaskan Eskimo Cremonialism*. New York: J.J. Augustin.

_____ (1959). Alaskan Eskimo cultural values. *Polar Notes,* 1:35-48. Occasional publication of the Stefansson Collection.

LEWIN, B. D. (1950). *The Psychoanalysis of Elation*. New York: Norton.

LUBART, J. (1976). *Psychodynamic Problems of Adaptation-MacKenzie Delta Eskimos*. Ottawa, Northern Science Research Group, MDRP #7.

LUCIER, C. (1954). Buckland Eskimo myths. *University of Alaska Anthropological Papers,* 6, 2:89-117.

MAHLER, M. S., PINE, F., & BERGMAN, A. (1975). *The Psychological Birth of the Human Infant*. New York: Basic Books.

McKENNAN, R. A. (1959). *The Upper Tanana Indians*. The Yale University Publications in Anthropology, No. 55. New Haven: Yale University Press.

MILAN, F. A. (1964). The acculturation of the contemporary Eskimo of Wainwright, Alaska. *University of Alaska Anthropological Papers,* 11, 2:1-85.

MURDOCH, J. (1892). *Ethnological Results of the Point Barrow Expedition*. Washington, D.C. U.S. Bureau of American Ethnology, 9:3-441.

NELSON, E. W. (1899). *The Eskimo about Bering Strait*. Washington, D.C. U.S. Bureau of American Ethnology. 18th Annual Report. 1896-1897.

PARKER, S. (1962). Eskimo psychopathology in the context of Eskimo personality and culture. *American Anthropologist,* 64, 1:76-96.

PETTIT, G. A. (1956). Primitive education in North America. Berkeley, University of California Press, *Publications in American Archeology and Ethnography,* 43:1-182.

POSPISL, L. (1964). Law and societal structures among the Nunamiut Eskimo. In *Explorations in Cultural Anthropology,* W. H. Goodenough (ed.). New York: McGraw-Hill, pp. 395-431.

_____ (1971). *Anthropology of Law: A Comparative Theory.* New York: Harper and Row.

_____ (1972). *The Ethnology of Law.* McCaleb Module in Anthropology 12. New York: Addison-Wesley.

PRESTON, C. (1964). Psychological testing with Northwest Coast Alaskan Eskimos. *Genetic Psychology Monographs,* 69:323-419.

RICHARDS, R. A. (1949). *Arctic Mood.* Caldwell, Idaho: Cafton Printers.

RODAHL, K. (1963). *The Last of the Few.* New York: Harper and Row.

RASMUSSEN, K. (1952). *The Alaskan Eskimos.* Report of the 5th Thule Expedition, 1921-24, 10, 8:1-291. H. Ostermann (ed.). Copenhagen: Gyldendal.

SIMMONDS, P. L. (1852). *Sir John Franklin and the Arctic Regions.* Zirftalo: G. H. Derby.

SIMPSON, J. (1875). Observations on the Western Eskimo and the country they inhabit. In *Arctic Geography and Ethnology,* 233-275.

SPENCER, M. (1954). The child in the contemporary culture of the Barrow Eskimo. *1952 Alaska Science Conference Proceedings,* 3:130-132. College, Alaska.

SPENCER, R. F. (1959). *The North Alaskan Eskimo.* Smithsonian Institution Bureau of American Ethnology Bulletin 171. Washington, D.C., U.S. Government Printing Office.

STEFANSSON, V. (1913). *My Life with the Eskimos.* New York: MacMillan.

VAN DEN STEENHOVEN, G. (1959). *Legal Concepts Among the Netsilik Eskimos of Pelley Bay.* Ottawa. Northern Coordination and Research Centre.

VAN STONE, J. (1958). An Eskimo Community and the Outside World. *University of Alaska Anthropological Papers,* 7, 1'27-38.

_____ (1962). *Point Hope, an Eskimo Village in Transition.* Seattle: University of Washington Press.

PART II

RELIGION

3

The Cult Phenomenon: Psychoanalytic Perspective

W. W. MEISSNER, S. J.

The task of this paper is to bring some psychoanalytic perspective to the understanding of cult phenomena. The first step in such an undertaking is to try to gain some degree of conceptual clarity about cults and their relationship to other forms of organized religious expression.

The matter of definition is one with which the sociologists of religion have struggled at length. The church-sect typology derives from Max Weber. For Weber, a "church" was "a community organized by officials into an institution which bestows gifts of grace" (Gerth and Mills, 1946, p. 288). Church organization, therefore, was hierocratic, bureaucratic and hierarchical in authority structure. As Weber comments:

> For the church, being the holder of institutionalized grace, seeks to organize the religiosity of the masses and to put its own officially monopolized and mediated sacred values in the place of the autonomous and religious status qualifications of the religious virtuosos. (p. 288)

On these terms, Roman Catholicism would qualify as a "church," but, curiously, the Baptist Church would not. A sect, on the other hand, was a form of voluntary association of believers, similar in nature to more secular versions such as clubs or fraternal organizations.

Attempts to integrate empirical observations with Weber's ideal types have always presented difficulties. A somewhat different slant on the relationship between church and sect was given by Niebuhr (1929) who argued that a sect is a relatively unstable form of religious organization that, over time, is transformed into a church, which represents a more stable form of religious organization. However, the failure of the new church to meet the needs of many of its members sows the seeds of discontent, leading to further schism and the splitting off of new sects. In this way, Niebuhr envisioned an endless cycle of birth, transformation, splitting, and rebirth of religious movements in a constant process of division and cyclic reorganization.

Another step forward was made when Johnson (1963) argued that religious groups could be more effectively classified by appealing to a single attribute, namely the form of the relationship between the religious group and its social environment. He concluded on this basis that a church could be regarded as a religious group that accepted the social environment in which it existed, while a sect was a religious group that essentially rejected the social environment. This conceptualization reflects the degree to which a given religious group may be in a state of tension with its surrounding social environment. Consequently, not only established churches but also a variety of religious institutions occupy a more stable sector of the social structure and provide a cluster of roles, norms, values, activities and beliefs that contribute to and maintain the stability of social structure. Religious institutions have the capacity to adapt to social change.

But religious movements may have advancement of social changes as their goal, or, conversely, may aim at preventing social change. Religious movements, then, are forms of social movement that aim at the causing or preventing of change in a system of beliefs, values, symbols and practices that are religiously based and oriented. Moreover, analogously to the understanding of sects and churches, religious movements strive to become religious institutions and thus seek to become the dominant faith in their society. The degree of tension that is often associated with sect movement and sect formation is equivalent to a form of subcultural deviance marked by difference, antagonism, and separation (Stark and Bainbridge, 1979).

Niebuhr's approach to the formation of sects applies to schismatic religious movements that take their origin as an internal faction of another religious body. But this is not the only form of religious movement that exists in a high state of tension with the surrounding sociocultural environment. Such religious movements may have no prior history of organizational attachment to another religious group and may, in fact, lack any close cultural continuity or similarity to such groups. To the extent that they add some distinctive feature to the more familiar characteristics of religious groups in the culture, these nonschismatic, deviant religious groups may represent either a form of cultural innovation or may comprise a cultural importation in that they represent or form an extension of a religious body already established in some other cultural setting.

Consequently, both cults and sects may be regarded as deviant religious bodies that exist in a relatively high state of tension with the surrounding sociocultural environment. From this point of view, then, the sect is specifically a schismatic movement that breaks off from a previously existing religious organization. In this perspective, cults do not have such a prior tie with the previously existing religious body. The cult may be imported from an alien religious context, or it may have originated in the host society through innovation rather than by schism. In any case, the cult comes to represent something new in relationship to the existing religious movements in a given society. If it arises by innovation within the society, it brings to that culture a new revelation or insight justifying its claim that it is somehow different or unique. Usually, imported cults have little in common culturally with the already existing faiths. Consequently, while they may be ancient in their society of origin, they present themselves to the contemporary social context as novel and different.

While the sociological analysis and the distinction of church, sect, and cult maintain their validity, from another perspective, the cult phenomenon can be regarded as expressing a general tendency in human religious experience and in the organization of religious groups. From a psychological perspective, the cult phenomenon seems to be built into all forms of organized religious experience. In this sense, the cult phenomenon refers to the tendency within a religious organization to form factions or subgroupings that can then set up divergent or deviant elements of belief that are at variance or even in opposition to the generally accepted belief system of the religious organization.

Individual cults tend to arise in all religious organizations, even the most tightly and systematically organized and disciplined. In this regard the cult phenomenon is at the root of schismatic developments and thus comes to contribute to the development not only of deviant cults (in the sociological sense), but also to new religious sects. Of course, the internal tensions and variations within any religious group can arise from other sources than those pertaining strictly to the system of beliefs. Such variation may also come to express itself through modifications of ritual or liturgy, deviations in various forms of religious practice, or other matters of churchly discipline. However, usually the resultant grouping will only be regarded as a cult or sect when significant aspects of the belief system in question are affected.

An interesting phenomenon concerning such deviant religious subgroupings is the extent to which they tend to become the repository for psychopathology. Even to pose the question is to invite controversy. The amount of acrimony, vilification, contention, and even litigation that flows between religious groups in our society is often staggering, if not disedifying. In the areas of religious dialogue, the well-known "mote-beam" projection seems to be the rule rather than the exception.

Religious adherents are quick to find the mote in their neighbor's religious eye, but they are blind to the beam in their own.

I would think that despite the potential for disagreement in this area, we could reach some degree of consensus regarding the propensity for psychopathology to find its way into religious cults. If we remind ourselves that the cult phenomenon is not restricted to such deviant cult groups, but rather has its play in varying degree, within all forms of religious organization, we may be able to keep a better perspective and avoid the fallacy of the mote and the beam. In a recent discussion of pathological aspects of religious groups, Pruyser (1977) listed a number of aspects of cultic belief that seemed to reflect underlying psychopathology.

One such neurotic feature of religious movements is the sacrifice of intellect. In many cultic contexts, a blind and unquestioning faith is not only required but demanded. In the Middle Ages a blind faith in incubi, alchemy, or even the Messianic pretensions of a variety of self-appointed saviors was a dominant aspect of cultic manifestations. Norman Cohn in his excellent work *The Pursuit of the Millenium* (1970) has traced the origins and evolutions of a wide variety of such medieval Messianic cults. Even in our own day certain cults demand blind and totally accepting faith towards seemingly undeserving objects, such as an ignorant, obese adolescent from India or a right-wing agitator from South Korea. Similarly, within the charismatic movement, large numbers of Christians are able to see manifestations of the Holy Spirit in acts of babbling or having fits. It is as if to say that the spirit of love was devoid of intelligence or reason. Even in the more benign manifestations of fundamentalism or archaism that finds some manifestation in more established churches, there is a tendency to erect a dichotomy and opposition between faith and reason. Someone with a more balanced religious perspective might embrace the position that neither faith nor reason were mutually reducible; but, by the same token, he would not find it necessary to sacrifice one to the other.

Along with the sacrifice of intellect, in neurotic forms of religion there is often a subtle form of thought control which masks an underlying authoritarianism. As Pruyser (1977) observes, "Doctrinaire and authoritarian thought turns symbols into things, ideas into concrete entities, suggestions into decrees, leaving in the end nothing to the imagination—creating a closed system that holds people captive" (p. 335). Thus, the sacrifice of intellect is invariably accompanied by a surrender of freedom. The tendency to accept authoritarian imposition, along with the surrender of freedom, can also be encountered in the regressive surrender of ego controls and responsibility found in various forms of impulsive emotionality along with the attribution of such impulses, on the good side, to the motions of the spirit or, on the bad side, to the evil influence of the devil.

This constellation of characteristics is reminiscent of the attributes of the authoritarian personality (Adorno et al, 1950). The study of the authoritarian personality derived its impetus from the events of the Second World War and the holocaust. It began as a study of antisemitic attitudes, but was extended to a formulation of a style of personality that can express itself in a wide variety of forms of prejudice, ethnocentricity, conflicts over power and dependence, as well as conflicts over aggression. The sacrifice of intellect, the surrender of freedom, the retreat from responsibility by submission to the power of the leader, the frequent repression of aggressive impulses and their projection to the environment outside the cult, are all characteristics that are quite consistent with the authoritarian personality and suggest that similar basic configurations may be found in many cult members. The central tendency of such individuals to escape from the threat of freedom and responsibility by the surrender of their own independence and their submission to a powerful and often idealized external figure, force, or cause (Fromm, 1941), is almost a formula for cult participation. Moreover, the authoritarian personality comprises one of the important personality configurations that the paranoid process may take, a configuration that is both pathological in nature yet supported by social and cultural contexts (Meissner, 1978).

One aspect of cult involvement that deserves special comment is the fanaticism that is often observed in the behavior of cult members. Fanaticism can be analyzed both in terms of the commitment (in the sense of the intensity of emotional attachment to the group or to its leader or its goals) and in regard to the modification of the belief system that characterizes the cult group. Both of these elements may be present in relatively normal proportion; but if either becomes disproportionate, we encounter fanaticism. Cults may vary in the degree of fanaticism they demand from participating members. Correspondingly, the degree of fanaticism can vary within any religious group or movement; and the degree of fanaticism in any religious group tends to parallel the extent to which the cult phenomenon is operative in that group.

One aspect of the cult phenomenon which is of particular interest to psychoanalysis is the degree to which pathological narcissism becomes an operative factor. Cults set themselves apart as an elite or exclusive group set in opposition to outsiders. This claim for special status and elitism has a particular appeal to individuals suffering from feelings of shame and inferiority relating to narcissistic personality defects. It should be noted that in the organization and sustaining of this elite status, paranoid mechanisms play a central role insofar that they project undesirable or feared qualities to the outside of the group and, correspondingly, preserve the qualities of self-enhancement and idealizing aggrandizement within the group. Consequently, participation in the cult often offers relief for inner feelings of inadequacy, powerlessness, ennui, emptiness, or meaninglessness. Kohut's (1976) recent discussion of idealization in the "cult" of psychoanalysis has its analogous application here. He writes:

> . . . The idealization of a group model protects the individual member of the group against certain states of narcissistic disequilibrium which are experienced as envy, jealousy, and rage. If these narcissistic tensions remain undischarged, they are exquisitely painful; if, however, they are discharged (through actions especially motivated by narcissistic rage) then they are socially dangerous. . . . [If, furthermore, the imago of the leader] . . . has been securely included in the [member's] idealized superego and has thus become a part of the self, then he can disregard contemporary competitors, they are not a threat to his own narcissistic security, and he can avoid suffering the painful narcissistic injuries which the comparison with the actual rivals for the goals of his narcissistic strivings might inflict on him. (p. 389)

Characteristic of the cult phenomenon, then, is its offer to the potential convert of a charismatic leader with whom he has the opportunity to both identify and idealize. Cultists will often speak reverently of the presence of the leader. The Guru Mahara Ji followers use a special Hindi term, the *Darshan,* to describe the physical experience of a high or a particular form of excitement that the follower experiences in the presence of the Guru. Undoubtedly, the experience has libidinal and hysterical components, but these are intimately connected with narcissistic dynamics. The leader of Guru's presentation of himself as an object to be idealized obviously responds to a deep inner need in his followers. We can infer that the more total the acceptance and subjection to the leader is built into the cult ethic, the more profoundly disturbed is the level of narcissistic and personality defect in the followers who accept it.

At this juncture, we are on familiar ground. In Freud's (1921) discussion of group psychology, he focused on the quality of the relationship to the leader as a central aspect of the group phenomenon. In Freud's view, the identification with the leader was based on a form of aim-inhibited sexual love. The outcome of this attachment was a form of idealization of the object, similar to the state of being in love. The idealized object was consequently introjected and, in Freud's terms, takes the place of the ego ideal. Thus, a basic aspect of the group formation is the replacement of the ego ideal in the group members by the idealization of the leader and identification with him. Freud's way of putting it was that "a number of individuals . . . have substituted one and the same object for their ego-ideal, and consequently have identified themselves with one another in their ego." (p. 116)

It is also obvious that in a variety of more pathological cult contexts, the cult leader tends to exploit this narcissistic attachment, often in the interest of personal aggrandizement or enrichment. The dynamics here are also readily recognized as group variants of the narcissistic transferences that have been delineated by Kohut (1971). Perhaps it would be premature to conclude that all members of such cults were narcissitic personalities or that they suffered from relatively severe narcissistic defects. But to the extent that the cult involves such transparently narcissistic dynamics, we can conclude that the cult phenomenon tunes in on basic narcissistic needs and processes that may be more broadly endemic in the susceptible population. By the same token, it may be reasonable to infer that individuals with diagnosable narcissistic pathology may, indeed, be more susceptible to the cult influence.

The strength of these dynamics and their influence over individual psychic life and human behavior is something that we often tend to underestimate. The power of such inner forces was dramatically brought to mind by the tragic events at Jonestown. We can wonder what it was that drove those unfortunate souls to join the People's Church. What was it that gave Jim Jones such an absolute and unquestioned power that he could demand the ultimate sacrifice of death from his followers? What was it that allowed them to accept his psychotic delusions as an acceptable and authentic belief system? There seems to be little doubt that Jim Jones was psychotic, paranoid, and delusional. He believed he knew the exact time of the atomic holocaust. He thought himself to be an object of a conspiracy aimed at his overthrow and the destruction of himself and the People's Church. He believed, and insisted, that he was the only legitimate sexual object in his church. We can only conclude that belonging to the People's Church and acceptance of its delusional belief system must have touched the deepest roots of the human existence of these people. We would also have to conclude that powerful underlying narcissistic needs lay at the heart of this human need, and that the belonging and belief of the People's Church must have provided a sense of purposefulness and meaningfulness to the lives of otherwise empty and deprived people. That motivation was sufficiently powerful to allow them to sacrifice their lives in the interest of sustaining it.

Available evidence seems to indicate a significant degree of psychopathology and emotional distress in cult converts. Not only do they manifest higher scores than normal comparison groups on measures of neurotic distress, but they also have greater incidences of psychiatric problems as reflected in a higher percentage of seeking prior psychiatric assistance or hospitalization for emotional problems (Galanter et al., 1979). Among members of the Unification Church (followers of Reverend Sun Myung Moon), preconversion measures of distress are higher than postconversion measures. The greatest improvement was reported by those who experienced the most commitment to the movement. Similar findings have been documented in members of Eastern religious cults (Galanter and Buckley, 1978). Proselytizing efforts for conversion and pressures for commitment have been compared to brainwashing (Ungerleider and Wellisch, 1979). The group ethos and the commitment to it by conversion provide the basis for a new integration of the individual's life experience, providing a sense of belonging, participation, meaning, and purpose that changes the participants' sense of self and the meaning of their existence. Cult participants generally manifest a "strong ideological hunger" (Lifton, 1956) for which the cult provides sustenance, as well as relief from inner turmoil. Among those who drop out, needs are less intense. Cult adherents tend to find greater emotional relief and stability in the cult and can more easily identify with the cult leader and thus minimize the sense of domination and submission (Ungerleider and Wellisch, 1979).

In order to concretize some of these observations, I would like to examine briefly the phenomenon of the cargo cults that flourished during the Second World War and its aftermath in Melanesia, particularly in parts of Dutch New Guinea. The advantage of focusing on the cargo cults is that they are of relatively recent origin and their roots are not obscure; they are also sufficiently removed from our own cultural context that we can look at them with considerable objectivity. Moreover, the cargo cults seem to manifest many of the essential elements that arise in the wide spectrum of forms of cult formation. Such millenial cults arise within many cultural contexts, with varying degrees of involvement in political or economic processes. If they can be regarded as symptomatic expressions of underlying psychopathology, they can also play a role as precursors of political revolutions that may have a positive and constructive outcome (Lidz et al, 1973; Worsley, 1968).

The cargo cults actually had their roots in the 19th century, emerging under the impact of Dutch civilization on the indigenous population. But the cults received a tremendous impetus during the Second World War when western armed forces littered the island with surplus cargo and military equipment. According to the cult belief, this wealth of cargo actually belonged to the dead ancestors of the tribe who were lured into giving the cargo to the white foreigners, rather than to the native Melanesians for whom it had originally been intended. The cults aim at restoring a past set of conditions which involve regaining the good will of their ancestors so they would bestow the blessings of cargo on the cult members. The central belief is that the spirits of the dead will return and one day bring with them the cargo of modern goods intended for the cult adherents. The cargo cults are revivalistic, insofar as they look to a restoration of a former golden age in which they will be united with their honored ancestors, and milleniarist, in that they anticipate the coming of a golden age at some unspecified time in the future.

Other features of the cargo cults include the aggrandizement and idealization of the cult leader who is uniquely blessed with the ability to aggregate significant amounts of cargo, marking him as especially honored by the spirits of the dead while stamping him with the aura of leadership and magical power. The leadership role of these cult figures is reinforced by the expectation of the appearance of one or more prophets who have received special revelations from God, from Christ, or from the dead ancestors. These prophets will be appointed to prescribe magical rituals which will ensure provision of the cargo. In some cults, the believers have been directed to destroy all their belongings; in others they have been ordered to hand over all of their wordly possessions to the cult leader. Only in this way will they be found eligible to receive the wealth of the cargo. Many of the cults foster a belief in the imminent coming of Christ.

Often the cargo cult leaders were relatively disturbed men who had held some minor position involved with missionary work. They had assisted the missionaries and had incompletely assimilated church teaching into their own idiosyncratic belief system. The misunderstandings of the Christian message was basic, but understandable in terms of the convictions of the natives. Obviously, the Europeans had superior rituals for obtaining the cargo. Church membership was in the interest of gaining access to the cargo, finding the secret ritual that would induce the ancestors to bestow the goods that the Europeans received on the members. Giving up their own native beliefs and ritualistic practices, they took on those of the missionaries. But still, no cargo!

Certain stylized and extreme cult behaviors, including the speaking in tongues and convulsive seizures, may be taken as signs of God's blessings or of the good will of the dead ancestors. The prime example of this is the Vailala madness, which was first reported in 1919 in the Gulf Division of Papua. The movement attained a brief popularity followed by several periods of waxing and waning, finally subsiding in about 1931 (Worsley, 1968). Adherents of the cult were affected by shaking, contortions, loss of limb control, often uttering a completely meaningless melange of nonsense syllables and pidgin English. Whole villages could be afflicted by this delirium (LaBarre, 1972).

The magistrate treated the affected cases as a form of madness. He feared that the strange and violent behavior might prove harmful to its victims. Along with the hysterical contortions, loss of bodily control and speaking in tongues, the sacred ceremonial objects that had been pre-served for generations were hurled from the holy men's houses and then burned. The cult members claimed that messages had come from the ancestors that the white man had no right to all the goods, and that soon the white man would be driven away and everything would belong to the natives. Soon a large ship would arrive bringing the ancestors back with an abundance of cargo (Rowley, 1965).

The stimulus for such crisis cults often arises in a context of the im-pingement of a superior or more advanced culture on a weaker or more primitive culture (LaBarre, 1971). The striking parallel to the origin of the cargo cults was the spawning of crisis cults among American Indians during the demise of their civilization in the face of the onslaught of the white man. LaBarre (1972) has described the origin of the Ghost Dance movements as the "final catastrophe of Indian cultures in the United States" (p. 227). Here, too, the vision of the prophet, granted him by the Great Spirit, was that the earth would swallow up the white man, leaving behind all his houses and goods for the red man. Even the dead chiefs of the tribe were to return and drive the whites from the land.

The question arises why such a cult should exist at all? In analyzing the cultural basis of these cults, Schwartz (1973) has argued that the cargo cult is a type-response to culture contact that occurs in the context of an area-wide paranoid ethos underlying the Melanesian culture. This paranoid ethos was undoubtedly persistent through the cultural evolu-tion of these societies, where it persists as a potential which becomes sporadically reactivated in certain modern contexts. Its ideology, forms of socialization, and institutionalization are specific to the Melanesian culture. Factors contributing to it in Melanesia would derive from the uncertainty of life, stemming from a short life span and a relatively high infant mortality. The paranoid ethos, also influenced by the uncertainty of various forms of native production, adds to the insecurity of life and economic well-being. But more basic to the Melanesian culture, the paranoid ethos is connected with an extreme atomism of social and political life, accompanied by the continuing and pervasive influence of war, including the practice of raiding among tribes and villages. In addi-tion, there is an uncertainty of tribal alliances, and an instability of village and clan cohesion (Worsley, 1968).

The paranoid strain that runs through a Melanesian society is rein-forced by the trust and distrust found within Melanesian family struc-ture. There is a dichotomy between the owner and the stranger that runs through Melanesian society. This split is exacerbated in the context of matrilineal succession. Conditioned by both unilineal organization and unilocal residence, the divided family tends to treat either husband or wife as stranger, outsider, a possible spy, and an agent of that individual's family or kin. Thus, either husband or wife can be left outside the circle of trust. Within this divided system, there is a competition for the loyalty of the children. Indeed, marriage payments are often regarded as paying off the family of the bride so they will lay no future claim to the children of the marriage. In addition to these factors, in Melanesian society there is a dominant principle of solidarity between siblings of the opposite sex. Consequently, the cleavage between husband and wife and the attitude of hostile suspicion that arises between them is reinforced by the competitive tug of loyalties on the part of a man to his sisters, and on the part of the woman to her brothers.

There is a considerable variation of expression of these motifs among Melanesian societies. There is also a considerable difference in the extent to which individuals internalize this paranoid ethos. The paranoid disposition may rarely reach the level of intensity found among the Dobu (Fortune, 1932), but where this ethos prevails, the paranoid propensity in individuals can interact in subtle and pervasive ways with the more institutionalized paranoia embedded in social structures. The diffusion of paranoid fantasies and their interaction with social processes has been documented in Europe of the later Middle Ages (Cohn, 1970) and even in our own society (Hofstadter, 1965). In a broad sense such implicit and diffuse paranoid trends may be an important component of the bedrock of social processes and religious institutionalizations (Meissner, 1978).

Religion plays its role in this paranoid ethos. In the Melanesian belief, it is primarily the dead who are active in the affairs of the living, and spirits occupy every conceivable feature of the environment. Schwartz (1973) comments on the impact of this belief system in the following terms:

> The living and the dead, human and nonhuman beings, inhabit the behavioral environment of Melanesians. Moral supervision is exercised by the dead of a person's own group, with sanctions of illness and threats of death. There are attacks by the malicious ghosts of other groups and by the deceptive and cannibalistic-ogre-spirits that inhabit the bush. There is sorcery and countersorcery. A person may be cursed by certain categories of his own kin who may have the power to inflict barrenness, even death, on members of the family.

> These are the core elements of Melanesian religion. It may be characterized in part by the familiar notion of "animism" in which all effects have some animate or personalistic cause. Fortune (1935) and others have described the moral burden, anxiety, and interpersonal uncertainty of trust that encumbers a society when it requires

a personalistic explanation of all sickness, death, and misfortune. Secularization, culturally implemented in notions such as luck, chance, accident, coincidence, and impersonal causes, partly relieves this burden. (p. 165).

The circle of trust for these believers is narrow. Outside of it fear is everywhere. The Melanesians tend to fear other natives more intensely than the white man who, though often an object of formal hostility, is also considered to be outside the magico-religious system. Closer enemies are more advantageous. The objectives of the cult are safety, longevity and wealth. The dead are not so much worshipped as they are respected and even feared. The relationship between the living and the dead is almost contractual, insofar as the dead provide protection and welfare for the living in return for the maintenance of their memories and their actual remains by the living. In this cult, religion and magic are virtually coextensive, based on the use of "supernatural" means for attaining the welfare of the living. Christianity was absorbed but in a syncretistic manner by which many new concepts were integrated. The Christian notion of heaven and hell, which seemed so remote and impersonal, was essentially rejected. Heaven, in its way, is a distraction from the primary business of the dead; that is, to provide satisfaction for the living. Hell itself is translated into terms of exclusion from the cargo. The doctrine of the Fall is not taken as a sin of disobediance or of the presumption to divine status, but rather as an exclusion from the redemption that restored the cargo to the white man.

I would like to relate these aspects of the cult phenomenon to elements of the paranoid process (Meissner, 1978). As I have previously suggested, aspects of the paranoid process play an important role, not only in the development of individual personality and its pathological aberrations, but they find a significant expression in various aspects of human social and cultural endeavor. Religion is no exception to this general finding and, in fact, may represent the primary cultural vehicle in and through which the mechanisms of the paranoid process come to express themselves.

The primary elements of the paranoid process that I would focus on for this present discussion are the following: (1) the *core introjects* around which the subject's inner world is structured; these introjects represent critical internalizations of significant object relations in the patient's developmental history and provide the basis for the organization and integration of the self-system; (2) *projections* that derive from the core introjects and contribute to the progressive modification and differentiation of object-representations and their correlative object-relations; and finally, (3) the *paranoid construction* by which the meaningful and sustaining patterns of environmental reference are cognitively organized to provide a congruent context for the support of specific projections. The integration of these projections within the framework provided by the paranoid construction gives rise to the subject's projective system (Meissner, 1978).

In applying this analysis to the cult phenomenon, and specifically to the cargo cults, we can start at the periphery, as it were, and work our way back to more central psychoanalytic concerns. We can begin, therefore, with the paranoid construction. In the cargo cults, there is an elaborate cognitive construction, namely the belief system, which sustains and integrates the organization of the cult, which can be regarded as a complex paranoid construction. We have already discussed some of the specifics of this belief system, particularly the belief in the dead spirits of the ancestors, the promise of the reward of the cargo, the investment of cult leaders with special magical powers and privileged relationships with the ancestors, animistic beliefs regarding the role of the ancestors in almost every aspect of human life and experience, the elaborate beliefs and various cultic practices of sorcery, and even the integration of elements of Christian belief systems in the form of expectations of a final coming in which the blessings of the cargo are to be bestowed on all true believers.

In terms of the paranoid process, the paranoid construction has a very specific purpose and motivation. It serves specifically to integrate and sustain the projections that arise within its context (which are sustained and reinforced by aspects of the paranoid construction) and, at the same time, reciprocally give life, strength, and power to the overriding projective system of which both the paranoid construction and the underlying projections are vital components. The projections in the cargo cults are not difficult to delineate. They take the form of the pervasive animism that is so characteristic of these cults, particularly in the form of the projective characteristics of the dead ancestors. These spirits of the dead are personalized and given unique and special qualities which ultimately derive from the projective propensity of the believers. Thus, the ancestors are regarded as powerful, influential, threatening, capable in magical ways of bringing good will and blessings to the believers or, correspondingly, they are seen as having destructive and malicious powers to bring illness, pain, loss and destruction to those same believers. The projections are also evident in the qualities attributed to the cult leader, particularly the idealization and aggrandizement with which he is cloaked.

Without attempting to analyze such projections in detail, it can be said that aspects of the internal psychic economy of individual believers tends to find its way into such projective systems along the primary dimensions of narcissism and aggression. Thus, in the cargo cults it is the magical power and aggrandizement with their benign and powerfully destructive qualities that find their way into the projective system. The projection of these aspects of the internal introjective configurations leaves behind elements of vulnerability, powerlessness, fearful impoverishment, and inferiority as the core elements around which the inner psychic world of the believer is organized. The result of this alignment can leave little other alternative than to reinforce the helplessness and dependence of the believer, and to make this reliance on the belief system of the cult and of the empowered figure of the cult leader an intense and powerful psychological necessity. Salvation, both from the evil external projective forces and from the inner sense of helplessness and vulnerability, is achieved by way of attachment to and perfect subjection to the powerful and idealized leader.

A further point that emerges from consideration of the cargo cults is that the cultic experience itself derives from, expresses, and reflects a more widely prevalent paranoid disposition that seems characteristic of the culture in which the cults flourish. It is as though the cargo cults themselves distill and concentrate elements of fear, distrust, insecurity, constant dread of hostile spiritual influences, as well as the threat of enemies, into the belief system of the cults.

In a general sense, the cult is a reflection and a derivative of the culture in which it arises. If we shift the cultural and geographic contexts of our consideration, we can move to the southern tier of the United States where we encounter a cult which seems no less bizarre in its manifestations, and at the same time even more pathological in its cultural context than the seemingly more primitive cargo cults. I refer to the snake handling cults which have been so vividly described and analyzed by La Barre (1969).

The origin of the snake cult can be traced to 1909 when its founder, George Went Hensley of Tennessee, discovered a unique inspiration in his meditation on the text from Mark:

And these signs shall follow them that believe; in my name shall they cast out devils; they shall speak with new tongues; they shall take up serpents; and if they drink any deadly thing, it shall not hurt them; they shall lay hands on the sick, and they shall recover. (16: 17-18)

Hensley's inspiration and subsequent preaching gave rise to a series of cults which contained many of the familiar signs we have already identified in the cargo cults. The cult meetings abounded with trances, "seizures," hysterical behaviors of twitchings and convulsings, and even the familiar speaking in tongues. The new element, consistent with the scriptural prescription, was the handling of snakes. Poisonous snakes were captured in the wild and were handled by the devotees of the snake cult in all manner of close physical contact—allowing the snakes to twine around the arms, neck and head of the participants. The snake's head came close to the believer's face, even to the point that the snake was able to lick the participant's nose with his forked tongue.

The wonder is that a higher degree of mayhem and fatality did not result than is, in fact, recorded. But if the number of snake bites and fatalities seemed fewer than one might expect, nonetheless, snake bites and deaths there were. Hensley himself was fatally bitten in 1955 (La Barre, 1972). The obvious dangers and threats to the community posed by the presence of poisonous snakes prompted official intervention by police and the passage of a number of state laws forbidding the practices of these cults. At least for a time, such opposition was taken as persecution, which only intensified the fanaticism of the cult members. Again, in unquestioning acceptance of the scriptural injunction, cult members were known to swallow a number of potentially fatal poisons with predictable results.

The symbolism of the snakes is overdetermined, reflecting, at one level, phallic and oedipal dynamics and, at another level, the displacement of a more primitive oral aggression and wishes for oral incorporation. In commenting on the psychological significance these cult practices, La Barre (1969) writes:

Snakes *are* the gods, and *are* the deathless element in each man; snakes are essentially immortality . . . the snake is the "uncanny" creature, like the phallus possessed of an independent and autonomous will and life of its own. . . . Again, the snake placed tauntingly to the lips and mouth in the snake cult is another neurotic "return of the repressed"—but under talion danger again, for the castrated snake-phallus is not bitten but *bites*. This also fits the familiar infantile stance of paranoid projection: "It is not I but *he* who is evil and malevolent." But the feared father protects as well as punishes; if, then, in talion punishment the snake does not bite me, then I am, by very God, demonstrated to be guiltless (or have in any case escaped the wrath). Drinking poison is the identical gambit in parallel form: an oral incorporation of Power will not kill—if only one has faith in the somewhat witless benignity of the Power, or, alternately, if one has already incorporated the spiritual power of the father which will render the new incorporation powerless. But only the triumphant paranoiac drinks poison; most paranoids are afraid of "poisons", i.e., talion punishment for guilty oral wishes. (pp. 107–108)

La Barre also provides us with a portrait of a cult leader, in the person of Beauregard Barefoot. The personality of the cult leader and the manner in which it interacts with the dynamics of the cult participants is a fascinating subject on which the paranoid process can shed some light. Barefoot is described as a psychopathic personality in whom paranoid mechanisms play a predominant role along with psychopathic defenses. The manner in which psychopathic traits reflect aspects of the paranoid process has been discussed elsewhere (Meissner, 1978). La Barre focuses on the introjection of a severe and punitive superego derived from a rigid, hard-working, and severely compulsive father. The defense against this intolerable superego introject appeared as a re-externalization in the form of external superego or paranoid persecutors. Barefoot was able to find such persecutory and repressive figures (modelled after his father introject) in God, the police, the courts, the state, and society at large. The same externalization comes into play in regard to the snake. As La Barre (1969) comments:

The snake must be dominated, but is still potentially dangerous; as unteachable as the psychopathic id, the snake is also made into one's still external supergo-judge, a dramatized and symbolized Fate. Reality itself is systematically distorted to fill this role in Beauregard's private drama, and his acting-out is skillfully contrived to seduce the needed punishments from society. Nowhere more than in the psychopath is a man's personality equivalent to his fate. (p. 145)

Mixed with this externalizing and paranoid core, Barefoot also displays a variety of narcissistic traits—"flamboyance, exhibitionism, dramatic flare, sensitivity to and preoccupation with the opinions of others, rashness, impulsiveness, slyness, ambition, quick temper, daredevil tendencies, and responsiveness to shame rather than to guilt" (p. 146). There is an element of tempting fate in his approach to life and to his religion. Handling the snake is a way of tempting fate and almost counterphobically coming to grips with the dangerous and destructive projection. Each service and each handling of the snake becomes a gamble with fate. Barefoot must skirt the possibility of danger and destruction. Sexuality and danger become interwoven, and the challenge is to triumph by gaining pleasure without paying a price. The all-powerful and the all-knowing God can be outwitted.

In his dealings with authorities, whether in the form of the police or the other state officials, Barefoot is both fearful and provocative. His relationship to other men is basically distrustful and suspicious, but, at times, he almost seems to seek their aggression and punishment. He is sensitive and demanding, hurt by the least rejection, and constantly seeking narcissistic support and gratification. His phallic omnipotent posture is hardly successful, with its labored exhibitionism and necessary testing of the limits.

La Barre has analyzed in detail the phallic symbolism of the snake cults. In many of the cultic practices, there is a poorly repressed and displaced expression of sexuality. La Barre notes that in this process there is a unique symbiosis of psychopathic and hysterical trends. The hysteric, for example, projects her sexual needs outside of herself into a phobic figure—he is the dirty old man, not she. Similarly, the psychopathic character projects sexuality into the phobic figure of the snake. The projective mechanism places the snake into the position of being a symbol in the service of an essentially paranoid process (Meissner, 1978). The snake thus becomes the evil one, the repository of evil lusts and unholy desires as well as hostile, seductive, sadistic and malignant intents.

And what of the people who form the congregation of the Hensleys and Barefoots? They are drawn from the population of poor, disenfranchised whites who populate the tobacco farms and mill villages, people who are economically marginal, the enslaved mill hands of a controlling and dominating economic structure, steeped in a religious tradition of repressive, rural fundamentalism. Mill workers lead monotonous and ritualized lives, and are held in the grip of a paternalistic economic system which offers them the promise of little more than low-paying jobs and semi-skilled labor. Power is almost totally in the hands of the ruling class of the village, particularly through its economic hold on all aspects and institutions of civic life.

There is little in the millhand's life that allows decision-making, whether in regard to his work in the mill or in the civic affairs of the village. He is almost totally dependent on and subservient to his economic masters. Resentment is buried and expresses itself more in depression than in rebellion. Religion and family both preach the code of conformity. Children are quickly and severly punished, often as a displacement for the strain of resentments their parents can express in no other way. Religion teaches a doctrine of total submission to the will of God. Clinically, depression and passive-aggressive tendencies are the recurrent themes. Blind obedience and rigid conformity are the socially accepted norms. Strangers, outsiders, anything new or different are held with suspicion and are to be avoided. The religious norm is a life of poverty and deprivation under a God who is stern and punishing, particularly to dissenters of all kinds. Obedience is essential to gain the rewards of the after-life, and the rules for such conformity are found unquestioningly and totally in the Holy Bible. As La Barre (1969) comments:

> Goaded by godly as well as by secular standards, the mill worker is puritanical, fanatic, narrow, and fundamentalist. Fate seems to have preordained him to be a textile worker. Even when he migrates from the South, he is lost, helpless, and without resources; when he goes to southern Michigan and Ohio industrial towns, he turns them into Southern places with his intransigent ethos. In *any* new situation, without adaptive resilience, he is functionally very much like the immigrant from a foreign country; and even in a Southern town he seems a rural primitive tribesman, with rigidly tribal values. (p. 167)

This rigid, fundamentalist creed forms a blindly embraced, desperately and unquestioningly maintained paranoid construction that provides the sustaining context for preserving the projective elaborations so necessary for protecting the inner sense of vulnerability and helplessness. Conversely, the creed sustains a sense, meaning, and purpose in an otherwise painful and disillusioning existence. (Meissner, 1978).

It is this poor white class of workers for the tobacco factories and textile mills that provides the basis for the snake-handling cults. It is in the snake cult that the psychology of the leader and the led finally meet. For both, leader and led alike, their approach to life is repressive and compulsive, joyless and denying. But in the snake-handling cult, they find the sources of strength, power, and an avenue for the discharge of long-repressed and otherwise frightening feelings. There is a reprieve from the gray and colorless deprivation of the economy and culture in which they live, and the way lies open to emotional salvation. There, at least, the individual can find some assurance that God loves him.

For Barefoot, there is the phallic-manipulative aggrandizement of masculine power. Filled with complete innocence and faith, he can seduce female communicants with his borrowed symbolic phallus. In the manipulation of the serpent and the hysterical domination, important psychic conflicts are being displaced and symbolically worked through in terms of the specific projective system of the snake-handling cult. Traumatic repressions and deprivations are abreacted, but sexuality, carnal desire, and phallic impulses are neither securely resolved nor mastered. They remain separate, discreet, dangerous and projected. The snake becomes the symbolic representative of the devil, evil incarnate and deathly dangerous. But the very danger, the very threat of death, exercises a fascination, since it comprises the projected, inadmissible, and hysterically acknowledge embodiment of one's own inner impulses and desires. The evil phallic part of one's self can only be mastered by the equally external and omnipotent "power of god."

The cargo cults of New Guinea and the snake-handling cults of the South serve to remind us that the cult phenomenon does not take place in a vacuum, but that it is influenced by and exercises an influence on the culture in which it flourishes. We have every right then, as analysts, to pose a question as to the extent to which the paranoid mechanisms we have been discussing may be found to be endemic not merely in deviant cultic religious expressions, but more generally within socially accepted and culturally adapted religious systems, as well as within the more general matrix of social and cultural processes themselves. From this point of view it would seem that the examination of the cult phenomenon serves only to open the door to a wide range of social and cultural exploration and discovery. It is the "tip of the iceberg" to which Freud called our attention so long ago.

There is a further point that requires special emphasis. The vulnerability, helplessness, and dependence which characterize and form the core dimension of the subject's introjective configuration provide the basic elements out of which the individual elaborates and sustains a sense of self. Correspondingly, the projective system, including the specific projections and the more general and more contextual paranoid construction, has as its inherent purpose the reinforcement and sustaining of this introjective configuration. In other words, the religious belief system, insofar as it functions as a paranoid construction, serves the important purpose of maintaining a sense of inner integrity and self-cohesion in the individual believer (Meissner, 1978). We are addressing ourselves at this point to a significant dimension of basic human motivation that has not been adequately appreciated by psychoanalytic theory until the recent, gradual emergence of a concept of the self and the understanding of the motivations directly related to the organization and maintaining of that sense of self.

The upshot is that adherence to such a religious belief system has important implications for sustaining a sense of inner cohesiveness and identity that may have greater intrinsic power as a motivating force than only libidinal or narcissistic needs. Viewing religious adherence (and particularly, the sometimes fanatic adherence of cult members) from this perspective offers another vantage point and another dimension to our understanding of these powerful forces. Something similar may be said about the phenomenon of psychotic conviction and adherence to delusional beliefs. The most powerful and convincing dimension (at least subjectively) for such patients may well be that the delusional system is somehow required for the maintaining of a sense of inner coherence and some semblance of a self-system.

An additional function of the paranoid construction, beyond its sustaining and integrating the projective elements, is that adherence to such a system provides a context within which the individual can begin to find purpose, meaning, and a sense of belonging that adds value and purpose to his existence. This may, in fact, be one of the most powerful elements underlying the adherence to religious belief systems. In regard to the cult phenomenon specifically, the intense need of individuals to find such self-completion and self-direction in external involvements and beliefs may reflect an underlying lack of structure and failure of effective internalizations stemming from a wide variety of developmental levels.

At the same time, this need is not necessarily pathological. In fact, it can be asserted that such a need is endemic to the human condition. To find meaning, purpose, acceptance, and a sense of belonging is a quest that is basic to human life. Consequently, to the extent that religious systems respond to such a basic human need, they may be providing a most important function in the sustaining of human life. We have placed the major focus in this discussion on the more pathological aspects of the cult phenomenon. However, at the same time we must remind ourselves that these processes and mechanisms have an inherent potential for human growth and strength, and that in very meaningful ways they can provide the vehicle for positive and constructive adaptations.

BIBLIOGRAPHY

ADORNO, T. W., FRENKEL-BRUNSWICK, E., LEVINSON, D. J., & SANFORD, R. N. (1950). *The Authoritarian Personality*. New York: Harper.
COHN, N. (1970). *The Pursuit of the Millenium: Revolutionary Millenarians and Mystical Anarchists of the Middle Ages*. New York: Oxford University Press.
FORTUNE, R. (1932). *Sorcerers of Dobu: The Social Anthropology of the Dobu Islanders of the Western Pacific*. New York: Dutton.
_____ (1935). *Manus Religion: An Ethnological Study of the Manus Natives of the Admiralty Islands*. Omaha: University of Nebraska Press.
FREUD, S. (1921). Group psychology and the analysis of the ego. *S.E.*, 18:65–143. London: Hogarth Press.
FROMM, E. (1941). *Escape from Freedom*. New York: Holt, Rinehart and Winston.
GERTH, H. H. & MILLS, C. W., eds. (1946). *From Max Weber: Essays in Sociology*. New York: Oxford University Press.
GALANTER, M. & BUCKLEY, P. (1978). Evangelical religion and meditation: Psychotherapeutic effects. *Journal of Nervous and Mental Diseases*, 166:685–691.
_____, RABKIN, R., RABKIN, J., & DEUTSCH, A. (1979). The "Moonies": A psychological study of conversion and membership in a contemporary religious sect. *American Journal of Psychiatry*, 136:165–170.
HOFSTADTER, R. (1965). *The Paranoid Style in American Politics*. New York: Knopf.

JOHNSON, B. (1963). On church and sect. *American Sociological Review,* 28:539-549.

KOHUT, H. (1971). *The Analysis of the Self.* New York: International Universities Press.

_____ (1976). Creativeness, charisma, group psychology: Reflections on the self-analysis of Freud. In *Freud: The Fusion of Science and Humanism,* Psychological Issues, Monograph 34/35, pp. 379-425. J. E. Gedo & G. H. Pollock (eds.). New York: International Universities Press.

LA BARRE, W. (1969). *They Shall Take Up Serpents.* New York: Schocken.

_____ (1971). Materials for a history of studies of crisis cults: A bibliographic essay. *Current Anthropology,* 12:3-44.

_____ (1972). *The Ghost Dance: Origins of Religion.* London: George Allen and Unwin.

LIDZ, R. W., LIDZ, T., & BURTON-BRADLEY, B. (1973). Cargo cultism. *Journal of Nervous and Mental Diseases,* 157:370-388.

LIFTON, R. J. (1956). *Thought Reform and the Psychology of Totalism.* New York: Norton.

MEISSNER, W. W. (1978). *The Paranoid Process.* New York: Jason Aronson, Inc.

NIEBUHR, H. R. (1929). *The Social Sources of Denominationalism.* New York: Holt.

PRUYSER, P. W. (1977). The seamy side of current religious beliefs. *Bulletin of the Menninger Clinic,* 41:329-348.

ROWLEY, C. G. (1965). *The New Guinea Villager.* Melbourne: F.W. Cheshire.

SCHWARTZ, T. (1973). Cult and context: The paranoid ethos in Melanesia. *Ethos,* 1:153-174.

STARK, R. & BAINBRIDGE, W. S. (1979). Of churches, sects, and cults: Preliminary concepts for a theory of religious movements. *Journal for the Scientific Study of Religion,* 18:117-133.

UNGERLEIDER, J. T. & WELLISCH, D. K. (1979). Coercive persuasion (brainwashing), religious cults, and deprogramming. *American Journal of Psychiatry,* 136:279-282.

WORSLEY, P. (1968). *The Trumpet Shall Sound: A Study of "Cargo" Cults in Melanesia.* New York: Schocken Books.

4

Freud and Religion: A History and Reappraisal*

EDWIN R. WALLACE, IV

For an *ir*religious, not *a*religious man, Freud was close to religion all his life. His father, Jakob, was a religious man—even if not a particularly proselytizing one. Freud remembered visits to the Catholic Church with his nanny and her lectures to him on heaven and hell. He recalled vividly an early exposure to the Philippson Bible and spoke (Freud, 1925a, p. 8) of his "deep engrossment in the Bible story." Jones (1957), p. 350) asserts that Freud remained "very conversant with the Bible and was always ready to quote *from either testament* [my italics.]."[1] From age seven to thirteen he received Hebrew lessons from Professor Hammerschlag, though he later denied any knowledge of that language. It is not known whether he had a Bar Mitzvah, but he received a Bar Mitzvah present (Falk, 1977). In his twenties he weighed the possibility (in part for practical reasons and in part to avoid the Judaic marriage ceremony) of a conversion to Christianity. Freud was always fascinated by the city of the Popes. "Next Easter in Rome" was one of his favorite expressions to Fliess, a curious twist on "next year in Jerusalem." Did Freud long to go to Rome as supplicant or conqueror? There are those (e.g., Dempsey, 1956) who maintain that it was as the former, that Freud harbored a repressed desire to embrace Catholicism. Five days before Christmas, in 1883, Freud wrote Martha that he was captivated by Titian's head of Christ, the "Maundy Money," (E. Freud, 1960, pp. 82–83).

---

*Abbreviated versions of this paper were presented at the Johns Hopkins University Institute of the History of Medicine in 1978 and at the Fall, 1979 Meeting of the American Psychoanalytic Association. I will use the word "religion" in a general sense although what I have to say applies most closely to its Christian and Judaic varieties, with which Freud himself was most concerned.

1. Granting this familiarity, the virtual absence in Freud's corpus of verbatim citations of the prophets is striking. Philip Rieff (personal communication) pointed this out to me and cogently suggested that it might be viewed as yet another expression of Freud's hostility toward religion. Similarly, Grollman (1965, p. 52) reminds us that there is not one single reference to the Talmud in Freud's extensive writings.

"I would love to have gone away with it, but there were too many people about . . . so I went away with a full heart." These letters to his fiancee contain numerous, not disrespectful, references to "God," the "Lord," the "Almighty." When in Italy he spent many hours contemplating Michelangelo's Moses, a figure with whom he strongly identified. In 1935 he (in Pfeiffer, 1972, p. 205) admitted to Lou Andreas-Salomé that all his life he was pursued by the problem of the historical Moses. His written considerations of religion began in 1895, and then spanned his entire career. At least three booklength works—*Totem and Taboo, The Future of an Illusion,* and *Moses and Monotheism*—deal largely or wholly with the subject. The gods of antiquity adorned his study. In 1907 he became an editor of the *Zeitschrift für Religionpsychologie.* The psychology of religion was to have been one of the subjects taught at his fantasied psychoanalytic university. Then religion is a frequent topic in the letters to Jung, himself the son of a Protestant pastor. For the last thirty years of his life one of Freud's closest associates and warmest friends was a Swiss minister, Pfister. In 1935 Freud (p. 72) admitted that "My interest, after making a lifelong *détour* through the natural sciences, medicine, and psychotherapy, returned to the cultural problems which had fascinated me *long before, when I was a youth scarcely old enough for thinking* [my italics]"—and foremost among these problems was religion.

Freud's approach to religion is a topic which pervades not only his thinking in general, but participates in the knotty problem of the relationship between religion and psychiatry as well; a thorough study of this encounter would amount to a history and theory of modernity itself. An article of this length, treating so complicated an issue, and combining intellectual history, "psychohistory," and criticism is bound to give the reader too little of all three. My primary aim is to produce a concise history of Freud's thinking and attitudes on religion, to point out the problems therein, and to present the opinions of some of our most creative thinkers on the topic. For the convenience of the reader, I have divided the essay into sections: the first presents Freud's ideas and attitudes themselves, the second criticizes them, and the third examines their determinants. A subsequent paper studies the thorny question of the compatibility between psychoanalysis and religion (Wallace, 1983a).

FREUD'S VIEW ON RELIGION

One of the strongest themes in Freud's treatment of the subject is a diagnostic one. Prior to 1900, Freud had treated patients whose symptoms had religious content or who suffered from conflicts of religious doubt. In 1901 he began diagnosing religion itself. Before finishing, he had compared it to a psychosis (paranoia), a neurosis (obsessional disease), an infantile neurosis, and had dubbed it a manifestation of, and attempt to resolve, the Oedipus complex. This equation of religion and psychopathology, although expounded by Freud in its most sophisticated version, of course was nothing new. Several authors, at least two of whom Freud had read by 1873—Nietzsche and Feuerbach (Gedo and Wolf, 1976, p. 12)—had broached this idea. For instance, Feuerbach called theology "pathology hidden from itself" (Acton, 1955, pp. 120-122).

Although Freud had theorized as early as 1897 that myths are projections of the "dim inner perception of our own psychical apparatus," (Bonaparte et al., 1954, p. 237), it was in *The Psychopathology of Everyday Life* (1901, pp. 258-259) that he introduced his conceptualization of religion as paranoia:

I believe that a very large part of the mythological view of the world, which extends a long way into the most modern religions, is nothing but psychology projected onto the external world . . . When human beings began to think, they were, as is well known, forced to explain the external world anthropomorphically by means of a multitude of personalities in their own image; chance events, which they interpreted superstitiously, were thus actions and manifestations of persons. They behaved, therefore, *just like paranoiacs* [my italics].

These ideas were of course extended in *Totem and Taboo* (1913) and *The Future of an Illusion* (1927). In that former work he (p. 92) writes:

Spirits and demons . . . are only projections of man's own emotional impulses. He turns his emotional cathexes into persons, he peoples the world with them and meets his internal mental processes again outside himself—*in just the same way as that intelligent paranoiac,* Schreber, found a reflection of the attachments and detachments of his libido in the vicissitudes of his confabulated 'rays of God' [my italics]!

This concept of projection was used to account for God's negative counterpart, the Devil, as much as for God himself. In a 1909 meeting of the Vienna Psychoanalytic Society, where Hugo Heller presented a paper on Satan, Freud (in Nunberg and Federn, 1967, p. 122) conceptualized the Devil as "the personification of the unconscious and repressed instincts" and reiterated that the notion is "nothing but a mass fantasy, constructed along the lines of a paranoid delusion.'' Such ideas reappear in *Totem and Taboo* (Freud, 1913, p. 92) and of course in "A Seventeenth-Century Demonological Neurosis" (1923a, p. 72). In this latter paper Freud (p. 86) also introduced his idea that "God and the Devil were originally identical—were a single figure which was later split into two figures with opposite attributes. In the earliest ages God himself still possessed all the terrifying features which were afterwards combined to form a counterpart of him.'' This idea smacks of the line of reasoning in which Freud (1913, p. 67) viewed taboo as having a "double meaning from the very first" and in which he (1911a) asserted the antithetical nature of primal words.

Very early in his career Freud had been exposed to several authors who had anticipated, in part, his notion of religion as projection. Darwin (1871, Vol. I, p. 132), in *The Descent of Man,* which Freud possessed by 1877, said that "savages would naturally attribute to the spirits the same passions, etc., etc., and the same affections that they themselves feel.'' Hume (1757, p. 317) had written on the "universal tendency among mankind to conceive all beings like themselves, and to transfer to every object those qualities with which they are familiarly acquainted, and of which they are intimately conscious.'' Freud would read this quote both in Hume's *Essays Literary, Moral and Political,* which he possessed as early as 1879, and in Tylor's *Primitive Culture,* which he cited both in *The Interpretation of Dreams* and in *Totem and Taboo.* Tylor (1871, Vol. I, p. 416) himself saw myth as the "history of its authors, not of its subjects.'' Spencer (1898), another author whom Freud had read before 1900, stressed man's anthropomorphization of nature. While still in the *Gymnasium* Freud had probably read Xenophanes trenchant dictum: "if the ox could paint a picture, his god would look like an ox" (Dodds, 1951, p. 181).

But well before he had read Hume, Tylor, or Spencer, Freud had encountered Feuerbach's (1841, p. 13) dictum that "theology is anthropology." "Religion is man's earliest and also indirect form of self-knowledge. . . . Man first of all sees his nature as out of himself, before he finds it in himself. . ." Nietzsche (1878, p. 29) had posited that "the human intellect, on the basis of human needs, of human emotions, has caused this phenomenon [religion] and has carried its erroneous fundamental conception into things." No more than Freud did he (ibid, p. 56) spare religion the "cruel sight of the psychological dissecting table.'' Nietzsche saw the ideal as a "sublimation" of the base and conceptualized morality, not as divine endowment, but rather as actions deemed good or bad on account of their consequences to the community. His (1880, p. 224) refinement of this anticipates—indeed probably influenced—Freud's work in the area:

The sum-total of our conscience is all that has regularly been demanded of us, without reason, in the days of our childhood, by people whom we respected or feared. . . . The belief in authority is the source of conscience, which is therefore not the voice of God in man but the voice of some men in man.

In 1907 Freud enriched his psychopathology paradigm by the comparison of religion to obsessional neurosis: "I am certainly not the first person to have been struck by the resemblance between what are called obsessive actions in sufferers from nervous afflictions and the observances by means of which believers give expression to their piety. . . . The resemblance, however, seems to me to be more than a superficial one." Freud (p. 119) then enumerated the similarities and differences between religious and neurotic ritual, the former including the "qualms of conscience brought on by their neglect" and the "conscientiousness with which they are carried out in every detail," the latter the greater variability of obsessional actions among individuals and their private, rather than public, nature; an ostensible difference—the significance and symbolism of religious ceremonial as opposed to the senselessness of neurotic—disappears on closer analysis.

In the same vein, Freud viewed religious rituals, like symptoms, as compromise formations—between the repressed instinct and the repressing forces. Thus the religious, like the obsessional ceremonial is not only a defense against a sexual or aggressive drive, it is also a disguised instinctual gratification. "One remembers how commonly all the acts which religion forbids—the expressions of the instincts it has suppressed—are committed precisely in the name of, and ostensibly for the sake of, religion" (Freud, 1907a, p. 125). An extreme example would be the Rat Man's behavior (Freud, 1909a, p. 193):

The conflict between love and hatred showed itself in our patient by other signs as well. At the time of the revival of his piety he made up prayers for himself, which took up more and more time and eventually lasted for an hour and a half. The reason for this was that he found, like an inverted Balaam, that something always inserted itself into his pious phrases and turned them into their opposite, e.g., if he said 'May God protect him', an evil spirit would hurriedly insinuate a 'not'.

Freud further demonstrated the compromise formation of religion in *Totem and Taboo* (1913), where he reiterated the similarity between religion and obsessional neurosis, contrasting the preponderance of sexual determinants in the latter with the combination of "egoistic and erotic" elements in the former.

Freud's tendency to view religion as a "universal obsessional neurosis" is perhaps partly related, as Pfister (in Meng and E. Freud, 1963, p. 122) suggests, to "the fact that [Freud] grew up in proximity to pathological forms of religion and regarded these as 'religion'." Doubtless Freud felt the Catholic Church shared responsibility for the repressive (hence potentially neurotogenic) and hypocritical environment of Vienna. In any event, it was the proximity of the Catholic Church that allowed him to equate "religion" with "ritual."

The "omnipotence of thoughts," a mechanism common to all neurotics but particularly favored, Freud felt, by obsessionals, was also recruited to explain the phenomena of animism and religion. Freud felt magic proceeded by the mechanism of the omnipotence of thoughts. Freud had discovered this "over-valuation of mental processes" in the Rat Man, who actually coined the term "omnipotence of thoughts." "If he thought of someone, he would be sure to meet that very person immediately afterwards, as though by magic. . . . If, without any really serious intention, he swore at some stranger, he might be sure that the man would die soon afterwards, so that he would feel responsible for his death" (Freud, 1913, p. 85). Freud explained this as a survival into adulthood of infantile megalomania; he saw omnipotence of thoughts as a remnant of the narcissistic sexualization of thought.

Although the Rat Man may have initiated the train of thought that led Freud to his conception of magic as omnipotence of thoughts, much earlier Freud had encountered the similar ideas of Tylor (1871, pp. 115-116): "Man, as yet in a low intellectual condition, having come to associate in thought those things which he found by experience to be connected in fact, proceeded erroneously to invert this action, and to conclude that association in thought must involve a similar connection to reality." Frazer (1911, p. 52), whom Freud would read later, continued this line of thought and based magic on the association of ideas by similarity or by contiguity—"homeopathic" and "contagious", respectively.

In *Totem and Taboo* Freud (1913, p. 88) examined the vicissitudes throughout history of this "omnipotence of thoughts":

> At the animistic stage men ascribe omnipotence to themselves. At the religious stage they transfer it to the gods but do not seriously abandon it themselves, for they reserve the power of influencing the gods in a variety of ways according to their wishes. The scientific view of the universe no longer affords any room for human omnipotence; men have acknowledged their smallness and submitted resignedly to death and to the other necessities of nature.

In 1927 Freud (a, p. 43) compared religion to the childhood neurosis through which all adults had to pass. But if Freud felt religion was a collective neurosis, he was unsure whether it guarded against, or contributed to, individual neurosis, whether it was beneficial or inimical to society. In the very work in which he broached his psychopathology paradigm of religion, Freud (1907a, p. 127) opined that "a progressive renunciation of constitutional instincts [which he would come to consider one of the foundations of social cohesion] . . . is effected by [society's] religions, in that they require the individual to sacrifice his instinctual pleasure to the Deity." This idea reappears in " 'Civilized' Sexual Morality and Modern Nervousness" (1908, p. 187) in which Freud notes "the [instinctual] renunciation has been a progressive one in the course of the evolution of civilization. The single steps in it were sanctioned by religion; the piece of instinctual satisfaction which each person had renounced was offered to the Deity as a sacrifice, and the communal property thus acquired was declared 'sacred'." This was furthered "by means of the promise of compensation in a future existence." But in reinforcing repression is religion really acting in the service of civilization? "In what relation do the possible injurious effects of this [instinctual] renunciation stand to its exploitation in the cultural field?" (Freud, 1908, p. 193). This is the question that remained in the background of all Freud's work on social cohesion (Wallace, 1977a). His answer in 1908 (p. 196) was a tentative one and reflects the uncertainty with which he always approached this imponderable. "I must confess that I am unable to balance gain against loss correctly on this point, but I could advance a great many considerations on the side of the loss."

In the *Leonardo,* Freud (1910a, p. 79) suggested more vigorously that religion might be a determinant of neurosis. "We know very well that the intellectual weakness which has been acquired in this way [by the religious prohibition of thought] gives an effective impulse to the outbreak of a neurotic illness." Thus religion has a twofold role in contributing to neurosis: reinforcing excessive instinctual repression, and the prohibition of thought. This verdict is interesting in the light of Freud's statements only several months earlier in 1909 to the Swiss pastor-analyst, Pfister regarding "the happy state of earlier times when religious faith stifled the neuroses" (Meng and E. Freud, 1963, p. 16). These letters to Pfister continue for thirty years and faithfully reflect Freud's ambivalence on the subject. In the same year of the Leonardo essay Freud (1910b, p. 140) would write of the "extraordinary increase in neurosis since the power of religion has waned."

In *Group Psychology* Freud (1921a, p. 142) owned that "even those who do not regret the disappearance of religious illusions from the civilized world of to-day will admit that so long as they were in force they offered those who were bound by them the most powerful protection against the danger of neurosis." In *The Future of an Illusion* (1927), Freud's ambivalence on these questions would be reflected in a dialogue between himself and a fictive, pro-religion antagonist (the latter probably a composite of Pfister and Binswanger).

In the Wolf Man case history Freud credited the Bible story with allaying his patient's childhood neurosis. As a result of his mother's religious instruction "the wolf phobia quickly vanished, and instead of sexuality being repudiated with anxiety, a higher method of suppressing it made its appearance. Piety became the dominant force in the child's life" (Freud, 1918, p. 114). Continuing, Freud (pp. 114-115) wrote:

> Apart from these pathological phenomena [obsessive exaggeration of religious ceremonial], it may be said that in the present case religion achieved all the aims for the sake of which it is included in the education of the individual. It put a restraint on his sexual impulsions by affording them a sublimation and a safe mooring; it lowered the importance of his family relationships, and thus protected him from the threat of isolation by giving him access to the great community of mankind. The untamed and fear-ridden child became social, well-behaved, and amenable to education.

In a 1919 addendum to his Leonardo monograph Freud (1910a, p. 123) explained this "protection against neurotic illness, which religion vouchsafes" by its removal of the "parental complex, on which the sense of guilt in individuals as well as in the whole human race depends, and [its] dispos[al] of it, while the unbeliever has to grapple with the problem on his own." Freud may have unconsciously regretted (and resented) that he could not have dispatched his own oedipal conflict by religious conversion, but that way was not open to him. In *Moses and Monotheism* Freud (1939, p. 193) confessed "how we who have little belief envy those who are convinced of the existence of a Supreme Power, for whom the world holds no problems because he himself has created all its institutions." And although Freud (in Meng and E. Freud, 1963, p. 126) would boast that "analysis is not satisfied with success produced by suggestion, but investigates the origin and justification for the transference," he (ibid, pp. 39-40) envied Pfister the ability to "sublimate the [patient's] transference onto religion and ethics." Subsequently, we will examine in greater detail how Freud (ibid, p. 118) opposes the moralism of psychoanalysis to that of religion, "the crooked cure," "a piece of infantilism which only a few are capable of overcoming."

In 1910 (a, p. 123) Freud derived the individual's attitude toward the Deity from that toward his father in childhood:

Psycho-analysis has made us familiar with the intimate connection between the father-complex and belief in God; it has shown us that a personal God is, psychologically, nothing other than an exalted father, and it brings us evidence everyday of how young people lose their religious beliefs as soon as their father's authority breaks down. Thus, we recognize that the roots of the need for religion are in the parental complex.

In 1913 he reiterated this idea and added that oedipal ambivalence toward the actual father is displaced onto God. Spencer (1898, Vol. 11, p. 286) had stressed both these elements—that the Heavenly Father is an exalted version of the earthly one, and that man's attitude toward Deity is ambivalent. Hume (1757) as well spoke of this ambivalence.

Not being content to account for religion with ontogenetic factors alone, Freud (1913) introduced phylogenetic ones as well. At man's dawn he was said to have lived in a horde, dominated by the tyrannical primal father who maintained jealous possession of the women, condemning the sons to a life of celibacy and impotence. One day the young men, overcome with dissatisfaction, united and slew and ate the primal father. This was no sooner done than remorse and longing for the father set in. The memory of, and guilt over, this deed, genetically transmitted, were then said to determine each subsequent religion—including Christianity, Freud (pp. 135–136) reiterated in 1939:

Original sin and redemption by the sacrifice of a victim became the foundation stones of the new religion founded by Paul. . . . Its main content was, it is true, reconciliation with God the Father, atonement for the crime committed against him; but the other side of the emotional relation showed itself in the fact that the son, who had taken the atonement on himself, became a god himself beside the father and, actually, in place of the father. Christianity, having arisen out of a father-religion, became a son-religion. It has not escaped the fact of having to get rid of the father [compromise formation on the world-historical plane!].

This constitutes what Freud termed the "historical truth" of religion. The Eucharist was conceptualized as a reenactment of the eating of the primal father. In positing that "God the Father once walked upon earth in bodily form" (which, incidentally, is also what Christianity says!), Freud (1919, p. 262) arrives at a position similar to that of his great Viennese anthropological antagonist, Father Schmidt (1912-1955), who stoutly maintained that monotheism was the pristine form of religion and that polytheism was a later degenerate form.

Since this is the hypothesis with which Freud claimed to have explained the very origin of religion, let me discuss its probable determinants, which I (1980a) have written of elsewhere. To begin with, by 1900 Freud had been exposed to the Lamarckian and biogenetic bases of his theory in the work of Darwin (1868, 1872), Nietzsche (1878), Baldwin (1895), Carus (1853, 1856), and others. And these men, including the cultural evolutionists that Freud (1900, p. 2) cited in 1900, espoused a psychical version of these "laws" as well. For example, Darwin (1872, p. 245) asserted that "every human brain passes in the course of its development through the same stages as those occurring in the lower vertebrate animals." He (1868, p. 451) clearly thought that humans could inherit complicated behavioral traits—including idiosyncratic mannerisms and habits, as well as "complex mental attributes." Freud remained a staunch Lamarckian even though the books of Weismann (1892), which delivered telling blows to the idea, lay on his shelves and even though in later years Ernest Jones tried hard to dissuade him from a Lamarckian stance.

Freud was influenced by Frazer's (1911, Vol. II, pp. 312-313) discussions on the slaying of kings and representatives of deities and by Robertson Smith's (1891, p. 29-30, 226–227) ideas on the communal significance of the sacramental totem meal. Freud's (1909b) and Ferenczi's (1913) work on phobic patients, which also formed the basis for Freud's *ontogenetic* theory of totemism, gave added impetus to Freud's general thesis on religion.

Freud was indebted to Darwin (1871, Vol. II, p. 760), again, for the notion that the horde was man's earliest form of social organization. Atkinson (1903, pp. 220-221), an obscure New Caledonian rancher turned anthropological theorist, furnished the idea—or at least lifted it from a latent state in Freud—that the ruler of this horde was slain by his sons because of sexual jealousy.

I feel that these influences constituted the *cognitive* building blocks of Freud's hypothesis, but that the fuel to assemble them as he did came principally from *noncognitive* factors—his father conflict, which I will discuss later, his feelings about the defections of Adler, Stekel, and Jung, who represented the rebellious sons while Freud was the primal father (Ostow, 1978), and, finally, his attitude toward mechanistic science.

To elaborate upon the last factor, it is well known that Freud cut his teeth on the mechanistic tenets of mid-nineteenth century German materialistic medicine. He had worked with one of the founders of this approach (Brücke) and imbibed this spirit in deep draughts. Freud's first scientific work was very much in this vein and he would have remained with Brücke had finances permitted. Even after leaving Brücke's Institute, he continued his neuroanatomical studies and moved into psychiatry only through the more scientifically respectable field of neurology. Even after abandoning his attempts to base psychiatry firmly on the principles of neurology and neuroanatomy, he always cherished the idea that one day psychopathology would be reduced to anatomy and physiology. After formulating psychological theories of hysteria and obsessional neurosis, he retained a category, the "actual neuroses," caused, he felt, by sexual toxins.

To a man of this scientific temperament and training, a man who constantly battled (as I will demonstrate) against strong speculative and philosophical trends in himself, it was much easier to believe that his hysterics' accounts were recollections of *real* events, rather than fantasies. Later Freud was shocked when he discovered they were fantasies after all: "I was for some time completely at a loss. My confidence alike in my technique and in its results suffered a severe blow. . . ." (Freud, 1925, p. 34), Even though he redeemed himself with the doctrine of *psychic* reality, was he not farther from Brücke's material reality than ever before? Grinstein (1968) has interpreted Freud's dream of self dissection as punishment for leaving Brücke's strict materialistic path. From that time forward, I believe, Freud was consciously and unconsciously preoccupied with returning to that path.

Freud had read many euhemerist authors and, in a broad sense his initial belief in the reality of his hysterics' remembrances exhibits a euhemerist trend. If the very nuclear complex (Oedipus) of neurosis could not be founded on ontogenetic history, would not the next best idea be to ground it on phylogenetic history? Has not the idea of the phylogenetic transmission of the memory of, and remorse over, the primal crime, virtually based psychology (and sociology) on biology? However, if Freud's intention was to return to Brücke's actuality, then his hypothesis backfired on him; even though the fantasies retain a certain reality after all, it is the sort of reality that makes each neurotic an epiphenomenon of a long past event. Like Jung, whom he may have been unconsciously copying, Freud stood the individual on his head in favor of the archetype. He is farther from his cherished actual reality than ever.

But the child experiences another attitude toward the father aside from the hostility which Freud wrote of in *Totem and Taboo*—i.e., dependency—which he felt contributed to man's conception of the Deity. Freud submitted this thesis in the *Leonardo* and developed it further in the *Future of an Illusion* (1927a, p. 24). It was a polemic against religion in the best Enlightenment tradition:

> When the growing individual finds that he is destined to remain a child forever, that he can never do without protection against

strange superior powers, he lends those powers the features belonging to the figure of his father; he creates for himself the gods whom he dreads, whom he seeks to propitiate, and whom he nevertheless entrusts with his own protection. Thus, his longing for a father is a motive identical with his need for protection against the consequences of human weakness.

Here, too, Freud was influenced by Feuerbach (and, through Feuerbach, Schleiermacher[2] as well). Feuerbach saw religion as infantile and emphasized its element of wishfulfillment (which Freud termed "illusion") and dependency.

In addition to Freud's analogies between religion on the one hand, and neurosis, psychosis, and infantilism on the other, and his view of religion as an ontogenetic and phylogenetic precipitate of the Oedipus complex, he emphasized the role of primary process thought in myth and religion, comparing them to dreams. Here he was influenced by Feuerbach and Tylor. Feuerbach had written, "Religion is the dream of waking consciousness; dreaming is the key to the mysteries of religion." (Acton, 1955, pp. 120-122). Tylor (1871, p. 282) saw the "myth-making function" as common to primitives, ancients, children, poets, and the insane.

Like Nietzsche, Freud used the concept of religion as a sublimation of lower drives. In the *Leonardo,* Freud (1910, p. 96) said, also undoubtedly influenced by Robert Knight's book, *A Discourse on the Worship of Priapus* (1786) (which, as he wrote Jung, he had recently read): "Originally [the genitals] were worshipped as gods and transmitted the divine nature of their functions to all newly learned human activities. As a result of the sublimation of their basic nature there arose innumerable divinities . . ." (McGuire, 1974, p. 276). As William James (1901, p. 27) points out, by 1900 many writers had attempted to derive religious phenomena from the sexual impulses.

As to another prominent aspect of Western religion, the idea of Paradise, Freud (1900, p. 254) called it a "group phantasy of the childhood of the individual." In the 1909 edition of *The Interpretation of Dreams* he (1900, p. 400 fn) reduced the belief in immortality to "phantasies and unconscious thoughts about life in the womb" which "afford the deepest unconscious basis for the belief in survival after death, which merely represents a projection into the future of this uncanny life before birth." Two years later, Freud (1911b, p. 223) theorized,

---

2. As to Freud's early familiarity with other theologians, I am indebted to John Gach for showing me a copy of the radical Protestant theologian David Strauss' biography of Ulrich von Hütten (published in Leipzig in 1871) which Freud inscribed and presented to his friend Heinrich Braun on the occasion of the latter's birthday in 1872!

"The doctrine of reward in the after-life for the—voluntary or enforced—renunciation of earthly pleasures is nothing other than a
mythical projection of this revolution [substitution of the reality principle for the pleasure principle] in the mind."

A CRITIQUE OF FREUD'S VIEWS ON RELIGION

In order to facilitate the task of psychopathologizing religion, Freud
first confronted it on his own terms. He reduced the manifestations of
religion to ritual and a few beliefs of the common folk. Mysticism, which
he admitted he never really understood, was explained as a reactivation
of the infant's lack of ego boundaries at the mother's breast (Freud
1930a, pp. 65-72). And a year before his death, he (1938, p. 300) conceptualized it as "the obscure self-perception of the realm outside the
ego, of the id." Religious philosophy (theology), which he (1930a, p. 74)
termed "pitiful rearguard actions" and whose greatest representatives he
never read or at least never quoted was dismissed in a few sentences
(1927a, p. 32):

> Where questions of religion are concerned people are guilty of
> every sort of dishonesty and intellectual misdemeanor. Philos-
> ophers stretch the meaning of words until they retain scarcely
> anything of their original sense. They give the name 'God' to some
> vague abstraction which they have created for themselves. Having
> done so, they can pose before all the world as deists, as believers in
> God, and they can boast that they have recognized a higher, purer
> concept of God, notwithstanding that their God is nothing more
> than an insubstantial shadow and no longer the mighty personality
> of religious doctrines . . .

I believe there is a good deal of subjectivity—implicit and explicit—in
all Freud's considerations of religion. At times he (1927a, p. 14) was
positive—terming religion "perhaps the most important item in the
psychical inventory of civilization." He (1921a, pp. 134-135) praised the
novel nature of the group ties in the Catholic Church where "Identification [with Christ] has to be added to where object-choice has taken place,
and object-love where there is identification." Freud (1912, p. 188)
spoke of the beneficent effect of Christian asceticism on the sensually
debased love of pagan antiquity. Then he (1921a, p. 91) referred approvingly to St. Paul's concept of love and compared it to his own. The
primal parricide hypothesis, with which he seemingly disposed of religion
as a "survival", may well have been a function of the positive side of his

ambivalence as well. Although on the one hand he reduced the transcendental to the mundane, on the other he dignified religion by providing it an ancient lineage and a foundation in concrete reality and in mankind's recurrent psychological dispositions. He (1926a, pp. 273-274, 1930b, p. XV, E. Freud, 1975, pp. 202-203) could even wax eloquent on the faith of his ancestors. Although Freud generally felt there was no point of reconciliation between religion and psychoanalysis, and although he could never understand how some people, like Pfister, could practice both, in *The Future of an Illusion,* the very work in which he was so harshly polemical against religion, he (1927a, pp. 36-37) asserted that psychoanalysis is an "impartial instrument" which can be used as much to defend, as to attack, religion.

However, more often he was negative. But Freud was *never* affectively neutral on the subject. In other words, he was not, in any sense of the term a "post-religious" man. For example, "the whole thing is so patently infantile, so foreign to reality, that to anyone with a friendly attitude to humanity it is painful to think that the majority of mortals will never be able to rise above this view of life" (Freud, 1930a, p. 74). He (ibid, p. 102) attacked the very Pauline ethic he had praised elsewhere on the grounds that it was psychologically unworkable. Although he lived out his own life in fairly strict accord with traditional Judaeo-Christian morality, in his writings it is clear that he was ambivalent toward it.[3] When he wanted to express a particularly sharp criticism of Jung's psychology, he (1914, p. 37) charged that it was "permeated with religious ideas." Freud even went so far as to brand any asking of the so-called "big questions" as pathological: "The moment a man questions the meaning and value of life, he is sick, since objectively neither has any existence; by asking this question one is merely admitting to a store of unsatisfied libido to which something else must have happened, a kind of fermentation leading to sadness and depression" (E. Freud, 1960, p. 436). Elsewhere he (1930a, p. 75) said one has "a right to dismiss the question [of the meaning of life], for it seems to derive from the human presumptuousness....Nobody talks about the purpose of the life of animals..."

His characterizations of religions as "neurotic relics" (1927a, p. 44), "mass delusions" (1930a, p. 81), and "blissful hallucinatory confusion" (1927a, p. 43) support Ackerknecht's (1943, pp. 58-61) accusation that there are "hidden moral judgements" in this diagnostic labelling: "We think that the custom of covering moral judgements with a pseudo-scientific and psychopathological nomenclature is no advance at all and

---

3. Freud's relationship to religious ethics is a rich and complicated one which is treated in my subsequent essay (Wallace, 1983a).

is equally bad for both of them: morals and science..." Similar moral judgements are present in Freud's conceptualization (1913, p. 90) of religion as the phase of man's history that corresponds to the infantile stage of individual development, while "the scientific phase would have an exact counterpart in the stage at which an individual has reached maturity, has renounced the pleasure principle, adjusted himself to reality and turned to the external world for the object of his desires." His (1927a, p. 43) idea that "it is to be supposed that a turning away from religion is bound to occur with the fatal inevitability of a process of growth" might have been penned by Comte or Spencer.

Quite apart from its moralizing quality Freud's psychopathologizing of religion is open to criticism on purely methodological grounds. First and foremost, it ignores the questions of history and sociocultural context. Second, it pays insufficient attention to adaptiveness as a point of differentiation between disease and normality. Third, it makes no distinction between the concept of the "individual" and that of the "institution," presupposes the existence of a mass mind, relies on an exaggerated concept of psychic unity, gives insufficient attention to the conscious aspects of myth and ritual, and inadequately treats the phenomenology of religious experience. Fourth, it violates sound psychoanalytic methodology itself. Finally, it attempts to give "scientific" answers to metaphysical questions.

My discussion will reflect the evident overlap among these points. However, let us begin with the first criticism, which Ackerknecht clearly grasped in 1943 (pp. 58-61).:

Once we stop at a typical statement of the 'psychopathological school' as the following [incidentally, attributed to Devereux]: *'Primitive' religion and in general 'quaint' primitive areas are organized schizophrenia* [Ackerknecht's italics] and think it over it is not very difficult to realize the full consequences of this tendency for science: When (primitive) religion is but 'organized schizophrenia', then there is left no room or necessity for history, anthropology, sociology, etc. God's earth was, and is, but a gigantic state hospital and pathography becomes the unique and universal science.

Years earlier, William James (1901, pp. 21-38), in a work Freud very likely encountered, had criticized, under the rubric of "medical materialism," psychiatric reductionism of religious experience.

In 1930 Erich Fromm accepted the importance of Freud's thesis that obsessional mechanisms operate in religion but demonstrated that they are not the whole story. Fromm showed how one cannot understand the

transformations in Judaic, and then Christian, theology without knowing the corresponding changes in the social-historical circumstances of
the times. It is on Freud's equation of religion with obsessionalism that
Rieff (1953, p. 109) chose to center a critique in which he points out that
Freud collapsed public reference into the private domain. "The historical
value context of social actions is assimilated to unconscious motivations.
A nun telling her beads and a neurotic counting buttons on his clothing
are both viewed as engaged in obsessional actions. The cultural context
of the nun's action is dismissed as superficial..." It may be, I might add,
that the nun *is* engaged in defensive operations, but that in no way
negates the other determinants of, and functions served by, her actions.
Psychological mechanisms, Rieff (p. 111) warns, are incomplete explanations of social action unless they are placed within their objective contexts. Culture itself, he feels, may pick up a given personality type and
subsume it to its own ends, extend it into the socially meaningful. For example, there is no "prophetic personality type." Prophecy cannot be
understood psychologically, but historically (p. 116)—"as a publicly
shared interpretive tradition, which has selected out and transformed the
most varied psychological material and organized it into a common contribution."

LeVine (1973) reminds us that any explanation of social behavior must
take into account institutional as well as personality determinants. He
advocates that we conceptualize religious behaviors as compromises between intrapsychic factors and current normative pressures, with the
relative weight of each set of factors varying from individual to individual. If Freud had realized the full implications of his doctrine of
overdetermination then he would have seen the precariousness of explaining religious behavior with reference to personality factors alone.

But *even if* one accepts that Freud's "mental mechanisms" are the
whole story of religion and that religious behaviors are nothing more
than compromise formations between the forces of repression and those
striving for expression, it does not follow from this that religion is
therefore "psychopathological." Freud's failure to realize this was in
part an unfortunate heritage from those early days of psychoanalysis
when conflict itself was considered pathological—exemplified in the very
title of Freud's second book on normal psychology, *The Psychopathology of Everyday Life*. We now appreciate, as Freud himself did
later, that intrapsychic conflict, compromise formation, and overdetermination or "multiple function" are ubiquitous and that any concept of
psychopathology that does not also take adaptation into account is
seriously limited.

Similarly, ego psychology has taught us that defense, or rather mental, mechanisms are *not* pathological *per se*. They can occur prior to any

use for defensive purposes (e.g., intellectualization) and can, in fact, be quite *adaptive*. Even mechanisms apparently as abnormal as dissociation are not pathological *in and of themselves*—but only with reference to the sociocultural-historical context within which they arise. In some cultures, such phenomena are not only considered normal, but are highly rewarded and sought after. Many studies show that trance subjects, outside of their states of altered consciousness, are usually psychologically indistinguishable from their fellows who do not enter trances (Belo, 1960). Embedded as he was in his Viennese matrix, Freud never appreciated the cultural relativity of psychopathology.

Although Freud eventually arrived at a conception of the psyche that stressed the continuum between normality and pathology, the fact that he began his study of psychology at its abnormal pole initially strengthened his tendency to psychopathologize. By contrast, if Freud has first recognized–conceptualized the mental mechanisms and dynamics that operate in all of us, and only afterward examined their exaggeration in those whom Western European society labelled "pathological," then it would have been harder for him to fall into errors such as extrapolating from the identification of *obsessional mechanisms* in religious ritual to the diagnosis of religion as an *obsessive-compulsive neurosis* itself. Interestingly enough, Freud recognized such mistakes when they occurred in Abraham's work on Ikhnaton, although he could not see them in his own (H. Abraham & E. Freud, 1965, pp. 118-119).

Turning now to the issue of adaptation, Spiro (1965, pp. 109-111) speaks to the relationship between religion and psychopathology, with specific reference to Burmese monasticism. He notes that, although "phenotypically" the behavior of the monk resembles that of the schizophrenic, "genotypically" it is quite different. The differences are illustrative of the general factors which distinguish between religious and psychopathological behavior: the origin of the psychotic's conflict is idiosyncratic, while that of the monk is rooted in modal features of his society; the psychotic solves his problems with idiosyncratic, private defenses, and the monk uses institutional means; psychotic behavior is inconsistent with the fulfillment of a normal social role, while monastic behavior is not only appropriate but socially valued; the psychotic's behavior isolates him from his fellows, while the monk's integrates him with his; and finally, the psychotic's world view is incompatible with that of his culture, while the monk's is not.

Thus, *adaptiveness*—both to society and to one's own intrapsychic needs—is evidently Spiro's major criterion. Not only is Burmese monastic behavior *not* maladaptive, but it "permits the resolution of emotional conflict" and thereby "reduces the probability of the occurrence of other, nonsanctioned means by which these conflicts might be expressed and resolved" (p. 112). In other words, by adopting a set of socially provided and sanctioned defense mechanisms—monasticism—the monk is relieved of the necessity of devising his own. Unlike Spiro, and James (1901), and Boisen (1936) before him, Freud failed to use adaptiveness as a criterion for distinguishing between individual psychopathology and institutionalized behavior like religion. And this despite the fact that, as we have seen, in several places Freud credited religion with a role in the development of civilization.[4]

As I have suggested, one can criticize Freud's psychopathologizing of religion on *grounds derived in part from psychoanalysis itself.* LeVine (1973, p. 273) has indicated that in his cultural work, Freud failed to use the most powerful tool he possessed—the clinical method of psychoanalysis. A question such as "whether the normal person [read "religionist"] under stress regresses to a projective fantasy that includes the same sexual and other content found in the paranoid delusion is an *empirical* [my italics] one, and I assume there is great individual variation in this regard." To put it another way, whether a person engaged in prayer is paranoid or whether a ritualist is obsessional can only be determined from a clinical examination of the particular individual and not merely from the knowledge that he is a religionist (see also Meissner, 1976). What Freud did was transfer insights arrived at in the clinical setting *directly* to the cultural arena and then treat these speculations as if they had the same validity as the empirically based propositions of clinical psychoanalysis. Thus, as George Gross (personal communication) has helped me to understand, he transferred *insights* derived at by way of the analytic method but not the *method* itself.

The next methodological criticism, somewhat related to the previous one, is that Freud failed to distinguish adequately between individuals and institutions. LeVine (1973, p. 209) has warned us that "individuals, and only individuals, can be psychoanalyzed. Customs, institutions and organizations cannot be, and any attempt to do so involves dispensing with those elements in the clinical method that give psychoanalytic assessments their validity."

When one analyzes the individual practitioners of any ritual, he will most certainly find that, as Cora Dubois wrote (1937, p. 247), not all of

---

4. In Freud's (in Nunberg and Federn, 1967, pp. 122-123) comments at the aforementioned 1909 meeting of the Vienna Psychoanalytic Association, there occurs a rare instance in which he did more than simply pay lip service to questions of adaptation and sociohistorical factors. In his discussion of Satan, he focused on the history of deities and the transformation of abandoned gods into devils. He touched on the "racial problem" which determines what color the Devil will assume. Finally, he saw the Devil as in part a "justification fantasy," enabling Christians to deal with the upsurge in repression during the Reformation.

them share the same attitude toward their highly formalized behavior. More recently the anthropologist Kracke (1979, p. 227) has issued a similar caveat: The analyst, in his day to day practice, does not even assume that "a particular *social* [my italics] form—shaking hands or payment for the analytic hour—has an identical unconscious meaning for all analytic patients." Freud was aware of this in his clinical, but unfortunately not in his cultural, work.

We are dealing with much the same problem in the psychoanalytic interpretation of myth. Psychoanalyst Charles Brenner (1976, pp. 160-161), has warned us that though there are "some stories, myths, and religious legends whose relation to the common instinctual wishes and conflicts of childhood is direct and unambiguous", "most stories and myths, however, are ambiguous." "They have," he continues, "a multiple appeal and can 'mean' quite different things to different people." Kracke (1979, p. 228) expresses similar, but stronger, sentiments, reminding us that myths stem, not from some "communal psyche," but from the varied fantasies of multiple *individuals*.

Since different social roles carry different tensions, create different needs, and offer different satisfactions for the individuals involved, it seems that each society would need, at any given point, several sets of myths—myths corresponding to the dominant needs and anxieties of its various members. Boyer (1979) has documented this among the Chiricahua and Mescalero Apaches (see also Arlow, 1961).

Just as myths differ as they correspond to the needs of the various roles within their particular society, they also alter in response to changing sociohistorical (especially technoeconomic) circumstances. Kardiner (1939, p. 103) points out that myths have a "functional relationship to the social organization" and that as their usefulness is exhausted, they undergo revision. Because of this, Kardiner (p. 105) states plainly that it is hazardous to draw on mythology as a source for historical reconstruction—to use, for example, current totemic myth and ritual or the Oedipus story to infer a primal parricide in man's dawn. "If folklore gives us clues about the current social tension we can draw conclusions about 'origins' only if we have the complete record of the changes in folklore and myths."

Sapir (1918, p. 527) has emphasized that meanings in the cultural sphere change not only from person to person but throughout time as well. This is something that every clinician recognizes in the individual domain—over the course of time the initially prepotent determinant of a patient's symptom can become all but supplanted by subsequent motives. Freud (1905, p. 53) himself wrote, "In the course of years a symptom can change its meaning or its chief meaning, or the leading role can pass from one meaning to another." Nevertheless, even though

Freud knew this, he had trouble keeping it in mind, tending to view the prototypic determinants as the decisive ones—in both his psychology and his anthropology. Hence, by implication for the cultural sphere, even if one considers totemic practices to be the forerunners of modern religions (a very controversial notion), and even if one accepts Freud's oedipal explanation of their origin, it does not follow that the same motivations and meanings will continue to be decisive for any or all of the present day participants. In fact they may, but this can only be determined empirically (clinically).

Returning now more directly to Freud's ahistoricism, Weinstein and Platt (1973, p. 3) observe that for Freud "the oedipal drama is inevitably and immutably the decisive reality, and what is important in and for man occurs independently of specific social structures and without reference to historical time." Ricoeur (1970, p. 243) opines that for Freud "there is no history of religion: religion's theme is the indestructability of its own origins; religion is the area where the most dramatic emotional configurations [the Oedipus complex and the primal parricide] are unsurpassable . . . it is the area of emotive repetition. *That is why in principle the gaps in this history are unessential* [my italics]." Rieff (1951, pp. 26-39) tells us that in Freud's view "there had to be a *Kairos,* that crucial time in the past that is decisive for what then must come after." The Freudian *Kairos* is the primal crime; all subsequent history is repetition, "the eternal return of the repressed." To this way of thinking it is plain that there can be but one *Kairos.* "Each subsequent *Kairos* is epigonal (e.g. Moses, Christ), and thus more and more spurious, inauthentic, at least unrevealing of any new psychic states."

Generally, in his sociocultural writings, Freud is concerned, undoubtedly influenced in part by the cultural evolutionists, with elucidating the earliest history—the very origins—of cultural institutions. It is precisely in such areas that speculation can reign supreme and where one can be left with either fanciful phylogenetic reconstructions, or projections of determinants of present day psychosocial constellations into the remotest past. Most social scientists, including psychoanalysts, now believe that the current state of complex social systems can hardly be explained simply by reference to their initial conditions (even if these conditions are known), just as we feel that historical explanation must proceed backward, and in short steps—the way Freud proceeded in his *clinical* work but not, unfortunately, in his *cultural.*

Where Freud did not have a Kairotic or cyclical conception of religion's history, he adopted the cultural evolutionists' formula that religion developed through a fixed and unilinear progression from animism and magic on down to its contemporary Western varieties; totemism also was deemed a well nigh universal precursor of "more advanced" religious forms. Freud's ahistorical errors in his study of religion are part and parcel of the errors in his entire approach to culture; I have examined these in great detail in recent works (Wallace, 1980b, Wallace, 1983b). Basically, Freud's mistakes derive, apart from the above noted displacement of psychoanalytic insights from office to culture, from too rigid an adherence to the cornerstone doctrines of cultural evolutionism—psychic unity, the comparative method, the notion that cultures everywhere develop along a fixed and unilinear evolutionary scheme, psychic Lamarckism and the biogenetic law, the idea that contemporary "primitive" cultures may be equated with those of prehistoric men, and the doctrine of survivals.

Although it is an integral part of his ahistorical approach to religion, I will resist the temptation to begin a detailed criticism of Freud's thinking on totemism since a proper treatment of this topic is far beyond the limits of this paper and it has been treated elsewhere at great length (Boyer, 1979, Wallace, 1983b). Suffice it to say, more recent evidence points out serious deficits in the work of the cultural evolutionists upon whom Freud relied; the data suggests that totemism is best not conceptualized as a unitary phenomenon (see Goldenweiser, as early as 1910), and that totemic practices in no way have as hoary a history as Freud supposed.

Implicit in much of the discussion thus far has been Freud's over reliance on the doctrine of psychic unity, which allowed him to extrapolate from the findings in himself and a relatively small number of *fin de siècle* European patients to whole populations, many of them *non Westerners,* whom he had never seen, much less analyzed. Also implied in Freud's approach—particularly in the parricide hypothesis and the theses of *Moses and Monotheism*—is the assumption that society can be treated as the human mind writ large. From at least 1913 on I can find no evidence that Freud had any doubt about the validity of such analogizing, although he (Jones, 1957, p. 313) was well aware that there were criticisms of it. Freud (1939, p. 100) felt his procedure was justified because, once we assume the Lamarckian transmission of archaic memory traces, "we have bridged the gulf between individual and group psychology: we can deal with people as we do with an individual neurotic."

One must be extremely cautious about applying the dynamic model, developed to explain the behaviors of the human individual, to groups, cultures, or nations. One can speak of the "unconscious" of a particular nation or civilization, as Freud and many subsequent psychohistorians have done, only *metaphorically.* Units as large as most modern nations and societies are composed of many different individuals, representing different trends and potentialities, concentrating and carrying some aspects of their society's history more than others. By and large, it is only with the smallest and most homogeneous societies that one can speak, with any semblance of correctness, of a "group unconscious." And then what one is referring to is, of course, not some magical collective mind, but the *common elements,* due to shared experiences and methods of child rearing, in the unconsciouses of the *individuals* involved. All this may seem obvious, but unfortunately some "psychohistorians" have not kept these caveats in mind and have reified abstractions such as the "national unconscious," etc. There is of course no better example of all this than *Moses and Monotheism,* where Freud (1939, p. 80) subsumes centuries of Jewish religious history to the formula. "Early trauma—defence—latency—outbreak of neurotic illness—partial return of the repressed."

Another major methodological criticism concerns Freud's lifelong tendency to view unconscious factors as somehow more *real* than conscious ones. As Victor Turner (1967, p. 34) points out, Freud, in contrast to those who place great emphasis on knowing the conscious indigenous interpretations of symbol and ritual, regards such interpretations as though they were identical with the rationalizations by which neurotics explain and justify their symptomatic behavior. "The psychoanalyst," he asserts (p. 250), "must cease to regard interpretations, beliefs and dogmas as mere rationalizations when, often enough, these refer to social and natural realities." Earlier, Kardiner (1939, p. 750) had made the same complaint about the analytic anthropologist's "contempt for the uses of the conscious systems."

I feel that the distinction between conscious and unconscious is one of the most important points of differentiation between religious and psychopathological behavior. It is, as Maritain (1957, p. 241) and Zilboorg (1956, pp. 180-188) point out, the disclosure of guilt concerning actions of which the religionist is deeply conscious that separates confession from the analysis of an unconscious and neurotic sense of guilt. It is the consciously intentional incorporation of the symbolic body of Christ and the tranquil state which often ensues that differentiates communion from the unconscious identification with the lost, ambivalently loved object and resultant state of euphoria or despondency in mania or melancholia (Zilboorg, 1955, pp. 161-167). Now this is not to say that the Eucharist or confessional cannot become vehicles for the expression of, and/or defense against, neurotic or psychotic trends, but that this is the case no more invalidates or devalues religion than the pathological use of any other cultural institution invalidates or devalues it. The Catholic Church, with its concept of "scrupulosity" has long sensed that neurotic issues can contaminate religious practices. Similarly, although it is true that religious asceticism can subserve neurotic and unconscious trends, this is by no means always the case, and one cannot lose sight of the considerable difference between the conscious and deliberate suppression of sexuality of the celibate priest or nun and the unconscious repression and impotence or frigidity of the neurotic. Freud himself may have been aware of this important distinction (conscious versus unconscious) between religion and neurosis. Gay (1975, pp. 493-507) indicates that in Freud's 1907 essay on religion he constantly uses the term *Unterdrückung* (suppression) in reference to religious behavior and *Verdrängung* (repression) in reference to neurotic.

Closely related to the previous criticism is Freud's insufficient attention to the *phenomenology* of religious experience and how it compares and contrasts with that of psychopathology. Having observed apparent similarities in the behaviors of obsessional neurotics and religious ritualists, he did not go on to ask whether their subjective experiences were actually the same. Consequently, he overlooked important distinctions between symptom and ritual, such as the *ego dystonic and ego alien* nature of the former and the *ego syntonic* of the latter. In seeking to comprehend and communicate the quality of religious experience, which he (1930a, p. 65) claimed never to have had himself, by recourse to a number of prosaic analogies, Freud was following in the time honored tradition of many theologians and mystics. Where he parted ways with them was in his conviction that such analogies exhaustively described and explained the phenomenology of religious states. The theologian Otto (1917, pp. 6-11) warned that, while affects such as love, trust, fear, dependency, etc., help elucidate the nature of religious experience, they do not fully comprehend it. There remains, he felt, a significant overplus of emotion (the "numinous") incomparable, and irreducible, to any other category of human experience.

Finally, if Freud treated the sociocultural, historical, and phenomenological aspects of religion too reductionistically, he did the same with its metaphysics. In other words, for him it was not only that his mental mechanisms and dynamics contribute to our understanding of religion but that they *are* the religious phenomena *themselves*.

Guirdham (1959, pp. 27-29) has acknowledged the importance of Freud's psychological explanations of religious behavior, but denies that they are the whole story or that they vitiate in any way the truth or value of religious experience: "religion must of necessity employ for its expression the mental and emotional attributes we possess . . . the fact that certain well-established psychiatric mechanisms are utilized in religious feeling does not in any sense imply that the latter is neither genuine nor divine." Similarly, he says, merely because religious feeling depends in part on the "repression and deviation of the sexual instinct, this does not mean it is spurious or abnormal." Likewise, Tillich (1957, pp. 106-107) asserts that "In every act of genuine faith the body participates because genuine faith is a passionate act . . . The same is true of the unconscious strivings, the so-called instincts of man's psyche." Küng (1979, p. 77) agrees, and points out that merely because the childhood attitudes toward the father and projection participate in one's attitude toward God, this does not mean that God does not exist.

Although Tillich (ibid, p. 83) feels that Freud was right to deny concepts like "soul" a place in his new psychology since they had not been produced by his own scientific work, he was wrong in attacking forms of faith in the name of scientific psychology. "The truth of man's eternal meaning lies in a dimension other than the truth of adequate psychological concepts" (p. 84). Zilboorg (1953, pp. 104-116) agrees that Freud erred in trying to give scientific or pseudo-scientific answers to metaphysical questions. In actuality, says Tillich (p. 84), Freud was opposing not science, but faith, to faith.

The religionist can scientifically demonstrate the truth of his theology no more than Freud can prove that there is not, *after all the psychological factors have been removed,* a God-implanted "drive" to religion or a transcendental reality that corresponds to religious beliefs. If one were to stay thoroughly and consistently scientific, then he would have to remain agnostic on all the so-called "big questions." This, as we have seen and shall see, Freud could not do. His attitude toward the truth of religion was characterized by the same certainty as was his stance toward psychoanalysis and the mechanistic world-view.

To recapitulate, because of its extreme psychological reductionism, ahistoricism, lack of attention to social factors, failure to take adaptiveness into sufficient account, and moralism, I feel that Freud's equation of religion and psychopathology is unsound. In making statements like "The states of possession correspond to our neuroses," Freud (1922, p. 73) is partly responsible for the view of Zilboorg (1941), Devereux (1956), Alexander and Selesnick (1966), and many others that witches, shamans, and medicine men are necessarily the products of or are suffering from mental disorder. Rosen (1968), Jackson and Jackson (1970), Hoch (1974), Hippler (1976), and others have demonstrated that witches were more likely to be socially deviant than mentally ill and that primitive healers and seers, while often exceptional individuals in many respects, are usually no more psychopathological by the standards of their culture (or by ours) than their fellows. Macfarlane (1970) demonstrated that Tudor-Stuart witches were usually economically unproductive, almsseeking pariahs rather than mentally deranged, and that it was more often their accusers who were using the more reality-distorting mental mechanisms—projection and omnipotence of thoughts. In a study of the Mescalero Apache, Boyer et al. (1964) even found that these shamans, if culturally deviant, are deviant in the direction of mental health. (See also Boyer 1962 and Boyer, Boyer and De Vos 1982.)

Freud's mistake was that, having correctly observed the commonalities in religious and neurotic behaviors, he emphasized them to the exclusion of the differences. Even in his 1907 paper he took the trouble to point out two of them—the greater individual variability in neurotic, as opposed to religious, ritual, and the private nature of neurosis versus the public nature of religion—and, as I have indicated, he may have been aware of a third (suppression versus repression). If Freud had done more than pay lip service to his own caveats, then many of the pitfalls in his work in this area would have been avoided. For example, he (1927a, p. 43) warned, "these [psychopathological explanations of religion] are only analogies, by the help of which we endeavor to understand a *social* [my italics] phenomenon; the pathology of the individual does not supply us with a fully valid counterpart." Merely because something is an "illusion," that is to say "derived from human wishes," does not mean that it is necessarily false or in contradiction to reality, he (p. 31) admitted in the same work: "Just as they [religious propositions] cannot be proved, so they cannot be refuted" (ibid). As early as 1913 (p. 157 fn.), in *Totem and Taboo,* he reminded himself that his theories had not exhausted the explanation of religious phenomena, but only added a new facet to them. Unfortunately, such bits of awareness did not emerge in Freud's writings, where he generally ignored the differences between religion and neurosis and proceeded as if his explanations *were* the only ones. This was in part because, like many highly original thinkers, he did not wish to dilute his point, but also because of more personal reasons which I shall consider in a moment.[5]

Despite its weaknesses, there are important implications of Freud's theorizing on religion. Perhaps the most seminal legacy of his problematic parallels between psychopathology and religion is the idea that *psychological mechanisms can be institutionalized by society.* This pro-

---

5. However, is it not possible, if one is so inclined, to turn Freud's psychopathologizing of religion on its head? Do not his analogies between religion and neurosis contain the seeds for a true inverse reduction of neurosis to religion—the idea of neurosis as a substitute for religion, as an attempt to meet needs otherwise met by religion, or even as the religious process gone awry? I am thinking particularly of Freud's (1907a) conceptualization of obsession-alism as a "private religion," of his 1913 formulation of obsessional neurosis as a caricature of religion, and of the following passage in *Group Psychology* (1921a, p. 142): "If he is left to himself, a neurotic is obliged to replace by his own symptom formations the great group formations from which he is excluded. He creates his own world of imagination for himself, his own religion, his own system of delusions, and thus recapitulates the institutions of humanity in a distorted way..." To some extent Jung (1938) engaged in this inverse reductionism. For him, neuroses were basically religious phenomena.

vides a link—the surest one that Freud gave us—between personality and culture. One other invaluable bequest is his ontogenetic theory of religion—*the idea that needs and tensions from early childhood can contribute to the formation of cultural systems.* This is of course one of the foundations upon which Kardiner (1939) laid what is still one of the most sophisticated attempts to relate culture to personality.

DETERMINANTS OF FREUD'S VIEWS ON RELIGION

In the previous sections of this paper I have attempted to document that Freud's attitude toward religion was ambivalent, though largely antipathetic. I believe that this ambivalence cannot be explained by reference to cognitive factors alone, but that noncognitive, less rational factors must be taken into account as well. Zilboorg (1953, 1955, 1958, 1959) has adduced additional evidence that Freud's attitude toward religion was not conflict-free. By way of example, he cites Freud's forgetting of the word "Menorah," his inability to recall the name of a painter of the Last Judgment—Signorelli, and his substitution of the word "nature" for "God" in a quotation from Shakespeare. Zilboorg even asserts (though he does not cite his source and I cannot confirm it) that Freud's claim to have begun practice on Easter Day, 1886 was a misrecollection since he actually opened his office in May, and Easter fell on April 25th of that year.

What are the wellsprings of this ambivalence? They are indeed many and in this essay I can do little more than enumerate those I consider to be particularly important.

Perhaps foremost among them is Freud's discomfort with his own speculative, superstitious or, as I (Wallace, 1978a) have called them, "mystical", trends. Jones (1955, p. 33) understood that Freud's "unrestrained imagination" was something "over which his highly developed capacity for self-criticism had to exert the strictest control." Jung (1961, p. 152) asserted that Freud was engaged in a "flight from himself, or from that other side of him which might perhaps be called mystical." Wittels (1931, pp. 79-80) puts it poetically: "I think that Freud, the fearless man who released the hell-hound out of Hades, is afraid of the song in his own heart. . . . In Freud's mentality the mystical gift of the seer is continually at war with the need for mechanical investigation..." Although from time to time Freud acknowledged the unmistakable appearance of these elements in himself, fearful that they might tarnish the scientific respectability of psychoanalysis, he never subjected them to his usual thorough analysis. Since it is crucial to my thesis that the reader realize the full importance of these factors in Freud, I will expand upon them at some length.

Apart from some superstitious phenomena connected with his fiancee, Martha Bernays, these tendencies first express themselves in Freud's death anxieties and preoccupation with death dates. The initial reference to this *Todesangst* is in 1894 in a letter to Fliess, (Bonaparte et al, 1954). The anxiety would persist, with frequent exacerbations (ages 41, 42, 51, 61, 62, 81) throughout his life. Its appearance in 1893–1894 was intimately related to his father conflict—occurring shortly after the death of the ambivalently cathected father imago, Meynert; shortly after the death of Brücke, the greatest intellectual authority in Freud's life but also the man who advised him to abandon his scientific career and whose status Freud must have envied; at a time when Freud was still plagued with guilt concerning his role in the cocaine addiction of the deceased friend and benefactor Fleischl; when the friendship with the fatherly Breuer was deteriorating; when the ambivalent relationship with Fliess was becoming more intense; and when the health of Freud's own father was rapidly declining. On a trip to Greece in 1904, during the apex of the Swoboda-Weininger difficulties with Fliess, the death ages 61 and 62 figured prominently in the most superstitious week of Freud's life. He explained the repeated appearance of these numbers (on baggage checks, hotel rooms, etc.) partly by his heightened unconscious sensitivity to them but partly by a more mystical "compliance of chance" (McGuire, 1974, p. 220). Freud's preoccupation with death dates continued; examples are too numerous to mention (see Wallace, 1978a, 1978b). Suffice it to say that, in addition to his father conflict, Freud's exposure to the numerological tradition in Judaism also played a part, as he surmised himself (in McGuire, 1974, p. 220).

Superstitious behavior continued. In 1905 Freud smashed a small marble Venus in his collection to avert disaster when his eldest daughter was near death. Years later, in 1925, he lost his eyeglasses in the woods as an apotropaic against evil to his daughter, Anna, then on a journey by train. On seeing a man who bore him an unusual likeness, Freud feared it as an omen of death (Jones, 1957).

Besides superstitions, Freud's "mystical" currents manifested themselves in certain highly speculative ideas such as the primal parricide hypothesis (1913), the Thanatos theory (1920a), and the thesis of *Moses and Monotheism* (1939). Certainly the parricide idea is as mystical, in its own way, as the phenomena—such as the Eucharist—it was invented to explain. Though Freud professed a marked antipathy to all of speculative philosophy—and particularly its religious branch, it would be hard to find anything more philosophical, indeed metaphysical, than the Eros-Thanatos construction. Though he criticized philosophy and religion for their lack of empiricism, *Moses and Monotheism,* with its reliance on a handful of dubious sources, is hardly a work in the empiricist vein.

In fact, though Freud's official attitude toward philosophy was quite negative, his underlying sentiments were the reverse. Although he generally depicted himself as a strict scientist, in his youth Freud read a great deal of philosophy (Gedo and Wolf, 1976). At the University of Vienna he took four semesters of that subject under Franz Brentano (Siegfried Bernfeld, 1951) and even considered following his M.D. with a Ph.D. in philosophy (Fancher, 1977)! In 1896 he wrote Fliess that he "secretly" nursed the hope of arriving by the "circuitous" route of medicine at *"my own original objective, philosophy* [my italics]" (Bonaparte et al., 1954, p. 141).

The romantic elements in Freud's education—and we now know of his considerable exposure to latter day German romantic literature, philosophy, and psychiatry—must have contributed greatly to his speculative trends.

Besides personal superstitions and highly speculative thinking, Freud's "mysticism" manifested itself in his infatuation with the occult and parapsychology. In 1908, at the Vienna Psychoanalytic Society, Freud presented three cases which ostensibly illustrated thought-transference, but which, on analysis, disclosed more prosaic explanations. Here Freud's skepticism prevailed; but with Ferenczi he visited several soothsayers and mediums, at least one of whom, Frau Seidler, he believed to have telepathic powers. Furthermore, he gave credence to some of Ferenczi's descriptions of paranormal experiences with patients and even described some with his own. He had "a few remarkable experiences which might easily have been explained on the hypothesis of telepathic thought-transference" (Freud, 1901, pp. 261-262). In 1932 Freud (p. 55) would posit that telepathy was "the original, archaic method of communication between individuals and that in the course of phylogenetic evolution it has been replaced. . . . But the older method might have persisted in the background and still be able to put itself into effect under certain conditions."

The idea of a kernel of truth in occultism attracted Freud. It cooperated, says Jones (1957, p. 380), "with more personal motives in his unconscious to incline him toward accepting a belief in telepathy." In 1911 Freud became a corresponding member of the British Society for Psychical Research; in September, 1913 he told Lou Andreas-Salomé about several cases of thought transmission; and, in September, 1915 he was made an Honorary Fellow of the American Society of Psychical Research. Indeed, in 1921 he was invited to join the advisory council of the American Psychical Institute. Though declining, he wrote its Director that "If I were at the beginning of a scientific career, instead of, as now, at its end I would perhaps choose no other field of work [parapsychology], in spite of all difficulties" (Fodor, 1971, p. 84).

Jones (1957, p. 381) well remembered the late night occasions when Freud regaled him with tales of the occult and supernatural. When Jones reproached him for his credulity, Freud would retort, "There are more things in heaven and earth than are dreamed of in your philosophy." In one particularly significant episode, Jones closed the conversation with, "...if one could believe in mental processes floating in the air, one could go on to a belief in angels." Freud stunned Jones with his intense gaze and only half joking response, "quite so, even *der liebe Gott*!"

But Freud's interest in parapsychology, like his interest in religion and philosophy, was not conflict-free. Thus, when plying Jones with stories of the occult, he would disclaim, "I don't like it at all but there is some truth in it" (Jones, 1957, p. 381). In a 1909 letter Freud chided Jung for his interest in the occult, but then went on to describe "paranormal" experiences of his own (McGuire, 1974, pp. 218-220). Although on the one hand in a work on telepathy he (1921b, p. 177) confessed that "It no longer seems possible to keep away from the study of what are known as 'occult' phenomena—of facts, that is that profess to speak in favor of the real existence of psychical forces other than the human and animal minds with which we are familiar," on the other, he (p. 179) warned the analyst to discipline himself against "allowing his interest to be drawn away on to occult phenomena." Freud's (p. 180) misgiving that occultists might use scientific inquiry "only as a ladder to raise them over the head of science" and that there "may follow a fearful collapse of critical thought, of determinist standards and of mechanistic science" seems a bit extreme in 1921, and suggests that it was principally his own mystical tendencies of which he feared losing control. Freud's ambivalence prevented "Psychoanalysis and Telepathy" from being published in his lifetime. Even when writing it he could not remember the third illustrative case he had wished to include! (See Freud, 1932, p. 49 for this case). "Dreams and Telepathy," written the next year (1922), began and ended with overstated disclaimers which, in the face of an otherwise friendly treatment of the material, suggest that Freud was in strong conflict concerning his desire to believe in the phenomena he described. Finally, and most interestingly, when asked by Dr. George Lawton if he had in fact written to the Director of the American Psychical Institute stating that if he had had his life to live again, he would have devoted it to parapsychology, Freud strenuously denied writing the letter (Fodor, 1971, p. 83)!

One of the unconscious devices which Freud used to deal with his conflict with these interests is that of "projective identification". From 1894 to 1912, the two most important figures in Freud's life were both scientists with strong mystical leanings—Fliess and Jung. Although Freud at first may not have recognized the mystical undercurrents in Fliess, they became readily apparent as time passed. Freud's acceptance of and (at times) encouragement of, and collusion with, these elements in Fliess suggest that he was doing much more than simply tolerating them. In addition to providing a transference-like object for Freud, Fliess was a personification of the mystical trends in Freud himself-just as Jung was subsequently. Freud's ambivalence toward these trends in himself played itself out in the relationship with Fliess. At first he vicariously enjoyed Fliess' numerology, while later he condemned it; in the end, this formed one of the primary reasons for the dissolution of their friendship. By projecting these elements onto Fliess, Freud was able to avoid acknowledging them as his own, to experience the conflict as being outside himself. Although in the 1901 edition of *The Psychopathology of Everyday Life* he (1901, p. 250fn) came close to accepting them in himself; in the 1907 edition he tended to shift the responsibility to Fliess.

The same dynamic was operating in the relationship with Jung whose interest in the occult and religion personified Freud's own. During Jung's 1909 visit to Vienna, both men were stunned by a bizarre noise from Freud's bookcase. Jung predicted it would repeat itself and, when it did, told the startled Freud that it was a parapsychological phenomenon (Jung, 1961, pp. 155-166). Freud (ibid, p. 155) vehemently dismissed this explanation and later challenged (p. 150) Jung to make his sexual theory a "dogma—a bulwark—against the black tide of mud—of occultism." This stands in sharp contrast to the letters in which Freud applauded and encouraged Jung's parapsychological researches and suggests to me, as it did to Jung, that the "black tide of mud...of occultism" that Freud feared was his own.

In fine, Freud had strong superstitious and speculative sides to his personality which his allegiance to Brücke's materialism prevented him from recognizing fully. Freud never adequately applied his classic early analysis of the occult and supernatural to his own psychic life. His failure to come to grips with this less rationalistic-positivistic current in himself not only robbed him of considerable self-insight (and probably creativity) and caused him to laden psychoanalysis with more of his materialist prehistory than was to its benefit, but biased his treatment of art, philosophy, and, most especially, *religion*. Freud reviled in the religionist what he could not accept in himself.

Second, we must consider the fact of Freud's Jewishness. There is a good deal of obscurity about Freud's religious upbringing. Freud's great grandfather and grandfather had been rabbis in an area of Galicia noted for its Chassidic influences. Before Sigmund's birth his father, a wool merchant, had moved the family to Priborg, a small town in Moravia with less than a hundred Jews. His father's piety in Freud's youth is of some dispute, although in his old age, Jakob spent much of his time poring over the Torah and Talmud. Sigmund's son Martin recalls participating in a *seder* at his grandfather's house. Although we have no record that Jakob ever actually denied his faith, Freud recalls a very "un-Jewish" upbringing (E. Freud, 1960, p. 395). But, although his father seems to have always maintained at least a superficial adherence to Judaism, Freud's mother may not have retained even this degree of devotion. In old age she would invite her children and grandchildren over on the Christian feast days—never the Jewish.

Marthe Robert (1976, p. 21) has probably accurately captured the state of affairs in the Freud household. "[Jakob] had taken a first decisive step away from the orthodox Judaism of his ancestors but had made no attempt to find a new spiritual home in which he and his children could sink roots. Thus he left the most gifted of his sons in an ambiguous position, halfway between the complete break with Judaism that would have been logical and the full allegiance that was no longer possible." This, coupled with the fact that Freud's Jewishness was a source of academic and social disabilities, must have left him with a good deal of hostility toward his faith and his father. This hostility—toward both father and Judaism—is very apparent in parts of *Moses and Monotheism,* where he robs the Jews of their traditional culture hero, Moses, with whom of course Freud also identified (Wallace, 1977b). His need to believe that Moses was murdered was such that when Rabbi Yahuda in 1938 told Freud that Sellin, the author from whom Freud had drawn this idea, later recanted, Freud only shrugged his shoulders and retorted "It might be true all the same" (in Jones, 1957, p. 373). His interest in Jewish jokes and anecdotes expresses both his affection for the Jewish people and, since these stories often depict his fellow Jews in a ridiculous or unfavorable light, his hostility. His ambivalent preoccupation with the Zionist leader, Herzl, is probably a further reflection of his attitude toward Judaism (Falk, 1977).

The positive feelings for Judaism that Freud did possess (exemplified by his opinion that their religion was in part responsible for the survival of the Jewish people) may account for the fact that his tirades against religion were always directed more strongly against Christianity than Judaism. This special animus against Christianity was strengthened by Freud's three categories of knowledge of Christian usage of Jews: historical, family historical (his father's account of having his hat knocked off by a Christian), and personal (subjection to anti-Semitic insults, delay in appointment to an extraordinary professorship, etc.). Furthermore, any feeling for Judaism that Freud had acquired probably helped align him against Christian elements such as the dependent ethic,[6]

---

6. By "dependent ethic" I mean the idea that man's moral behavior is dependent on his belief in a rewarding and punitive deity. In Judaism there is heightened emphasis on just behavior being its own reward. Freud would also have been exposed to the

nonintellectual or mystical trends, belief in immortality, and ascetic or body-denying tendencies. Bakan (1958) has argued for a profound influence of Judaism on the form and content of psychoanalysis itself. Several others have pointed out the affinities between Freudian dream interpretation and Talmudic exegesis; Freud (1900, p. 514) himself, referring to his relentless search for the hidden meaning in dreams, says, "we have treated as Holy Writ what previous writers have regarded as arbitrary improvisation." Rieff (1959) compares psychoanalysis to religious hermeneutics. Analogical forms of reasoning are prominent both in psychoanalysis and Judaic scholarship. Did Freud unconsciously view himself as continuing in the fine rabbinic tradition of his forefathers?

Intertwined with Freud's ambivalence toward Judaism was his ambivalence toward his father. Freud had commented several times on the latter, and it was only months after his father's death that Freud felt the need to begin his self-analysis. In a previous paper, I (1978b) have examined Freud's father conflict as it manifested itself in his dreams, his relationships to Breuer, Meynert, Fleischl, Fliess, and Jung, his death anxiety and preoccupation with death dates, and some of his more speculative ideas and writings (the parricide hypothesis and *Moses and Monotheism*). The evidence for his father conflict is overwhelming. Freud had commented on the turning away from God that often accompanies rebellion against the authority of the earthly father. I am by no means the first to suggest that this rebellion was a powerful determinant of Freud's aversion to religion. This dynamic is represented, as Jung (1961, p. 157) and Freud himself (in Schur, 1972, p. 268) thought, in Freud's two syncopal episodes in the presence of Jung. The second of these (1912) followed Freud's accusation that the Swiss psychoanalysts had failed to acknowledge some of his recent work *and* Jung's disagreement with Freud's *reduction of Ikhnaton's monotheistic reform* to a manifestation of Ikhnaton's father conflict.

Freud's father conflict is nowhere better exemplified than in the theory which he proposed to explain the very origin of religion—the "primal parricide." It is no accident that this hypothesis was penned in the last, turbulent days of Freud's friendship with Jung—a relationship characterized by a complicated oscillation of the father-son roles (Wallace, 1980c). Freud's ambivalence toward Jung found expression in his attitude toward *Totem and Taboo* in 1913; although (on May 13, 1913) he hoped it would divide him from Jung "as an acid does a salt," (two weeks later) he feared the totem work would "hasten the break against my will" (Jones, 1955, p. 354).

Enlightenment preoccupation with the independent ethic; he may have read Feuerbach's (1838) biography of Bayle, a key proponent of this idea. See *The Future of an Illusion* (1927, p. 39) for Freud's comments against the dependent ethic.

Ferenczi and Jones opined that Freud's original elation about *Totem and Taboo* represented his excitement at killing and eating the father, and that his doubts were the reaction to the fantasied deed. Since Freud (1913, p. 149) had termed the modern nuclear family a "restoration of the former primal horde," then its father—including Jakob—must be a reincarnation of the primal father. When Jones (1955, p. 354) asked him "why the man who wrote *The Interpretation of Dreams* could now have such doubts about *Totem and Taboo,*" Freud (ibid.) replied, *"Then I described the wish to kill one's father, and now I have been describing the actual killing; after all it's a big step from a wish to a deed* [my italics]." Freud was alternately the murdered father (slain by Jung) and the murdering son (slaying his father and Jung).

By raising his personal dynamic (father conflict) to the level of a phylogenetic universal, based on a long past deed, Freud is distancing himself from his patricidal rage, reactivated by the recalcitrant Jung, but he is metaphorically expressing its importance (by calling it a primal fact of world history) in his own psychic life. The characterization of the primal parricide as an irrevocable heritability reflects Freud's partial awareness of his own dynamic—the fatalistic inevitability that he must reenact the father conflict and suffer the guilt. Furthermore, the hypothesis may have been a way of undoing his previous attribution of guilt to fathers (when he believed his hysterics' fantasies): in other words, it was the sons, not the fathers, who had committed a crime. However, the element of compromise formation is plain enough for, by depicting the primal father as a brutal tyrant, in a sense Freud has justified the murderous behavior of the sons.

In a previous paper I (1977b) have attempted to demonstrate that Freud's father conflict was an equally strong determinant of *Moses and Monotheism,* a work begun when Freud was approaching 81, the age his father died and one of his own superstitious death dates. The significance of the father in Freud's psychological life also helps explain why he emphasized the paternal elements in religion, as opposed to the maternal (which were more stressed by Bachofen [1861] and others whom Freud had read).[7]

---

7. Freud's ambivalence toward his father and toward Judaism probably accounts in part for his hesitancy in publishing *The Future of an Illusion* and *Moses and Monotheism.* I am inclined to feel that this was an even more powerful reason than his stated one—fear of damaging the psychoanalytic cause in Catholic Austria. This ambivalence may also account for the curious fact that Freud broke off the writing of *Totem and Taboo* before completing what he had originally set out to do in that volume—proffer a theory of religion from its origins up to its contemporary Western varieties. This is what he had to say on the matter in 1913 (p. 146): "A great number of *powerful motives* [my italics] restrain me from any attempt at picturing the further development of religions from their origin in totemism to their condition today." Freud waited twenty-five years before writing *Moses and Monotheism,* the final chapter of *Totem and Taboo.*

Fourth, Freud's contact with neurotics doubtless gave him more exposure to the pathological rather than to the normal manifestations of religion. He had seen those who had experienced its baneful, not its strengthening effects. Much of Freud's life's work was a battle against repression and hypocrisy which he, like other good Enlightenment thinkers, saw represented by the Catholic Church and, perhaps to a lesser degree, by rabbinic Judaism.

Fifth, one cannot dismiss Zilboorg's (1958) contention that Freud's Catholic nanny had an impact on his attitudes. Although she taught Freud the Catholic religion and professed it herself, she was a thief and Freud's seductress. A good deal of disillusionment must have followed her dismissal from the Freud family. "Did not Freud as a child believe in his nurse, only to be disappointed and to find his faith shattered into the dust of eternal disappearance?" (Zilboorg, 1958, p. 241). Zilboorg (ibid.) suggests that when Freud writes contemptuously of the religion of the common man, it is this nurse's faith he has in mind. She could have helped jaundice Freud's view of religion in general and of Catholicism in particular.

A sixth factor, also put forward by Zilboorg (1958), may have been Freud's ambivalence toward his infant brother, Julius, who died in Freud's second year. Guilty feelings over his murderous wishes caused Freud, on the one hand, to want to believe in the resurrection in order to undo the death but, on the other, to disbelieve in it because, if Julius returned, so would Freud's rage.

Seventh, Freud's extreme discomfort with his own dependency doubtless contributed to his distaste for any religious manifestation of it. Jones (1955, p. 420) had said "freedom and independence were lifeblood to him. . . . When I asked him why he minded old age so much he said it was because it made him dependent on others." Freud wrote Abraham that helplessness and poverty were his two chief fears (H. Abraham & E. Freud, 1965, p. 268). One could speculate that this distaste for dependency was determined by several factors, including early losses (the nanny, childhood companions and home in Moravia, the father-brother Philip), later losses (Fliess and Jung), and disillusionment with his father. Freud's emphasis on the competitive, Oedipal, elements in his reaction to his own father's death, allowed him to give short shrift to his equally, if not more, important genuine sense of loss and longing for the father. Similar defensiveness may explain his (1913) focus on the negative pole of primitives' ambivalence toward their dead, when the very sources Freud used (see Jevons, 1896) contain as many examples of their fondness for, and attempt to hold on to, the dead as of their anger and fear toward them. Aversion to the passive-feminine role toward the father was also important; Freud remarked that "the overcoming of his 'homosexuality' had brought him a greater self-dependence" (Jones, 1955, p. 420). Freud also confided to Jones (1953, p. 317) that his second fainting episode with Jung was in part a "piece of unruly homosexual feeling." Several of Freud's dreams exhibit him in a passive-homosexual attitude toward the father and some of his comments about Dostoevsky's supposed latent homosexuality seem to be as much a projection of Freud's dynamics as an appreciation of Dostoevsky's (Wallace, 1978b). Freud's attempt to deny these passive, submissive, and dependent aspects of his personality may have contributed to his difficulties with close male friends. Rieff (1959, p. 293) notes that in at least three works (the Schreber and Wolf Man cases and the paper on masochism), Freud characterizes the religious attitude as basically feminine and submissive; the piety of Schreber and the Wolf Man was diagnosed as a manifestation of a passive homosexual attitude toward the father. If Spector (1972, p. 63) and Norman Atkins (personal communication) are correct about Freud's wish-fear of symbiosis with his mother, then this could have been a further determinant of Freud's aversion to dependency. Freud's early agoraphobia, his later train "phobia," and to some extent, his death anxieties, may well have been in part a function of this conflict concerning dependency.

Last, but certainly not least, of the factors determining Freud's antipathy to religion was his view, despite his assertions to the contrary, of psychoanalysis as a *Weltanschauung*. It was a new mode of interpretation that intruded itself into the subject matter of all the *Geisteswissenschaften,* and, as such, it had to oppose all other modes of interpretation—including the religious mode. So unique was it that Freud (in Jones, 1975, p. 289) felt it even merited its own university (seminary?) (Jones, 1975), p. 289). Psychoanalysis was an exegetical discipline that reduced all religious phenomena to its own categories of conceptualization. God is projection, prayer is omnipotence of thoughts and wishfulfillment, ritual is obsessionality. The moral treatment without illusions, psychoanalysis, was opposed to the religious, or "crooked" cure (*Schiefheiligung*) (Freud, 1921a, p. 142). That Freud first opened his office on Easter Sunday (whatever else it may signify—identification with Christ, ridicule of Christianity, etc.) may have partly symbolized the fact that here was the birth of a new and world-saving doctrine, opposing itself to the old.[8] Freud's lifelong identification with Moses is well known. When he crowned Jung his successor it was, to use Freud's (in McGuire, 1974, p. 218) own words, "*in*

---

8. I have cited Zilboorg to the effect that this was a misrecollection. Even if Zilboorg is right and this is a paramnesia, it would still speak to the *psychical reality* of Freud's preoccupation with Easter.

partibus infidelium [in the midst of the infidel]," and he consoled Jung that he would live to see the "Promised Land" (triumph of psychoanalysis) though Freud himself would not. Freud compared his work to that of a priest on more than one occasion, termed (1927b) the analyst a "secular pastoral worker" (*Seelesorger*), and dubbed the "Catholic fathers" "our predecessors in psycho-analysis" (Meng and E. Freud, 1963, p. 21). He admitted that faith, in the form of the positive transference to the therapist, played a role in the analytic, just as in the religious, cure.

Fromm (1972), Roazen (1971), and others have written on the religious overtones of the psychoanalytic movement. Freud told Binswanger (1955, p. 9) that Adler and Jung defected because "they too wanted to be Popes." On the eve of his departure from Vienna, Freud said, "After the destruction of the Temple in Jerusalem by Titus, Rabbi Jochanan ben Sakkai asked for permission to open a school at Jabneh for the study of the Torah. We are going to do the same" (Jones, 1957, p. 221). Some analysts continue to call the analytic institute the "Shul." While it would be absurd to maintain that psychoanalysis is a religion in the strict sense of the term, nevertheless, *if we lend the same significance to words that Freud did,* then how can we assume otherwise than that, at least to some degree, albeit largely unconsciously, Freud saw himself laboring in the service of a new priesthood and a new temple?

I feel that the very social-historical circumstances that helped bring psychoanalysis to life were in part responsible for Freud's need to treat it as world-view. For most of Western history, as Rieff (1959, 1966) suggests, neurosis could be expressed within the added security of a collective symbolism—a symbolism which was not only expressive but, since it was compelling and reintegrative with the group and its traditions, therapeutic as well. Such "therapies of commitment", as he terms them, can only exist in communities which retain viable systems of symbolic integration—whether they be philosophies, religions, or social-political ideologies. Of course the recent centuries have been the scene of a progressive breakdown of such communities and their ideals. Analysis, says Rieff (p. 73), arose in response to the need for a therapy that would no longer depend for its effect upon the symbolic return to a "positive community." Of his cure, Freud himself (1926b, p. 256) said, "We do not seek to bring him relief by receiving him into the Catholic, Protestant, or socialist community. We seek rather to enrich him from his own internal sources..."

Intuitively, Freud recognized the demise of these communities, their ideals, and their curative powers, and the relationship between these factors and the prevalence of neurosis. Did he not speculate that the incidence of neurosis had risen with the decline of religion? Whereas

formerly religion had operated as a socially furnished vehicle for compromise formation, by Freud's time it was failing in this function and the
attempts at compromise (expression, defense, and resolution) had
become more idiosyncratic and less adaptive.

Suffering acutely from his own neurosis, Freud was still inaccessible,
for a variety of psychodynamic and sociohistorical reasons, to what was
left of those systems of symbolic integration—Judaism and Christianity—that would otherwise have been available to him. Freud thereby
found himself in a position that was growing increasingly common in the
Western world. His commitment to the scientific community and its
materialistic ideal seemed to offer a compromise for awhile, but inevitably Freud's neurosis asserted itself—forcing him to become the first
analyst and the first analysand. Thus, as Freud suggested to Pfister, it is
no accident that psychoanalysis was discovered by a "*godless* Jew [my
italics]" (Meng and E. Freud, 1963, p. 63).

The developer of psychoanalysis, like Luther, sensed clearly in himself
the needs and tensions present but only dimly felt in others. He raised his
own patienthood to the level of the universal and, by curing himself,
cured many others as well (Erikson, 1958). But Freud cured himself not
merely by *analysis,* but by *commitment* as well—commitment to a new
way of looking at the world which would come to occupy the *center of
his life.* It was a system that would become more all embracing each year,
moving quickly from the counsulting room to culture and history at
large.

Although Freud derided the religious person's need for certainty and
applauded (see Jones, 1955, p. 419) the scientist's ability to live without
it, I believe he needed certainty as much as the religionist. He once told a
disciple that, in psychoanalysis "we possess the truth; I am as sure of it
as fifteen years ago" (Jones, 1955, p. 148) William James (1901, p. 47)
defined religion, very broadly, as a "solemn attitude toward whatever is
felt to be the primal truth." By this definition Freud's attitude toward his
creation was a religious one. It is in this light that we should recall Jung's
(1961, p. 150) insightful opinion that for Freud the theory of sexuality
was a sort of "numinosum." In some ways, Freud's last instinct theory,
like his preoccupation with the occult and telepathy, may also have functioned as a sort of surrogate religion; at times *Beyond the Pleasure Principle* reads like a religious or philosophical tract. Far from being merely
human instincts, Eros and Thanatos were conceptualized as global principles of organic functioning. Freud even used frankly religious terminology—the "Nirvana Principle"—to carry his speculations. I have
previously suggested that Freud's death instinct idea, although formulated before the diagnosis of his cancer, became a spiritual-emotional
support in his long battle with that disease (Wallace, 1976). "...It is

easier to submit to a remorseless law of nature, to the sublime Ananke . . . than to a chance which might perhaps have been escaped..." (Freud, 1920a, p. 45). This attitude of respectful submission toward what Freud variously termed "Ananke", "Fate", "Necessity", "Reality", the "death instinct" (god-terms all) is, contrary to Freud's (1927a, pp. 32-33) protestations, in many respects a religious attitude. It is likely that the "unconscious" itself functioned equivalently as another "god-term" for Freud. Never to be grasped directly and yet powerfully present in the psyche of each human being and "knowable", after a fashion, through it derivatives, Freud's "unconscious" bore certain resemblances to many mystics' conception of God. The "unconscious," with the overlapping concept of the "id," seemed to be assigned the same explanatory power in Freud's theory and therapy as God is in religion.

Thus far we have been discussing the therapeutic symbolism by means of which Freud, discovering that his neurosis was a universal affair, was reintegrated into mankind's symbolic community. But he was reintegrated with an *actual,* as well as an abstract, community—the Psychological Wednesday Evenings, from which grew the Vienna Psychoanalytic Society in 1908, and an international organization by 1910. I maintain that there is not a considerable difference between the organization Freud founded for himself and more traditional therapeutic communities. In gathering this group of mostly Jewish young men, in part Freud may have been providing himself with an ersatz for the Judaic community that was inaccessible to him, as well as living out his lifelong identification with Moses. Although he was concerned with the dissemination of his doctrine, he was even more preoccupied with the degree of cohesion among, and depth of conviction in, his disciples. "As a rule," he (1932, p. 153) said, "psycho-analysis either possesses a doctor entirely or not at all."

My thesis is that *because psychoanalysis for Freud (largely unconsciously) partook of the character of a "positive community" with its own therapeutic and reintegrative symbolism, he had to oppose it to all the more traditional "positive communities" and commitment therapies—foremost among which was religion.*[9]

Besides psychoanalysis, "science" and "reason" were what one might call "god-terms" for Freud. In *The Future of an Illusion,* Freud (1927a, p. 54) referred to "Our *god* [my italics] Logos" and in that work poetic paeans to science appear. In an 1899 letter to Fliess, Freud referred to the

---

9. It is these currents in Freud's attitude toward psychoanalysis that probably account, in part, for his (see Freud, 1930a, p. 74) fondness for that well known quote by Goethe: "He who possesses science and art also has religion; but he who possesses neither of those two, let him have religion!"

" 'religion of science' " which had replaced the " 'old religion' " (Bonaparte et al., 1954, p. 276). Zilboorg (1953, p. 107-109) sees inordinate faith in science and human reason, "scientism", as a function of human narcissism; Freud (1927a, pp. 52-53) himself was aware of the illusory aspects of such a stance. Even though he eventually went far beyond them, Freud always subscribed to the fundamental tenets of German materialistic science. "Analysts are at bottom incorrigible mechanists and materialists...," he wrote in 1921b (pp. 178-179). The "pious" oath of Brücke and DuBois-Reymond might have been his own (Jones, 1953, pp. 40-41):

> No other forces than the common physical-chemical ones are active within the organism. In those cases which cannot be explained by these forces one has either to find the specific way or form of their action by means of the physical-mathematical model or to assume new forces equal in dignity to the chemical-physical forces inherent in matter, reducible to the force of attraction and repulsion.

Another factor which, paradoxically (in light of the statements I have previously made about Freud's attitude toward Judaism), might have met Freud's needs for meaning and certainty in his own life was his virtually mystical reverence for his Jewish identity; he expressed this poetically on several occasions (1925a, p. 9; 1925c, p. 292; 1926, pp. 273-274). He was a member of B'nai B'rith, and most of his friends were Jewish. He boasted (1925b, p. 291) to the editor of the Jewish Press Center in Zurich that he had always retained his membership in the "Jewish denomination [*Judischen Konfession*]." He (Meng and E. Freud, 1963, p. 76) wrote to Pfister that of all the Christian saints he was especially attracted to Paul because of his "genuinely Jewish character."

On a different score, the questions and concerns about immortality that beset many men were partly alleviated in Freud by the secure knowledge that he had attained literary-scientific immortality and that his creation, psychoanalysis, would live on beyond him. Very possibly Freud's characterization of the unconscious as timeless and his phylogenetic theories also helped meet deep seated needs to believe in immortality. The idea that some of our complexes (e.g., the oedipal) and symbols are based on universal and perennially heritable memories amounts to smuggling psychic immortality into the psychoanalytic synthesis. I feel that we must consider the following words in this light (Freud, 1923b, p. 38): "Thus in the id, which is capable of being inherited, are harbored residues of the existences of countless egos; and, when the ego forms its super-ego out of the id, *it may perhaps only be reviving shapes of former egos and be bringing them to resurrection* [my italics]." In *Beyond the Pleasure Principle*, he speculated about cellular immortality. Furthermore, his preoccupation with death dates may, as Norman Atkins (personal communication) suggests, have given him a feeling of control over his mortality. Freud's interest in the occult and telepathy perhaps met needs (including those for immortality) which in others find fulfillment in the transcendental. In this context, recall Freud's response to Jones' accusation that one could as well believe in angels as in telepathy. It may be, as Suzanne Bernfeld (1951) suggests, that Freud's passion for archeology, which concerns itself with the dead and buried, was a reflection of his concerns with death. Surrounding himself by objects—many of them religious—resurrected from long dead civilizations may have given him a sense of immortality and of the numinosum. The Gradiva monograph (Freud, 1907b) and the short paper on Diana of the Ephesians (Freud, 1911c) both deal with the theme of death and resurrection.

Nevertheless, for all these devices and for all the equanimity with which Freud approached his final hour, I suspect that he never really came to terms with death. Certainly his lifelong preoccupation with death dates would lend some credence to this hypothesis. The aforementioned slip, in which Freud substituted "Nature" for "God" in a quotation from Shakespeare, occurred in a discussion about death. Freud would often take leave of friends with "Good-bye, you may never see me again" (in Jones, 1957, p. 279). Then it was his reaction to a death—of his father—that prompted his very self-analysis. On seeing a woman whom he mistook for a deceased patient the thought overtook him, "So after all it's true that the dead can come back to life" (Freud, 1907b, p. 7). On awakening from the syncopal episode in 1912, he uttered, "How sweet it must be to die." (Jones, 1953, p. 317). Freud once admitted that not a day passed without the thought of death (Jones, 1957, p. 279). Jones (ibid) says that Freud was "prepossessed by thoughts about death, more so than any other great man . . . except perhaps Sir Thomas Browne and Montaigne." Freud (1901, p. 260fn) attributed much of his own superstitious behavior to "suppressed ambition (*immortality*) [my italics]." Freud (1913, p. 87) quoted Schopenhauer approvingly that "the problem of death stands at the outset of every philosophy." I submit that his (1915, p. 289) notion that for the unconscious there is no concept of death and his (1923b, p. 58) reductionistic reconceptualization of death fears as castration anxiety in part also reflect these discomforts. If Freud indeed had a deepseated longing for a belief in the immortality of the soul, and at the same time a mechanistic world view that prevented him from indulging it, then there could have resulted a conflict of insuperable importance in his life. Being denied what he needed most—a belief in personal immortality—would have left him with a good deal of rage toward both the religionist who was secure in this belief and toward his own mechanistic science. By displacement, it may have been religion rather than science which bore the brunt of this hostility.

In sum then, rather than refusing to ask the "sick" questions about the meaning and purpose of existence, Freud's entire life was devoted to answering them. But this is hardly a criticism of him, for I feel that such questions spring not merely from ontogenetic and neurotic sources, but from an irreducible need in mankind—a need related to concern about mortality-immortality, but in some ways even overriding it.

Conclusion

In summary, nowhere else in his corpus does Freud lose his analytic neutrality as much as when he approaches religion. Although it would do an injustice to the complexity of Freud's affective and intellectual stance to ignore that he could, as we have seen, be positive on the subject at times, I feel that the predominant attitude in his work on religion is clearly negative. While his aim ostensibly was merely to show the light that could be cast on religion (like any other cultural institution) by psychoanalysis, *actually* he was using psychoanalysis with polemical intent—to *explain away* the phenomena under observation. Thus, it was not only that mechanisms such as projection, undoing, omnipotence of thought, and wishfulfillment contribute to our understanding of religion—and I feel that they do—but that they *are* the religious phenomena themselves. At one stroke this dismisses not only any question of the truth or value of religious experience, but the need to understand its history and it social-economic environment as well. In marked contrast was Freud's ability to speak of the ontogenetic factors (e.g., infantile scoptophilia, the desire to know where babies come from, etc.) in scientific enterprise without implying that they exhausted the explanations for science or in any way lessened its dignity.

But on the reverse side of this coin is a message for the theologian. Just as Freud's psychological explanations of religion do not necessarily negate the theological, so the theological explanations do not necessarily negate the psychological. If there be a transcendental reality, then man must respond to it with all the levels of his being—including the psychobiological. William W. Meissner, a psychoanalyst and a priest, was a discussant at a presentation of this paper. Meissner believes that if psychoanalysis tends to be too reductionistic in its approach to religion, theology tends to be too antireductionistic and jumps too quickly to the highest level of explanation. Theologians, he opines, fear too strongly that an explanation from "below" will destroy the "higher level" explanation. I would agree with Meissner that each level of explanation is not necessarily incompatible and recent approaches in psychoanalysis—ego and self psychology—have much more to offer the student of religion than the older, predominantly id, psychology of Freud's day. The theologian, just as the cultural scientist, must keep in mind the distinction between Freud's reductionistic, too simplistic application of psychoanalysis to culture and his attitude to religion on the other hand, and his more empirically based *psychology* on the other. He must not let the former disillusion him about the latter. Furthermore, to refute his less substantiated sociocultural work is *not* to disprove his theories of individual psychology. It is Freud's basic *psychology* and not his specific works on religion that have the most to offer the theologian and clergyman.

In my opinion there is much that psychoanalysis can contribute to the elucidation of religious phenomena. It can clarify the relationship between an individual's religious beliefs and the rest of his psychical economy—including the degree of intrapsychic rootedness of these convictions and the quality of their integration with the rest of his psychic apparatus. It can disclose conflicts for which religious convictions serve as the vehicle of expression or defense or in which these convictions contribute force to one side or the other. It can uncover the history of each individual's religious beliefs, the childhood object cathexes and identifications that are associated with and help determine the final form of these beliefs—i.e., the transferential aspects of one's attitude toward the object of his devotion. Finally, it can comment upon the role of one's religion in overall adaptation (or maladaptation) to the internal and external environments.

In fine, psychoanalysis is on most solid ground when it is investigating the *psychological* meaning of the religious beliefs of *any given practitioner*—i.e., the more or less idiosyncratic (because of childhood history and constitution) contribution of each religionist to what is otherwise a cultural affair. Only from the cumulative results of such laborious, *clinically based,* studies can dynamic psychiatry make meaningful statements about religion and religionists *in general.* What psychoanalysis can *never* do is comment upon whether, after all the psychodynamic factors are removed, there is an ultimate justification for religious faith.

If Freud wanted to damage the religious Weltanschauung—and there can be little doubt that he did—then it would have been sufficient for him to propound his ontogenetic theory of religion without psychopathologizing. By basing religion on man's dependency in childhood, Freud provided one more cogent secular explanation for the universality of religion—one more thesis that bypassed the need to postulate an irreducible "drive" to religion or a fundamental human awareness of a supernatural reality. Now, a theorem like Freud's, as I said a moment ago, does not "disprove" religious tenets but, like all the other secular explanations of human and nonhuman phenomena that had been previously explained by reference to the supernatural, the net effect is a further contribution to religion's loss of esteem.

In conclusion, although I know of no instance where Freud was disrespectful of the religious convictions of his patients, friends, or associates as individuals,[10] he never forgave *mankind* for exhibiting religious trends—in contrast, for example, to Jung, who said (1933, p. 122), "I do not, however, hold myself responsible for the fact that man has, everywhere and always, spontaneously developed religious forms of expression, and that the human psyche from time immemorial has been shot through with religious feelings and ideas." On the other hand, if Freud could have maintained throughout an attitude toward religion consistent with the following statement, then much that is problematic in his work in this area would not have appeared (Freud, 1925c, p. 218):

> The suggestion that art, religion, and social order originated in part in a contribution from the sexual instincts was represented by the opponents of analysis as a degradation of the highest cultural values...the fact is that the existence of these other [non-sexual] interests in men had never been disputed by me and that *nothing can be altered in the value of a cultural achievement by its being shown to have been derived from elementary animal instinctual sources* [my italics].

Nevertheless, for all the difficulties inherent in Freud's approach to religion, the fact remains that *any theologian who pretends to a semblance of honesty and intellectual integrity must come to terms with Freudian psychology.* I believe this is the case quite apart from whether it has any potential usefulness to him. No religion can ignore the psychology of its practitioners and, insofar as this is the state of affairs, then theologians must come to grips with psychoanalysis, the theory which bears the closest correspondence to that rich and many-faceted reality known as "mind." If Feuerbach was, to borrow Marx's words, the "fiery brook" through which the nineteenth century philosopher and

---

10. For just a few examples of his respectfulness to individual religionists I would refer the reader to Freud's correspondence with Pfister, the biography by Binswanger, and Freud's (1928b, p. 170) reply to an American physician who described his conversion experience.

theologian had to pass, then Freud is their "fiery brook" of the twentieth.

BIBLIOGRAPHY

ABRAHAM, H. & FREUD, E. (1965). *The Letters of Sigmund Freud and Karl Abraham (1907-1926).* Tr. B. Marsh, H. Abraham, New York: Basic Books.
ACKERKNECHT, E. (1943). The shaman and primitive psychopathology in general. In *Medicine and Ethnology: Selected Essays.* Baltimore: The Johns Hopkins University Press, 1971.
ACTON, H. (1955). *The Illusion of the Epoch.* Toronto: Burns and MacEachern.
ALEXANDER, F. & SELESNICK, S. C. (1966). *The History of Psychiatry.* New York: Mentor Books.
ARLOW, J. (1961). Ego psychology and the study of mythology. *Journal of the American Psychoanalytic Association,* 9:371-393.
ATKINSON, J. (1903). Primal law. Appendix to A. Lang's *Social Origins.* London: Longmans, Green.
BACHOFEN, J. (1861). *Das Mutterrecht.* Gesammelte Werke, Volume II. Basel: Benno Schwabe, 1948.
BAKAN, D. (1958). *Sigmund Freud and the Jewish Mystical Tradition.* Princeton, N.J.: Van Nostrand.
BALDWIN, M. (1895). *Mental Development.* New York: Macmillan.
BELO, J. (1960). *Trance in Bali.* New York: Columbia University Press.
BERNFELD, SIEGFRIED (1951). Sigmund Freud, M.D. *International Journal of Psycho-Analysis,* 32:204-217.
BERNFELD, SUZANNE (1951). Freud and archaeology. *American Imago,* 8:107-128.
BINSWANGER, L. (1955). *Sigmund Freud: Reminiscences of a Friendship.* Tr. N. Guterman, New York: Grune and Stratton, 1957.
BOISEN, A. C. (1936). *The Exploration of the Inner World.* New York: Harper.
BONAPARTE, M., FREUD, A., & KRIS, E. (1954). *The Origins of Psycho-Analysis: Letters to Wilhelm Fliess, Drafts and Notes: 1887-1902.* New York: Basic Books, 1977.
BOYER, L. B. (1962). Remarks on the personality of shamans: With special reference to the Apache of the Mescalero Indian Reservation. In *The Psychoanalytic Study of Society,* 2:233-254.
————— (1978). On aspects of the mutual influences of anthropology and psychoanalysis. *Journal of Psychological Anthropology,* 1:265-296.
————— (1979). *Childhood and Folklore. A Psychoanalytic Study of Apache Personality.* New York: Library of Psychological Anthropology.
—————, BOYER, R. M., & DE VOS, G. A. (1982). An Apache woman's account of her recent acquisition of the shamanistic status. *Journal of Psychoanalytic Anthropology,* 5:299-331.
—————, KLOPFER, B., BRAWER, F. B., & KAWAI, H. (1964). Comparisons of the shamans and pseudoshamans of the Apaches of the Mescalero Indian Reservation. *Journal of Projective Techniques and Personality Assessment,* 28:173-180.
BRENNER, C. (1976). *Psychoanalytic Technique and Psychic Conflict.* New York: International Universities Press.
BUBER, M. (1965). *The Knowledge of Man,* M. Friedman (ed.), tr. by M. Friedman & R. Smith, New York: Harper and Row.
CARUS, C. (1853). *Symbolik der Menschlichen Gestalt, ein Handbuch zur Menschenkenntnis.* Leipzig: F. A. Brockhaus.

CARUS, C. (1856). *Organon der Erkenntniss der Natur und des Geistes.* Leipzig: F. A. Brockhaus.

DARWIN, C. (1868). *The Variation of Plants and Animals Under Domestication,* Vol. 1. New York: D. Appleton, 1883.

──────── (1871). *The Descent of Man,* Vol. 1. New York: American Home, 1902.

DEMPSEY, P. C. (1956). *Freud, Psychoanalysis, Catholicism.* Cork, Ireland: Mercier Press.

DEVEREUX, G. (1956). Normal and Abnormal: the key problem of psychiatric anthropology. In *Some Uses of Anthropology: Theoretical and Applied.* Washington: Anthropolitical Society of Washington, pp. 23–48.

DODDS, E. R. (1951). *The Greeks and the Irrational.* Berkeley: University of California Press, 1973.

DuBOIS, C. C. (1937). Some anthropological perspectives on psychoanalysis. *Psychoanalytic Review,* 24:246–263.

ERIKSON, E. (1958). *Young Man Luther.* New York: Norton.

FALK, A. (1977). Freud and Herzl. *Midstream,* (1977 volume): 3–24.

FANCHER, R. (1977). Brentano's *Psychology From an Empirical Standpoint* and Freud's early metapsychology. *Journal of the History of the Behavioral Sciences,* 13:207–227.

FERENCZI, S. C. (1913). A Little Chanticleer. In Ferenczi's *Sex in Psychoanalysis.* New York: Basic Books, 1950.

FEUERBACH, L. (1841). *The Essence of Christianity.* London: John Chapman, 1854.

──────── (1838). *Pierre Bayle: Ein Beitrag zur Geschichte der Philosophie der Menschheit,* Vol. 4. Gesammelte Werke. Berlin: Akademie-Verlag, 1967.

FODOR, N. (1971). *Freud, Jung, and Occultism.* New Hyde Park, New York: University Books.

FRAZER, J. (1911). *The Magic Art,* Vol. I. New York: Macmillan, 1935.

FREUD, E., ed. (1960). *The Letters of Sigmund Freud.* New York: Basic Books, 1975.

FREUD, S. (1900). The interpretation of dreams. *S.E.,* Vols. 4 and 5. London: Hogarth Press.

──────── (1901). The psychopathology of everyday life. *S.E.,* Vol. 6. London: Hogarth Press.

──────── (1905). Fragment of an analysis of a case of hysteria. *S.E.,* 7:15–122. London: Hogarth Press.

──────── (1907a). Obsessive actions and religious practices. *S.E.,* 9:117–127. London: Hogarth Press.

──────── (1907b). Delusions and dreams in Jensen's "Gradiva." *S.E.,* 9:7–93. London: Hogarth Press.

──────── (1908). "Civilized" sexual morality and modern nervousness. *S.E.,* 9:181–204. London: Hogarth Press.

──────── (1909a). Notes upon a case of obsessional neurosis. *S.E.,* 10:155–249. London: Hogarth Press.

──────── (1909b). Analysis of a phobia in a five-year old boy. *S.E.,* 10:5–147. London: Hogarth Press.

──────── (1910a). Leonardo Da Vinci and a memory of his childhood. *S.E.,* 11:63–137. London: Hogarth Press.

──────── (1910b). The future prospects of psycho-analytic therapy. *S.E.,* 11:141–151. London: Hogarth Press.

──────── (1911a). The antithetical meaning of primal words. *S.E.,* 11:155–161. London: Hogarth Press.

———— (1911b). Formulations on two principles of mental functioning. *S.E.*, 1:218–226. London: Hogarth Press.

———— (1911c). Great is Diana of the Ephesians. *S.E.*, 12:342–344.

———— (1912). On the universal tendency to debasement in the sphere of love. *S.E.*, 11:179–190. London: Hogarth Press.

———— (1913). Totem and taboo. *S.E.*, 13:1–161. London: Hogarth Press.

———— (1914). On the history of the psycho-analytic movement. *S.E.*, 14:7–66. London: Hogarth Press.

———— (1915). Thoughts for the times on war and death. *S.E.*, 14:275–300. London: Hogarth Press.

———— (1918). From the history of an infantile neurosis. *S.E.*, 17:7–122. London: Hogarth Press.

———— (1919). Preface to Reik's *Ritual: Psycho-analytic studies. S. E.*, 17:259–263. London: Hogarth Press.

———— (1920a). Beyond the pleasure principle. *S.E.*, 18:7–64. London: Hogarth Press.

———— (1920b). The psychogenesis of a case of homosexuality in a woman. *S.E.*, 18:147–172. London: Hogarth Press.

———— (1921a). Group psychology and the analysis of the ego. *S.E.*, 18:69–143. London: Hogarth Press.

———— (1921b). Psycho-analysis and telepathy. *S.E.*, 18:177–193. London: Hogarth Press.

———— (1922). Dreams and telepathy. *S.E.*, 18:197–220. London: Hogarth Press.

———— (1923a). A seventeenth century demonological neurosis. *S.E.*, 19:72–105. London: Hogarth Press.

———— (1923b). The ego and the id. *S.E.*, 19:12–66. London: Hogarth Press.

———— (1925a). An autobiographical study. *S.E.*, 20:7–70. London: Hogarth Press.

———— (1925b). Letter to the editor of the Jewish Press Centre in Zürich. *S.E.*, 19:291. London: Hogarth Press.

———— (1925c). On the occasion of the opening of the Hebrew University. *S.E.*, 19:292. London: Hogarth Press.

———— (1925d). The resistances to psycho-analysis. *S.E.*, 19:213–222. London: Hogarth Press.

———— (1926a). Address to the society of B'nai B'rith. *S.E.*, 20:273–274. London: Hogarth Press.

———— (1926b). The question of lay analysis. *S.E.*, 20:183–258. London: Hogarth Press.

———— (1927a). The future of an illusion. *S.E.*, 21:5–56. London: Hogarth Press.

———— (1927b). Postscript to the question of lay analysis. *S.E.*, 20:251–257. London: Hogarth Press.

———— (1928a). Dostoevsky and parricide. *S.E.*, 21:177–194. London: Hogarth Press.

———— (1928b). A religious experience. *S.E.*, 21:169–172. London: Hogarth Press.

———— (1930a). Civilization and its discontents. *S.E.*, 21:64–145. London: Hogarth Press.

———— (1930b). Preface to the Hebrew Translation of *Totem and taboo. S.E.*, 13:XV. London: Hogarth Press.

———— (1932). New introductory lectures on psycho-analysis. *S.E.*, 22:7–182. London: Hogarth Press.

———— (1935). Postscript to an autobiographical study. *S.E.*, 20:71–74. London: Hogarth Press.

———— (1938). Findings, ideas, problems. *S.E.*, 23:299–300. London: Hogarth Press.

———— (1939). Moses and monotheism. *S.E.*, 23:60–137. London: Hogarth Press.

FROMM, E. (1930). *The Dogma of Christ and Other Essays on Religion, Psychology, and Culture.* New York: Holt, Rinehart, and Winston, 1963.

_____ (1972). *Sigmund Freud's Mission.* New York: Harper Colophon Books.

GAY, V. P. (1975). Psychopathology and ritual: Freud's essay on Obsessive actions and religious practice. *Psychoanalytic Review,* 62:493–507.

GEDO, J. & WOLF, E. (1976). From the history of introspective psychology: The humanist strain. In *Freud: The Fusion of Science and Humanism.* Psychological Issues Monograph 34/35. J. Gedo & G. Pollock (eds.). New York: International Universities Press.

GOLDENWEISER, A. (1910). Totemism, an analytical study. *Journal of American Folk-Lore,* 23:179–293.

GRINSTEIN, A. C. (1968). *On Sigmund Freud's Dreams.* Detroit: Wayne State University Press.

GROLLMAN, E. (1965). *Judaism in Sigmund Freud's World.* New York: Appleton-Century.

GUIRDHAM, A. (1959). *Christ and Freud.* London: Allen and Unwin.

HIPPLER, A. E. (1976). Shamans, curers, and personality: Suggestions toward a theoretical model. In *Culture-Bound Syndromes, Ethnopsychiatry, and Alternate Therapies,* W. Lebra (ed.). Honolulu: Univ. of Hawaii Press, pp. 103–114.

HOCH, E. (1974). Pir, faqir, and the psychotherapist. *The Human Context,* 6:668–677.

HUME, D. (1757). The natural history of religion. In Hume's *Essays Literary, Moral, and Political.* London: Longmans, Green, 1875.

JACKSON, S. & JACKSON, J. (1970). Primitive medicine and the historiography of psychiatry. In *Psychiatry and Its History: Methodological Problems in Research,* G. Mora & J. Brand (eds.). Springfield, Ill.: Charles C. Thomas, 1970, pp. 195–222.

JAMES, W. (1901). *The Varieties of Religious Experience.* New York: The New American Library, 1958.

JEVONS, F. (1896). *An Introduction to the History of Religion.* London: Methuen.

JONES, E. (1953). *The Life and Work of Sigmund Freud, Vol. I: The Formative Years and the Great Discoveries 1856–1900.* New York: Basic Books.

_____ (1955). *The Life and Work of Sigmund Freud, Vol. II: Years of Maturity 1901–1919.* New York: Basic Books.

_____ (1957). *The Life and Work of Sigmund Freud, Vol. III: The Last Phase 1919–1939.* New York: Basic Books.

JUNG, C. (1933). *Modern Man in Search of a Soul.* New York: Harcourt, Brace, and World.

_____ (1938). *Psychology and Religion.* New Haven: Yale University Press, 1976.

_____ (1961). *Memories, Dreams, Reflections.* New York: Vintage, 1965.

KARDINER, A. (1939). *The Individual and His Society.* New York: Columbia Univ. Press, 1961.

KNIGHT, R. (1786). *A Discourse on the Workshop of Priapus.* New York: The Julian Press, 1957.

KRACKE, W. (1979). Review of Róheim's *Children of the Desert. Journal of the Am. Psa. Assn.,* 27:223–231.

KÜNG, H. (1979). *Freud and the Problem of God.* New Haven: Yale University Press.

LeVINE, R. (1973). *Culture, Behavior, and Personality.* Chicago: Aldine.

MacFARLANE, A. (1970). *Witchcraft in Tudor and Stuart England: A Regional and Comparative Study.* New York: Harper and Row.

MARITAIN, J. (1957). Freudianism and psychoanalysis: A Thomist view. In *Freud and the Twentieth Century,* B. Nelson (ed.). New York: World Pub. Co.

MEISSNER, W. (1976). "The function of consensus", *Contemporary Psychoanalysis,* 12:81–87.

MENG, H. & FREUD, E., eds. (1963). *Psychoanalysis and Faith: The Letters of Sigmund Freud and Oskar Pfister.* New York: Basic Books.

McGUIRE, W., ed. (1974). *The Freud/Jung Letters: The Correspondence Between*

Sigmund Freud and C. G. Jung. (Bollingen Series XCIV). Trs. R. Manheim & R. Hull. Princeton, N.J.: Princeton University Press.

NIETZSCHE, F. (1878). Human, All-Too-Human, Part I, Vol. 6, (1880), Part II, Vol. 7, *The Complete Works of Friedrich Nietzsche,* O. Levy (ed.). Edinburgh and London: T. N. Fowles, 1910.

NUNBERG, H. & FEDERN, E., eds. (1967). *Minutes of the Vienna Psychoanalytic Society,* Vol. II. New York: International Universities Press.

OTTO, R. (1917). *The Idea of the Holy* Translated by J. Harvey. Oxford: Oxford University Press, 1978.

OSTOW, R. (1978). Autobiographical sources of Freud's social thought. *Psychiatric Journal of the University of Ottawa,* 2:169–180.

PFEIFFER, E., ed. (1972). *Sigmund Freud and Lou Andreas-Salome Letters.* New York: Harcourt, Brace, Jovanovich.

RICOEUR, P. (1970). *Freud and Philosophy.* New Haven: Yale University Press.

RIEFF, P. (1951). The meaning of history and religion in Freud's thought. In *Psychoanalysis and History,* B. Mazlish (ed.). New York: Grosset and Dunlap, 1971.

_____ (1953). History, psychoanalysis, and the social sciences. *Ethics* (1953): 107–120.

_____ (1959). *Freud: The Mind of the Moralist.* New York: Anchor Books, 1961.

_____ (1966). *The Triumph of the Therapeutic.* New York: Harper, 1968.

ROAZEN, P. (1971). *Freud and His Followers.* New York: New American Library, 1976.

ROBERT, M. (1976). *From Oedipus to Moses: Freud's Jewish Identity.* New York: Anchor Books.

ROSEN, G. (1968). *Madness in Society.* Chicago: Univ. of Chicago Press.

SAPIR, E. (1918). Review of H. A. Alexander's "The Mythology of All Races", Vol. XI: Latin American. In *Selected Writings of Edward Sapir,* D. Mandelbaum (ed.). Berkeley: Univ. of Cal. Press, 1973.

SCHMIDT, W. (1912-1955). *Der Ursprung der Gottsidee, eine Historisch-Kritische Positive Studie,* 12 volumes. Munster: Aschendorff.

SCHUR, M. (1972). *Freud: Living and Dying.* New York: International Universities Press.

SMITH, R. (1891). *Lectures on the Religion of the Semites,* 2nd Edition. New York: MacMillan, 1927.

SPECTOR, J. (1972). *The Aesthetics of Freud.* New York: McGraw-Hill.

SPENCER, H. (1898). *Principles of sociology,* 3 vols., Vols. I, II. New York: D. Appleton.

SPIRO, M. (1965). Religious systems as culturally constituted defense mechanisms. In *Context and Meaning in Cultural Anthropology,* M. Spiro (ed.). New York: Free Press.

TILLICH, P. (1957). *The Dynamics of Faith.* New York: Harper.

TURNER, V. (1967). *The Forest of Symbols: Aspects of Ndemba Ritual.* Ithaca: Cornell University Press.

TYLOR, E. (1871). *Primitive Culture,* Vol. I. New York: Henry Holt, 1874.

WALLACE, E. (1976). Thanatos—A reevaluation. *Psychiatry,* 39:386–393.

_____ (1977a). The development of Freud's ideas on social cohesion. *Psychiatry,* 40:232–241.

_____ (1977b). The psychodynamic determinants of *Moses and Monotheism. Psychiatry,* 40:79–87.

_____ (1978a). Freud's mysticism and its psychodynamic determinants. *Bulletin of the Menninger Clinic,* 42:203–222.

_____ (1978b). Freud's father conflict: The history of a dynamic. *Psychiatry,* 41:33–56.

_____ (1980a). The primal parricide. *Bulletin of the History of Medicine,* 54:153–165.

_____ (1980b). Freud and cultural evolutionism. In *Essays in the History of Psychiatry: A Tenth Anniversary Supplementary Volume to the "Psychiatric Forum",* E. Wallace & L. Pressley (eds.). Columbia, S.C.: S.C. Department of Mental Health, pp. 184–201.

_____ (1980c). A commentary on the Freud-Jung letters. *Psychoanalytic Review,* 67:111–138.

_____ (1983a). "Reflections on the Relationship Between Psychoanalysis and Christianity," *Pastoral Psychology,* Vol. 31, No. 3.

_____ (1983b). *Freud and Anthropology: A History and Reappraisal.* New York: Psychological Issues Monograph #55, International Universities Press.

WEINSTEIN, F. & PLATT, G. (1973). *Psychoanalytic Sociology.* Baltimore: Johns Hopkins University Press.

WEISMANN, A. (1892). *Das Keimplasm: eine Theorie der Vererbung.* Jena: G. Fischer.

WITTELS, F. (1931). *Freud and His Time.* New York: Liveright.

ZILBOORG, G. (1941). *A History of Medical Psychology.* New York: W. W. Norton.

_____ (1950). A psychiatric consideration of the ascetic ideal. *Psychoanalysis and Religion,* M. S. Zilboorg (ed.). New York: Farrar, Straus and Cudahy, 1962, pp. 63–79.

_____ (1953). Scientific psychopathology and religious issues. In *Psychoanalysis and Religion,* M. S. Zilboorg (ed.). New York: Farrar, Straus and Cudahy, 1962, pp. 104–116.

_____ (1955). Some denials and assertions of religious faith. In *Psychoanalysis and Religion.* M. S. Zilboorg (ed.). New York: Farrar, Straus and Cudahy, 1962, pp. 140–168.

_____ (1956). The sense of guilt. In *Psychoanalysis and Religion,* M. S. Zilboorg (ed.). New York: Farrar, Straus and Cudahy, 1962, pp. 169–188.

_____ (1958). *Freud and Religion. A Restatement of an Old Controversy.* Westminster, Md.: Newman Press; London: Geoffrey Chapman.

_____ (1959). Psychoanalysis and religion. *Pastoral Psychology,* 10(98):41–48.

5

An Outcome Study of Intensive Mindfulness Meditation

DANIEL P. BROWN[1] and JACK ENGLER[2]

DEFINING MEDITATION

The trend of current research is to define meditation primarily according to the model of stress reduction. Such a model is a likely consequence of psychophysiological investigations of meditation. Another trend is to define meditation according to models of psychotherapy (Goleman, 1976; Goleman and Schwartz, 1976). Such studies may offer us useful information about the applicability of meditation to Western-defined systems of mental health. However these studies do not tell us much about the essential phenomena of meditation as conceived in the East, nor about an Eastern understanding of meditation in mental health.

The assumptions underlying this study are very different in that cognitive and developmental theories have been used to understand the Eastern contemplative systems. All of the contemplative systems involve training of attention. Therefore, these traditional meditation systems may be interpreted accurately according to what Western psychologists have recently called cognitive skill training. Contemporary cognitive

1. Associate Director of Psychology, The Cambridge Hospital, Cambridge, MA, Instructor, Department of Psychiatry, Harvard Medical School; Adjunct Assistant Professor, Simmons College School of Social Work, Boston, MA.

Rorschach data on the American meditators was collected under a post-doctoral Training Grant in Social-Behavioral Sciences (NIMH–#T32MH14246–04) through Harvard Medical School under the supervision of Elliot Mishler, Ph.D. The author wishes to acknowledge the inspiration of Dr. Charles Ducey, Director of Psychological Services, The Cambridge Hospital, who supervised the data collection, as well as contributing greatly to an understanding of Rorschach scoring and interpretation. The author also wishes to thank the staff of the Insight Meditation Society, especially

Michael Grady and James Roy, for not only allowing this data to be collected but dedicating themselves to organizing and ensuring the data collection. The author would also like to thank all of the teachers at the Insight Meditation Society for their cooperation in this study, especially Dr. Jack Kornfield, whose training as both a meditation teacher and a psychologist allowed him to be a model for the integration of eastern and western psychologies, thereby making the project of collecting research data in a quasi-monastic setting credible to the meditation students. Thanks are also given to Joseph Goldstein, resident teacher at IMS, who was kind and patient enough to read a draft of this paper and offer corrections so that the final draft presented an understanding of Buddhist practice that was free of serious distortions and misunderstandings. Finally the author would like to thank the following people for their careful reading of the paper and their offering of helpful suggestions: Drs. Roger Walsh & Dean Shapiro, Charles Ducey, Ph.D., Bennett Simon, M.D., Gerald Epstein, M.D., Paul Fulton, M.A., Erika Fromm, Ph.D.

2.   Formerly, Board of Religious Studies, University of California, Santa Cruz; Fellow Division of Religion and Psychiatry, The Menninger Foundation, Topeka, Ks., currently, Psychology Fellow, McLean Hospital/Harvard Medical School, Belmont, MA. Fulbright Research Fellowship to India in 1976–77, through the University of Chicago. The author wishes to thank first of all Prof. Don Browning and Prof. Frank Reynolds of the Divinity School, The University of Chicago, who supervised the planning of this research and have kept faith through its many vicissitudes; also Ven. Dr. U Jagara Bhivamsa, Prof. of Pali at the Nalanda Pali Institute of Post-Graduate Buddhist Studies, Nalanda, who supervised the actual execution of the project in the field. The author would also like to acknowledge Ven. Nyanaponika Mahathera of Sri Lanka, who first introduced him to this tradition and suggested the site for research; and Dr. Jack Kornfield and Mr. Joseph Goldstein, resident teachers at the Insight Meditation Society who ensured that the proper foundation for the research was laid before leaving and who suggested the only approach by which the author was able to gain access to this group of subjects. The many friends and colleagues in Asia to whom the author is indebted are too numerous to mention. He would like to thank two in particular who contributed directly to the data collection as test consultants: Dr. Manas Raychaudhari, Prof. of Clinical Psychology at Rabindra Bharati University, Calcutta, for the Rorschach; and Dr. Uma Chowdury, Prof. of Clinical Psychology at the All-India Institute for Public Hygiene, Calcutta, for the Thematic Apperception Test. Dr. Chowdury is herself the author of Indian adaptation of the TAT used in this study. The author also wants to acknowledge the Ven. Mahasi Savadaw, the head of this teaching lineage, for his invitation to study at Thathana Veiktha and for his active support of this research. Most of all, the author wants to thank the subjects of this study who volunteered several months of their time during the hottest months of the hot season, under conditions which are difficult to imagine at this distance and under the press of family and professional lives, without complaint. Two especially deserve his thanks: the teacher; who represents the Masters Group in this paper, who made her home available for the bulk of the interviewing and testing; and her teacher, who was the author's own mentor and main "informant" throughout his stay in Asia, and who first identified the Ss for this study and then solicited their cooperation on the author's behalf. Lastly, he would like to acknowledge and thank Ms. Jellemieke Stauthamer of the Wright Institute in Berkeley, who collaborated in every phase of this study, especially the data collection. In the interviewing and testing, she opened the study in a unique way to the lives of women which are not shared with men, especially in Asia.

psychologists are just beginning to recognize the importance of such cognitive skill training as attention deployment (Neisser, 1975) and its implication for mental health and sense of well being (Csikszentmihalyi, 1980). Whereas cognitive psychologists are just beginning to research attention deployment in some depth, the long-term effects of intensive attention-training are as yet unexplored by experimental psychology. In contrast, for the most part Eastern contemplative systems are descriptions of the long-term effects of intensive attention-training. Such attention training may trigger an atypical developmental sequence complete with an invariant sequence of stages wherein each stage represents a distinct alteration in cognitive and perceptual structures, and each a distinct subjective experience.

Therefore, meditation may be conceived according to a stage model, much like stage models used in such developmental psychologies as Werner, Piaget, and Kohlberg. This is not to say that the path of meditation recapituates child development. It *is* to say that a stage model may be useful in understanding meditation as it has been for understanding child development.

The idea of a stage model came from a very detailed study of indigenous Buddhist meditation practitioners and the authoritative textual traditions in which their practices have been recorded.

The outstanding feature of meditation in most of these textual traditions is its conception in terms of a stage model. Each major tradition we have studied in their original languages presents an unfolding of meditation experience in terms of stages: for example, the *Mahamudra* in the Tibetan Mahayana Buddhist tradition (Brown, 1977); the *Visuddhimagga* in the Pali Theravanda Buddhist tradition (Nyanamoli, 1976); and the *Yoga Sutras* in the Sanskrit Hindu tradition (Mishra, 1963). One is struck by great similarities in these stage models. The models are sufficiently close to suggest an underlying common invariant sequence of stages, despite vast cultural and linguistic differences as well as different styles of practice (Brown, 1981). Although such convergence remains to be established on empirical grounds, the idea of conceiving meditation in terms of a stage model is intuitively appealing. The traditions themselves, like Theravada Buddhism, describe the practice in terms of the metaphors of "path" (magga) and "development" (bhāvanā).

The current study is about one such stage model, the Theravada Buddhist tradition. We have had the good fortune to be able to conduct extensive investigations on contemporary practitioners of this meditation. According to this tradition, there are three major divisions of the entire system of meditation: Preliminary Training, also referred to as Moral Training (sīla); the second is called Concentration Training (samādhi); and the third is termed Insight Training (paññā). The former is recommended for beginners; the latter two comprise meditation in its more restricted sense of formal sitting practice.

Each of these divisions or stages represents a different set of practices leading to a distinct goal. Each involves a very different kind of psychological transformation. The *Preliminary practices* include the study of the teachings, following of ethical percepts, and training in basic awareness of one's daily activities and the flow of one's internal experience. These preliminaries also include learning meditative postures, learning to sit quietly in order to observe and thereby calm one's thoughts, and learning to observe the flow of one's internal experience when free from distraction. *Concentration practice* is defined in terms of one-pointed attention, the ability to hold attention on an object steady without distraction. This is said to result in a relative reduction in thinking and higher perceptual processes. The fully concentrated meditator has learned to develop a deep concentrated state called *samādhi* in which awareness is held continuously and steadily upon very subtle activities of the mind, at a level simpler than that of thinking or perceptual pattern recognition. *Insight practice* is the most important. All earlier stages are preparations. The meditator has trained his awareness to observe the subtle workings of his mind and is now in a position to genuinely know how the mind works at its most refined levels. There are a number of individual stages of insight, all of which are quite technically defined. The yogi is said to learn fundamental truths regarding the operations of the mind. His awareness is said to become so refined that he begins to explore the interface of mind/universe and the universal laws governing the workings of both. He explores how events come into existence and how they pass away. In so doing, he learns that there is no real boundary between the mind-inside and the universe-outside.

Eventually, a fundamental non-dual awareness will intuitively and experientially understand the operations of the mind/universe. Insight training eventually leads to a radical transformation of experience, self-understanding, and psychological functioning called enlightenment. Moreover, there seems to be several such transformations, four stages of enlightenment in all. According to Buddhist psychology, specific *trait-changes* occur at each of the stages of enlightenment which lead to increasing psychological well-being. The change experienced at stages of practice prior to enlightenment are considered to be only *state-changes,* however important they may seem to be. The trait-changes resulting from enlightenment are said to be irreversible and are the real goals of the practice. The state-changes at earlier stages of meditation are reversible and may be lost when meditation is no longer practiced. Those readers who wish to study translations of the classical accounts of the stages of meditation in Theravda Buddhism are referred elsewhere (Nyanamoli, 1976; Mahasi Sayadaw, 1965; Mishra, 1963).

THE PROBLEM OF VALIDATION

The problem with the traditional Buddhist accounts of the stages of meditation is their status as subjective reports. These texts may contain archaic historical artifacts which have no validity in terms of describing the experience of contemporary meditators. Or, the texts may represent experiences very similar to those of present-day meditators, but the descriptions of experience may be the consequences of rigid belief systems, i.e., merely expectation effects. Then again, the texts may be descriptions of stages of meditation experience that have external validity. The task of our current research was to determine just what sort of validity these textual accounts have.

In order to approach the issue of validity, interviews were first conducted with contemporary indigenous practitioners to see if their experiences were consistent with those in the classical texts (Kornfield, 1976; Engler, 1983). Questionnaires were also designed to quantify these experiences (Brown, Twemlow, Engler, Maliszewski and Stauthamer, 1978). Secondly, an attempt was made to compare the textual accounts to constructs drawn from specific traditions of western psychology, particularly cognitive psychology. In a previous study (Brown, 1977), learning meditation was likened to the acquisition of cognitive skills, specifically, skill in attention deployment and awareness training. Those who persist in the attention and awareness training undergo a set of meditation experiences which unfold in a very discrete manner, perhaps in discernable stages. In that study the stages were viewed according to a deconstructivist cognitive/developmental stage model, i.e., one in which more complex thinking and perceptual processes are deconstructed during meditation so that more subtle levels of information-processing can be observed. Although the focus of that study was theoretical and not empirical, a case was made that the traditional textual accounts may depict a sequence of cognitive changes that could indeed have construct validity.

Such theoretical work is only a preliminary step toward validation. Does the yogi "really" alter his attitudes, behavior, and awareness during the preliminary stages of practice? Does he "really" reduce thinking and perceptual processes during concentration practice? Does he "really" become aware of the most subtle workings of his mind and the universe during insight practice? What "really" changes during and following enlightenment? The objective of a validation study is to establish independent empirical measures of the alleged cognitive changes described in the traditional texts and in the subjective reports and questionnaires of contemporary practitioners. The Rorschach may not seem to be a likely choice for such a validation study. In fact, the Rorschach was originally used as a personality measure. However, we began to notice that practitioners at different levels of the process gave records that appeared very distinct. In fact, the Rorschach records seemed to correlate with particular stages of meditation. Common features were more outstanding than individual differences at each level of practice. This unexpected observation raised the further question whether perhaps there were qualitative features (and quantitive variables) on the Rorschach that discriminated between the major divisions or stages of the practice. If so, this would be an initial step toward establishing the possible validity of the stage-model of meditation. In the current study, the Rorschach is used as a stage-sensitive instrument by administering it to criterion groups defined according to their level of practice. The main reason that the Rorschach was useful as a validating instrument was that we used it as a measure of cognitive and perceptual change, not as a personality measure, as it is so often used.

THE POPULATION OF MEDITATORS

Finding a proper instrument to test the validity of the textual accounts of the stages of meditation is insufficient unless the research is able to select a sample of meditators who indeed have experience comparable to those in the traditional texts. A fundamental problem with contemporary meditation research is the failure to use subjects who have acquired sufficient training in the cognitive skills specific to meditation. Most experiments use naive subjects, often college students, who are experienced meditators of a given discipline, e.g., Zen or Transcendental Meditation. But even these experienced meditators, by traditional criteria, are beginners. For example, Maupin (1965) conducted a Rorschach study of Zen meditators. He used naive college students who were given ten 45-minute sessions in breath concentration. It is very doubtful that these subjects perfected concentrative skills in ten sessions. Nevertheless, Maupin concluded that these subjects experienced an increase in primary process thinking along with a greater capacity to tolerate it. While this may indeed be an effect of meditation, it may very well be a beginner's effect. Inexperienced subjects manifest the general effects of a hypoaroused state of consciousness (Brown, 1977). Similar reports of increased primary process thinking have been reported for another hypoaroused state, hypnotic trance (Fromm, Oberlander and Grunewald, 1970). Effects such as increased primary process may have little to do with effects of meditation in what the tradition would define as more experienced subjects.

In one cross-sectional study which attempted to control for *level of experience,* Davidson, Goleman and Schwartz (1976) segregated their subjects into beginning, short-term, and long-term meditation groups. The criterion for the long-term group was 2 or more years of regular practice in either transcendental meditation or Buddist breath concentration. Such cross-sectional studies attempted across criterion groups typically employ a purely temporal factor—length of time meditating—as a means to discriminate beginning, intermediate, and advanced subjects. As all teachers of meditation and most students are painfully aware, however, length of time one has practiced is no index to depth of practice or acquisition of skill. This relationship is highly variable and indeterminate. This kind of global and rather artifical tripartite grouping on the basis of time has been resorted to in the absence of more appropriate criterion measures derived from the practice itself.

The current study does not rely on length of practice as the sole criterion of selection, although it does not abandon this. Initially, subjects were selected who had sufficient experience in intensive meditation in a well defined tradition. Intensive practice served as the initial criterion. Moreover, teacher ratings and self-reports on questionnaires were used as primary criteria to further delineate the level of experience of subjects from among this group of intensive meditators according to the textual model of stages of meditation. Goleman (1971) already pointed to the need for a cartography of meditation a decade ago. Without it, he notes, the researcher cannot know what he is comparing to what: what variables he is actually measuring, whether they are relevant, and what their interrelationship is. By cartography, however, Goleman largely meant a typology of techniques (Goleman, 1977). What we mean by cartography is the textual model of the *stages* of meditation. Presumably, the teachers are cognizant of the traditional accounts of the stages of meditation, and are alleged to be capable of discerning through interview the type of experiences and level of skill a given subject has achieved. Certain responses to questionnaire items also disclose the level of skill.

The present study in both its Asian and American components draws upon meditators in the context of a well-defined tradition, not a college population. It utilizes meditators who attend intensive retreats of several weeks or months duration. The daily routine involves a continuous alternation between periods of sitting and periods of walking meditation, usually 1 hour in length to start, over a span of 18 hours. There are two meals before noon and a 1 hour discourse in the evening. Subjects practice from 14–16 hours a day continuously for the length of the retreat. They adopt traditional Buddhist precepts such as silence and abstinence from sex or substance use. They do not interact with other meditators. There is no eye contact. They do not write or talk except for a 15-minute interview with the one of the teachers on alternative days. This routine is defined as *intensive meditation* and is the basic structure for both short-term and long-term retreats. During this time practitioners have the opportunity to work uninterruptedly toward the acquisition of meditative skills and to cultivate the kind of stage-specific training and mental development (*bhāvanā*) which this tradition of meditation aims at.

The instructions for formal periods of sitting and walking meditation follow the traditional mindfulness instructions of one of the major Burmese teaching lineages, that of the Venerable Mahasi Sayadaw (Mahasi Sayadaw, 1972; Goldstein, 1976). The practice begins in this tradition with an initial concentration exercise. Attention is focused on the in/out movement of the breath at the tip of the nostrils or the rise and fall of the abdomen. After an initial period when some degree of concentration is developed, new classes of objects are then added in a series: bodily sensations, emotions, thoughts, images, memories, perceptions and the hedonic tone of the pleasant, unpleasant, or neutral quality of each moment of experience. The meditator is instructed to become aware of the exact moment any of these objects occur as long as it occurs in his stream of consciousness. When no other object presents itself to awareness, attention is returned to the basic meditation object, the breath. It is mainly this process—the extension of the range of attention to a variety of objects in their momentary arising and passing away—that now converts this exercise from a concentrative to a mindfulness technique.

The second instruction in this tradition of practice is that attention should be "bare." Objects are to be attended to without reaction: without evaluation, judgment, selection, comment, or any kind of cognitive or emotional elaboration. If any of these types of mental reaction occur over and above mere perception of the object, the student is instructed to make them, in turn, the object of "bare attention" or "choiceless awareness." The specific object chosen is not nearly as important as this quality of detached, non-reactive observation with which it is registered in awareness. *Bare attention,* then, denotes a noninterpretive, non-judgemental awareness of one's predominant experience, moment by moment. Emphasis is on the *process* by which a particular event occurs, *not* on the individual *content* itself. Walking meditation is done in the same way, with the movement of the feet taken as the basic meditation object with awareness expanded to include all other events which occur, as they occur, during the walking. Equally important, the student is instructed to remain mindful of each and every other activity he engages in throughout the day, as he does it. In effect then, meditation is continuous and is ideally carried on without a break from rising to sleeping. This continuity in practice is the single most important factor in developing and maintaining that high degree of concentration which facilitates the development of insight.

The present study combines data from three independent projects: a *Three Month Study* of intensive meditation; data collection on *Advanced Western Students;* and a *South Asian Study* of enlightened masters. Through combining the data, we hoped to have Rorschachs that represented all the major stages of practice, from beginners to enlightened masters. The first project used Western students. The research was conducted at the Insight Meditation Society center in Barre, Massachusetts. This center offers a series of 2-week courses throughout the year and a 3-month fall retreat annually. Data were collected at one of these 3-month retreats. The second project also took place at the same center. In addition to the 3-month meditators, data were collected from the staff and teachers of the retreat center and from advanced meditators who visited the center throughout the year. The third project took place in South Asia. The subjects of this independent study included a number of well-known meditation masters in the same teaching lineage. Thus, data are available from meditators at nearly all levels of practice, from beginners to enlightened masters. Primary emphasis is given here to the longitudinal data from the *Three Month Study* with some illustrations of very advanced practice drawn from the data of the *Advanced Western Students* from the Insight Meditation Society, and the *South Asian Study*. However, because data were combined from three independent projects some mention must be made of the different assumptions made, and designs used, in each of these projects as they affect the conclusions of this paper.

THE THREE MONTH STUDY

A total of 30 subjects on the same 3-month retreat from mid-September to mid-December, 1978, were used. Of the 30 tested, only one dropped out. Six had attended a previous 3-month retreat. For 24, it was their first intensive retreat of this length. The design was intended to distinguish between expectation effects and meditation effects. In an excellent study, Smith (1976) demonstrated that most of the enthusiastic claims about meditation outcomes were largely instances of *expectation of change* and not due to the specific meditation skills, e.g., concentration on a mantra. In order to distinguish between meditation and expectation effects, the staff of the Insight Meditation Society served as a control. The staff live in the same setting for the same length of time as the retreat meditators. They adopt the same belief system and attend each of the evening discourses. They expect the meditation to work and they devote a minimum of 2 hours a day to meditation along with the retreat meditators. The main difference between the staff and retreat meditators is the amount of daily practice (2 hrs. vs. 14–16 hrs.). Differences between the groups presumably are suggestive of the treatment effect (intensive meditation) and not simply of expectation when it is assumed that both groups expect that the meditation they are practicing will result in some positive change. The unusual Rorschach findings reported in this study were found only in the meditation group, not in the control group, thereby suggesting that the findings are not entirely attributable to expectation.

The instruments used in the study were primarily the Profile of Meditation Experience and the Rorschach. The Profile is a 600-item questionnaire designed to discriminate different types of meditation as well as different levels within the same type of meditation. It was administered together with a Social Desirability Scale (Crowne & Marlowe, 1960) and a demographic sheet. The Rorschach was administered individually in the traditional manner by a half-dozen Rorschach clinicians, only one of whom was familiar with the hypotheses of the experiment to minimize experimenter bias.

The original design of the experiment called for a comparison of type of individuals, as measured by factor analytic ratings of a personality rating scale for the Rorschach, with patterns of response on the Profile. The intention was to find out whether different types of individuals had different experiences with the same instructions through the course of the 3-month retreat. Originally, only a few post-Rorschachs were planned to see if any changes might occur. None were expected. Much to our surprise, these post-Rorschach measures looked so dramatically different that post-Rorschachs were collected from all subjects. Rorschachs were collected, then, from all subjects at the beginning and end of the 3-month retreat. Since the meditators had not talked for the entire period, the concluding phase of the retreat was a 5-day transition period in which they were allowed to talk and interact with other meditators and staff but were also expected to continue their meditation. The post-Rorschachs were collected between the first and second day of the transition period, i.e., after the retreatants became used to talking again, but before the state of consciousness accumulated from 3 months of continuous practice had been disrupted. Only the post-Rorschachs are reported for the current study.

THE ADVANCED WESTERN MEDITATORS

The teachers at the Insight Meditation Society nominated a small group of Western students whom they felt had a "deep" practice. Whenever these students visited the retreat center data were collected in the same manner as in the *Three Month Study*.

THE SOUTH ASIAN STUDY

No such longitudinal pre/post design was possible in the *South Asian Study,* nor was it possible to employ control groups. The study was conducted on the basis of two different assumptions from the *Three Month Study*. First, meditation research, including the *Three Month Study,* had not had access to the more advanced subjects as classically defined by the experience of enlightenment. Second, the experience of enlightenment was used as the sole criterion of selection, a criterion which superceded length of practice or even teacher ratings of practice as in the *Three Month Study*. An experience of enlightenment was based on consensual teacher nomination. According to the tradition of mindfulness meditation, enlightenment is said to result in permanent and irreversible changes in perception and experience. The tradition distinguishes between what in Western psychology might be called state and trait changes (Davidson, Goleman and Schwartz, 1976). In the tradition, trait effects are said to be the result *only* of enlightenment and not of prior stages of practice. Meditation can produce both state and trait changes but these are not to be confounded. The tradition itself makes this distinction and forcibly emphasizes it in warning of the dangers of self-delusion. The yogi may mistake state effects for trait effects and suffer subsequent disillusionment and discouragement to the detriment of his practice (*Yoga Sutras* IV.27; *Visuddhimagga,* IV, 86f. xxiii.2). Similarly, if the researcher accepts this assumption, then enlightenment must be used as a criterion independent of level of skill or stage of practice. The changes alleged to occur as a result of enlightenment must be studies in their own right.

In this Theravada Buddhist tradition there are four distinct stages of enlightenment. Since irreversible trait effects are said to occur at *each* of these four stages and only there, experience of one or more of the subsequent stages of enlightenment became a secondary criterion. As can be appreciated, this required a rather special group of subjects. At the time this study was conceived, such a group could only be found in Asia. Understandably these were individuals who had already completed a certain course of training. No pre-test measures were available for them, nor were they tested just after a period of intensive meditation as in the *Three Month Study*. In fact, this was the first time any such group of yogis had agreed to be subjects for research at all, in South Asia as well as in the West.

Because a longitudinal design was not possible under the circumstances, an individual case study approach was taken instead, based on precedents in ethnographic research using similar research instruments (Boyer et al., 1964a, b). By an "ideographic" case study method as it has been employed in studies of child development (Flavell, 1963, Mahler et al., 1975), it was hoped to discover nomothetic principles in the individual case examples. Eight subjects, including two teachers, were nominated by two masters. The masters themselves also agreed to participate in the study, making a total of n = 10: eight women, mostly mothers and housewives, and two men. All were middle-aged. All practiced the same type of Burmese Satipatthana-vipassana or mindfulness meditation in the lineage of the Ven. Mahasi Sayadaw of Rangoon (Kornfield, 1977) on which the subsequent 3-month study of western meditators at the Insight Meditation Society was also based. According to teacher-rating, five subects had attained first enlightenment, four had attained second, and one had attained third. In interesting contrast to the western group of meditators, most of these Asian yogis had a minimum of prior retreat experience; most of their practice was done at home in the context of daily family and vocational activities. In all but one case, the actual experience of enlightenment did occur during a retreat, but a retreat of short duration and often the only retreat the individual had attended. The length of time from first beginning practice to the experience of enlightenment ranged from 6 days to 3 years. This contrasts again with the relatively slow rate of progress experienced by most of the western meditators in our larger study.

The instruments used in the *South Asian Study* included the same instruments used in the study of American meditators at the Insight Meditation Society with some additions. First, a case history was obtained from each practitioner. Because married women in Asia will discuss certain subjects only with another married woman, to ensure completeness of data collection the case history interviews with the female subjects were conducted by Ms. Jellemieke Stauthamer, a clinical psychologist. For the same reason, a trilingual married woman, Mrs. Maitri Chatterjee, was chosen from the many interviewed to be an interpreter. Next, a series of semi-structured interviews were conducted on the meditative experience of each individual. An attempt was made to obtain separate protocols for the meditative process itself and for its experienced outcomes in the form of self-reports. The Rorschach was then administered by a colleague and Rorschach clinician from the host culture who was neither a Buddhist nor familiar with this system of meditation and its claims, nor known to the subjects. This was followed by administration of the Thematic Apperception Test (TAT) in its Indian form (Chowdury, 1960) in a separate session.[3] The interviewing and testing were carried out over a 4-month period either in the rooms of two of the teachers or in the hall adjoining the nearby Buddhist temple. All interviews and tests were tape-recorded and translations subsequently checked for accuracy by an independent interpreter. Finally, the Profile of Meditation Experience was translated into the language of the host culture, independently checked for accuracy, and administered.

THE CURRENT STUDY: CRITERION GROUPING

An attempt was made to establish clear criterion groups in order to see if the pattern of responses on the Rorschachs were different in each of the criterion groups. The five groups that were established followed the traditional divisions of the stages of practice: (1) beginners; (2) samadhi group; (3) insight group; (4) advanced insight group (attainment of at least first enlightenment); (5) masters (attainment of the higher stages of enlightenment as defined in Theravada Buddhism, e.g., Nyanamoli, 1975). The criterion groups were established by two independent modes of assessment: objective ratings by four teachers for the western group and by two masters for the Asian group; and patterns of response on the Profile of Meditation Experience. The four teachers rated each of the 30 western subjects on the 3-month retreat along three different scales:[4] a) use of the practice to work on emotional problems; b) depth of concentration (proficiency in samadhi); c) depth of insight. The scale end-points were 1 and 10. A rating of 1 meant "little" and 10 meant "great." Anchor points were given a specific meaning. For example, 1 meant very little concentration; very little insight; and very little evidence for working on emotional problems. A rating of 5 meant moderate concentration

---

3. The Indian version of the TAT was selected over the Murray set after considerable consultation with clinicians of the host country who had worked with both and after a small pilot study confirmed the appropriateness of the Indian version for this subject population.

4. The effective reliability for the rating by the four teachers was 0.98. This does not necessarily mean that the teachers are highly reliable, independent judges of the students' meditation progress. This high correlation may be an artifact of the fact that the four teachers probably talked among each other about each student's progress daily durng the 3 months of the retreat and probably had reached some informal consensus concerning their progress prior to the ratings.

(beginner's samadhi); moderate insight ("easy" insights such as perception of the constant change of mental events); and moderate evidence of working on emotional problems. A rating of 10 meant deep concentration (Access Samadhi); deep insight (realization of the stage of Arising and Passing Away, or the stage of Equanimity);[5] and considerable evidence of working on emotional problems. In addition, certain key questions on the Profile of Meditation Experience were used as an independent means to differentiate groups. The Profile contains certain questions regarding types of insight. Several of these latter questions are worded so they are only intelligible to those who have had the direct experience of the stage, such as the experience of the state called "Access" or the state called "Arising and Passing Away." Students who answered these questions as "sometimes, often, usually, or always" characteristic of their current practice (post-retreat) were sorted into groups. A given subject had to meet both teacher rating and questionnaire criteria in order to be placed within a given group.

The *beginners group* consisted of 15 subjects who received a mean rating of 6 or more by the teachers on the scale of Emotional Problems. The *samadhi group* consisted of 13 subjects who met the dual criteria of receiving a mean rating of 6 or more by the teachers and a minimum self-report of "sometimes" or more on the Profile questions concerning concentration and samadhi. These 13 subjects were defined as having accomplished some level of samadhi, from Beginner's samadhi to Access Samadhi, but no attempt was made to ascertain the exact level of samadhi. Similarly, the *insight group* consisted of three subjects who met the dual criteria of a mean rating of 6 or more by the teachers and a minimum self-report of "sometimes" or more on the Profile questions regarding levels of insight. There were some differences between the teacher and self-ratings of insight. The teachers were more liberal in their ratings. They included relatively "easy" insights, such as perception of the constant change of events, in their high ratings. A total of 11 subjects were given a mean rating of 6 or more by the teachers. However, according to the Profile, eight of these subjects had only the "easier" insights. Only three had actually progressed to the more advanced Insight stages as classically defined.

Thus, in the *Three Month Study,* using the very same instructions, subjects varied markedly at the end of their 3 practice months. The great majority were still working through the problems of the beginning stage. About half had progressed to the next major stage of practice, the

---

5. Technical terms like "Access Samadhi," Arising and Passing Away" and "Equanimity" refer to stages recognized by tradition (Nyanamoli, 1976) and adopted by the teachers (Mahasi Sayadaw, 1965) in their assessment of the student's progress. They will be discussed in some detail later in the text.

samadhi stage. These subjects had become genuine meditators by traditional standards. Some of these same subjects also began to experience pre-access levels of insight. Others, though relatively weak in their concentration, developed stronger mindfulness and insight. The reason for this variation is due at least in part to the dual set of instructions used: concentration on the breath and mindfulness of any or all categories of objects. It may also be partly due to the fact that a given meditation object like the breath can be used to develop either concentration or insight. Subjects differed in their use of these instructions during 3 months. Those who felt scattered tended to practice more concentration. Those who desired insight practiced more mindfulness. The reason why so many meditators achieved samadhi is explained by tradition: both concentrative skills and mindfulness skills can lead to the attainment of at least beginner's samadhi, although concentrative skills are necessary to deepen the samadhi state. The reason why so few reached the Insight Series of meditations is also explained. These require considerable time to master. In addition, they follow after attainment of access-samadhi. This is supported by the strong positive correlations between concentration and insight on the Profile. All three subjects in the Insight Group had at least 5 years of previous experience with the same instructions. All three had also received very high ratings on concentration by the teachers. Thus, it seems that those who practice mindfulness without achieving optimal concentration reach a plateau at the pre-access levels of insight, while those who practice concentration without sufficient mindfulness tend to lose their "state effects" after the retreat ends. It is difficult for each student to find the optimal balance, so the variation after 3 months is great.

Nevertheless, it was possible to establish strict criterion groups for the traditionally defined levels of samadhi and insight. Because of the small number of subjects in the insight group, these data were pooled with data from advanced subjects collected outside the retreat, yet meeting the same strict criteria. This still only brought the total n to 7, which suggests the difficulty of attaining the classical or post-access stages where the fundamental insights into the very workings of the mind are perceived during meditation in the Theravada tradition.

A fourth group was designated the *advanced insight group.* It consists of advanced western meditators who have reached at least the first of the four stages of enlightenment as recognized by their Asian teachers. A fifth group was designated the *master's group.* The tradition recognizes a fundamental difference between the first two and the last two "Paths" or stages of enlightenment. This is based on qualitative differences in degree of difficulty in attainment, extent of trait change, expressed in terms of the "fetters" or "defilements" (kilesa) permanently eliminated from the personality, all of which are claimed to radically differentiate the second from the third Path. In accordance with this principle, the master's group is defined in this study as those who have attained either the third or fourth Path, either the penultimate or ultimate stage of enlightenment, a group defined by a single individual. Contemporary Theravada Buddhists recognize a number of such *ariyas* or "ones worthy of praise" but data are available for only one, an individual residing in South Asia and a subject in the South Asian Study. The following table summarizes the data:

CRITERION GROUP

	Beginner's Group Group	Samadhi Group	Insight Group	Advanced Insight Group	Master's Group
Three Month Study	15*	13	3**	—	—
Advanced Student's Study	—	—	4	4	—
South Asian Study	—	—	—	(9)***	1

*There is some overlap between the Beginner's and Samadhi Groups (five subjects).

**There is some overlap between the Samadhi and Insight Groups (three subjects). All three subjects in the Insight Group also met the criteria for the Samadhi Group, but are included only in the latter. This means that a total of seven subjects did not meet the dual criteria for *any* group and are not included in this study.

***The enlightened subjects in the Advanced Insight Group are derived from a pool of the Advanced Insight Meditation Society and South Asian groups. A total of nine more Rorschachs have been collected. These have not been included however. Only Rorschachs from Westerners are included in order to circumvent the difficulties of cross-cultural Rorschach interpretation.

DATA ANALYSIS

A number of traditional and non-traditional procedures were used for scoring the Rorschach. These included scoring of: *determinants* (a version of the Exner system (Exner, 1974), modified in that it uses the Mayman system (Mayman, 1970) for scoring form-level and the Binder system (Binder, 1932) for shading; *formal variables* (Holt and Havel, 1960; Watkins and Stauffacher, 1975); and the *fabulization scale* (Mayman, 1960). Because of the unusualness of the post-Rorschachs, a non-traditional scoring manual was developed by the senior author, the Manual of Feature-Dominated Responses (unpublished). The blind scoring and quantitative analysis of nearly 80 such Rorschachs according to all the stated scoring systems was time consuming and complicated. What follows is only a preliminary report on data representative of the outstanding features on the Rorschachs in the respective criterion groups. By outstanding features is meant those *qualitative features* of Rorschachs which are characteristic of a given criterion group and relatively uncharacteristic of the remaining pool of Rorschachs. Clear-cut qualitative features are readily apparent for each group so that in a pilot study clinicians and experimentalists were blindly able to sort these Rorschachs into the appropriate *a priori* groupings. What follows is a summary of these qualitative features.

The value of a purely qualitative analysis of these Rorschachs may be questioned. Quantitative analysis may indeed inspire more confidence in the determination of the question of validity. However, quantification alone will not facilitate interpretation of the unusual features of these Rorschachs. Therefore, the first approach to an analysis of the data is qualitative. Those who put confidence only in formal experimental designs and statistical methods to the neglect of qualitative evidence are reminded of the recent warnings against overconfidence in experimentation and statistics by Donald Campbell (1975). Campbell has reconsidered the value of qualitative evidence, such as case studies, especially when an investigator has a "superior acquaintance" with the context in which the data are collected. In fact, that is exactly the situation in the present case. The authors are familiar with the cultural context of the practice, know the languages, have read or translated the authoritative texts, and have engaged in actual practice. In addition, the senior author is also a practicing clinical psychologist with extensive experience using the Rorschach as both an experimental and clinical instrument. In addition to his academic position, the junior author is also a teacher in the Theravada Buddhist tradition on which this study is based, though he was not on the Insight Meditation Society staff during the period when data for this study were collected. This is exactly the kind of "acquaintance" with the phenomena that Campbell says may lead to more valid interpretation as long as the investigator remains critical of his own interpretive processes. At any rate, it is hoped that such an approach will help to understand this very unusual Rorschach data.

RESULTS

Beginners Group

The beginners Group consisted of 15 Rorschachs collected immediately after 3 months of intensive meditation. Basically, these Rorschachs were not different from the respective Rorschachs collected from the same subjects just prior to the meditation retreat. The only differences were a slight decrease in productivity across subjects and a noticeable increase in drive-dominated responses for some subjects (Holt & Havell, 1960).

Samadhi Group

The most outstanding characteristic of the samadhi Rorschach is its seeming *unproductivity* and *paucity of associative elaborations.* Recall that the test instructions require the subject to describe what the inkblot "looks like." Meditators in deep samadhi experience these instructions as being somewhat incongruous with the functioning of their altered state of consciousness. Many complained that it "took too much energy" to produce images and associations while perceiving the inkblot. One subject said:

> I just lack the kind of motivation or interest to look for stuff . . . I could force things, but that's about it . . . it [3 months of meditation] really wiped out my interest in trying to find things. If I decided to engage it more, it just sends off all these associations, but I'm just not interested in these . . . It's as if cognitive layering and motivation are connected somehow.[6] (I.W)

When asked if he could say what the inkblot "looked like" if he tried, he said that he could produce images; and indeed, he was able to produce a record virtually as productive as his pre-test Rorschach. He added, however, that to generate such images required "go [ing] into various levels of perceptual layering," that is, "break[ing] down [perception] into its [perceptual] patterns and concepts". As with this subject, all the subjects in the Samadhi Group showed a decrease in their overall productivity. Since the task demand presumably was contrary to the actual organization of their perceptual experience, their very accommodation to the instructions biased the results so that even this degree of productivity is probably inflated, comprising a response to task requirements rather than to perceptual functioning.

What does the subject experience? Subjects in the Samadhi Group distinguished between three levels of their perceptual processes: the *perceptual features* of the inkblot, *internal images* given in response to these features, i.e., the content applied to the inkblot, and *associative elaborations* of these images. During the samadhi state, the subject's

---

6. The notation following each student response indicates the card number and the specific location of the response on that card (following Exner, 1974).

focus of attention was primarily on the perceptual features of the ink-blot, and only secondarily on the images and associations that might follow from these. Each Rorschach in the Samadhi Group was characterized by a mixture of responses in the three categories, though the overall tendency was to comment on the pure perceptual features of the inkblot. To them, the inkblot "looked like" an inkblot. The same subject says:

> . . . the meditation has wiped out all the interpretive stuff on top of the raw perception . . . like, there's this thing out here, but then [when asked to make it look like something] I go into it, into the various levels of perceptual layering. (I.W)

Those units of perception involving images and association were often given some qualification, the kind of qualification not usually found in normal and pathological Rorschachs. For example, subjects were careful to distinguish images and associations from the raw perceptual features. Some distinguished their memory from perception with comments such as, "I remember it from last time, but I don't *really* see it there." Some distinguished their associative processes from perception with comments like, "My association to it is a bat, that was my first thought, and then I elaborated it." Many adopted a critical attitude toward their own image. They felt the image was non-veridical. Percepts, even those of good form-level, were often qualified with statements such as, "It doesn't really look like that . . . I'm just projecting." At times, subjects were unable to find words to label or describe a particular unit of an inkblot's features, even when their attention was fixed on it. Comments in such cases were similar: "I know what it is, but I can't put a name on it"; "It's real interesting but it's nothing I've seen before."

Nevertheless, subjects were able to report specific images for most of the cards, though not for all. These images, however, were quite *fluidly perceived.* Subjects complained, for instance, that the images "kept changing." While describing a particular image, it was not unusual for it to change into something else; it sometimes changed so rapidly that it was difficult to specify a single image:

> It's becoming so many different things so quickly, they go before the words come out. (II.W)

Or subjects reported simultaneous images for the same areas of the blot:

> It's alot of things at once—could be a bat, a butterfly, a flying man. (I.W)

The focus of attention was less on the actual image and more on the *process* by which the image manifested itself in their stream of consciousness. For example, one subject said, "It's just beginning to become something . . . [pause] . . . a bat." (I.W)

The most unusual finding, yet characteristic of the entire Samadhi Group, is the high frequency of comments on the *pure perceptual features* of the inkblot. In traditional scoring language, these subjects used many pure determinants: form-domination, pure color (chromatic and achromatic), pure shading, and pure inanimate movement. Form-dominated responses were those in which the subject became fascinated with the various shapes and configurations of a given inkblot in their own right, without attempting to associate to them. They spent as much time commenting on the shapes, edges and outlines of the blot in the post-test as they did producing images in the pre-test. For example:

> One of the things I focus upon is the outline of the blot, the different variations, up and down, the little patterns, the little ridges of the blot...then, I see um...ah...a human pelvis. (I.D4)

Comments on chromatic colors as colors were equally common:

> It's as though more, more comes from the color...it's a remarkably stronger input, an incredible set of impressions (from each color on card IX).

And on achromatic color as well:

> Most about this one is the color, the shades, the heaviness of the dark with the contrast to the white, and the shades of grey. (IV.W)

Among the pure perceptual responses, the most unusual finding was the high incidence of pure shading responses and color-shading responses, often in combination with pure inanimate movement:

> So many quick changes . . . my focus was somewhere else [than the images] . . . it's easier to look at the movement . . . the vibration, the texture and the movement . . . occasionally more obvious forms come up, but what comes up is the ones I remember I saw [in the pre-test] . . . but within the ink itself, there's so much movement . . . like sometimes there were these faces and eyes. But they changed so quickly that when I tried to say something it was no longer there. (X.W; Dd33)

Another subject gives a similar report:

One of the things that's real striking about the picture is just the variations in shading. It just keeps sort of moving [laughs], with the grays . . . There's sort of these pink blotches [red in black area] like it's sort of full of motion, um, sort of like it makes my eyes move around so it's hard to focus . . . my attention keeps shifting to the different variations of the light gray, the dark gray . . . the outlines are really fascinating, especially in the center where there's a space. (II.W; DS5)

This subject actually became fascinated with the stipple effect which constitutes the printing of the card!

Each subject varied in the relative production of specific images, fluid patterns and pure perceptual features for all ten cards. Some subjects commented that some cards favored "obvious" images while other subjects did not. As an example of such variation, the entire passages—the actual test response and the inquiry—are given with cards VIII–IX for a single subject. This subject saw "two rats and a woman's dress" on card VIII and "two eyes and a rabbit" on card IX in the pre-test. Post-test responses—pure perceptual features—are not clearly related to pre-test responses, but rather are a function of samadhi effects:

VII 23" 52"   Well the color, all of it . . .
colors against the white color, they're striking . . .
[Form?] all the different forms of the color, each shading of color has a certain form to it. [What might it look like?] Nothing, nothing at all . . . last time I was struck very much with this one . . . I tried to find something, and turned it around and around . . . once somebody told me that you were real bright if you turned it around . . . I never forgot that, so I did. [This time?] This time the colors were enough . . . very plea-

sant, pretty, doesn't look like a thing to me . . . but there is part of it that takes on a very distinct form . . . (VIII.W)

2. rodents climbing

They look exactly like rodents. [How so?] The shape . . . the feeling I get of the way they're climbing, moving their feet, tail, faces . . . (VIII.D1)

IX. 8'' 50''
1. hazy color...movement

The shadings make it hazy . . . very, very light color here . . . and it gets more darker or clearer . . . there's [DS8] a movement to it . . . very fast movement [?] the lines . . . the shading gives the illusion of it moving very quickly. [Did it suggest anything to you?] No, not at all, other than a moving form. [Does it look like anything?] No. (IX.W)

This illustration is intended to reemphasize the main feature of this group of protocols: the unproductivity and relative paucity of the associative process which characterizes the samadhi state. The "animals" on card VIII are one of the easiest and most popular responses on the entire test because the features of the card closely resemble an animal form. Despite the strong stimulus-pull, the immediate impact of the card on this subject is *not* the obvious pattern, but rather the pure perceptual features of color and form.

The Insight Group

The Rorschachs of the Insight Group point in a direction nearly opposite to that of the Samadhi Group. They are primarily characterized by *increased productivity* and *richness of associative elaborations*. These meditators experience the test instructions as an opportunity to exercise the apparently increased availability of their associative and imaginal processes, while keeping these closely and realistically attuned to the perceptual features of the inkblot.

The average response/card was 10, but only because the cut-off point was also 10. Whereas repeated measures of normal and clinical Rorschachs evidence many of the same responses, the post-test responses in this group showed little overlap with pre-test responses. These meditators claimed that their productivity per card was unlimited, that their minds were constantly turning over. One said:

> When I can't see anything else I hang out with it for a while . . . allow space . . . I stay with my awareness of not seeing anything . . . then, more images come . . .

This openness to the flow of internal associations and images is characteristic of the Insight Group. The experiences may be likened to the extemporaneous music of a jazz musician.

Moreover, most of the associations are richly fabulized, with a great variability and intensity of affect. Color symbolism, or better, the metaphoric use of color, abounds. The content shows great cultural diversity. One of the more unusual features of these long, elaborate associations, in light of their richness, is the relative absence of looseness. Subjects employ one of the two styles of elaboration, the empathetic or the creative. In the *empathetic style,* the subject puts himself fully into his percept, especially the human movement percept. Note, for example, not only the attention to subtle perceptual detail but also the successful construction of a scene with its own affective quality:

Response:

I see . . . um the head of someone who's sitting at a piano . . . it's funny, I don't really see the piano. It's almost like the posture of the head reminds me of someone who's intently playing the piano . . . his shoulders and the arms feel like they're in the position of someone playing the piano . . . and I see some little tiny dots, shapes of ink above the head that remind me of musical notes . . . and it's like a visual image of the music that's being played . . . the person has kind of unkempt hair as musicians sometimes do . . . scraggly

Inquiry:

Actually on this side it's a bit more distant. Really couldn't see the piano [?] general physical shape . . . couple of things, one a certain postural attitude, that reminded me of somebody intensely playing the piano, postural attitude, the shoulders, mainly . . . kind of like the neck and head is what I saw and then the outline of the head suggesting hair that's kind of flying in a lot of different directions . . . like I tend to associate with musicians or players that really put a lot of energy into their music, and with a beard that hair . . . and a short beard . . . and I just get the sense of someone who's just playing ah . . . a real intense, basically fairly happy um . . . kind of music, probably jazz, or possibly classical. (I.D6 V)

kind of suggested the same thing . . . so these little dots up here . . . these spots kind of struck me as being musical notes, and then that became a visual image of what was happening . . .

This illustrates the slow unfolding of a single perception until the subject gets a certain "feel" for it.

In the *creative style,* the subject also slowly unfolds his elaboration of a single percept but changes his perspective on the same image one or more times during the response. Often, the subject ascribes several very different affective states to the same image:

Response:

First, I see a woman in the middle with her hands raised in supplication, a very aspiring movement. It's either in supplication or in praise, maybe both . . . it's not to God, it's not to anyone or anything out there, it's more a movement of the heart with the feeling of great joy, great tenderness, great longing . . . it started off as a very chaste image and it's becoming more sensual now, as I look at it, but it still has that, that quality and the person is still in that position I described . . . (I.D4)

Inquiry:

It's a combination of shape and shading . . . the transparency here [?] [D4], shape, her hips here, thighs and hips. I don't associate to this other gray area here, just the inner form [supplication?], the erect posture and the hands raised to the heavens. I don't mean heaven and earth in the traditional sense [becomes more central?]. I was more aware of the shape of the form, the hips, the breasts, the figure of the woman as a very ideal figure.

Note that in each case, the subject never departs from the original percept.

Note also that the original percept is a classic example of a qualitatively distinct mode of reality testing that Mayman (1970) has called the F + in which:

the subject maintains an objective, realistic, appropriately critical attitude toward a given response. He stays close to the determining influence of the blots and maximizes the fit between the associated idea and the blot outline. His associations, however rich, will form themselves around the outline he finds in the inkblots.

These protocols also contain a high incidence of original responses. Thus, the subjects are able to manifest a high degree of congruency between the flow of their internal world, moment-by-moment, and the changing demands of external reality. This *enhanced reality attunement* is clearly illustrated in the following response to the same area of the same card as the Samadhi Rorschach, where the subject saw only color and "rodents climbing." Note the contrast also in productivity and in the richness of elaboration:

> This is a wonderful one, too . . . sideways this is again, the red figure is a four-legged animal, like a mountain lion and now he's running, leaping over a real rocky and difficult terrain . . . there's a sense of great energy and power in him, but the most wonderful thing of all is how sure-footed he is . . . a great sense of flight . . . he always lands on just the right crop of rock . . . never misses . . . always instinctively sure of his footing so he'll be able to go on like that, wonderful mastery and wonderful fit between the animal and his world, kind of perfect harmony between them, even though it's very dynamic, leaping, he always does it . . . here, he's in flight . . . just landed with the front paw and the back paw is still in the air and he's feeling, not very reflective, just doing it spontaneously. He's feeling the great energy and lightness and challenge. He loves the challenge because he's equal to it, but it's always keeping him out there on his limit . . . With this is another wonderful thing. It has to do with the colors again, a progression in his progress from warm wonderful colors to colder, finally very cold colors. In other words, he started from a place of warmth and security and as he started from there, he can carry it out and conquer the cold, insecure place because he himself is in the pink, the color of the heat, light, energy, warmth . . . and so he can go out and master the cold of the world again... (VIII D1, with inquiry)

There are also some remarkably life-affirming insights contained within these fabulized human movement percepts:

> I see two, I see two heads. It's like a large being, a tall person and a shorter person . . . a tall rather massive person and a smaller . . . could be an adult and a child . . . a father and a son or . . . probably a father and a son . . . that's what it reminds me of . . . and they're just sitting quietly together looking off into the distance . . . very at ease with each other . . . and there's a lot of real warmth between them, just a real feeling of connectedness . . . the feeling of knowing the limitations of the communication that can come between them . . . accepting those limits, not finding them painful, and just being real happy with what is there . . . and the limits are really the

limits that are . . . not like generational, but the limits that are there between any two people whatever their relationship might be . . . the limits of two people trying to communicate to each other . . . there's a certain place where that breaks down and you just can't get any closer, where you can't bridge the gap anymore, and yet you can come to a real deep acceptance of that limitation. (IV D1, without inquiry)

Another example concerns the acceptance of both the limitations of and the potential freedom in the roles, status and particular circumstances of one's life:

[laughs, laughs again] this is nice, I turned it over and here I see a kind of ghoul . . . these are his eyes, his long sort of nose, beginning of a mouth, here, the wings are drooping over some kind of pole there, as though they are liquid . . . he's trying to look very ghoulish but in fact is nice and friendly, it's just a pretense he's putting up . . . he doesn't want to look so ghoulish . . . he has just managed to temporarily frighten these two little creatures on the side and they're trying to run away from him because they're a little scared, but that won't last . . . no, in fact they're emanations of his own substance, forms of himself that he sends out into the world to do his work . . . and to try to encompass all the other beings . . . but some . . . they will be able to do that too . . . and others, they won't be, and it all depends not on what *he* does, but on how we see him . . . if we see him as ghoulish and frightening them, then we are taken in and we become terrified and lost and if we see him as just another old creature whose game it is . . . who's role it is just to try to terrify people . . . that's who it is, that's what he does . . . then, we're not terrified. In fact, I feel very accepting of him and even very kindly disposed toward him and he knows that I know so he's having kind of a secret laugh with me, but he's still trying to scare me because that's what he has to do . . . (VIII, response #5 test response only, without inquiry, D2)

The reader may wish to compare the mountain lion and ghoul to the previous excerpt from the Samadhi Rorschach. Both of these responses are from Card VIII of the same subject (responses #5-6). The difference between these and the previous example of a samadhi response to the same card are obvious.

Nevertheless, these insight Rorschachs are not without conflicts, such as the fusion of sexual and aggressive impulses found in this response by the subject who provided the mountain lion and ghoul:

and this which I first saw as just the two trunks of the elephant, this I see as a circumcised penis; at first I saw it very solitary, just sort of proud of itself to be there, but now I'm beginning to see it in connection with the two red spaces above as though it's thrusting up through, between them, but they seem a little as though they could damage it, could hurt it, as though they were two twin creatures with little paws, little legs outstretched wanting to pounce on it, maybe claw it . . . the feeling it seems to have, flinches a little anticipating that, but it's going to keep on moving, thrusting, moving upward anyway and finally the two little creatures will withdraw their paws and snuggle against it because their shapes will fit right down in here—see the contours match here —and this will come up and it will fit snug and come together [fits red into white spaces] and it will be all right, it will be a very nice experience and a feeling of real union and sharing and closeness. (II D4 without inquiry)

ADVANCED INSIGHT GROUP

The Advanced Insight Group consisted of four Rorschachs collected from western-born students of mindfulness meditation. These advanced practitioners are alleged to have achieved at least the first stage of enlightenment as defined by the tradition. Unlike the previous groups, these Rorschachs were *not* collected after a period of intensive meditation. One might think that few valid statements could be made from only four such protocols. Nevertheless, three of the four[7] showed a remarkable consistency, enough consistency to warrant a preliminary statement about Rorschachs from enlightened practitioners.

These Rorschachs do not evidence the same outstanding qualitative features as found in the Samadhi and Insight Groups. At first glance they appear to be more like the Rorschachs of the Beginners Group. The range of content is quite varied. Responses are nearly always images with brief associative elaborations and are seldom dominated by the pure perceptual features of the inkblots, as was true for the Samadhi Group. Responses also lack the richness of associative elaboration so characteristic of the Insight Group.

---

7. The fourth Rorschach was very different. It contained over 100 responses. The responses were specific in their content with very little evidence of either feature-dominated responses (pure shapes, colors and shading) or rich associative elaboration, as was true for the samadhi and Insight Groups respectively. There were, however, an unusually high number of aggression-dominated responses.

Nevertheless, there do appear to be certain qualitative features that distinguish this group of protocols which we are calling "residual effects." We hypothesize them to be the consequences of having previously mastered both the samadhi and insight practices. Like the Rorschachs of the Samadhi Group, these Rorschachs contain occasional but less frequent references to the perceptual features of the inkblots, notably the shapes, symmetry, color, and variations in shading. Responsivity to achromatic color and shading variations is also quite high, as was true for the Samadhi Group. Such responses are, however, seldom pure shading responses. Instead, the shading is more likely to be interpreted as a certain *quality* or *state of mind* such as "pain . . . beauty," "dark and heavy," "unpleasantness," to draw examples from Rorschachs of the respective advanced practitioners. The use of inanimate movement responses, alone and in conjunction with color and shading, is also quite high, much higher in fact than in any other group. At least 10–20% of the total responses were inanimate movement responses for each of the four subjects. No subject's record contained less than a raw count of eight such responses. Compared to norms, this is extraordinarily high. Furthermore, these Rorschachs evidence residual effects akin to the effects in the Insight Group. Productivity was high for each of the subjects (total number of responses ranged from 55 to over 100). In contrast to those of the Insight Group, these responses showed less variation in subsequent testing.

If these Rorschachs are not strikingly different from those of the previous criterion groups, especially the Beginners Group, what then is distinctive about them? The most unusual feature, clearly present in a number of responses on three of the four Rorschachs, is the degree to which they perceive the inkblots as an *interaction of form and energy* or *form and space*. That is, in several responses *each* of the subjects perceived the inkblot primarily as *energy-in-motion* or as *empty space*. Such responses were, of course, distributed among the variety of specific images on all the cards. However, the subjects saw the specific images (content) and the energy-in-motion (process) as distinct but interrelated "levels" of perception.

A range of 5–20% of the content for each of the protocols referred specifically to various perceptions of energy. For example.

> movies that I saw in science class which were talked about . . . let's see . . . talked about organism . . . um . . . atoms and molecules, and kind of a changing energy, changing energy. (IX. shading in D1)

Most often, content was given in conjunction with inanimate movement or inanimate movement/shading responses. In this respect, the subject's sensitivity to inanimate movement and shading was somewhat different from comparable responses in the Samadhi Group. Whereas meditators during samadhi are likely to see the shapes themselves (or shading itself) moving on the card, these subjects seldom saw this. Instead, the movement and shading was usually "interpreted," i.e., it was given content, and usually the content referred to some manifestation of energy.

These energy responses might best be seen as representing *various "levels" of energy organization*. On the simplest level are responses referring to *pure space from which energy unfolded*. For example:

the space between each form serves a purpose, not too compressed, and yet gives enough space for each quality to be its own and yet have enough room to exchange its own individual energy. However, it's a natural source of energy, unfolding and extending to take certain forms, um . . . almost feels more explo . . . I don't know if explosive is the right word. Let's say, such a strong source that it could come from that center core, that central orange, and go up into the blue and just push off just a little so that it could have its definite, um, shape and function . . . (VIII.DdS28)

On the next level are responses depicting the activity of the *molecules* of the universe or the *primal elements* within the body:[8]

and the pink and the orange [D2] add to the beauty of the skeleton [DS3] and it amost indicates evolution, like the top, the blue, the gray, [D4] seem to indicate more of the beginning. Um, I just got the image of when there was fire, but not fire like bright red, but say, the *heat element* and more of the beginnings . . . prehuman . . . prehuman qualities, when the elements were just doing their dance . . . Fire wasn't quite the right word, but it was indicative of primary elements just forming . . . kind of like when, when all of the elements are in a huge interplay and then that linking between the orange of this division, at the very core say of this picture; and then also the orange kind of feeding into the blue color, right, the orange root into the blue, um, color. It feeds into the blue like evolution . . . it's becoming skeletal features, [DS3] then here, the bear . . . [D1] it's like the evolutionary force is feeding into them and their back foot is on the primary elements . . . just one foot as if having that as a link . . . it's like that primary element on either side is making a circle so that the elements feeding into the skeletal,

8. Extension, cohension, heat and motion, traditionally symbolized as earth, water, fire, and air in yogic physics (Narada, 1975).

feeding into the animal and with the animal's foot back into its primary source . . . (VIII)

At still another level are responses indicating the *types of energy organization within the human body,* as conceptualized by any one of traditional eastern systems of energy yoga (Dasgupta, 1946; Eliade, 1969; Varenne, 1976; Avalon, 1931). Such responses include diffuse body energies such as a "life-force" (X), as well as energies that have specific directions to the body (III). According to yogic physiology, the body is said to contain both diffuse and specific energy. The latter is said to flow through normally invisible but perceptible subtle channels. Note that the organization of energy into specific currents represents a more complex form of energy than that of the primal elements. Also, *all* of the subjects made references to the main "centers" of energy within the body. Again, according to yogic physiology, the body energies are said to be concentrated in specific centers called "chakras." Here we note a futher organization of energy, now into specific, quasi-stable locations:

I see the different colors . . . going up the different energy centers of the body, starting with the whole pelvic region [D2] . . . the abdomen, chest, [5] and head [D4] and each color representing the different energy in that part of the body. (VIII.W)

In addition to these more common references to internal "yogic" anatomy, two of the subjects also made reference to a type of energy more akin to western physiological processes, such as the energy of *cell division* or that of *chromosomes dividing:*

It looks like a chromosome splitting in half . . . creating itself. (VI.D1 with D12 as division]

Even more common were responses akin to what western psychology has called *drive energy*:

I see a vagina [D12] and ovaries or some kind of organs, [D11] internal organs . . . internal organs . . . I see [something] very phallic . . . [D2] a lot of thrusting energy I get from it . . . I see like an energy flow [shading of D12] between like, ah, the vagina and the penis . . . it's like one continuum, the flow of energy between them, sexual energy . . . (VI)

Such direct references to sexual energy were found on all four protocols. One also made comparable references to aggressive energy.

Finally, there were a number of responses depicting the type of *energy that is bound up within inanimate objects,* thereby causing them to move. Typical responses were spinning tops (II DS5) or airplanes (II DS5). Note however that these responses, in which form predominates over movement, are quite rare in each of the four protocols.

By way of summary, all of these energy responses can be represented along an energy/form continuum, with pure empty space at one end, form-dominated energy at the other, and the various intermediate levels of energy organization in between:

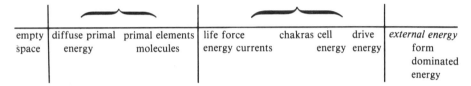

empty space	diffuse primal energy	primal elements molecules	life force energy currents	chakras cell energy	drive energy	*external energy* form dominated energy

What is implicit in such responses is an understanding of the *interrelationship of form and energy/space.* The most striking feature of *all* these subjects' Rorschachs is the extent to which they view their own internal imagery merely as manifestations or *emanations of energy/space.* Here is a typical but highly clear example:

> I feel the energy coming from that [Dd26], the whole energy of the picture . . . there's an intensity, a certain power of it, and everything else is just a dancing manifestation of that energy coming out. (VII.WV)

We here see that the advanced practitioners have a perspective that is quite unlike that of the previous group. They see all of their percepts merely as emanations of energy, as part of the "dance of the mind." In fact, the subjects sometimes reported that *such a transformation from energy/space into form actually took place before their eyes* during the test. Recall the responses about the evolutionary force. That subject saw the primal elements transform into skeletal forms, and into full animals (bears). Here is an example from another subject:

> Seems like there's a whole vortex of energy swirling around that central core, [Dd21] that's um, more stable, that's just spinning around it [motions] now it looks like some sort of beings sort of dancing around, um, this blob in the center [laughs, amused at response]. Um . . . something that is just pure energy, not a figure, the figures are sort of dancing around it . . . so somehow it feels more like the center, then becomes these dancing creatures, dancing around the center, and then when it gets to be just energy again, it's dizzy, spinning and um, very strong . . . (VIII.W)

Here the energy-in-motion becomes immediately organized into external appearances, in this case dancing creatures (lions). Another subject gave a very similar response to the same card, adding that the animals (bears in that case) on the side (D1) were not exactly "solid." This subject, along with another, also gave responses which illustrate an interesting variation of the same theme. For these subjects, the energy became organized into quasi-stable mind-states rather than external forms:

> I see a face now. [DS8] It's hard to describe . . . the eyes are very clear and exposed, the eyelids go vertical, not sideways . . . tongue, uvula, shoulders . . . [Dds22] it's like an X-ray scene. He's looking with X-ray vision . . . these are clouds happening in his head; [shading of Dd22] forces of the kinds of energies in his mind, some dark, some light, like a chakra is opening and a lot of energy is pouring in, a lot of light. He's talking, saying something important, but it's also already clear and doesn't need to be said . . . now he's laughing at himself. (IX)

Sometimes particular qualities of mind were specified. Here is an example from another:

> that um dark part, and the red at the top seem more painful, [D2] and the red at the bottom . . . an element of pain, but also an element of beauty [D3] [inquiry] it's more of the planetary sufferings and like ecology and the things man does to man [beauty?]. The red seemed to balance out and be a statement of beauty or truth. (II)

Although responses pertaining to mind-states are rare, it is important to point out that they hardly ever occur in the records of the Beginner's Samadhi or Insight Groups. They occur occasionally in the protocols of these advanced practitioners and will become even more important in records of the Master's Group.

While the subjects more often comment on the actual process by which forms and images come into existence, they also comment, though less often, on the *reverse process,* namely, *how forms and images dissolve into space.* For example, one subject saw a number of typical images on Card X, such as dancing insects. Then there followed a distinct shift in perception. The subject began to see the card as mere color and form and noticed that the colors and forms seemed to move inward, concentrating themselves at the center blue region of the card. The subject explained that all the forms and colors were connected by a "unifying force" by which the seemingly separate images on the card tended to "flow" back into the center region of "localized energy." (D3) Upon their return, the subject noted another perceptual shift, namely, a figure-around reversal. She ended up seeing only the white (former background) of the card, as if all the colors and forms had become absorbed into it. Such *figure-ground reversals* and *movement toward the central unifying point* were other distinctive features of these Rorschachs.

In sum, the most distinctive feature of these subjects' Rorschachs is their unique perspective in which they *actually witness energy/space in the moment-by-moment process of arising and organizing into forms and images; and conversely, witness the forms and images becoming absorbed back into energy/space.* Here is one response which stands out as a particularly clear example of an advanced practitioners' perception of the momentary arising and passing of phenomena:

> sort of like just energy forces and um like molecules . . . something like the energy of molecules . . . very much like a microscopic view . . . in some way there are more patterns of energy . . . there are different energies in the different, the different colors . . . it looks like it's a view into the body where there's energy, there's movement, but it's steady because it's guided by a life-force . . . there is arising and passing away of these different elements. [Inquiry] the colors seemed very alive and suggested life and they seemed very basic or elemental—both the shapes and size. They don't have heavy substance, you know; they each, um, are relatively fragile [different colors suggested different elements?] yeah . . . and then it started to seem just like a vibration, really not a swelling movement but a pulsation, just a coming and going of um kind of elemental bits [laughs because of word choice] of life [laughs] [arising and passing away of elements?] It was very far out when it happened . . . I can't um . . . some of that was because of the suggestion of the spinal column (previous response) [D14] . . . um it reminded me somewhat of those electron microscope pictures of the body and I just had this sense of movement of it all. (X.W)

One might expect certain consequences from seeing form as a manifestation of energy, from seeing the world as not particularly solid and durable. Some evidence for this may be found in the form-level scores on these Rorschachs. Using the Mayman criteria for scoring form-level (Mayman, 1970), the Rorschachs of the advanced practitioners evidence a high percent of vaguely and amorphously perceived forms; while the number of weak, spoiled or poor forms is quite low (from 20–25% vague, amorphous responses on each of the four records). The reason, of course, is due to the high number of energy responses and qualities of mind, all of which get a vague or amorphous form-level score. According to Mayman, vaguely and amorphously perceived responses are interpreted as a noncommittal hold on reality. These data suggest a rather different interpretation, what might be called the *relativization of perception.* No particular feature on an inkblot, or aspect of external reality, is compelling enough to suggest perception of solid and durable forms.

The way this unique perspective is developed seems to be related to awareness of one's bodily and mental processes. For example, the number of references to bodily parts and internal organs (especially the spinal column and sex organs) and the psychic energy centers within the body is very high. Examining the flow of associations in each Rorschach, one discovers something interesting. In one Rorschach, every response involving the unfolding and transformation of energy/space into form was immediately preceded by an image of a bodily part or internal organ. A Buddhist interpretation of this contiguity between body and energy responses is that penetrating awareness of bodily (and mental) processes becomes a vehicle through which to observe the fundamental energy transformations of body/mind/universe.

While emphasizing the distinctive features of these Rorschachs, it is important to keep in mind that the responses discussed above constitute only a small proportion of the total Rorschach record for each advanced practitioner. The remainder of the imagery is quite varied. Examination of all the imagery reveals that advanced practitioners at this first stage of enlightenment are *not without intrapsychic conflict.* Using the Holt system for scoring drive-dominated content and defenses there is consistently low but scorable number of aggression-related responses in the protocols of three of the four advanced practitioners. Overall, there appears to be an *intensification of sexual drive states,* relative to beginners and insight practitioners, even though the experience of aggression seems to diminish for most. To some degree concern with the awareness and management of impulses was characteristic for all the advanced practitioners.

In addition, each of these Rorschachs evidenced *idiosyncratic conflictual themes* such as fear of rejection, struggle with dependency and needs for nurturance, fear and doubt regarding heterosexual relationships, and fear of destructiveness. All of these issues are related to intimacy. They may reflect long-standing difficulties. But they may reflect instead the peculiar role of an enlightened person in the context of modern western culture—a culture where eager students idealize such individuals as "gurus" while these same individuals struggle to uphold the ethical standards of the Buddhist teachings. The result of the struggle is that intimate relationships become more problematic. To emphasize: The unusual feature of these Rorschachs is *not* that these people are without conflict, but rather they are relatively *non-defensive in experiencing such conflicts.* Vivid drive-dominated content was often present while minimal or no defense was employed against it (using Holt defense scoring criteria). This empirical finding is supported by the directness and matter-of-factness with which these advanced practitioners talked about personal problems during a follow-up interview. They tended to see their own sexual and aggressive drives, as well as their individual dynamics, as intense mind-states which could be experienced and acted on with awareness, but which were not necessarily compelling or invested in to any great degree.

The Master's Group

The single Rorschach in this group is included because of its unusualness. It is the only one available on the final stages of "development" (*bhāvanā*), that is, from someone who had attained all, or all but one, of the four levels of enlightenment and has allegedly undergone a cognitive-emotional restructuring that has completely, or almost completely, eliminated suffering from their human experience. It should not be necessary to emphasize the extraordinary uniqueness and potential signficance of data from this range of experience. This Rorschach was collected in South Asia, and for reasons of confidentiality cannot be further identified. Analysis of this Rorschach re-opens all the complicated problems of cross-cultural Rorschach interpretation (Hsu, 1972). Nevertheless, several features are so striking that they are worthy of comment. The first is its notable *shift in perspective.* Of the 32 total number of responses, 13 pertain to specific states of mind (41%) and three to states of the ordinary and non-ordinary world (9%). Whereas most "normal" Rorschach subjects unquestioningly accept the physical "reality" of an inkblot and then project their imagings onto it, this master sees an *inkblot itself as a projection of the mind.* All the various stages of the mind and the world that might be articulated are themselves a kind of immediate reality. So also, in a certain sense, the testing situation is a projection of the mind. The master, therefore, uses the situation as an occasion to teach about the various states of the mind and cosmos, especially those that enable others to alleviate their suffering.

The second unusual feature of the protocol is its *integrative style.* Each of the 10 cards, as they are presented, are utilized in the service of a systematic discourse on the Buddhist teachings pertaining to the alleviation of human suffering. Thus, Card I sets the stage with four images of humans and beasts in their everyday life of suffering. Card II depicts a picture of the mind in its angered state, and Card III depicts the creatures of hell, the hellish state of mind produced by anger in this life, or the plane on which an angry person is believed to take birth in the future, both in accordance with the Buddhist teachings on karmic action based on hatred. Cards IV–V depict the ignorance and craving of the mind, believed to be the two root causes of suffering in Buddhist psychology. So far, the master has set forth the traditional doctrine of the Three Poisons: anger, craving, and ignorance. Card VI illustrates how the same mind and body can be used to gain liberation:

1. A pillar. It has taken the form of truth. This pillar is the process of getting at or discovering the human mind. (D 5)
2. Inside there is envy, disease, sorrow and hatred in the form of black shapes. (W)
3. A human torso. (Dd 25)
4. After conquering truth, the mind has become clean and white. (D 11)

Card VII gives the results of the practice.

1. I see a body [here, which reminds me of] a temple. (D 6) The mind, here, like a cavern. I can also call this [with the portion identified as 'mind' inside it] the physical body [term used implies a lack of respect in the original language].
2. From it, wings have spread—the impulses. (D 10)
3. Ultimately, this body has gone up to the temple [identifies a second temple, D 8]. At the end of spiritual practice, the mind can travel in two temples [i.e., the first is the human body, once the source of the impulses but now the master of them; the second is the temple at the end of spiritual practice].

The remainder of the cards depict the enjoyment of the perfected practice as well as the consequences of practice that is not perfected.

Integrating all 10 cards into a single associative theme is an extremely rare finding. Note that the master achieves this without any significant departure from reality testing and without ignoring the realistic features of the inkblot, though there is considerable reliance on shading responses and vague and amorphously perceived form.

Discussion

In each of the criterion groups, there are unique qualitative features in the Rorschachs which are distinctly different from those of the other groups. This finding in itself suggests that there are indeed different stages of the practice. Even more interesting is the fact that the specific qualitative features of the Rorschachs for each group are *consistent with the classical descriptions* of the psychological changes most characteristic of that stage of practice. Thus the Beginner's Rorschach is understandable in light of the classical descriptions of the preliminary stage of moral training; the Samadhi Rorschach in terms of the classical descriptions of the stage of concentration leading to access concentration and samadhi; the Insight Rorschachs in terms of the classical stages of insight; and the Advanced and Masters' Rorschachs in terms of enduring trait changes upon attainment of the classical stages of enlightenment. The classical descriptions used in this study are those found in the *Visuddhimagga* (Nyanamoli, 1976) and in the *Progress of Insight* (Mahasi Sayadaw, 1965). Such convergence of the Rorschach qualitative features on the one hand and the classical descriptions on the other may be an important step toward establishing the cross-cultural validation of the psychological changes at each major stage of the practice. What follows is a brief discussion of the convergence in each instance.

THE BEGINNER'S GROUP

The qualitative features of the post-Rorschachs of the 15 subjects in the Beginner's Group were not especially different from the pre-Rorschachs, with one important exception. The Rorschachs of a significant number of these subjects manifested an increased incidence of drive-dominated content as well as significant changes in the formal aspects of their verbalizations (Holt and Havel, 1960; Watkins and Stauffacher, 1975).

These findings are consistent with those of Maupin (1965). Using the Rorschach, Maupin reported an increase in primary process thinking and tolerance for unrealistic experience in beginning zen students. Maupin also found that such an increase in primary process thinking and tolerance predicated a successful response to meditation while attentional measures did not. Maupin concludes:

> Capacity for regression and tolerance for unrealistic experience significantly predicted response to meditation, while attention measures did not. Once issues related to comfort in the face of strange inner experience are resolved, attention functions necessary to the exercise probably become available.

Thus, at the start of meditation practice, the naive subject is introduced, perhaps for the first time, to the vast world of his internal experience. Maupin correctly points out that, whereas the beginning meditator's task may be to train attention, most are readily distracted from that task by the very strangeness of their internal world.

There is a characteristic storminess to the beginner's experience. Subjective reports of an increased awareness of fantasy and daydreaming, of incessant thinking, and of lability of affect abound in the literature (Mahasi Sayadaw, 1965; Walsh, 1977, 1978). Objective measures such as primary process scores on the Rorschach lend some validity to these reports. Likewise, Davidson, Goleman and Schwartz (1976) have reported an increase in state-anxiety for the beginning meditator, in contrast to a decrease for the advanced meditator. Overall, the beginner's experience is largely a matter of *adaptation to the flow of internal experience,* an adaptation that is perhaps necessary and anxiety-producing in a culture that lays so much stress on external adaptation and reality-boundness at the expense of imaginative involvement (Hilgard, 1970). It is necessary to keep in mind that this phase of adaptation, though necessary, has very little to do directly with meditation in the formal sense.

The beginning meditator's introduction to his internal world is not essentially different from the naive subject's who begins exploration of other hypoaroused states, e.g., self-hypnosis, reverie, and free association. For example, using the Rorschach, a similar increase in primary process thinking has been reported for hypnotized subjects (Fromm, Oberlander and Grunewald, 1970) and for patients who had undergone psychoanalysis (Rehyer, 1969). Using questionnaires, an increased awareness of imagery was reported for self-hypnosis (Fromm et al., 1981). According to these findings, adaptation to the internal milieu may be a common feature of *any* hypoaroused state of consciousness and may have little to do with the "specificity" of meditation per se (Tart, 1975).

The implication is that beginners, in a strict sense, are not necessarily "meditating" even when they appear to be sitting in a meditation posture for some period of time. What then are they doing? This question was recently put to an esteemed Asian Buddhist teacher of this practice. He was asked why only a very few of the, say, 60 students who meditate intensively for 3 months in this country reach the more advanced stages of concentration and insight according to classical criteria; whereas the majority of students who meditate the same way for a comparable length of time in certain meditation centers in South Asia are reported to reach these advanced states.[9] He attributed the differences in part to variations

---

9. This was confirmed in the South Asian study, for example, at Thathana Yeiktha in Rangoon, Burma, the major teaching center of this tradition of practice and the residence of the Ven. Mahasi Sayadaw.

in cultural beliefs and to the degree of conviction and understanding the students bring to practice. In addition, he said, "Many western students do not meditate. They do therapy . . . they do not go deep with the mindfulness." The answer is to the point. It suggests a *difference between adaptation and attentional training,* mindfulness in this case. Much in line with Maupin's findings, it seems that many westerners become so fascinated with the content of their internal world, understandably perhaps since it is often their first real conscious encounter with it—fantasies, personal problems, emotional reactions, thoughts—that they become preoccupied with an exploration of this content. In effect, they fail to go beyond the content and proceed to the necessary task of training concentration, mindfulness and related processes of attention. This form of *self-exploratory therapy* often gets confounded in both practice and in the theoretical and research literature with *formal meditation,* defined in terms of the specific training of attentional skills.

In order to avoid such confusion, many eastern systems have devised a more or less elaborate system of "preliminary practices" to be carried out before formal meditation. These practices are often referred to as the stage of Moral Training.[10] They often consist of an elaborate set of instructions for changing attitudes about self and world, thorough exploration of internal states, and the regulation of external behavior through precepts. They demand nothing less than a radical change in one's view of oneself, an exploration of and working through the qualities of one's internal milieu, and a thorough behavioral change. Considerable time may be spent in these practices—several years is not uncommon in some traditional systems—before formal training in meditation is begun.

It is indeed remarkable that formal meditation has become so popular in this country while the preliminary moral training has been largely ignored. The psychological changes characteristic of the preliminary practices are the necessary precondition to formal meditation. What happens when they are skipped over? One can predict that the beginner is destined to "work through" these changes during meditation itself. Consequently the preliminary therapeutic change and the stages of formal meditation become confounded. In this country, meditation is indeed a form of "therapy" for many.

Unfortunately, this makes it more difficult for even the most sincere students of meditation to advance in the more formal practice. Outcome studies have shown that expectations play a significant role, whether in

---

10. Cf. the Yamas and Niyamas, the first two "limbs" or stages of "eight-limbed" astanga or raj yoga (*Yoga Sutras,* II.27–43); and the cultivation of sila as the first of the threefold division of training or mental culture (bhavana) in the standard structure of Buddhist practice (*Visuddhimagga,* Section I).

therapeutic outcomes (Frank, 1962) or meditation outcomes (Smith, 1976). Once the cultural belief that formal meditation is a variety of therapy becomes firmly entrenched, students are likely to engage the content of their internal milieu at the expense of attentional training, even during intensive practice. Such students are unlikely to advance at a very rapid rate in the more characteristic features of formal meditation. Perhaps this is one reason why over half of the experimental subjects were still exploring emotional issues after 3 months of continuous 16 hr./day practice. Some, however, who become less distracted by the content and proceed to train their attention may advance. The self-reports and Rorschachs of the Samadhi Group are illustrative of such advance.

The Samadhi Group

The Rorschach data of the Samadhi Group might be considered in light of the classical descriptions of the psychological changes occurring in first set of formal meditations, the stages of concentration. These classical stages have been described in detail elsewhere, along with comparisons with constructs from western cognitive and perceptual psychology (Brown, 1977). Briefly, according to the tradition, formal meditation begins when the yogi trains his posture and learns to quiet his mind so that internal events, such as thoughts and imagery, and external events, such as sights and sounds, no longer distract the meditator from an ongoing awareness of the internal milieu. The meditator begins by concentrating on some object, such as the breath. As his concentration becomes more steady, with fewer lapses in attention, the meditator slowly and systematically expands the range of his awareness to the moment-by-moment recognition of the changing events in the internal milieu. As he becomes more skilled, he is able to become aware of events very quickly, so quickly that he is aware not so much of the *content* but of the very *process* of moment-by-moment change. At times he may experience a relative cessation of specific visual, auditory, and other perceptual patterns during the meditation while remaining uninterruptedly aware that some moment-by-moment change is occurring in the flux of stimuli prior to their coalescence into particular patterns of objects. These changes mark the onset of samadhi.[11]

---

11.   In some systems, these stages are kept relatively distinct. In some Mahayana Buddhist systems such as Mahamudra, for example, the postural and thought changes are described separately in a set of Exercises called the "Three Isolations." The succeeding perceptual changes are described in another set of exercises called "Concentration on Gross Objects." In the Theravadin Buddhist *Visuddhimagga,* the Burmese style of mindfulness that the meditators of this study employed, all of the respective changes are collapsed into a single set of instructions consisting of concentration on the breath followed by mindfulness of all types of events, moment-by-moment.

There are different stages or refinements of samadhi. *Beginner's Samadhi* is here defined according to two criteria: the object of awareness and the quality of that awareness. With respect to the object of awareness, Beginner's Samadhi is characterized by relative freedom from distracting thoughts. If thoughts occur, they are recognized immediately and subside upon being noticed. As with thoughts, the yogi is struck by the immediate awareness of all forms of sense data. Though specific gross perceptual patterns may occur, e.g., a sight or sound, emphasis is on registration of the impact, not on the pattern. For example, in glancing at a specific object like one's hand or hearing a specific sound like a bell, the yogi is more aware that he has glanced at something or that a sound has occurred than he is of the content of the sight or sound. Nevertheless, in Beginner's Samadhi there is a distinct tendency to become lost in a given thought or in the interpretation of a moment of sense data and thereby lose awareness of the immediate sensory impact. Second, with respect to the quality of awareness, Beginner's Samadhi is characterized by a relative steadiness. The yogi's awareness is relatively continuous. During each sitting period, there are fewer periods of non-awareness, that is, of becoming distracted by or lost in the content.

The next stage of samadhi in this system is *Access Samadhi*. With respect to the object of awareness, Access is characterized by a distinct lack of thinking and recognizable perceptual patterns. The yogi has "stopped the mind," at least in the sense of its so-called "higher operations": thinking and pattern recognition. The yogi keeps his awareness at the more subtle level of the *actual moment of occurrence or immediate impact* of a thought or of a sensory stimulus. Thus, instead of recognizing specific thoughts, images or perceptual patterns (as still occurs in Beginner's Samadhi), the yogi is aware only of their moment of impact. Each discrete event is experienced more as a subtle movement or vibration at the very onset of its occurrence. Although the yogi is aware of a myriad of discrete events happening moment-by-moment, he no longer elaborates the cognitive or perceptual content of such events. The meditation period is experienced as a succession of discrete events: pulses, flashes, vibrations or movements without specific pattern or form. With respect to awareness itself, Access is now characterized by completely stable and steady attention. Though mental and bodily events occur moment-by-moment in uninterrupted succession, attention remains fixed on each discrete moment. Awareness of one event is immediately followed by awareness of another without break for the duration of the sitting period, or for as long as this level of concentration remains. This succession of moments of awareness is called "momentary concentration" (Mahasi Sayadaw, 1965).

The essential distinction between these levels of Samadhi, however, is the grossness or subtleness of the object of awareness on the one hand, and the degree of uninterrupted awareness on the other. Steadiness is most important. Once stabilized, the more advanced yogi can hold his samadhi at different levels, from gross to subtle, for the purpose of insight at each level. He may, for example, purposely allow the gross content of the mind to return in full force, especially thoughts, feelings, and meaningful perceptual patterns, in order to deepen insight into the nature of mental and bodily processes. However, this skilled yogi's steady awareness continues in the midst of the various content. Now, there is little difficulty with the distraction which was such a problem for the beginning meditator.

The Rorschach data from the Samadhi Group are consistent with these classical descriptions of samadhi. Recall that these Rorschachs were characterized by: (1) a paucity of associative elaborations; (b) a significant decrease in the production of internal images; (c) a concentration on the pure perceptual features of the inkblot. Despite the experimenter demand to produce images and associations, the subjects are believed to have partially maintained their state of samadhi during the testing. This is hypothesized to account for the marked reduction in the availability of ideational and pattern recognition components of perception, concomitant with an increased awareness of the immediate impact of the inkblot. Thus, the yogis were primarily attentive to, and occasionally absorbed in, the pure perceptual features, e.g., outlines, colors, shading, and inanimate movement.

Although the data analysis is not yet complete, an attempt will be made to correlate the level of samadhi (as measured by teachers ratings and discriminatory items on the Profile of Meditation Experience) with the pure determinant scores on the Rorschachs of the Samadhi Group. It is hypothesized that the Rorschachs from those in Beginner's Samadhi are likely to produce more internal images and less pure determinant responses, while those of the more advanced Access Samadhi will produce fewer internal images and more pure determinant responses. In addition, it is hypothesized that the pure inanimate movement response, or inanimate movement in combination with shading, is a specific predictor of Access Samadhi. A high incidence of such responses was found only in a few subjects and only in the post-Rorschachs of the Samadhi Group. Shading and inanimate movement responses are the least understood of all the Rorschach determinants, no doubt because of their rarity of occurrence. It has been pointed out that shading responses may indicate a sensitivity to subtle perceptual nuances (Schachtel, 1966). According to the data from the samadhi group, we might interpret these findings in terms of an increased sensitivity to the subtle undercurrents of perception, namely, awareness of a perceptual field in constant but subtle change. Thus, yogis at the level of Access Samadhi may "see" the ink-blots merely as a field of continuous changing events, a pulsing swirling mass. They do not "see" bats, butterflies, or other specific perceptual patterns.[12]

Whether such fine distinctions can be made empirically remains to be established. Nevertheless, it is at least clear from the data that the yogis' awareness in this group is at the level of the immediate perceptual impact of the inkblot, not at the level of an elaboration or interpretation of that sensory impact. Because such pure determinant Rorschach responses are highly atypical of either normal or clinical Rorschachs, and are uncharacteristic of both the pre-test Rorschachs of the same subjects and the Rorschachs of the control group as well, these Rorschach responses may be seen as evidence validating the classical description and existence of the state of samadhi as a definite kind of perceptual event or level of perceptual experience.

The Insight Group

In the classical stages of meditation, Access Samadhi is merely a prerequisite for *Insight Meditation.* Just as a scientist may painstakingly construct a sensitive electronic instrument to measure some process, similarly, in order to gain insight into the fundamental workings of the mind, the meditator has carefully prepared himself through the refinement and steadying of attention with its accompanying shifts in levels of perception. The meditator is now ready to proceed to the Stages of Insight. Because the descriptions of these stages are technical, the reader is referred elsewhere (Nyanamoli, 1976; Mahasi Sayadaw, 1965). Suffice it to say that the foundation of all "insight" in Buddhism is direct experience and understanding of the three "lakkhanas" or "marks" of existence: impermanence, suffering, and selflessness or nonentityness. According to the tradition, an experiential understanding of these marks powerful enough to lead to enduring trait-changes and intrapsychic structural change is possible only after having achieved Access Samadhi.

In each discrete moment of awareness the meditator notices *both* the mental or bodily event *and* his awareness of that event. In a single meditation session he is likely to experience thousands of such individual and separate moments of awareness because his attention is now refined enough to perceive increasingly discrete and rapidly changing mind-

---

12. Fluidness of perception was also found in Rorschachs administered during hypnotic trance and marihuana intoxication (personal communication, Erika Fromm, Ph.D., Chicago, August, 1980). Dr. Fromm believes that fluid Rorschach percepts may be characteristic of many altered states of consciousness, not just meditation.

moments. When this level of moment-by-moment change is actually experienced, the meditator is led to a profound and radical understanding
of the impermanence (*anicca*) of all events. He may also notice a tendency to react to the events, to prefer some or to reject others. This reactive
tendency disrupts the clear perception of the moment-by-moment flow
and, in fact, has the effect of blocking the flow itself in an attempt to
resist it—to hold on or push away. The continual experience of this with
clear awareness eventually leads to an understanding of the suffering
(*dukkha*) inherent in the normal reactive mind and its relationship to lik-
ing and disliking, attraction and aversion. Furthermore, as discrete
events/movements of awareness arise and cease in rapid succession, the
yogi finds it increasingly difficult to locate anything or anyone that could
be either the agent of these events or the recipient of their effects. He
cannot find any enduring or substantial agent behind the events to which
they could be attributed. At this level the only observable reality is the
flow of events themselves. From this perspective of constant change,
what was once a solid body, a durable perceptual object such as a tree, a
fixed idea, or even a fixed point of observation, no longer appear
substantial, durable or existent in their own right. By viewing this changing process, the yogi comes to understand the lack of intrinsic durable
nature of the selflessness (*anattā*) of mind, body, and external perceptions. These insights into the fundamental operations of the mind and its
"marks" result in a profound reorganization of the mediator's experience called, in the *Visuddhimagga,* "Purification of View."

At first it is easier to obtain these insights by holding awareness at the
level of Access, i.e., at the level of the subtle moment-by-moment pulsa-
tion of events. Eventually, the meditator is able to sustain the same insights even when allowing his awareness to return to the ordinary gross
content of experience such as specific thoughts, bodily sensations, or
perceptual patterns. With perfectly uninterrupted and steady awareness,
he observes this varied content moment-by-moment and thereby deepens
his insight into the three characteristics of all mental and bodily processes. This is called, again in the terminology of the *Visuddhimagga*,
"Overcoming Doubt." Eventually, the very manner in which these
events are perceived to arise undergoes a series of significant shifts, both
in duration as well as in vividness. Regardless of the content, the events
flash by very quickly, like pulses of light, moment-by-moment. The
beginning and ending of each event is clearly perceived. This is called
"Knowledge of the Arising and Passing Away" of events and is a key
stage in Insight Meditation (Nyanamoli, 1976).

The moment-by-moment arising and passing away of bodily and mental events and the concomitant moment-by-moment awareness of them
eventually "break up." This is called the experience of "Dissolution."
Only the unbelievably rapid and successive passing away of discrete

events and the awareness of them are perceived. Their arising is no longer noticeable. Events and awareness of the events seem to vanish and disappear together moment-by-moment. The net effect of this level of perception is either to experience reality as a state of continual and ongoing dissolution, moment-by-moment; or to experience forms and percepts as literally void—to have no perception, for instance, of a form at all like one's arm or leg or even entire body, or of an external object like a tree.

The first reaction to this experience is often one of exhilaration or ecstasy. If so, it is usually short-lived. Soon it is followed in subsequent stages of practice by states of fear and terror, misery and disgust, as the implications of this discovery become apparent. These are affective reactions to the experience of reality as a condition of continual dissolution or radical impermanence, but they are not affective states in the normal sense. The yogi's awareness remains steady and balanced behind these affects. They are experienced fully and observed as mind-states, but without further reaction. They in turn become objects of bare attention and continue to be observed with uninterrupted mindfulness towards further insight. They are technically described as "knowledges" (ñānas) rather than affects and are considered separate stages in the insight series.

In subsequent meditation, events reoccur. The yogi is not only aware of each event which occurs within consciousness but is also aware of its context, i.e., he is aware that each event is located within the entire fabric of a cosmos comprised of an infinite number of potential interactions. From this wider perspective called "dependent origination" all potential events are again seen to break up rapidly. Eventually the meditator's attitude changes toward these dissolving events. He comes to realize that no event could possibly serve as an object of satisfaction or fulfillment. Precisely for this reason, he then experiences a profound desire for deliverance from them, from which this stage derives its technical name, "Desire For Deliverance." He subsequently begins to re-examine these events with renewed effort and dedication: this is the stage of "Re-Observation For the Purpose of Deliverance." With continued practice he next realizes what is technically called "Equanimity About Formations": a perfectly balanced, *effortless,* and *non-reactive awareness* of each rapidly changing and vanishing event moment-by-moment, with a clear perception of their impermanence, unsatisfactoriness, and nonentityness. Despite great individual variation at the level of gross content, there is no difference at the subtlest level of awareness or reaction to any events. Awareness proceeds spontaneously, without any reference to an individual self or personal history. A fundamental shift in time/space organization has occurred so that the yogi is now aware of the continuous occurrence of all the potential events of the mind/cosmos.

These classical descriptions of the stages of insight in Theravada

Buddhism can be compared to the Rorschachs produced by the Insight Group. Recall that the insight Rorschachs were characterized by: (a) increased productivity; (b) richness of associative elaboration with shifts in affect; (c) realistic attunement of the image and the blot. These Rorschachs are strikingly different from those of the Samadhi group. In fact, in some respects they are nearly opposite. In interpreting these data, we assume that a meditator skilled in insight is likely to allow a very great variety of content to pass through his mind during a single meditation session. With uninterrupted and steady awareness, and without reaction, he simply notices the great richness of the unfolding mind states. He notices the play of mental events from all the sensory and cognitive modes moment-by-moment, all dependently arising according to their respective causes and conditions.[13] In a test situation like the Rorschach, one would predict this state of non-reactive, moment-to-moment awareness to affect Rorschach performance. According to our understanding of the insight stages, the striking increase in productivity as well as its richness is not at all surprising. In response to a given ink-blot, one would expect a great richness of content to arise moment-by-moment. The unfolding of such rich content would be seemingly endless with nothing experienced as especially durable or lasting. Nevertheless, just as the Buddhist texts claims that such events arise by causes and conditions, so also the meditators were sensitive to and aware of the relative stimulus-pull of each Rorschach card. In the same way, they were finely attuned to the reality features of the blots. Moreover, during the Insight Stages the yogi is less likely to be restricted by any form of reaction to these subtle events, by any selection or rejection of them. Thus, it is not surprising to find a distinct quality of non-defensiveness in Rorschachs of such practitioners. There is an acceptance and matter-of-factness concerning what would normally be conflictual sexual and aggressive material. Furthermore, the experienced absence of any solid or durable self behind the flow of mental and physical events is consistent with the advanced yogi's capacity to switch perspectives on the same response, a pattern atypical of normal and clinical Rorschachs. Nevertheless, despite the impersonal nature of the experience of insights such as insubstantiality, these Rorschachs are deeply human and fraught with the richness of the living process contrary to the stereotypical and erroneous notions of nonentityness as a void state. One need only glance at the Rorschachs of these subjects to see that we are dealing with a very unusual quality and richness of life experience.

---

13.   This is the central doctrine, common to all Buddhist schools, of Dependent Origination and has its origin and confirmation at this level of practice.

Advanced Insight Group

At a specifiable point—when the mind is perfectly balanced, insight into the three marks is clear in each moment of perception, and all forms of desire consequently are suspended—the most fundamental shift of all occurs. Awareness, previously tied to each momentary event, now passes beyond these events. During this moment, all conceptual distinctions and ordinary understandings of the "mind" fall away. All objects of awareness and individual acts of awareness cease. There is only stillness and vastness, "the Supreme Silence" as one Asian teacher described it, without disturbance by any event whatsoever but with pure awareness. This profound shift is called the *Cessation Experience* (*nirodha*) and is the First or Basic Moment of Enlightenment. It is technically called "Entering the Path (*magga*)" or Stream (to *nirvana*). When this Path-Moment (literally *sotāpatti* or "stream-entry") is experienced, certain erroneous conceptions about the nature of reality and certain emotional defilements (*kilesa*) are eradicated. This moment is followed by yet another shift, called Fruition (*phala*), in which the "fruit" of Path-entry is experienced: mind remains silent and at peace. This is followed in quick succession by a moment of Reviewing (paccavekkhana) in which awareness of the content of the meditator's individual experience returns and he becomes reflexively aware of the extraordinary thing that has happened to him. As ordinary mental events pass through awareness, the meditator simply lets this relative content run its own course while his awareness is no longer bound to it. The state immediately following Path-Fruition-Reviewing is typically one of great lightness and joy which may last several days. The important fact, however, is that *enduring trait changes* are said to occur upon enlightenment.

Several options are available to the meditator at this point. He may simply return to his daily affairs. If he does, he may or may not continue formal practice.[14] Whether he does or not however, the gains of this experience of First Path are thought to be permanent. If the meditator continues practice on the other hand, either in the context of his daily life or in further intensive retreat settings, two courses are open to him. He may remain on the level attained at First Path and practice to develop what is technically termed the "Maturity of Fruition." This refers to the ability to reenter the state of awareness he experienced at the initial moments of both Path and Fruition. Both of these are moments of Cessation in which all ordinary perceptual, cognitive, affective, and motivational ac-

---

14. The second author encountered a number of practitioners in South and Southeast Asia who did not feel the need to pursue the practice further after attaining First Path or first enlightenment. This is not considered unusual or unacceptable.

tivity ceases. Each lasts only a brief moment before ordinary consciousness and mental activity resumes. Phenomenologically they are both experienced as a state of supreme silence. The difference between them lies in the power of the Path-moment proceding Fruition. It is at that point that the fundamental and irreversible shift or change in the meditator takes place. This is expressed as a "change-of-lineage" (*gotrabhū*) and is traditionally defined in terms of the specific "fetters" (*saṁyojanas*) or perceptual-cognitive and affective modalities that are permanently eliminated at that stage of enlightenment (Nyanomoli, 1976).[15] The experience of Path and the changes associated with it are accordingly said to occur only once at each stage of enlightenment, four times in all. With continued training, the silent and peaceful mental state of Fruition, on the other hand, can be re-experienced indefinitely. This is termed "entering the Fruition state." With practice, the meditator can learn to re-experience the Fruition state at will for extended periods of time.[16]

The other course open to the individual who wants to continue meditation is to practice for a subsequent Path experience, each of which defines a progressively more advanced stage of enlightenment. There are three further Paths or stages of enlightenment in this tradition. Each is attained in the same manner. If the yogi chooses to work for Second Path, for instance, he must begin by formally and deliberately renouncing the Fruition-state of the First Path. This is a consequential decision. According to tradition and confirmation provided by self-reports in the South Asian study, once having made this renunciation he will never experience the Fruition of First Path again, whether or not he is successful in attaining Second Path. Attainment of a prior Path does not guarantee attainment of the succeeding Path. After making his renunciation, he returns to the stage of Arising and Passing Away. He must then pass through all the subsequent stages of insight a second time until he once more experiences a Path-moment at their conclusion. Again, stage-specific trait-changes will occur. Additional and different emotional defilements will permanently disappear from his psychic organization. This Path-moment will be followed by moments of Fruition and Reviewing. He may discontinue practice or, choosing to continue, either

15. The experience of Path is also thought to affect one's rebirth status in specific ways as well, but this concentration lies outside the perspective of this study (cf. Nyanamoli, 1976, XIII; Narada, 1975).

16. According to his degree of "mastery," the meditator can enter Fruition when he wants, where he wants, for as long as he wants (subject to an upper limit of 7 days), leaving it at the time he resolves or prior to entering it (Nyanamoli, 1975, XXIII). This claim was confirmed in the self-reports of a number of the subjects in the South Asian study.

cultivate Fruition or practice for the Third and finally the Fourth Path, which is said to produce a final state of perfect wisdom, compassion, and freedom from any kind of suffering. Each stage of enlightenment is more difficult to attain than the previous one. The yogi passes through the same stages of practice prior to the experience of Path each time; but the experience becomes more intense, the suffering greater, as more deeply rooted fetters are extinguished and insight into the nature of reality grows.[17] Though theoretically possible (as all the advanced practitioners and masters in this study maintain) the South Asian study in indigenous Buddhist cultures, where a higher incidence of such attainments is still to be expected, disclosed that few meditators attain all four Paths.

The Rorschachs of the Advanced Insight Group can be interpreted by considering the consequences of enlightenment specified by the tradition. Enlightenment is said to be followed by a return to ordinary mental experience, though one's perspective is radically altered. One might expect such Rorschachs to reflect the idiosyncrasies of character and mental content for each of the respective practitioners. One would also expect such Rorschachs to retain some of the features of enlightenment specified by tradition. These features are: a) changes in the conception of reality, following the Cessation experience; b) eradication of certain defilements upon Path experience. The four Rorschachs, though a small sample, are consistent with the classical accounts of the trait changes said to follow the enlightenment experience.

Recall that these enlightenment Rorschachs did not evidence a high degree of the unusual qualitative features of the samadhi and insight Rorschachs. They are not especially distinct from the Rorschachs of the pre-test population of the *Three Month Study*. Their lack of immediate distinctiveness poses some interesting issues for interpretation. One might conclude either that the outcomes of long-term meditation are psychologically insignificant or a function of unstable state-changes. Or, one might conclude that the Rorschach is unable to measure those psychological outcomes, whatever they may be. From another standpoint, the very mundaneness of these Rorschachs could be interpreted as a highly significant finding. Consistent with the classical descriptions of enlightenment, especially the stage of Reviewing following enlightenment, the practitioner is said to retain his ordinary mind. Though his perspective is radically different, nevertheless the content of his ex-

---

17. There appears to be some similarity between this repetitive process at deeper and deeper levels of meditation and a similar phenomenon sometimes encountered in psychoanalytically oriented psychotherapy where, for example, a given problem such as oedipal guilt may be worked through in successive stages at different phases of an individual's life history under qualitatively more severe forms of stress (personal communication, Dr. Richard Weiser, California School of Professional Psychology).

perience is as it was prior to meditation, though he may no longer react to it with the usual emotional attitudes of attraction, aversion, or indifference. There is a famous Zen saying which speaks directly to this point:

> Before I began meditating, mountains were mountains and rivers were rivers. After I began meditating, mountains were no longer mountains and rivers were no longer rivers. Once I finished meditating, mountains were once again mountains and rivers were once again rivers.

In the language of the present tests from the advanced practitioners, "Rorschachs are once again Rorschachs." The advanced practitioner lives out his idiosyncratic life history, though in the context of a relativized perception of the self and object world.

Though these are for the most part seemingly mundane Rorschachs, each contains evidence that the enlightened person is said to manifest *awareness on different levels*. On the *mundane* level, such a person continues to perceive solid and enduring forms in the external world as well as habitual mind-states such as emotions and attitudes. To the extent that perception has been relativized by enlightenment, on an *absolute* level these external forms and mental states are no longer viewed as solid and durable. They exist only in a relative sense.

These alleged changes may be reflected in the Rorschachs. For enlightened subjects, the inkblots do indeed "look like" specific images such as butterflies, bats, etc., and yet these images as well as mind-states such as pain and pleasure are perceived merely as manifestations of energy/space. Such subjects perceive content but also energy processes in the inkblots. One possible interpretation is that the enlightened practitioner has come to understand something fundamental about the process by which this perceived world comes into existence in our ordinary awareness.

While retaining an ability to perceive external forms and ordinary mental experience on both these levels—as relatively real but ultimately mere configurations of changing energy/space—the enlightened practitioner becomes free of the constraints of non-vertical perception or attachment to external forms or internal mind-states. One alleged outcome is that the enlightened person sees that man's place in the universe is not self-contained but is located within a fabric of many other modes of existence and potential interactions, all of which are interrelated and mutually conditioned. He comes to understand, experientially, the doctrine of dependent origination.[18] Life becomes multi-dimensional and

---

18. This perception that each individual form is ultimately void of substance and, further, that the uniqueness of each form arises from the fact that it exists in relation to every

multi-determined in its dynamism and manifestation. This mode of perception leads to a deeper acceptance of human life and death, now set within the context of an unfolding universe in which there is both form and emptiness. Here is an example of a Rorschach response which illustrates this *non-attached, contextualist* mode of perception:

> It looks like a combination caterpillar-butterfly. It seems to be in motion. It gives me the feeling of this creature, this being, walking through the meadow or through a field of grass. It has the feeling of being at home with what it's doing . . . simple and right, at one with what it's doing. It's just its movement. (I,W)

Human life in its most ordinary form is now perceived as precious.

The Rorschachs also contain evidence that the enlightened practitioner *may experience conflict differently.* One very important discovery from these Rorschachs is that the enlightened practitioners are *not* without conflict in a clinical sense.[19] They show evidence for the experience of drive states and conflictual themes such as fears, dependency struggles, and so forth. They are, however, less defensive in their awareness of and presentation of such conflicts. Enlightenment does not mean a person becomes conflict-free.[20]

According to the tradition, only certain defilements are removed upon the experience of *First Path.* What changes is *not so much the amount or*

---

other form is systematically formulated in the most central of all Buddhist teachings in both Theravada and Mahayana, the doctrine of Dependent Origination. In the work which probably represents the culmination of Indian Mahayana, the *Avatsamsaka Sutra,* it is expressed metaphorically in the image of a vast network of gems or crystals, like a spider's web at dawn, in which each gem reflects all the others and in which a touch at any point vibrates through the entire network and affects every other point. This net of gems is the Dharmadhatu, the universe, the realm of innumerable "dharmas" or "events," individual configurations empty of substance and continually in process. The same perception underlies Whitehead's notion of "actual occasion," the nearest equivalent in contemporary philosophical thought. This is also the quantum mechanical vision of the universe which underlies modern physics.

19. This may explain why some of the more controversial and reportedly enlightened teachers and gurus currently in the United States seem to have rather active sexual involvements, problems with aggression, and so forth.

20. According to the tradition, the experience of underlying personal conflicts is actually likely to intensify between the second and third experience of enlightenment. This contradicts one major misconception in both western and eastern cultures. It is often mistakenly assumed by western students of meditation that enlightenment solves all of one's problems. Asian teachers know this is not so. But they in turn point almost exclusively to the remaining "fetters" or "defilements" that will be eliminated only with the attainment of further degrees of enlightenment. They are often unaware of the extent to which psychodynamic conflicts continue at least, the earlier enlightenment stages' though, as pointed out, individuals at these stages may better manager the effects of such conflicts even without specific psychological insight into their nature.

nature of conflict but the awareness of it. In a manner of speaking, during enlightenment, the locus of awareness transcends conflict. Awareness "goes to the other shore" so that it is longer influenced by any mental content. After enlightenment, the context, including conflictual issues, returns. In this sense, enlightenment provides sufficient distance, or better, a vastly different perspective, while one continues to play out the repetitive dynamic themes of life history. There is greater awareness of and openness to conflict but, paradoxically, less reaction at the same time in an impulsive, identificatory, and therefore painful way. Awareness is less caught up at this stage in the relative play of conflictual content or, indeed, in any type of content. For example, problems concerning sexual intimacy are more likely to be seen as "stages of mind." The individual may observe these clearly for what they are and thereby have more freedom in his/her possible reactions to such states. He/she may note that intense desire until it passes, like every other transient mental state; or he/she may act on it, but with full awareness.[21]

One reported effect of first enlightenment is said to be immediate awareness of any "unwholesome" mental state. Mindfulness is said to automatically intervene between impulse or thought and action in such cases. This mechanism of delay, combined with clear and impartial observation, allows a new freedom from drive and a new freedom for well-considered and appropriate action. In this sense, suffering diminishes while conflictual content nevertheless recurs as long as one has not yet attained the subsequent enlightenments.

If these traditional accounts of the effects of first enlightenment are considered in psychodynamic terms, one might say that such enlightened individuals exhibit a loosening of defense with a decreased susceptibility to the usual effects of unbound drive energy or the lifting of repression because they no longer have the power to compel reaction, i.e., to produce an affective or drive state which must be acted upon or defended against. The model of defense seems, then, not well suited to explain these processes; similarly, the notion of insight. Enlightened practitioners do not necessarily have greater psychological insight into the specific nature of conflicts. Many may tolerate and naturally allow conflictual mind states to pass. The degree to which enlightened persons achieve psychological insight varies according to the degree of psychological sophistication of the individual (cf. also Carrington and Ephron, 1975). There is apparently less need to "see through" on the level of content what can be "let go of" on the level of process.

It seems that a dynamic/defense model is not truly suited to these data because of the subtle but pervasive changes that occur at enlightenment.

---

21.   With respect to such passions there are no dictates in terms of social role. One may be monk, lay person, or tantric adept. The only dictate is clear awareness.

One could adopt a rather skeptical view toward these data and diagnose these advanced practitioners as possessing serious pathology according to the defense model. The evidence for conflict in these Rorschachs would support an argument. One could interpret the samadhi and insight Rorschachs, for instance, in light of the operation of extreme obsessive defenses such as isolation and intellectualization respectively. Similarly, the preoccupation with energy, especially bodily energy, could be interpreted as somatization. Certainly, preoccupation with the body is often a pathological symptom. Yet, if these data were so interpreted, something very important would be lost. Such an interpretation fails to take seriously what traditional Buddhist texts mean when they speak of the changes that come from enlightenment: the change in locus of awareness and the intervention of mindfulness between impulse, thought, and action.

Enlightenment has been poorly understood in the psychoanalytic literature. It has been seen as an extreme form of regression to fusion with the mother-representation (Simmel, 1944; Zilboorg, 1938). Recall that this view of enlightenment was derived from a psychoanalytic interpretation of rather poorly translated texts; it was not derived from in-depth study of enlightened individuals. Here, a distinction must be made between *fantasied or wished-for enlightenment* and the *experience of enlightenment*. This distinction has not been clear in clinical studies of meditators nor in the popular literature on meditation. Currently there are many young meditators in America. Some may be isolated schizoid or psychotic individuals who use meditation in the service of defense; others are members of cults who use meditation as a culturally constituted defense system (Spiro, 1965). In both instances, we are speaking about enlightenment as either an individual or shared fantasy; not about the *experience* of enlightenment. Thus, it is not surprising that psychoanalysis of such individuals reveals serious pathology, e.g., tendencies toward identity dissolution, wishes for fusion, and body narcissism.[22]

However, a similar pathological interpretation of those who have the *experience of enlightenment* is more problematic, for here we are talking about *trait changes that are predicted regardless of pre-existing personality make-up* and degree of pathology. Some pathology may even remain at this first level of enlightenment for those with pre-existing personality disorders. In fact, the tradition *predicts* it would remain until the higher stages of enlightenment. There are some individuals in the South Asian group, for example, who evidence the kind of pathology in question. But only some; others are distinctly healthy.

One solution is to seek some sort of behavioral validation, or, to quote

---

22. These patients, suffering from narcissistic personality disorders, were reported by L. Bryce Boyer, personal communication, May, 1980.

William James' famous criterion, "by their fruits ye shall know them" (James, 1958). Many of the enlightened individuals, despite remaining conflicts, are warm, related, non-defensive individuals, who hold responsible and ethical positions as teachers, administrators, and businessmen. Several Rorschach administrators, who frequently gave clinical Rorschachs, commented on the test behavior of these individuals by noting the ease of administration and the unusual cooperativeness of the subjects within an engaging and friendly atmosphere. When the community at large and unbiased Rorschach administrators rate these individuals as such, it is difficult to justify an extreme pathological interpretation of their Rorschachs. This methodological fallacy—to read pathology into Rorschachs without taking into account adaptation and adjustment—has been mentioned elsewhere (Spain, 1972). While it is possible to rule out biased pathological interpretation, this is not to say that some enlightened individuals may not still evidence serious pathology at this stage.

Another solution is to rethink current models of the relative position of meditation and normal adult development, or meditation and psychotherapy insofar as therapy reinstitutes the normal developmental process (Blanck and Blanck, 1974). First, meditation is different from normal development and/or psychotherapy; it is also something more. While meditation apparently parallels some of the processes and accomplishes some of the goals of conventional therapies in alleviating intrapsychic conflict and facilitating mature object relations, it aims at a perceptual shift and a goal-state which is not aimed at or even envisaged in most psychotherapeutic models of mental health and development. However, meditation and psychotherapy cannot be positioned on a spectrum in any mutually exclusive way, as though both simply pointed to a different range of human development (Rama et al., 1976). Not only do post-enlightenment stages of meditation apparently affect the manifestation and management of neurotic and even borderline conditions, but these types of conflict continue to be experienced after first enlightenment.[23] This suggests either that psychological maturity and the path to enlightenment are perhaps two complementary but not entirely unrelated lines of growth; or that indeed they do represent different

---

23. There is an analogous situation perhaps on the border between neurotic and psychotic levels of organization. Recent exploration of the borderline and narcissistic conditions has led to a recognition that different "developmental lines" (A. Freud, 1963) can be simultaneously structured at different levels of organization so that, e.g., a personality generally organized at a neurotic level can be seriously impaired and infiltrated by developmental deficits in specific psychic functions (Blanck and Blanck, 1979). The potential relevance of this finding and of this kind of thinking to meditation development has not yet been explored.

"levels" or ranges of health/growth along a continuum, but with much more complex relationships between them than have previously been imagined. It may be, for instance, that still higher stages of enlightenment may indirectly affect the intrapsychic structural foundations of neurotic or borderline level conflict and so resolve it, even though this is not their main intent.[24] This will be an issue for the next group of protocols. It is also one of the most important issues for future empirical research.

The Master's Group

Masters at the third stage of enlightenment are alleged to no longer be subject to sexual or aggressive impulses and painful affects. The fully enlightened master (fourth Path) is alleged to have perfected the mind and to be free from any kind of mental conflict or suffering. These two types of *"Ariyas"* constitute a unique group according to past tradition and current practice.[25] The single Rorschach of the master representing

---

24. A similar suggestion has been made by Wilbur (1977) in his cross-cultural integration of many of these same traditions into a unified spectrum model of consciousness, though he does not develop the point or analyze the mechanism by which this comes about. He states (Wilbur, 1977:272f): "In undercutting these dualisms (persona vs shadow, psyche vs soma), one simultaneously undercuts the support of the individual neuroses . . . In recognizing a depth of one's identity that goes beyond his individual and separate neuroses . . . Once this process quickens, the individual is no longer exclusively identified with just his separate self sense and hence is no longer exclusively tied to his purely personal problems. He can start to let go of his fears and anxieties, depressions and obsessions, and begin to view them with some clarity and impartiality." Again, the situation on lower levels of personality integration is apparently similar according to the most advanced clinical thinking. In discussing impairments in certain "developmental lines" which could ordinarily be expected to lead to borderline pathology, Blanck and Blanck (1979) point out, following Mahler et al., (1975), that "Affront at a given phase or subphase does not result in cessation of development. Although fixation and regression may occur in one of several developmental lines, the forward march of the totality of development and organization proceeds nonetheless. Sometimes, with favorable subsequent experience, the sweep of organization carries with it and may even repair the damage of an earlier process by subsuming it favorably" (Blanck and Blanck, 1979:134).

25. While collecting data in the South Asian component of this study, the second author was interrupted by the master when he began to ask an advanced subject to describe their practice for Third Path. He was told the question about attainment of higher Paths was not appropriate and was not generally asked. This happened only this once and contrasts with the rather extraordinary openness and frankness which all the subjects had shown throughout the study. This cooperation was itself extraordinary in light of the fact that traditionally these experiences are never discussed with anyone but one's teacher. To the best knowledge of the authors, no Asian practitioners at any state of enlightenment have agreed to be subjects of research before or since this study. This was the only question the author was not permitted to ask—or was not answered—in 6 months of interviewing and testing. No such prohibition applied to

this group[26] is certainly unusual. The interpretive question however is whether this protocol can be distinguished from the dogmatic opinions of a religious fundamentalist or the fixed delusions of the paranoid schizophrenic where one might also expect attempts to relate the various test cards into a single theme. There are differences. The decision to use the testing situation as an occasion to teach stands in direct contrast to the guardedness and constrictedness of a paranoid record. The personalized nature of paranoid delusion contrasts with the systematic presentation of a consensual body of teaching established by a cultural tradition. These are culture-dominated, not drive-dominated, percepts. The associations are consistent and integrated across all 10 cards rather than being loosely related from card to card. We know of no paranoid record that compares with its level of consistency and integration. It is a considerable feat to integrate all 10 cards into a single body of teaching over and against the varied stimulus-pull of 10 very different cards, and to do so without significant departure in reality testing.

One additional piece of evidence that might speak to the validity of the integrative style is its documentation in other field work. Though, to our knowledge, no other Rorschachs have even been reported for meditation masters, Rorschachs have been reported for advanced teachers from other spiritual traditions. For example, Boyer et al. (1964) administered the Rorschach to Apache shamans. He also collected indigenous ratings on the authenticity of the shamans by having the Indians themselves rate whether they felt a given shaman was real or fake. The Rorschachs of the pseudoshamans looked like pathological records. The records of the shamans rated authentic were atypical. In separate papers, Klopfer and Boyer (1961) and Boyer, Boyer and De Vos (1982) published the protocols of "real" shamans. They are surprisingly similar to our master's Rorschach. The shamans also used the 10 cards as an occasion to teach the examiner about their lived world-views, one about his ecstatic flights through the universe, and the other about her sense of experiencing the psychic functioning of operating as a shaman. The Klopfer-Boyer shaman also relied heavily on shading and amorphously used form. The authors were unclear as to the significance of the shading and saw it as pathological. We are not so sure, especially in light of the high use of shading by our subjects during Samadhi. Shading in very high incidence

---

questions about first or second Path experiences and the author obtained extensive autobiographical accounts of these moments of enlightenment. These are being incorporated in a subsequent study in preparation.

26. Though the author was not allowed to ask the question of attainment directly, data from the case history interview, corroborated by the Rorschach and the additional TAT protocols which were administered in the South Asian study, permits this classification.

for practitioners of altered states may be a valid indicator of the awareness of subtle internal and external nuances in stimuli that is a result of disciplined exploration of these states. The integrative style is perhaps an additional feature of those individuals who have carried their skill to its completion. One possible implication of such cross-cultural similarities is that this style may be suggestive of a "master's Rorschach" regardless of the spiritual tradition.[27] The master is not at all interested in expressing the individual content of his mind to an examiner. Out of compassion, the master is only interested in pointing a way for others to "see" reality more clearly in such a way that it alleviates their suffering. The test situation becomes a teaching situation whereby the examiner becomes a witness to a guided exploration of the transpersonal level of the mind/universe.

A second possible inference from the master's protocol is that intrapsychic structure has undergone a radical enduring reorganization. The protocol shows no evidence of sexual or aggressive drive conflicts, or indeed any evidence of instinctually based drive at all. Remarkable though it may seem, there may be no endopsychic structure in the sense of permanently opposed drives and controls. We assume that "a perfectly mature person" would be "a whole unified person whose internal psychic differentiation and organization would simply represent his diversified interests and abilities, within an overall good ego development and good object-relationships" (Guntrip, 1969).[28]

SUMMARY

These findings of course must be interpreted with some caution due to the influence of expectation effects and demand characteristics. An attempt was made to control for such effects in the data from the *Three Month Study* alone. There, a staff-control group was used based on the assumption that both meditators and staff expect their meditation to work. Differences between the meditators and staff-controls cannot be attributed to expectation alone, but more likely to differences in the amount of daily practice. Though such differences were confirmed, they were limited to the *Three Month Study*. This includes all the subjects in the Beginner's Group and the Samadhi Group, and part of the subjects

---

27. A similar integrative style in response not to Rorschach plates but to ambiguous figures was reported for a shaman in Fiji (Richard Katz, personal communication, August 1979).

28. Guntrip (1969:428) himself however goes on to say that, "We cannot, however, hope for such perfection." The Masters Group in this study suggested that such hope may actually not be misplaced.

in the Insight Group. It does not include subjects in the more interesting Advanced Insight Group and the Master's Group. Thus, because of the limits of data collection, it is impossible to rule out the operation of expectation effects and demand characteristics in these latter enlightened individuals. Still, the general purpose of this study—to illustrate an approach to the empirical validation of the classical scriptural accounts and current reports of meditation attainments using a single instrument, the Rorschach—has been fulfilled. The Rorschachs in the respective criterion groups were so obviously different they merited this report, even without the quantitative data analysis. These Rorschachs illustrate that the classical subjective reports of meditation stages are more than religious belief systems; they may be valid accounts of the perceptual changes that occur with the intensive meditation and these classical reports help us toward the goal of understanding perception and alleviating suffering.

As it happens, in addition to being a personality test, the Rorschach is an excellent measure of perception for such an investigation. Ducey (1975) has argued that the Rorschach is a measure of "self-created reality." The task requires a subject to attribute meaning to a set of ambiguous stimuli. In so doing, the experimenter learns something of how the subject constructs an inner representation of the world. This task is congruent with the meditator's own practice, namely, to analyze the process by which his mind works in creating the internal and external world. Much to our surprise, the unusual performance on these Rorschachs for most subjects seemed to indicate clearly most important changes in mental functioning that occur during the major stages of the meditative path.

To the extent these findings are valid, the prospect of quick advance along the path of meditation is not realistic. Note that after 3 months of continuous, intensive daily practice about half the subjects showed very little change, at least as defined in terms of formal meditation. The other half achieved some proficiency in concentration. Only three perfected access concentration and began to have insights similar to those described in the classical accounts of the insight series of meditations. In turn, only one of these advanced in the insight series to the stage of Equanimity, the stage prior to enlightenment. At least for western students this slow rate of progress is humbling; but it is also consistent with general patterns of growth. It should also inspire confidence. Such unusual and far-reaching transformations of perceptual organization and character structure could not possibly be the work of 3 months or even a year, nor could they be attained by short-cuts without an adequate foundation having been laid first. Patience, forebearance, and a long-enduring mind, or what one master has called "constancy" (Suzuki Roshi, 1970), are listed among the traditional "*paramis*" or "perfections" required of practitioners. On the other hand, the self-reports as well as the test data from both the South Asian and the American study seem to validate the hypothesis that meditation consists of something considerably more than stress-reduction or psychotherapy; its apparent goal-states are commensurate with the effort and perserverance that are undoubtedly required.

Meditation, then, is not exactly a form of therapy but a soteriology, i.e., a means of liberation. It is said to be an extensive path of development that leads to a particular end: total liberation from the experience of ordinary human suffering and genuine wisdom that comes from true perception of the nature of mind and its construction of reality. Western therapy utilizes ideational and affective processes as its vehicle of treatment toward the end of behavioral and affective change. This is *not* so of formal meditation. As seen in the Rorschachs, ideational and affective processes do not even occur to any significant degree during the initial development of samadhi, though much later they re-occur as objects of, not vehicles for, insight. Though meditation concerns itself with a thorough analysis of all mental operations—ideational, affective and perceptual—it is primarily an analysis of perception of the world and how ignorance of perceptual processes contributes to human suffering. Trait transformations are indeed very difficult to achieve.

What does all this mean? In an often quoted statement Freud once said that, at best, therapy can only help the patient exchange his neurotic suffering for ordinary human unhappiness. For Freud, suffering was an unavoidable consequence of various developmental vicissitudes in the origins and resolution of oedipal conflict, with the necessary renunciation of instinctual aims and subsequent compromise formation of the superego. This tendency to view intrapsychic conflict as not only developmentally inescapable but as institutionalized in the final organization of psychic structure was one of Freud's most fateful legacies to psychoanalysis. It has been accepted as a given in clinical thinking and practice. In light of emerging cross-cultural ethnopsychiatric data, one may justly wonder why. Is it one of the limiting assumptions that arise out of a certain paradigm and inhibit further growth of the science?

In recent years there has been a shift of emphasis in clinical theory from psychological illness to psychological health. Even though there is still no clear consensus on a definition of health or normality, there *is* a growing consensus that health is not simply the absence of illness. This was the problem Winnicott once said psychoanalysis had not yet faced: "What is life about, apart from illness?" The Charter of the World Health Organization defines health as "a state of complete physical, mental and social well-being and not merely the absence of infirmity." Freud once described such a norm as an "ideal fiction" because he believed he would find no instances of individuals who embodied it.

Other ethnopsychiatric systems, similar to the one we have investigated here, specify an actual method for its attainment and offer living individuals as evidence. The data of this study is anomalous in terms of most psychiatric and psychological paradigms. But one function of all anomalous findings is to force rethinking of limits, methods, and possibilities. This kind of ethnopsychiatric data suggests that our usual models of mental illness and health may ultimately reflect culture-bound assumptions and a restricted range of population groups and data samples on which our norms have heretofore been based.

Meditation may offer enduring and radical trait benefits only to a very few who attempt its practice, at least under present conditions. Yet, for those of us who have had occasion to come in contact with and study the few masters, like the one whose Rorschach is discussed here, they are indeed unusual and deeply compassionate individuals who appear to stand as rare, living examples of an ideal. The master in this study who completed this course of training is someone who no longer appears to suffer even "ordinary human unhappiness." Might civilization actually be possible, then, *without* discontents?

BIBLIOGRAPHY

AVALON, A. (1931). *The Serpent Power.* Madras: Ganesh & Co.

BINDER, H. (1932). *Die Helldunkeldeutungen in Psychodiagnostischem von Rorschach.* Zürich: Orell Füssli.

BLANCK, G. & BLANCK, R. (1974). *Ego Psychology: Theory and Practice.* New York: Columbia University Press.

_____ (1979). *Ego Psychology II: Psychoanalytic Developmental Psychology.* New York: Columbia University Press.

BOYER, L. B., BOYER, R. M., BRAWER, F. B., KAWAI, H., & KLOPFER, B. (1964a). Apache age groups. *Journal of Projective Techniques and Personality Assessment, 28:337-*342.

BOYER, L. B., BOYER, R. M., & De VOS, G. A. (1982). An Apache woman's account of her recent acquisition of the shamanistic status. *Journal of Psychoanalytic Anthropology,* 5:299-331.

BOYER, L. B., KLOPFER, B., BRAWER, F. B., & KAWAI, H. (1964b). Comparisons of the shamans and pseudoshamans of the Apache of the Mescalero Indian Reservation: A Rorschach study. *Journal of Projective Techniques and Personality Assessment,* 28:173-180.

BROWN, D. P. (1977). A Model for the Levels of Concentrative Meditation. *International Journal of Clinical and Experimental Hyponosis,* 25(4):236-273.

_____ (1981). Mahamudra meditation-stages and contemporary cognitive psychology: a study in comparative hermeneutics. Unpublished Doctoral Dissertation, The University of Chicago, Chicago, Illinois.

_____ , TWEMLOW, S., ENGLER, J., MALISZEWSKI, M., & STAUTHAMER, J. (1978). The Profile of Meditation Experience (POME), Form II. Psychological Test Copyright, Washington, D.C.

CAMPBELL, D. (1975). Degrees of freedom and the case study. In *Qualitative and Quan-*

titative Methods in Evaluation Research, T. Cook & C. Reichardt (eds.). Beverley Hills: Sage Publications.

CARRINGTON, P. & EPHRON, H. S. (1975). Meditation as an adjunct to psychotherapy. New dimensions in psychiatry: A world view. In *The World Biennial of Psychotherapy and Psychiatry,* S. Arieti & G. Chrzamowski (eds.). New York: Wiley, pp. 261-269.

CHOWDURY, U. (1960). *An Indian Modification of the Thematic Apperception Test.* Calcutta: Sree Saraswaty Press Ltd.

CROWNE, D. P. & MARLOWE, D. A. (1960). A new scale of social desirability independent of psychopathology. *Journal of Consulting Psychology,* 24:349-354.

CSIKSZENTMIHALYI, M. (1980). Attention and the structuring of reality. Invited address, Annual Meeting, The Society for Clinical and Experimental Hypnosis, Chicago, Illinois, October 11, 1980.

DASGUPTA, S. (1946). *Obscure Religious Cults.* Calcutta: F.K.L. Mukhopadhyay.

DAVIDSON, R. J., GOLEMAN, D., & SCHWARTZ, G. E. (1976). Attentional and affective concomitants of meditation: a cross-sectional study. *Journal of Abnormal Psychology,* 85:235-238.

DUCEY, C. (1975). Rorschach experiential and representation dimensions of object relations: a longitudinal study. Unpublished Doctoral Dissertation, Harvard University.

ELIADE, M. (1969). *Yoga: Immortality and Freedom.* New York: Bollingen Foundation, Inc.

ENGLER, J. (1981). The vicissitudes of the self according to psychoanalysis and Buddhism, Psychoanalysis and Contemporary Thought. New York: International Universities Press.

EXNER, J. E. (1974). *The Rorschach: A Comprehensive System.* New York: Wiley.

FLAVELL, J. H. (1963). *The Developmental Psychology of Jean Piaget.* Princeton, N.J.

FRANK, J. (1962). *Persuasion and Healing.* New York: Schocken Books.

FREUD, A. (1963). The concept of developmental lines. *The Psychoanalytic Study of the Child,* 18:245-265. New York: International Universities Press.

FROMM, E. F., BROWN, D. P., HURT, S., OBERLANDER, J., PFEIFFER, G., & BOXER, A. (1981). A phenomenological study of self-hypnosis. *International Journal of Clinical & Experimental Hypnosis,* 29(3):189-246.

FROMM, E. F., OBERLANDER, M. I., & GRUNEWALD, D. (1970). Perception and cognitive processes in different states of consciousness: the waking state and hypnosis. *Journal of Projective Techniques & Personality Assessment,* 34:375-387.

GOLDSTEIN, J. (1976). *The Experience of Insight: A Natural Unfolding.* Santa Cruz: Unity Press.

GOLEMAN, D. (1971). Meditation as Metatherapy. *Journal of Transpersonal Psychology,* 3:1-15.

_____ (1972). The Buddha on meditation and states of consciousness. Part I: The Teachings. *Journal of Transpersonal Psychology,* 4:1-44.

_____ (1976). Meditation and consciousness: an Asian approach to mental health. *American Journal of Psychotherapy,* 30:41-54.

_____ (1977). *The Varieties of the Meditative Experience.* New York: Dutton.

_____ & SCHWARTZ, G. E. (1976). Meditation as an intervention in stress reactivity. *Journal of Consulting and Clinical Psychology,* 44:456-466.

GUNTRIP, H. (1969). *Schizoid Phenomena, Object Relations and the Self.* New York: International Universities Press.

HILGARD, E. R. (1970). Issues bearing on recommendations from the behavioral and social sciences study committee. *American Psychologist,* 25(5):456-463.

HOLT, R. & HAVEL, J. (1960). A method for assessing primary and secondary process

224 DANIEL P. BROWN—JACK ENGLER

in the Rorschach. In *Rorschach Psychology,* M. A. Rickers-Ovsiankina (ed.). New York: Wiley.

HSU, F. L. K. (1972). *Psychological Anthropology.* Cambridge: Schenkman.

JAMES, W. (1958). *The Varieties of Religious Experience.* New York: Mentor Books.

KLOPFER, B. & BOYER, L. B. (1961). Notes on the personality structure of a North American Indian shaman: Rorschach interpretation. *Journal of Projective Techniques & Personality Assessment,* 25:170–178.

KORNFIELD, J. M. (1976). The psychology of mindfulness meditation. Unpublished Doctoral Dissertation, The Humanistic Psychology Institute. San Francisco, California.

_____ (1977). *Living Buddhist Masters.* Santa Cruz: Unity Press.

MAHASI SAYADAW (1965). *Progress of Insight.* Kandy: Buddhist Publication Society.

_____ (1972). *Practical Insight Meditation.* Santa Cruz: Unity Press.

MAHLER, M., PINE, F., & BERGMAN, A. (1975). *The Psychological Birth of the Human Infant.* New York: Basic Books.

MAUPIN, E. W. (1965). Individual differences in responses to a Zen meditation exercise. *Journal of Consulting Psychology,* 29:139–145.

MAYMAN, M. (1960). Measuring introversiveness on the Rorschach Test: the fabulization scale. Unpublished Manuscript.

_____ (1970). Reality contact, defense effectiveness and psychopathology in Rorschach form-level scores. In *Developments in the Rorschach Technique III: Aspects of Personality Structure,* B. Klopfer, M. Meyer, & F. Brawer (eds.). New York: Harcourt Brace Jovanovich, pp. 11–46.

MISHRA, R. M. (1963). *Yoga Sutras: The Textbook of Yoga Psychology.* Garden City: Anchor Press, 1963.

NARADA, T. (1975). *A Manual of Abhidhamma.* Kandy: Buddhist Publication Society.

NEISSER, U. (1975). *Cognition and Reality.* Ithaca, New York: Cornell University Press.

NYANAMOLI, B. (1976). *The Path of Purification.* A translation of the *Visuddhimagga* by Buddhaghosa. Berkeley: Shambala.

RAMA, S., BALLENTINE, R., & AJAYA, S. (1976). *Yoga and Psychotherapy.* Glenview, Illinois: Himalayan Institute.

REYHER, J. (1969). Electroencephalogram and rapid eye movements during free imagery and dream recall. *J. Abnorm. Psychol.,* 74:574–82.

SCHACHTEL, E. G. (1966). *Experiential Foundations of Rorschach's Test.* New York: Basic Books.

SIMMEL, E. (1944). Self-preservation and the death instinct. *Psychoanalytic Quarterly,* 13.

SMITH, J. C. (1976). Psychotherapeutic effects of TM with controls for expectation of relief and daily sitting. *Journal of Consulting & Clinical Psychology,* 44:630–637.

SPAIN, D. (1972). On the use of projective tests for research in psychological anthropology. In *Psychological Anthropology,* F.L.K. Hsu (ed.). Cambridge: Schenkman, pp., 267–328.

SPIRO, M. (1965). Religious systems as culturally constituted defense mechanisms. In *Context and Meaning in Cultural Anthropology,* M. Spiro (ed.). Glencoe: Free Press.

SUZUKI ROSHI (1970). *Zen Mind, Beginner's Mind.* New York: Weatherhill.

TART, C. (1975). *States of Consciousness.* New York: E. P. Dutton.

VARENNE, J. (1976). *Yoga and the Hindu Tradition.* Chicago: University of Chicago Press.

WALSH, R. (1977). Initial meditative experiences, Part I. *Journal of Transpersonal Psychology,* 9:151–152.

_____ (1978). Initial meditative experiences, Part II. *Journal of Transpersonal Psychology,* 10:1–28.

WATKINS, J. G. & STAUFFACHER, J. C. (1975). An index of pathological thinking in the Rorschach. In *Handbook of Rorschach Scales,* P. Lerner (ed.). New York: International Universities Press.

WILBUR, K. (1977). *The Spectrum of Consciousness.* Wheaton: Theosophical Publishing House.

ZILBOORG, G. (1938). The sense of immortality. *Psychoanalytic Quarterly,* 7.

PART III

HISTORY

6

Les Sanson: An Oedipal Footnote to the History of France

LAURIE ADAMS

For nearly two centuries capital punishment in France was carried out by six generations of executioners, all members of a single family, les Sanson. The first Sanson to enter this macabre profession, Charles (I), was born in 1635 and the last, Henri-Clement, received notice of his dismissal as executioner on March 18, 1847 (Sanson v. 1, 1876: ix).[1] These same two centuries witnessed the reigns of Louis XIV, XV, and XVI, the French Revolution, and a series of violent political shifts from the Terror to the Second Republic of 1848. It is with the royal family, the ministers, and the parliaments that most history books are concerned. Theirs were the history-making decisions. But on a lower rung of the social ladder is the man who has to carry out the decisions and uphold the laws handed down from above. Such were the Sansons. In killing and torturing, the Sansons were hated and feared. Yet they carried out the law of the land, and the will of the king and his judges. Even after the Revolution, they continued as executioners. The study of the Sansons, therefore, is a study in microhistory which nonetheless mirrors and encapsulates the more monumental events of the period.

This paper will focus on the Paris line of executioners, described in detail in the Sanson family memoirs.[2] Members of this line bore the title, *Monsieur de Paris,* while their relatives functioned as executioners in the

---

1. For introducing me to the Sanson memoirs, I am indebted to Lewis Lapham, former editor of *Harper's Magazine.* For several helpful suggestions in researching this paper, I have to thank not only Lewis Lapham but also Professors John Stead and Donald McNamara of the John Jay College of Criminal Justice (CUNY), N.Y.
2. There is some controversy concerning the authorship of various editions of the memoirs. Nevertheless, their substance is fairly consistent and, as the translator of the English version points out, Henri-Clement Sanson attested to their authenticity. Among the various ghost writers, the following have been advanced: Balzac, L'heritier de l'ain, Gregoire, and d'Olbereuse. See also Christophe, (1960), pp. 12–13, and Sanson v. 1, Introduction.

French provinces. The present discussion is limited to a few of the more salient aspects of this unusual family, without restrictions of historical data in so far as the memoirs themselves are continually interwoven with individual and collective family fantasy. Most of the available data about the Sansons, together with the very subject of execution by decapitation, lends itself to oedipal, rather than pre-oedipal, interpretation. As a result, the following study deals primarily with that stage of development, its later derivative expressions and metaphorical transformations. In addition, historical aspects of capital punishment, torture, and their psychological implications will be considered.

One might wonder how an entire family came to devote itself to such an unappealing profession, handing down the title from father to son. Henri-Clement, the alleged author of the memoirs, refers to his family's occupation in terms of royal succession, calling it a ''regency in the history of the scaffold.'' The family itself, and French society as a whole, acted as though the Sansons had legal claim to what was actually a *de facto* title. Indeed, the French government continued to appoint the eldest son of the reigning executioner to succeed his father. Despite the social and political upheavals of France, no head of state ever tampered with the Sansons' occupation. Although the Sansons occasionally feared that their position would be endangered by political events and/or their own royalist views, such worries always proved groundless. French society treated the family as a single unit, the members of which became taboo.

LES SANSON AND ASPECTS OF TABOO

The Sanson children spent little time in school, where they were treated as pariahs. Before the Revolution, the taboo was quite rigorously enforced, much as those described in primitive cultures, and rarely did a Sanson marry outside the executioner's ranks. Fortunately, since Sansons carried out executions all over France, the family was a large one. Members of the family had to live apart from society and, in some communities, were forced to paint their houses red. They had great difficulty finding lodging. Shopkeepers often refused to sell to them. In addition, anything delivered to the executioner, whether money or a message, was thrown on the ground, forcing him to kneel in order to recover it (Levy, 1976, p. 21).

The ambivalence of this taboo is evident in France's approval of capital punishment on the one hand while, on the other, her executioners lived as outcasts. A further indication of this cultural ambivalence was the fascination for the execution itself. So well attended were the executions that, in Paris, windowsill space was rented out to eager spectators.

The attraction of death by beheading explains, in large part, the repulsion felt for the executioner. Freud has shown that the taboo originates as a superego reaction against a powerful impulse. He further notes liguistic ambivalence in the fact that the very word "taboo" is a variation on certain primal words originally antithetical in meaning—in this case, "sacred" and "unclean" (Freud, 1913, p. 67). The Sanson family was treated in just this way, as sacred in their hold on their profession and as unclean in being avoided and untouchable.

Occasionally a Sanson tried to evade the taboo by educating his son anonymously in the French school system. Such attempts were inevitably doomed to failure as the child's true identity was always discovered. Of all the elder sons, only one declined to follow in his father's footsteps. Louis-Gabriel, son of a provincial executioner, left his parents' house in an attempt (like Oedipus) to escape his destiny. He went to another town, became a locksmith, married, and set up a business. But he sank into poverty because his name discouraged potential clients. Finally, the local government sheltered him in his father's house. The front door was painted red to keep people away (Levy, 1976, pp. 254-255).

This custom reveals yet another aspect of the ambivalence inherent in the taboo. The color red is usually related to the fear of blood. Freud discusses the blood taboo as both a prohibition against killing and a desire to kill. According to Freud, the horror of blood simultaneously prohibits "murder and forms a protective measure against the primal thirst for blood, primeval man's pleasure in killing" (Freud, 1910a, pp. 196-197). By its connection to blood, the red paint serves an apotropaic function. It alerts the passerby to the presence of the executioners (i.e. the killers), unconsciously warning him to avoid exposure to the temptations lurking within his id.

The Sansons responded to society's ambivalent attitude by instituting a reversal of the taboo. For example, they likened their own position to that of royalty; at first glance an unusual response but psychologically appropriate when one considers that the king in many primitive cultures is, indeed, taboo. The Sansons thus denied the degradation imposed on them by society, a degradation exemplified by having to kneel before communications from non-taboo persons. In the assumption of a regal image, the Sansons identified in fantasy with the real royal family, denying and reversing their taboo condition. Their political identification with royalty is further evident in the family claims to noble extraction. They traced the origin of their name, for example, to one "Sanson de Longueval"—from the village of Longval, where a Sanson had actually been no more than the vassal of a local seigneur (Levy, 1976, p. 18). The family also boasted a coat of arms—a broken bell, explained as an image of the name "Sans-son," meaning "without sound."

One Sanson was particularly rigorous in his efforts to legitimize the family position. Charles-Henri, the executioner who presided over the revolutionary scaffold and caused more heads to roll than any of his relatives, was also the Sanson who most energetically insisted on the identification with royalty. The family memoirs relate an incident in which Charles-Henri went to court to protest his taboo status. He had dined with a marquise, introducing himself to her as an *"Officier de Parlément."* Upon discovering that her companion was none other than the executioner of Paris, the marquise was overcome with emotion and washed her hands because Charles-Henri had touched them during dinner. In this reaction, the marquise expressed another aspect of the taboo—namely, its contagious nature. Unknowingly, she had transgressed the taboo, and her immediate need for expiation and cleansing derives from the fear of underlying temptation. The taboo object is avoided, precisely because it represents a wish that has been repressed, and the transgressor is in danger of being reinfected with the revived temptation (Reik, 1964, pp. 63–64).

The outraged marquise sought revenge and petitioned "Parlément" for an apology to be delivered with a rope around Sanson's neck. She further asked that he be identified by some mark or sign so that in the future the public would be able to avoid his company. Unable to find a lawyer, Charles-Henri conducted his own defense. His observations on the indispensable, even honorable, role of the executioner are quite predictable. In his brief to the court, he claims an affinity with the throne, which is protected by his functions as they protect the innocent, purging society of "the monsters who disturb its repose" (Sanson v. 1, 1876, p. 150). He reasserts the hereditary nobility of his family. More interesting psychologically are Sanson's observations on, and objections to, the horror which he and his office arouse in the public. In his defense, he resorts to the example of various Biblical heroes entrusted with executions and compares himself to soldiers and duellists who shed blood with impunity. He concludes by attributing society's repulsion for his office to fancy and prejudice rather than to logic and reason. In this, or course, he is correct; for he has focused on the fundamental ambivalence underlying the taboo. One cannot, however, legislate to the unconscious. The court retired and indefinitely adjourned the case (Sanson v. 1, 1876, p. 158).

In matters of dress, too, Charles-Henri denied his lowly status. He wore blue, corresponding to the color of aristocratic blood and, like the aristocracy, carried a sword. When reprimanded by the Public Prosecutor for this presumption, Charles-Henri adopted a distinctively-cut, green outfit. The result was that it became fashionable to dress à la Sanson (Manceron, 1977, p. 194). With regard to his title, as well as his dress, Charles-Henri wished to reverse his image. To no avail he tried to have the French word for executioner, "bourreau," outlawed since its connotations are extremely derogatory. A lawyer whom he consulted on the matter pointed out, incorrectly, that "bourreau" came from the Latin "borrea" meaning one who whips women. In fact, however, "bourreau" derives from the name of a man whose ownership of a certain property legally obligated him to carry out executions. But Charles-Henri persisted, taking his case as high as the king himself. In the end he was ridiculed and caricatured in the media as a royalist horrified by his own job (Levy, 1976, p. 81).

This tendency to royal pretense, which reaches its peak in the person of Charles-Henri, also pervades the language of the memoirs. These writings are filled with regal metaphor, though here, too, the ambivalence reasserts itself. On the one hand, the author refers to "the curse which had weighed on their race" (Sanson v. 1, 1876, p. x), and confesses to having washed his hands so as never again to be soiled by "the blood of my brethren" (Sanson v. 1, 1876, p. x). On the other hand, however, he speaks of the responsibility of each succeeding generation of Sansons to follow in the family footsteps. He cloaks his own sense of professional destiny in a royal mantle: "The sword of the law," he writes, "was transmitted from generation to generation in my family, as the sceptre in royal races" (Sanson v. 1, 1876, p. xv). Consistent with the royal fantasy of the Sanson family was the realistic circumstance that brought their "reign" over the scaffold to an end. Henri-Clement had no sons to succeed him; he had two daughters. One married a Paris doctor, thereby escaping the Sanson destiny in a way that was only possible for a woman—changing her name through marriage. The other daughter never married.

CHARLES (I) BECOMES AN EXECUTIONER

The events that propelled the first Sanson executioner into his unsavory profession are distinctly susceptible to oedipal interpretation. Like the family's attitude to its position in French society, the oedipal aspects of the way in which Charles (I) entered his profession are largely characterized by the defense of reversal.

Charles was born in 1635 in Abbeville. His brother, Jean-Baptiste, was eleven years his senior. Orphaned quite early, the two boys went to live with their maternal uncle, Pierre Brossier. Pierre's daughter, Colombe, was the same age as Charles. Despite the knowledge that Charles and Colombe had loved each other since childhood, Pierre insisted that his daughter marry Jean-Baptiste who was older and professionally better established than his brother. Disappointed, Charles left for Canada, and Jean-Baptiste, now the husband of Colombe, became blind and paralyzed. Later, Charles heard of Jean-Baptiste's death and returned for Colombe. But she also died.[3] On his way back, Charles was thrown from his horse and knocked unconscious. When he came to, he was found and tended by the Jouënne family. Charles subsequently fell in love with their daughter, Marguerite.

In the first part of the story, the account of Colombe and Jean-Baptiste, Charles Sanson relates what is essentially an oedipal failure on his part. If we reconstruct psychoanalytically his version of events, we encounter a man of twenty who has to yield before his elder brother. It is likely, given the eleven-year age difference between the brothers, that the elder would have assumed a fatherly role toward Charles, even more so since their parents died while they were children. Later, when their uncle ignored the protestations of love between Charles and Colombe, forcing his daughter to marry Jean-Baptiste, Charles' oedipal disappointment was compounded. He was, in effect, betrayed by two older men akin to father imagos who conspired to deprive him of the girl he loved.

In the second part of the story, Charles returns to France after several years abroad. He is now confronted with a repetition of his failure to win Colombe. Between these two romantic attachments to Colombe and Marguerite, Charles both goes away and is knocked unconscious. Dynamically, these two events can be interpreted as symbolizing the repression characteristic of latency that separates the incestuous oedipal love for Colombe from the more mature love for Marguerite. Nevertheless, Marguerite's father, and Marguerite herself, for reasons as yet unknown to Charles, deny him her hand in marriage. At this point, Charles' cousin Paul begins to boast of capturing the most beautiful girl in Dieppe. Charles recognizes the girl in question as Marguerite, for Paul wears a "marguerite" (French for "daisy") in his lapel. Paul's advances, like those of Charles', were unsuccessful. Paul confides to Charles his intention of giving Marguerite a sleeping potion and then raping her. After contemplating this news, Charles takes up his sword and repairs to the Jouënne house. There he finds his cousin with a friend. Charles draws his sword, wounds the would-be rapists, and chases them away. Charles then rapes the sleeping Marguerite himself.

In this highly melodramatic turn of events, Charles acts more assertively in pursuing his love object than he had with Colombe. Where he could not defeat his brother, he now draws his phallic sword and commits the rape himself.

Marguerite's character is endowed with several fairy-tale qualities. When Charles comes to see her after his recovery, she is in her garden.

---

3. See Christophe, ch. 2, for a more extensive account. The original manuscript of Charles (I) in which he describes these events is included in the *Memoirs* v. 1, ch. 2.

He has to observe her through a forest in order to remain hidden. And finally, her sleeping state at the time of the rape suggests the traditional symbolism of virginal latency, followed by sexual awakening like that of Snow White and Sleeping Beauty. These romanticized aspects of the Sanson memoirs, among many others, attest to the high degree of their fantasy content and highlight the combined historical and psychological interplay characteristic of fairy-tales. As a result, the Sanson story lends itself to an analysis of intrapsychic dynamics counterpointing a documentary historical approach. The overall family myth, (Kris, 1975, ch. 14) as well as the personal myth, becomes crucial in understanding the Sansons.

Though endowed with certain qualities of the traditional fairy-tale maiden, Marguerite is socially taboo because she is the executioner's daughter—a fact of which Charles is still ignorant. Marguerite thus shares a taboo condition with the oedipal mother that renders her sexually forbidden to the little boy. After the rape, Marguerite becomes a "fallen woman" thereby assuming the degraded role often assigned to the oedipal mother by her son (Freud, 1910a, p. 165ff). Eventually, Charles discovers the true profession of Marguerite's father. Charles unexpectedly walks in on a scene in which Master Jouënne tortures his daughter in an attempt to make her reveal the name of her seducer. Since she was asleep at the time of the rape, she cannot identify him. When Charles realizes what is going on, he offers to marry Marguerite. Her father agrees on condition that Charles become an executioner (Sanson v.1, 1876, pp. 4-21).

The scene of torture which Charles interrupts is shocking indeed. Like much of the account in Charles' manuscript, this description seems farfetched and fanciful, although when viewed psychologically the direct-displaced oedipal themes are entirely consistent with the manifest narrative. But the story is more complex; it is not only driven by oedipal forces. Marguerite's father, according to the manuscript, pounds nails through a boot into her foot, a standard form of torture during this period of French history. The fact that a father performs the torture on his own daughter however, hints not only at the traditional *"droit de signeur,"* but also at a fantasied, even pre-oedipal distortion of the primal scene. In this version, the image contains the fantasy that the father inflicts bodily harm on the woman during intercourse. It implies the fantasy that the female, in not possessing a penis, has been mutilated. The choice of the foot as the object of torture simultaneously recalls the early oedipal fantasy of the phallic mother. The element of unexpected interruption is also characteristic of both the typical traumatic primal scene and Charles Sanson's account. Finally, in rescuing Marguerite, Charles carries out that aspect of the oedipal fantasy in which the boy rescues his mother from what he believes to be the abuse of his father. In addition, the incestuous nature of this particular primal scene imagery (i.e., father and daughter) seems to prefigure the later historical reality of the Sanson family whose members were forced by their taboo condition to intermarry.

In assuming his father-in-law's profession, Charles is, in effect, pursuing his oedipal destiny of identification with the only "positive" father figure of his life. His own father (together with his mother), deserted him by dying, his uncle by denying him the hand of Colombe, and his elder brother by taking the hand of Colombe. Only Master Jouënne gives Charles access to a female love object. The castration symbolism inherent in Jouënne's profession corresponds with the oedipal boy's fantasy that his father's retaliation will take that form. Charles' implicit identification with the father-figure aggressor serves to ward off this threat, and puts him in a similarly castrating position, prefigured when he draws his sword and wounds his cousin, Paul. This action, in turn, may be seen as a symbolic repetition of what Charles must have *wished* to do when his brother took Colombe and earlier, when his father was sole possessor of his mother.

The hostile nature of Charles' wish is incorporated into his brother's name, John the Baptist, the Biblical figure who really did lose his head. Another aspect of the parallel between John the Baptist in the Bible and the story of Charles Sanson is the forbidding role of both the Baptist who condemned incest between Herod and Herodias, also first cousins, and Jean-Baptiste whose marriage to Colombe ended her "romance" with her own cousin Charles.[4] Clearly, these romantic situations in which Charles finds himself are all variations on the family romance theme. The outcome, however, unlike that of the typical family romance, is that he becomes an executioner instead of a king. Later on, the family romance seems to reassert itself in the royal pretensions of the Sansons, particularly those of Charles-Henri.

The multiple overdeterminism in both the family romance theme and the parallels with John the Baptist is characteristic of the Sanson memoirs. Like the repressed that returns, written records indicate that the Sansons and their contemporaries occasionally changed the first "*n*" of their name to an "*m*", thereby identifying themselves as "*Samson*" (Levy, 1976, pp. 123-124; France, 1912, p. 212). Again we find an unwitting reference to a well-known Biblical story of romance and symbolic

---

4. Freud cites a more recent example of oedipal fantasy paralleling the Biblical story of John the Baptist. In this case, a five-year old boy of Freud's acquaintance, angry at his father's return from the war, dreamed that his father was carrying his own head on a plate (Freud, 1900, p. 366).

castration. By virtue of the mechanism of upward displacement, Samson was symbolically castrated when Deliah cut off his hair and deprived him of his strength.[5] Later, Samson suffers a second symbolic castration when blinded by the Philistines. The sexual symbolism of the eye has been described by Ferenczi, (*Sex and Psychoanalysis,* pp. 228-233), and George Devereux (1973, pp. 36-49) has demonstrated on philological as well as on psychoanalytic grounds that the self-blinding of Oedipus represented castration. In the light of the eye's phallic association, it is interesting that neither French kings nor their legitimate children were allowed to wear eye-glasses until after 1830 (Manceron, 1977, p. 61). To do so would have implied an admission of physical weakness symbolically related to sexual impotence and thus unacceptable to an absolute monarch expected to produce an heir.

When Charles Sanson succeeds his father-in-law as executioner, he is at once identifying with him and also projecting his unconscious wish for castrating revenge against him—against his brother, uncle, cousin, and ultimately his own real father who died (and took his mother away). This repetition within his immediate family is surely reflected by the repeated beheadings that Charles was destined to perform for society.

Charles did marry Marguerite, only to have her die soon afterwards in childbirth. Their son, Charles (II), succeeded his father as executioner, and moved to Paris. In 1688, Charles (II) received his official appointment to *"l'état d'exécuteur des hautes oeuvres et sentences criminelles de nôtre dite ville, prévôste et vicomte de Paris...."* He was given no salary but he exercised the *"droit de havage,"* the right to take whatever he could carry from shops and markets. In fact, though, he took the goods not with his hands, which were considered stained with blood, but with a scoop.

AMBIVALENCE WITHIN THE FAMILY

Once Charles accepted the role of executioner, the Sanson fate was sealed. With relentless and unconsciously determined force, the Sansons bowed to all the demands of their destiny. They lived apart from French society despite repeated efforts to legitimize their position and reaffirm their claim to normal humanity.

The effect of the father's profession on the family life of the Sansons was extreme. Wives had to be chosen from within the ranks of France's

---

5. Cf. Freud (1900, p. 367) for a dream relating hair cutting to castration. Cf. also Kahr, (1972), for representations of Samson and Delilah in Renaissance and Baroque paintings.

executioners. The children were raised within the family circle and sometimes were introduced to the scaffold at a remarkably early age. One child officially obtained his father's position at the age of seven. Charles-Henri officiated for the first time at an execution at sixteen.

Implicit in the Sanson saga is the important role of the mother, although the Sanson women are not accorded as much attention in the literature as the men. In the absence of the relevant data, therefore, the present discussion deals primarily with the oedipal aspects of the family. One notable exception to this inattention was Marthe Dubut, wife of Charles (II) and mother of Jean-Baptiste Sanson (II). Marthe ruled her family with an iron hand, while transferring her ambitions narcissistically onto the Sanson men. She, more than any other, secured the Sanson's "hereditary" claim to the title of executioner. Charles (II)'s choice of this type of woman as a wife is perhaps related to the absence of his own mother, Marguerite, who died in childbirth. His father did not remarry until he was sixty-four. Charles was twenty-six when his father died and eight days later, he married Marthe. Marthe was also his step-mother's sister and thus literally as well as psychologically something of a mother substitute.

Charles (II) was the only Sanson who never openly expressed shame for his profession and, together with Marthe, he arranged for their son, Jean-Baptiste, to receive an official appointment as his successor—at the age of seven. From then on, Jean-Baptiste had to validate every execution by his presence at the scaffold. Perhaps another indication of Marthe's perverse determination appears in the very name given to her son, recalling both his father's uncle and the beheaded saint of the Bible. Dynamically, it would seem as though Marthe's sadistic castrating nature was revealed in the naming of her son while the denial of the wish persisted in the reverse—turning *him* into a beheader. In addition, the Sanson memoirs indicate that Marthe occupied a dual role of wife and mother to Jean-Baptiste, noting that after her husband's death, she sat opposite her son at all family dinners (Sanson v. 2, 1876, p. 142). Mother and son thus presided together in a manner usually reserved for married couples. Nor was Marthe's decapitating zeal confined to her son. When he retired, she repeated the favor for her grandson, Charles-Henri, by securing his official appointment when he was fifteen. When, a year later, he had to carry out his first execution, Marthe arrived at the scaffold to insure his success. Later, in 1757, when Damiens was sentenced to torture and death for the attempted assassination of Louis XV, even Charles-Henri faltered. He confessed to his grandmother that he was not up to the task, whereupon she summoned her other son from the provinces to act as substitute. She is reputed to have been very pleased that there were now *two* Sansons at the scaffold. Eventually, however,

Charles-Henri would have his day. He was destined to inherit the epithet, *"clef-voûte de la Revolution."*

Despite the apparent acceptance of their gory profession by most Sansons, the unconscious guilt accompanying it is evident in two characteristics that persisted from one generation to the next. Nearly all the executioners suffered some form of physical paralysis or other symbolically similar conversion symptom. This tendency appeared in the blindness and paralysis of Colombe's husband, Jean-Baptiste, even before the Sansons became executioners. Charles (I) came to tremble at the sight of blood, and *his* son, Charles (II), retired at forty-six because of poor health. Jean-Baptiste, Charles (I)'s son by Marthe Dubut, suffered an attack at thirty-five that paralyzed his right side. Even Charles-Henri, "keystone of the Revolution," tried to resign in favor of his son on grounds of poor health, but his request was ignored. His youngest son, Gabriel, was killed falling from the scaffold while showing a decapitated head to the crowd. At the height of the Terror, Charles-Henri, then aged fifty-five, again indicated that he was tired of his job. At last his gruesome tasks seemed to overwhelm him. His hands began to shake so much that he had to omit the pre-decapitation custom of cutting the victim's hair (Sanson v. 2, 1876, p. 171). On one occasion, according to his diary, he had to execute a young girl and he hallucinated blood on his dining room tablecloth (Sanson v. 2, 1876, p. 175).

Charles-Henri sent his eldest son, Henri, to be educated in the country under the name "de Longval." This plan to free Henri of the family's reputation miscarried when the son's true identity was discovered. Henri then joined the National Guard, hoping to avoid his destiny. Ulitmately, he resigned himself to his fate. By fifty-two, Henry developed pleurisy and *his* son, Henri-Clement, author of the memoirs, took over the family profession. Henri-Clement was twenty, as was his first victim. So anxious that he was unable to climb the scaffold, Henri-Clement stood below while an aide carried out the execution. Contemporary accounts describe the young Henri-Clement trembling as though the blade were falling on his own neck (Levy, 1976, p. 226). Of all the Sansons, the last was most outspoken in his guilt. Not only did he assemble the family memoirs, but he contracted an unhappy marriage and led a life of gambling and debauchery (Levy, 1976, p. 79).

In addition to their many physical symptoms, the self-destructive life of Henri-Clement, and even the death of Gabriel in 1792, the Sanson family displayed a curious form of rationalization: they all practiced medicine. In this activity, it would seem, they hoped to compensate for the executions. Through medicine, the Sansons found a kind of atonement for the (denied) guilt of their profession. The Sanson tendencies for somatization and the practice of medicine reflect the intense physical nature of the activity being denied. In the former case, the guilt is turned inward on the executioner's own body and expressed in physical symptoms, hallucinations, even "accidental" death. In the latter, the destruction itself is denied by the actualization of its opposite, healing, in the community. These typical defenses of reaction formation and conversion symptomatology, impelled by the executioner's guilt, are exemplified most vividly by the behavior of Charles-Henri.

As with everything else, Charles-Henri practiced denial with a greater flourish than his predecessors and successors. He sold the corpses of his victims to surgeons, thereby both enriching himself and furthering the cause of science. Also self-enriching was his reputed arrangement with Marie Grosholtz, the future Mme. Tussaud of the famous London waxworks, who made death masks of Charles-Henri's most famous victims. On the surface, he appeared to be most favorably inclined toward his job. It would seem, however, that he only proved to have erected the strongest defense, by denial. He tried vigorously to elevate the status of his job—in his dress, his court brief, etc.—and yet Charles-Henri forbade any mention of his profession at home (Levy, 1976, p. 79).

Perhaps the most striking evidence of Charles-Henri's unconscious conflicts emerged in his response to the beheading of Louis XVI. On January 21, 1793, Charles-Henri executed the king of France. The scaffold was moved to the Place de la Concorde for the occasion. Composed, exacting, and thorough as Charles-Henri was reported to have been by eye-witnesses, his internal reactions were otherwise. Every evening thereafter, Charles-Henri did penance. He knelt before the blade of the Guillotine and prayed for Louis's soul.

We can see parallels in this activity to the origins of certain religions. Freud has pointed out the sequence of killing, guilt, and atonement both in primitive religious practices and in Christianity itself (Freud, 1913). That the victim of the original killing is typically a father or father figure is consistent both with the underlying oedipal fantasy and with Louis's historical position as king of France. "God the Father," writes Freud, "once walked upon the earth in bodily form and exercised his sovereignty as chieftain of the primal horde until his sons united to slay him" (Freud, 1919b, p. 262). These events seem to be reenacted in the death of the French king. The bloodthirsty revolutionary uprising against Louis XVI and its accompanying massacres correspond to Freud's hypothetical organization of the cannibalistic primal horde brothers.

In the origin of religion as described by Freud (1913), the brothers atone for their act by making the dead father into a god. In France, a similar intense ambivalence is evident in subsequent historical turmoil—from the Terror to the Second Republic. Charles-Henri Sanson, who actually carried out the execution, atoned for his deed by establishing a private obsessional "religion," making a god out of his victim. It was one of the executioner's prerogatives to sell the clothing of his victims. At Louis's execution, Sanson is reported to have done just that. He also allegedly auctioned off his hat to the crowd (Jordan, 1979, p. 220). The parallel with the Roman soldiers who crucified Christ and then "parted his garments, casting lots" (*Matthew* 27:35), could not have escaped a devout Catholic like Sanson, thereby reinforcing his need to atone.

The conscious and unconscious motivations underlying Charles-Henri's private religion were not far removed from prevailing cultural notions of kingship prior to the French Revolution. Basic to the divine right of kings was the belief in the godlike nature of the monarch (Walzer, 1974, p. 17). In a metaphor of the body image, this concept was applied to the state. The king was the head of state and also the anatomical head of the body politic. The revolution thus decapitated more than a man called "king," it decapitated the state itself. The body metaphor was further expanded to include the Church. As an illustration of this point, Michael Walzer cites King James's "I am the husband, and all the whole land is my lawful wife," noting the derivation of such statements from Christ's mystical marriage to the Church (Walzer, 1974, p. 17). Just as Christ healed the multitudes, the kings of France, and other nations, were believed to possess magic curative power. The ideological connection between being a Christian king and a *"roi medecin"* was evident in the ritual "healing" by the mere touch of the king of thousands stricken with scrofula, a form of tuberculosis popularly called "the King's Evil." Louis XVI touched some twenty-four hundred scrofula victims on the day after his consecration in 1775 (Walzer, 1974, p. 20). Just as the king's touch was imbued with the power to heal, the executioner's touch had the reverse effect, namely spreading the contagion associated with his taboo status.

The king was also Christ-like by virtue of his connections with the sun around which revolves the universe. This is a traditional association covered by a vast literature.[6] Suffice it to say, in the Versailles of Louis XIV this connection was most splendidly celebrated. He called his throne room the *Salon d'Apollon* and his emblem of the sun darting its rays upon the world became a standard feature of the royal iconography

---

6. For an entire volume of studies of the sun's symbolic implications for ancient Egypt to the 19th century, see *Le Soleil à la Renaissance,* Presses universitaires de Bruxelles, Brussels (1965). On solar imagery in connection with Christ and kings see Lord (1976), ftns. 17, 18, 23). Cf. also Freud (1911), in which the rays of the sun act as impregnators sent by God the Father. Cf. also the relief sculptures of Akhenaton's reign in which the sun and its rays represent the god Aten.

(Voltaire, 1961, pp. 269-270; Blunt, 1953, p. 337). In a conscious imitation of the sun, the kings of France performed a daily ritual of rising and
setting. Therefore, when Charles-Henri Sanson executed Louis XVI, he
was not killing an ordinary criminal. He was killing an idea, a sym-
bology, an entire set of political, religious, and psychological concepts
that had prevailed for centuries. Unlike the aftermath of an assassination, there would be no heir to replace the dead king. "For all effects and
purposes," writes Walzer (1974, p. 26), "the revolution marks the end of
political fatherhood."

In Charles-Henri's prayer before the blade of the Guillotine, various
levels of the psychological history of the Sanson family were condensed
with certain universal historical fantasies about kings, gods, and fathers
into a private, obsessional religion. As a historical postscript, the Restoration (1815-1830) created a martyr cult out of Louis XVI's death.
January 21 was declared a national day of mourning and Louis's will was
the sacred text read at the official ceremony (Jordan, 1979, ch. XIII).

An Uncanny Profession

In October, 1830, Victor Hugo spoke against the death penalty in
Parliament, referring to the executioner as *"mal à l'aise au soleil du
juillet comme un oiseau de nuit en plein jour...."* (Levy, 1976, p. 236).
Later in the same speech, Hugo compares the executioner with a mouse
living in a dark hole, daring to come out only when the coast is clear
(Levy, 1976, p. 236). In these images, Hugo captures the subhuman,
shadowy, and hidden nature of the executioner who is associated with
qualities of darkness and night. As a sinister creature of the shadows, the
executioner assumes characteristics described by Freud in his essay, "The
Uncanny" (Freud, 1919a, pp. 219-256). Referring to the German word
"unheimlich" (meaning "unhomely"), Freud relates the uncanny to that
which is frightening and arouses a sense of "dread and horror" (Freud,
1919a, p. 219). Two themes from this complex essay are particularly relevant to an understanding of the executioner's character.

According to Freud, one of the most convincing ways to arouse feelings of the uncanny is to blur the boundaries between human and non-
human, the word he uses for the latter being "automaton" (Freud,
1919a, p. 227). The resulting uncertainty derives from childhood when
distinctions between living and inanimate objects are fluid (Freud,
1919a, p. 233). Dolls, as Freud notes, are a case in point, since children
use them to dramatize their ambivalent feelings. Subsequently, in adult
life, if this ambivalence is revived, a sense of the uncanny may result.
With regard to the horror inspired by the executioner's presence, as in

the instance of the marquise who unwittingly dined with Charles-Henri, an element of uncanniness is evoked. The sense of horror was intensified by the belief that Sanson carried out his duties without human emotion, as "automaton."

In at least two ways, dolls are related to the history of the scaffold in France and are specifically connected with the uncanny. Mme. Tussaud used the decapitated heads of Charles-Henri's victims to make death masks. In the adult response to her wax-work figures, which appeal to fantasies of mastering death, the line between life and death becomes blurred. A similar mechanism at a different level is apparent in ancient Egyptian techniques for preserving the material likeness of the deceased's face and body. The impact of the wax-works, like an encounter with the grave, may be expected to arouse an almost inevitable sense of the uncanny.[7]

Another episode in the scaffold's history dates from the invention of the Guillotine, when women began wearing Guillotine earrings and pendants, and children played with toys modelled after it. The games included little dolls in the image of decapitated celebrities who "lost their heads" in effigy. Some dolls were manufactured with a sweet red liqueur that flowed from the severed neck. Women would dip their handkerchiefs in the liquid (an activity replete with castration and cannibalistic symbolism), playing with the boundaries between life and death and thus arousing feelings of the uncanny. As the distinction between life and death was blurred, so too was the boundary between opposing factions that represented the ambivalence toward the entire subject and the methods of capital punishment. Perhaps because such a condition of blurring cannot long be tolerated, any more than we can exist in a continual state of dread and horror, one side of the ambivalence quickly reasserted itself. Joseph Guillotin, the doctor originally honored for his humane invention, ended by attracting the same hostility as the Sansons, taking its ignominy with him into posterity (Levy, 1976, pp. 107-108).

The second related theme which Freud discusses in his essay, has to do with another, opposite meaning of "uncanny," namely, "that which is familiar." In a popular sense, Freud means "familiar" as something from the past that comes back to haunt. Psychodynamically, however, he means a childhood past in which wishes, fears, and reality were interwoven, particularly with the idea of castration. The Sand Man is uncanny (Freud, 1919a, p. 227), for example, since it is he who tears out children's eyes as a poetic substitution for the castrating father. Similar-

---

7. A similar feeling is experienced by readers of Ira Levin's novel, *The Stepford Wives*, a story about women who are murdered and replaced by life-like robots who perform all the useful functions of the living women but do not react with the full range of human emotion. They are, in effect, automatons.

ly, fear of the evil eye and dismembered limbs, especially those that have
the power to move, can arouse the feeling of uncanniness (Freud, 1919a,
240-244). In this latter instance, we may be reminded of certain contemporary accounts of Sanson beheadings in which the decapitated head
seemed to express life-like emotion or the headless body trembled as if it
were still alive (Cf. the uncanny feelings aroused by Washington Irving's
Headless Horseman). In a humorous play on this theme, a patriot in
Anatole France's novel of revolutionary France, *Les Dieux Ont Soif,*
describes a political rival as one whom he would enjoy watching sneeze in
Sanson's basket.[8]

The connection of the executioner who beheads with the fantasied
castrating father of childhood is suggested by Victor Hugo's image of the
executioner as a creature of the night. For it is at night—when the visual
boundaries really are blurred—that the child's sexual fears (and wishes)
are likely to be most compelling. It is also at night that the child is most
likely to encounter the parental sexual activity that stimulates these
fears and wishes. Freud concludes his discussion thus: "An uncanny experience occurs either when infantile complexes which have been repressed are once more revived by some impression, or when primitive
beliefs which have been surmounted seem once more to be confirmed"
(Freud, 1919a, p. 249).

CONCLUSION ON AN OEDIPAL NOTE

In the history of France, as elsewhere, there was a progressive decrease
in the severity of corporal punishment. It is in the spirit of traditional
historical scholarship to underplay the inner psychological motivations
of history makers. Psychohistorians, on the other hand, are likely to be
accused of the reverse, of over-emphasizing the psychological
significance of an event without adequately taking into account external
issues. History is made by a constant interplay between these two currents so that neither may be discounted. While approaching French
history from the vantage point of the scaffold, we encounter a recorded
incident that highlights the connection between external social and
political upheavals and underlying oedipal and pre-oedipal forces.

In August, 1788, Charles-Henri Sanson was ordered to torture a man
named Louschart on the wheel. Louschart, a young revolutionary, had
decided to marry. His father, a staunch royalist, decided that *he* would
marry his son's fiancee in order to punish his son for his revolutionary

---

8. Cf. Anatole France, p. 212: *"Celui qui parle ainsi," s'écria-t-il, "est un f....aristo-
crate, que j'aurais plaisir à voir étérnuer dans le panier à Samson."*

ideas. An argument ensued in which Louschart's father threatened him with a hammer. Louschart wrested the hammer from his father and turned to leave. Just as he was going out the door, Louschart tossed the hammer over his shoulder, accidently hitting and killing his father (Levy, 1976, p. 86).

The predominating oedipal implications of this event in which father and son compete for the same woman are thinly disguised by the "accidental" nature of the father's death. That the French court recognized, at least unconsciously, the purposefulness of the impulse to kill the father is evident in its verdict. Throughout classical mythology too, one encounters examples of accident as a disguise for unconscious intent. Thus Oedipus killed Laius, though without "knowing" him to be his father. Perseus "accidently" killed his grandfather, Akrisios, by hitting him with a discus in the midst of an oedipal web of events. The popular English phrase, "to do something accidentally on purpose," speaks to the same issue.

With Louschart, the story's oedipal features parallel the political conflict between the revolutionary and the royalist factions of French society. The social implications of this event are visible in the public's reaction to it. For the first time in centuries, a group of men destroyed the scaffold, attacked the executioner, and set free his prisoner (Levy, 1976, p. 86). Charles-Henri barely escaped the angry crowd which broke up the wheel of torture and the scaffold and set them both on fire. The king pardoned Louschart. But the sentiments that would spark the Revolution less than twelve months later were already beyond containment. The unwitting oedipal nature of Louschart's crime and the harsh punishment meted out to him thus coincided with the broader social and political upheavals of the times. The unprecedented public reaction against his punishment reflects a more general repulsion for the repressive character of the monarchy and, as such, was one factor which prefigured the French Revolution.

APPENDIX: ON THE SYMBOLISM OF TORTURE

On a broad social level, the story of the Sanson family offers a unique view of the history of capital punishment and some of its accessory tortures in France. That the oedipal fantasy informs much of this history is apparent both from certain pre-decapitation rituals and the punishments reserved for parricides and regicides. However, in these too, since all murder victims were not equal, an underlying ambivalence may be suspected. Fathers and rulers were, in effect, the most important victims, a fact that derives from their unconscious totemistic role.

In June, 1791, France abolished torture and decreed that all capital punishment would be carried out by beheading. By the middle of the following century, France, like most of Europe, would see a major change in styles of punishment. Torture as a public spectacle would disappear and the body would cease to be the "major target of penal repression" (Foucault, 1979, pp. 7-8). Concurrent with this development was a decline in, and eventual elimination of, torture focusing on physical mutilations. Michel Foucault has discussed some of these developments in the French system of punishment, emphasizing the changing role of the king as sovereign power (Foucault, 1979, chs. 1 and 2). This change is also fraught with oedipal overtones, the understanding of which may serve to elucidate some aspects of the importance of the French Revolution for modern history.

According to Foucault, since every crime ultimately represented a rebellion against the person of the monarch, the punishment had to assume appropriate retaliatory form. "In the darkest region of the political field," writes Foucault, "the condemned man represents the symmetrical, inverted figure of the king" (1979, p. 29). He compares the public execution to a joust in which the executioner functions as the king's companion (1979, p. 52). The public nature of the execution and torture was intended to prevent future crime by example, becoming a ceremony which combined the crime itself with the "sovereign power that mastered it" (Foucault, 1979, p. 93). On the individual level, the parallel of this custom with the process of symptom formation and dreaming reveals itself in the condensation of id wish and superego punishment. As long as the crime was considered a personal attack on the king's body, the punishment had to be directed against the body of the perpetrator. In another sense, it could be said that primitive oedipal talion law still dominated the penal system. The end of sovereign vengeance in France roughly corresponds to the era of the Revolution (Foucault, 1979, pp. 73-74), when the body of the criminal ceased to be royal property and became the property of society (Foucault, 1979, p. 107).

These changes in French history evolve as king and God (represented by Church power) are forced to yield some of their authority to a broader social base. By 1905, France passed a law asserting the separation of Church and State, more than a century after the first and most important deposition of the earthly monarch. If we take France as an example, the implications of these events could be extended to a larger psychohistorical scale, though this would go beyond the scope of this paper. Suffice it to point out that there appears to be a parallel between authoritarian kingship, fanatical state religions, and punishment of criminals by physical mutilation. Thus, one finds that the evolution of punishment typically develops from private vengeance into public justice, from family blood feuds into central social authority (Imbert and Levasseur, 1972, pp. 10-14). Ancient Greek law exempted free men from torture; slaves were regarded as things,[9] i.e., property, like the prerevolutionary criminal in France. The penal law of the Roman Republic (from the 3rd century B.C.) abolished talion punishment and mutilation. They were revived in the 3rd century A.D. by the Empire (Imbert and Levasseur, 1972, p. 276) and reappeared in western feudal society. Even these scant examples seem to indicate the operation of primitive oedipal talion fantasies within those penal codes that officially sanction torture and mutilation.

To return to the example of France, a close look at the prerevolutionary mutilations and tortures reveals that they were as imbued with unconscious castration symbolism as decapitation itself (Freud, 1922, p. 273ff). This symbolism was reinforced by the intimate legal relationship between the type of crime committed and the social position of criminal and victim. Under the early French kings, for example, feared high personages could not be killed but could be blinded by the princes. The paranoid process underlying this custom suggests early childhood, when being seen or caught outright invokes real or fantasied punishment. The eye of the feared person is the offending organ which sees the bad behavior, as parents were once magically believed to know children's thoughts and thus to have power over them. Such narcissistic magic derives from a pre-oedipal past just as in the history of the French penal code the custom of blinding dates back to the earliest recorded kings. At a later stage of individual development, the eye may become attached to fantasies of phallic power and blinding to castration—whence the origin of the "evil eye." Indeed, in antiquity, erect stone phalli were often displayed before entrances as apotropaia against the evil eye.

Other mutilations than blinding, such as the removal of the tongue for blasphemy—speech against God and thus against the father—represent psychic parallels to blinding. In each case, an organ with phallic associations is removed in retaliation for offenses against powerful and important figures. The punishment of extracting Jews' teeth to force them to give up their gold contains the unconscious phallic symbolism of money. The phallicism of money is also elucidated by the similar etymology of the words "execute" and "executive," both from the Latin "ex(s)equi," meaning "to follow out" or "carry into effect." Thus, when an executive "axes" an employee, he deprives him of his power to earn money. Another derivative meaning of the word "axe" is "to

9. Cf. Imbert and Levasseur (1972, p. 169). This was more theoretical than actual as there were also instances of free men being tortured in ancient Greece.

economize,'' or "save money,'' while a "battle axe'' is a castrating, usually phallic, woman. In a similar manner, in old French law, the Jews lost their teeth while noblemen were deprived of their swords, by comparison a relatively mild form of symbolic castration.

The ritual cutting of the victim's hair prior to decapitation was rationalized as facilitating the work of the executioner. That this custom was more of a rite than an expedience is evident from the fact that Louis XVI was denied permission to cut his own hair in prison. He was told instead that it would be done by Sanson on the scaffold (Jordan, 1979, pp. 216–219).

The Guillotine was invented just before the Revolution and was considered a more humane way to die than by the axe. Not only was the blade more efficient because it was mechanized, it was also more democratic. Nevertheless, despite this socalled "civilized" advance, the associations to primitive aggressive castration fantasy relentlessly emerged. The hole through which the condemned placed his head, for example, was popularly called the "widow's window" (Jordan, 1979, p. 220). This term implies that only men were executed and thus is a reflection of the castration fantasy rather than the reality of the Guillotine's victims, many of whom, especially during the Revolution, were women. The very image of the hole itself, and the blade that severs head from neck, suggests an upwardly displaced version of the *vagina dentata* fantasy—even more so as "Guillotine" is a feminine noun in French.

A more disguised connection with castration symbolism appears in the pre-revolutionary punishment in which the left ear of a first offender was removed. Since the left ear was associated with the sexual organs, its removal was believed to render procreation impossible and thus prevent the recurrence of criminal tendencies in the next generation (Levy, 1976, p. 25). This curious belief is a condensation of several traditional Christian ideas with the unconscious mechanism of upward displacement that also accounts for the decapitation = castration equation. Ernest Jones (v. 2, 1964, pp. 266–357) has discussed the popular Christian notion current during the Middle Ages and Renaissance that Mary was impregnated through the ear by God's word, via the Holy Ghost. Thus, in many paintings of the *Annunciation,* the words of the Holy Ghost are literally (and concretely) represented on the picture plane emerging from the phallic dove into Mary's receptive ear (often the right one).

Developmentally, the concrete power of the word, like the belief in the omnipresent parental eyes, resides in an early, pre-genital level of fantasy which, at a later stage, becomes attached to the phallus. Hence the combination of word and phallus in the iconography of the *Annunciation.* Also incorporated in the removal of the left ear are traditional notions of left and right which predate Christianity—cf. Latin for "left" is "sinister"—and which were subsequently absorbed into the metaphor of Christian theology. To sit on the right hand of God, for example, denotes being saved while the Devil is likely to appear on one's left side. In Christian art, the *Last Judgment* scene is generally organized to correspond with the right-left fantasy so that the saved souls are on Christ's right while the damned are on his left. The sinful connotations of sex in Christianity are clearly related to the removal of the left ear as well as to certain less radical practices. It is still customary, for example, in predominately Catholic France, for the schools to try to change left-handed children over to right-handedness. Thus, the French word for law, "droit," also means "right," which brings us back to our subject.

It is surely significant that the French punishments for parricide and regicide assumed slightly different—and more severe—forms than those for other murders. Since all murder victims are equally dead, the laws against the perpetrator of parricide and regicide must reflect an unconscious communal sense of guilt for the very impulse that the laws attempt to control. Before the abolition of torture, parricides and regicides were drawn and quartered and then beheaded. Article 13 of the French penal code decreed that a parricide be led to the scaffold barefoot and in shirt-sleeves. In addition, his right hand would be cut off and his head covered with a black cloth (Levy, 1976, p. 231). It is evident from this parade of tortures for parricides and regicides, that the castration displacements were greatly multiplied. This increases both in the number and severity of their punishments, in the light of their unconscious connection to castration, points to the aggressive oedipal aspects of the crimes and the talion nature of the community's retaliation against them. The penal code thus assumes a cultural equivalent of the role of the harsh superego whose character derives in part from the child's fantasy of talion punishment for his repeated infantile aggressive impulses toward his father.

Another significant aspect of the punishment of parricides is the requirement that their heads be covered with a black cloth. In this custom, the parricide is symbolically deprived of his identity. The executioner himself was also a remarkably anonymous figure, reinforced in that character by his taboo status. This anonymity pervades the more general character of the executioner throughout European imagery. In this absence of identity, actual executioners are the equivalent of externalized cultural forms of death images as, for example, in Ingmar Bergman's film, *The Seventh Seal*. In addition, as has been described above, the executioner was depicted typically as sinister, brutal, and devoid of normal human emotions. In the particular case of the Sansons, Levy (1976, p. 229) attributes their safety during the extreme political shifts during and after the French Revolution to precisely this denial of their human condition. Hand in hand with this denial went the assumption that the Sansons had no social or political views although, in fact, they leaned toward the monarchy. Levy (1976, p. 191) notes that despite the increasing notoriety of Charles-Henri during the Revolution, there is not a single reliable likeness of him among the many drawings, engravings, paintings, etc. of that period. In contemporary accounts, he is referred to as "le bourreau," contrary to his own attempts to have that term outlawed. Even later, his grandson, Henri-Clement, became something of a celebrity among certain social liberals like Balzac, Dumas, and Benjamin Appert, who wanted to abolish capital punishment. Nevertheless, the visual anonymity persisted.

BIBLIOGRAPHY

BLUNT, A. (1953). *Art and Architecture in France 1500–1700*. London: Penguin Books.
CHRISTOPHE, R. (1960). *Les Sanson, Bourreaux de Père en Fils pendant deux siècles*. Paris: Fayard.
DEVEREUX, G. (1973). The self-blinding of Oidipous in Sophokles: *Oidipous Tyrannos*. *Journal of Hellenic Studies* XCIII:36–49.
FERENCZI, S. (no date). On eye symbolism. *Sex and Psychoanalysis*. New York: Dover.
FOUCAULT, M. (1979). *Discipline and Punishment*. New York: Vantage.
FRANCE, A. (1912). *Les Dieux Ont Soif*. Paris: Calmann-Levy.
FREUD, S. (1900). The *interpretation of dreams*. *S.E.*, 5. London: Hogarth Press.
_____ (1910a). The taboo of virginity. *S.E.*, 11. London: Hogarth Press.
_____ (1910b). A special type of object choice made by men. *S.E.*, 11. London: Hogarth Press.
_____ (1911). Psycho-analytic notes on an autobiographical account of a case of paranoia. *S.E.*, 12. London: Hogarth Press.
_____ (1913). Totem and Taboo. *S.E.*, 13. London: Hogarth Press.
_____ (1919a). The uncanny. *S.E.*, 17. London: Hogarth Press.
_____ (1919b). Preface to Reik's *Ritual*. *S.E.*, 17. London: Hogarth Press.
_____ (1922). Medusa's head. *S.E.*, 18. London: Hogarth Press.
IMBERT & LEVASSEUR, (1972). *Le Pouvoir, Les Juges et les Bourreaux*. Paris: Hachette.
JONES, E. (1964). The Madonna's conception through the ear. *Essays in Applied Psychoanalysis, II*. New York: IUP.
JORDAN, D. P. (1979). *The King's Trial*. Berkeley: California University Press.
KAHR, M. (1972). Delilah. *Art Bulletin*, LIV, #3:282–300.
KRIS, E. (1975). *Selected Papers of Ernst Kris*. London and New Haven: Yale University Press.
LEVY, B. (1976). *Les Sanson, Une Dynastie de Bourreaux*. Paris: Mercure de France.
LORD, C. (1976). Solar imagery in Filarete's *Bronze Doors to Saint Peter's*. *Gazette des Beaux Arts*, April, 143–150.
MANCERON, C. (1977). *Twilight of the Old Order*. New York: Knopf.
REIK, T. (1964). *Ritual*. New York: International Universities Press, Inc.
SANSON, H., ed. (1876). *Memoirs of the Sansons*. 2 Vols. London: Chatto and Windus.
VOLTAIRE. (1961). *The Age of Louis XIV*. London: Penguin Books.
WALZER, M. (1974). *Regicide and Revolution*. Cambridge: Harvard University Press.

PART IV

LITERATURE

7

Oscar Wilde and the Masks of Narcissus

KARL BECKSON

In so vulgar an age as this, we all need masks.

It is only when you give the poet a mask that he can tell you the truth.
(Letters, pp. 353, 759)

In January, 1895, Oscar Wilde, though decidedly not an ideal husband, was enjoying the success of his society comedy, *An Ideal Husband,* the theme of which involves a secret sin and public disgrace. The disaster of his life awaited him in April, the cruellest month, when he would be arrested, charged with homosexuality, and sentenced to two years at hard labor. But, in January, his wittiest dandy, Lord Goring, was uttering brilliant epigrams on the London stage and living up to his name by puncturing cherished notions. As a narcissist, Lord Goring is an inspired creation, a manifestation of Wilde himself, as we see him at the beginning of Act Three speaking to his servant, Phipps, who, affirming his master's observations, functions as a male Echo to Wilde's Narcissus:

Goring: Rather distinguished thing, Phipps. I am the only person of the smallest importance in London at present who wears a buttonhole.

Phipps: Yes, my lord. I have observed that.

Goring: You see, Phipps, Fashion is what one wears oneself. What is unfashionable is what other people wear.

Phipps: Yes, my lord.

Goring: Just as vulgarity is simply the conduct of other people.

Phipps: Yes, my lord.

Goring: And falsehoods the truths of other people.

Phipps: Yes, my lord.

Goring: Other people are quite dreadful. The only possible society is oneself.

Phipps: Yes, my lord.

Goring: To love oneself is the beginning of a lifelong romance, Phipps.

Phipps: Yes, my lord. (pp. 138-139)

The myth of Narcissus, as told in Ovid's *Metamorphoses,* is essentially a self-destructive homosexual fable with incestuous implications. Narcissus' father, the river god Cephisus, finding an object of desire in his own waters, ravishes Liriope, who gives birth to Narcissus. As Spotnitz and Resnikoff (1954) suggest, Narcissus wishes to merge not only with the self but also with the mother, for he gazes with desire into the water that is the source of his being. However, there is also the suggestion here of a primal scene fantasy (Freud, 1917), for Narcissus cannot take his eyes away from the procreative source. As we shall see, the ravisher father in the myth is important to Wilde's creative imagination, and the self-destructive Narcissus is significant in revealing Wilde's illusion concerning his own presumed self-sufficiency.

As an embodiment of Wilde's exhibitionistic narcissism, Lord Goring is described as a "flawless dandy," who, like all of Wilde's male dandies, believes that precise attention to trivial detail in dress confers moral superiority upon the wearer and that aesthetic form takes precedence over bourgeois sentiment and conventional morality. As Lord Goring says to his servant: "Extraordinary thing about the lower classes in England—they are always losing their relations." And Phipps, something of a dandy himself, replies: "Yes, my lord! They are extremely fortunate in that respect" (Wilde, 1895, p. 146).

Wilde derived his ideas concerning dandyism from such English and French forerunners as Beau Brummell, Byron, and Disraeli among the English, and among the French, Barbey d'Aurevilly and Baudelaire, whose exposition of dandyism was perhaps the most original of the nineteenth century. For Baudelaire, dandyism revealed the aristocracy of the spirit and raised the last heroic protest in an age of vulgar egalitarianism. Correct, precise dress, with only a touch of elegance, conferred a moral grace upon the wearer, whose physical body, nevertheless, retained the taint of original sin and inevitable corruption. The dandy, consequently, affected "a mask of indifference concealing inner despair" (Moers, 1960). Baudelaire merged dandyism with his conception of the artist, for both strove for perfect control and self-sufficiency. The idea of art for art's sake was thus associated with the cult of the self, which Baudelaire envisioned as equivalent to a religion, the devotees of which were committed to the quest for moral perfection that would raise them above the mediocrity of the masses.

In borrowing the style of Baudelairean dandyism and infusing it with his genius for paradoxical wit, Wilde transformed it into a mode for experiencing exquisite sensations that have about them the aura of sin. In addition, Wilde borrowed from Barbey the idea of shocking others while remaining impassive. What is implied here, however, is controlled aggression and anxiety (despite the mask of presumed indifference), narcissistic expansiveness, and a celebration of what Kohut (1971) calls the "grandiose self." In short, the narcissistic element of Wildean dandyism, both in his life and in his art, proceeded from the need, in Stolorow's (1975) functional definition of narcissism, to maintain cohesiveness, stability, and a positive self-representation.

Such strategies are paradoxically associated with the central themes of Wilde's "personal myth" (Kris, 1956), an elaborate masochistic fantasy of martyrdom, in which the self is eroticized, maimed, mutilated, and finally destroyed. This "myth," as we shall see, enriched his creative life and provided him with a self-fulfilling prophecy that he would faithfully enact. Indeed, Wilde wrote, "Every single work of art is the fulfillment of a prophecy. For every work of art is the conversion of an idea into an image. Every single human being should be the fulfillment of a prophecy. For every human being should be the realisation of some ideal..." (Hart-Davis, 1962, p. 481). At times, Wilde appeared brilliantly cohesive,[1] but in the crucial year of 1895, he was so divided by both intrapsychic conflict and a fragmented self that he could not, at the critical moment, save himself from disaster. As one character states in *An Ideal Husband:* "When the gods wish to punish us, they answer our prayers" (p. 84).

Unfortunately, little is known of Wilde's very early life which might shed light on his development. His family was one of the most distinguished and notorious in mid-nineteenth century Dublin. His father, an eye and ear surgeon with an international reputation, was also an archaeologist, a man of letters, and editor of the *Dublin Quarterly Journal of Medical Science.* His book, *Aural Surgery* (1853), was the standard textbook in Britain, the Continent, and America. He was one of the first physicians to examine the eardrum with the speculum, which had been invented in Vienna, and he introduced the technique of the incision for draining absesses from the mastoid. While still in his late thirties, Queen Victoria appointed him as Surgeon Oculist and Aurist in Ordinary, which meant that had the Queen required medical attention for

---

1. Kohut (1971, p. 4) has written: "Unlike the patients who suffer from these latter disorders [i.e., psychoses and borderline states], patients with narcissistic personality disturbances have in essence attained a cohesive self and have constructed cohesive idealized archaic objects."

an ailing eye or ear while in Ireland, Dr. Wilde would have been summoned. Primarily because of his exhausting work as Commissioner of
the Medical Census, in 1864 he was knighted Sir William Wilde.

Despite such acclaim, Sir William was often satirized by the press for
his unattractive appearance and for his imperious manner. A question
that reportedly circulated in Dublin at the time was "Why are Dr.
Wilde's nails black?" And the answer: "Because he scratches himself."
But important for our understanding of Oscar was Sir William's sexual
promiscuity. Though his sexual prowess would later become legendary
(indeed, it was rumored that he had a bastard in every cottage), he did, in
fact, have at least three illegitimate children before he married. One of
these was named Henry Wilson, whom Sir William educated and who,
like Sir William, became a Fellow of the Royal College of Surgeons, and
indeed became Sir William's assistant—an inspiring example of paternal
loyalty! Though Oscar called this illegitimate offspring "cousin" and indeed attended his funeral when he suddenly died at the age of thirty-nine,
it is likely that he knew—or at least suspected—the truth, for Sir
William's sexual proclivities were the subject of a scandal that filled Irish
newspapers in 1864, the year of his knighthood, when Oscar was ten
years old.

At the age of forty-nine, Sir William was involved in a libel suit
brought against Lady Wilde by a Mary Travers, the daughter of a professor of medical jurisprudence at Trinity College, Dublin. Ten years
before, Mary, at the age of nineteen, had been Sir William's patient. She
apparently became his mistress, and they were often seen together in
public; indeed, he even invited her on occasion to the Wilde home. Ob-
jecting to what appeared as an "intrigue" between the two, Lady Wilde
wrote a letter to Mary's father that became the basis for the suit. The ensuing trial was a major sensation of the time.[2] It is likely that this incident
had a profound effect on the fantasy life of the youthful Oscar, who
could not have been shielded from such a widely publicized event.

Lady Wilde, or "Speranza," as she had called herself earlier, had been
a leading figure in the Young Ireland revolutionary movement of the
1840s. As a poet—of no great ability—and as an agitator for independence from England, she had been widely regarded as a major
voice, but with her marriage to Sir William, she progressively settled into

2. Wyndham (1951, p. 100) quotes a ballad reportedly chanted by Trinity College stu-
dents at the time:
There's an oculist living in Merrion Square,
Who has skill that's unrivaled and talent that's rare;
And if you will listen, I'll try to reveal
The matter that caused poor Miss Travers to squeal!

domestic life and established a salon in the continental fashion, to which she invited writers and artists in rather eccentric dress covered with jewelry copied from ancient Celtic relics. Her imposing stature and lofty manner—no doubt a source of Wilde's character Lady Bracknell in *The Importance of Being Earnest*—impressed all who met her.[3] One of her visitors referred to Speranza as the "the gigantic lady . . . of the warlike songs" (White, 1967, p. 87). Wilde's own huge physical frame and the sense of his own destiny point to a deep identification with his mother. To be sure, Lady Wilde also contributed to the development of Oscar's personal myth, for, as an imagined savior of Ireland, she saw herself as a figure doomed and martyred, both in her public and private lives. When, for example, Oscar was born in 1854, she wrote to a friend: "A Joan of Arc was never meant for marriage, and so here I am bound heart and soul to the home hearth" (Wyndham, 1951, p. 50).

At the trial, Mary insisted that she had been raped by Sir William two years before, but she also admitted that she continued to see Sir William thereafter, obtained money from him, and accepted gifts of clothing. Since the evidence indicated that she was not a victim of the lascivious Sir William during their ten-year liaison, the jury awarded her a farthing's damages (a farthing was one fourth of a penny), the jury's estimate, presumably, of the value of her chastity.

Following the trial, Sir William spent most of the remaining years of his life at his country house at Moytura, in the west of Ireland, where he became more slovenly, drank to excess, and undertook archaeological exploration. During school holidays, the three Wilde children—Willie, Oscar, two years younger, and their sister, Isola—stayed with him and acted as his assistants in his explorations. At the end of his life (he died in 1876, at the age of sixty), Sir William suffered from severe depression.

Sir William's public disgrace and self-exile, we may assume, influenced the young Oscar, for the ravisher father and crucified figure were images that pervaded his own life and art as self-images. Schafer (1967, p.142) writes that "in the instance of 'borrowed guilt,' which refers explicitly to identifying with the guilt of a parent, not only a superego position is taken over, but also fantasies concerning id and ego tendencies and properties that warrant such guilt."

In the spring of 1867, when Oscar was twelve, his sister Isola, who was in her ninth year, died while visiting a relative. He was so profoundly disturbed by the loss that his mourning was expressed and preserved sym-

---

3. Lambert's (1967, p. 126) description of Lady Wilde is a remarkable foreshadowing of her son's behavior at the time of *his* trial. Speranza, Lambert writes, "went grandly into the courthouse, self-assured that she could reduce this wretched girl's case to nothing by her eloquence and the force of her personality."

bolically in a variety of ways, then, and later in his life. At the time of her death, he placed a lock of her hair, apparently blond, into an envelope, which he decorated with elaborate and revealing imagery, an envelope he reportedly kept until his death (Holland, 1960).

Reprinted from *Oscar Wilde: A Pictorial Biography*. London: Thames and Hudson, 1960.

The interesting features of this envelope are, first, the combinations of "O" (for Oscar) and "I" (for Isola) that are apparent in the wreaths at the top, and the combinations on either side of the two top crosses. Object loss and self-loss are clearly represented, but simultaneously there is a defensive merging of identities in a transcendent world. At the top of the envelope, the suggestive phrase, "My Isola's Hair," within the frame, or symbolic coffin, is the central organizing principle in the design, as though it were an incestuous or fetishistic emblem celebrating Oscar's love. (In one of the versions of the Narcissus myth—as told by the second-century Greek writer Pausanias—Narcissus had an identical twin sister, whom he loved. When she died, he would go to the spring seeking relief for his grief by gazing at his own image to recall his sister's). At the bottom of the envelope is a glittering crown (traditionally associated in Christian iconography with the Virgin Mary), an indicator, possibly, of a superego serving to control and master Oscar's fantasies and drives.

In later years, while in Italy, Wilde (1881, p. 57) wrote a poem, titled

"Requiescat," embodying the same sense of identification with the lost object:

> All her bright golden hair,
> Tarnished with rust,
> She that was young and fair
> Fallen to dust.
>
> . . . .
>
> Peace, peace, she cannot hear
> Lyre or sonnet,
> All my life's buried here,
> Heap earth upon it.

There is conceivably, double meaning in the word "lyre." On the manifest level, she cannot hear the musical instrument—but is Wilde once again revealing a repressed incestuous wish by suggesting that he could never tell Isola the truth concerning his desire?

The last lines of the poem—"All my life's buried here, Heap earth upon it"—recall Laertes' similar lines in *Hamlet,* when his sister Ophelia is buried. Shakespeare associations seem to have provided Wilde with an elaborate series of significant image patterns. In his novel, *The Picture of Dorian Gray,* another young virgin, Sibyl Vane, has acted the role of Ophelia in the theatre where Dorian discovers her. Her brother, Jim, whose affection seems to border on the incestuous, becomes an avenger when Sibyl kills herself as a result of Dorian's rejection, reminiscent of Ophelia's brother, Laertes, who undertakes revenge for the death of Ophelia, similarly rejected by Hamlet. These associated images—of brothers seeking revenge for the deaths of their virgin sisters—suggest that the young Oscar had developed a rescue or revenge fantasy concerning Isola and that the envelope containing her hair was a talisman. Did Wilde hold the disgraced Sir William "responsible" for her death because he had isolated himself from the family after the trial? Might Wilde have even had doubts as to the legitimacy of Isola herself—a justifiable preoccupation of the Wilde family? Wilde probably knew—or, at least, suspected—the truth concerning Sir William's two illegitimate daughters, twenty-four and twenty-one years of age, who were accidentally burned to death in 1871, when Oscar was seventeen. (They had been living with Sir William's eldest brother, a clergyman, for all of these years.) Wilde's preoccupation with illegitimacy is evident in *The Picture of Dorian Gray,* in which Jim Vane discovers that he and his sister Sibyl are both illegitimate, and in two of Wilde's society comedies, *Lady Windermere's Fan* and *A Woman of No Importance,* the plot depends on the exposure of such a secret.

Another depiction of Isola's death occurs in Wilde's (1881) poem, "Ballade de Marguerite," in which a boy in humble circumstances in the service of a noble family (Wilde's view of himself when young?) observes a funeral, which he discovers is Marguerite's (just as Hamlet, returning to Elsinore, finds himself a witness to Ophelia's funeral). In the poem, the boy exclaims:

> "O Mother, you know I loved her true:
> O Mother, hath one grave room for two?" (p. 162)

In *Hamlet,* Laertes, leaping into Ophelia's grave to embrace her, proclaims: "Now pile your dust upon the quick and the dead" (Act V, scene 1). The envelope with Isola's hair had provided the young Oscar with a similar symbolic merging, a narcissistic fusion defending against guilt and mourning.

In 1889, Wilde published a strange and revealing story titled "The Birthday of the Infanta," which appears to dramatize, in symbolic form, the relationship between the young Oscar and Isola as the mature Wilde perceived it. In the story, the Infanta, who has blond hair, is to be entertained on her twelfth birthday. The Infanta's father, the King, has visited the body of his embalmed, dead wife each month for the past twelve years, the precise age of the Infanta. (The young Oscar had regularly visited the grave of Isola.) Kneeling by the Queen's side, he seizes the "pale, jewelled" hands in a "wild agony of grief" and kisses the cold face. (In this story, and especially in *The Picture of Dorian Gray,* Wilde puns on his own name as though placing his personal signature upon the experience. For such a self-conscious writer as Wilde, it is inconceivable that he was unaware of the significance of so many puns on his name at critical points in his work.) In the "Infanta" story, the most unusual feature of the birthday celebration is a dancing dwarf, who had been discovered just the day before "running wild" in the forest. Fascinated by the Infanta, he cannot keep his eyes off her, and he dances for her alone. The Infanta rewards him by removing from her hair a white rose, traditionally associated with the Virgin Mary.

After she has retired, the dwarf, searching for her, enters a large room, at the far end of which he sees a figure whom he believes to be the Infanta, but he is mistaken. The narration describes his self-confrontation before a mirror (Wilde, 1889a, pp. 60-62).

> It was a monster, the most grotesque monster he had ever beheld. Not properly shaped, as all other people were, but hunchbacked, and crooked-limbed, with a huge lolling head and mane of black hair. The little dwarf frowned, and the monster frowned also. He

laughed, and it laughed with him, and held its hands to its sides, just as he himself was doing....When the truth dawned upon him, he gave a wild cry of despair and fell sobbing to the ground. So it was he who was misshapen and hunchbacked, foul to look at and grotesque. He himself was the monster, and it was at him that all the children had been laughing.

In a rage, the dwarf destroys the cherished rose, and crawling like "some wounded thing," dies broken-hearted.

An inversion of the Narcissus myth, the story may reveal an aspect of Wilde's self-representation, defensively employed, for if the Narcissus myth is, in part, a homosexual fantasy, Wilde's tale may be interpreted as the narcissist's defense. Having made the discovery of his grotesqueness, the dwarf knows that he will never be loved by the Infanta: he dies a mutilated, depersonalized "thing," an anticipation of Dorian Gray's grotesque end. Both characters reveal deep narcissistic and body image distortion.[4]

The idea of the grotesque dwarf was undoubtedly derived from Robert Louis Stevenson's *The Strange Case of Dr. Jekyll and Mr. Hyde,* which had appeared just three years before "The Birthday of the Infanta" and which Wilde had read. When Hyde emerges from the psyche of Dr. Jekyll, he is described as a dwarflike creature "with the imprint of deformity and decay," the emblem of evil. Did Wilde seize upon this image as an analogy to his own emergence from *his* father, a similarly respected and disgraced physician, who was himself dwarflike in appearance compared to the giantess Lady Wilde? The identification of the father and the son is indeed present in Stevenson's story, for Dr. Jekyll and Hyde are given that symbolic relationship.

In 1884, a year before the Criminal Law Amendment Act was passed making homosexuality a crime, Wilde married Constance Lloyd, whom he characterized in a letter to Lillie Langtry as "a grave, slight, violet-eyed little Artemis" (Hart-Davis, 1962, p. 154). There seems to have been considerable affection between them at least early in their marriage, but Wilde eventually lost interest in her; friends of the couple noted her lack of wit and Oscar's desire to dine out without her. Undoubtedly, Wilde believed, like Lord Henry in *The Picture of Dorian Gray,* that "the one charm of marriage is that it makes a life of deception absolutely necessary for both parties" (Wilde, 1891, p. 6). Bergler (1956, 99) has suggested that Wilde's marriage was "an unsuccessful attempt to escape his masochistic attachment to the image of a cruel giantess: his self-willed

---

4. Weill (1958, p. 18) writes that at the time of Wilde's trial "he presented himself as the grotesque and misshapen monster of his own unconscious self-image."

mother. To counteract this image, he unconsciously chose a nonentity who was too weak to be dangerous.''

In 1891, the seemingly inevitable movement toward disaster began: Wilde met Lord Alfred Douglas, who, he later wrote (Hart-Davis, 1962, p. 448), was the "true author of the hideous tragedy" of his life. Wilde had now encountered a disturbed narcissist[5] whom he professed to love, whom he recognized as the central destructive force in his life, but whom he felt helpless to resist. Later, Wilde wrote of Lord Alfred:

> My genius, my life as an artist, my work, and the quiet I needed for it, were nothing to him when matched with his unrestrained and coarse appetites for common profligate life: his greed for money: his incessant and violent scenes: his unimaginative selfishness....I curse myself night and day for my folly in allowing him to dominate my life.[6] (Hart-Davis, 1962, pp. 413-414)

Socarides (1978, p. 55) has written that at the root of the masochistic element in homosexuality is "an expression and fulfillment of the original masochistic relationship of the helpless child to the overwhelming, engulfing, overpowering, cruel mother to whom the child must submit in order to survive. This submission is perpetuated in the relationship with homosexual partners. The sexual object has been changed, but the sexual aim remains the same. Thus, his hope to escape from his masochistic enslavement to a woman (mother) by choosing a male partner is utterly defeated."

In 1891, Bosie, as Lord Alfred was called by his friends and relatives, was twenty-one; for Wilde, who was thirty-eight, Bosie was the embodiment of ideal self and ideal object, which mirrored his own grandiose and eroticized fantasies of power and privilege. Like Dorian Gray, the young, handsome, delicately effeminate, and aristocratic Bosie was Wilde's visible symbol of eternal youth—another instance, Wilde insisted, of Life imitating Art. In the novel, Lord Henry, who idolizes youth, expresses the fear Wilde often spoke of concerning the threat of dissolution and that partly accounts for his narcissistic defenses (Hart-Davis, 1962, p. 36): "The pulse of joy [Lord Henry states] that beats in us at twenty becomes sluggish. Our limbs fail, our senses rot. We degenerate into hideous puppets, haunted by the memory of the passions

---

5. Early in his friendship with Douglas, Wilde wrote to Robert Ross: "[Bosie] is quite like a narcissus—so white and gold" (Hart-Davis, 1962, p. 314).

6. In October, 1897, some five months following his release from Reading Gaol, Wilde wrote to his publisher: "[Bosie] is witty, graceful, lovely to look at, lovable to be with. He has also ruined my life, so I can't help loving him—it is the only thing to do" (*Letters,* p. 651).

of which we were too much afraid, and the exquisite temptations that we had not the courage to yield to. Youth! Youth! There is absolutely nothing in the world but youth!''

Wilde's compulsive homosexual relationships with Bosie, with casual pick-ups, and with numerous "renters"—that is, male prostitutes—seem to have been undertaken to maintain a sense of stability and defend against self-depletion and a progressive self-fragmentation. It was, he said, like "feasting with panthers" (Hart-Davis, 1962, p. 492). He placed himself, however, in ever-increasing danger with the law. As early as 1886, in a letter to a friend, he wrote what appears to be a description of his homosexual impulses and the penalty he was prepared to pay—once again the fantasy of martyrdom in the service of an eroticized need for cohesiveness (Hart-Davis, 1962):

> I myself would sacrifice everything for a new experience, and I know there is no such thing as a new experience at all. I think I would more readily die for what I do not believe in than for what I hold to be true. I would go the stake for a sensation and be a sceptic to the last! Only one thing remains infinitely fascinating to me, the mystery of moods. To be master of these moods is exquisite, to be mastered by them more exquisite still. Sometimes I think that the artistic life is a long and lovely suicide, and am not sorry that it is so.

The Picture of Dorian Gray dramatizes these elements and indeed depicts their outcome, for Dorian does, in fact, kill himself at the end, though manifestly his intent is to destroy only the split-off emblem of conscience and body self, his own portrait. Dorian deludes himself that he has succeeded in dividing his unchanging body from his multilated portrait, for both body and "soul" are reunited in the final act of self-destruction. The haunting last image of Dorian Gray is one of a self-mutilated creature, while the portrait is restored to its primal innocence and autonomy. Wilde's symbolic attempt to dissociate the damaging effects of his own autoeroticism and a punitive conscience is here dramatized as a failure.

Though the novel is not explicit in naming Dorian's sins, the suggestions are sufficient. The painter of Dorian's portrait, Basil Hallward, confesses that he has embodied in the painting the "secret of his own soul"—that is, his fatal attraction to Dorian. (Hart-Davis, 1962, p. 352) Wilde later stated that Hallward is "what I think I am." In so stating, Wilde confessed that the novel embodied the secret of *his* own soul, though in the early 1890s, Wilde's "secret" seemed more like a public advertisement. As Ekstein and Caruth (1972, p. 205) state, "It often turns out that the very method by which the secret is defended is also the means by which it is given away." When Hallward is finally shown the secret of Dorian's soul, the mutilated portrait, he urges Dorian to repent for his sins, but Dorian, in a rage over the loss of Hallward's esteem, kills him by stabbing him in the "great vein behind the ear." Curiously, this act recalls Sir William's operation on the mastoid; indeed, Grinstein (1970) suggests that Dorian's action reveals Wilde's "murderous rage against the father," for Hallward is Dorian's symbolic creator and super-ego representative. But the act also reveals Wilde's unconscious identification with the aggressor, the ravisher father, the surgeon with the tool.

In *The Picture of Dorian Gray,* Wilde destroys Dorian when splitting fails. In his play *Salomé,* he also destroys Salomé, another perverse narcissist,[7] in an attempt to stablize the self (Wilde, 1894a). When she appears on stage with the severed head of Jokanaan—that is, John the Baptist—her speech is filled with images of phallic destruction and manifest oral aggression, simultaneously suggesting the homosexual nightmare of the engulfing vagina (p. 427):

> Ah! thou wouldst not suffer me to kiss thy mouth, Jokanaan. Well, I will kiss it now. I will bite it with my teeth as one bites a ripe fruit. Yes, I will kiss thy mouth, Jokanaan....But wherefore dost thou not look at me, Jokanaan? Thine eyes that were so terrible, so full of rage and scorn, are shut now....Lift up thine eyelids, Jokanaan! Wherefore dost thou not look at me?...And thy tongue, that was like a red snake darting poison, it moves no more, it speaks no words, Jokanaan, that scarlet viper that spat its venom upon me. It is strange, is it not? How is it that the red viper stirs no longer.

Aubrey Beardsley's brilliant illustrations, which Wilde thought "quite wonderful," reveal much of the perversity and narcissism in this scene.

Salomé is clearly a castrating figure, but she is herself a prime candidate for mutilation, for in her desire to devour the resisting Jokanaan, she will bring about her own death. Jokanaan, the prophet of Salomé's death, is the same prophet who baptized Jesus and envisioned his saving mission—another indication that castration and crucifixion are intimately united in Wilde's imagination as two related forms of mutilation associated simultaneously with masochistic debasement and narcissistic elevation.

---

7. Of Salome, a character in the play says, "She is like a narcissus trembling in the wind" (Wilde, 1894a, p. 397).

Also of interest in the play is the recurring motif of incest that unites Salomé's mother, Herodias, to Herod, her former brother-in-law, who, according to ancient law, has married her illegally. In addition, Salomé's desire for Jokanaan has incestuous implications, for he is held prisoner in the same cistern that had held her own father for twelve years. Finally, Herod's desire for Salomé—another manifestation of the ravisher father—is seen as profane by the disapproving Herodias. When Herod observes Salomé absorbed with the severed head, he orders her execution, an action nowhere to be found in the Bible or in other versions of the story by such writers as Flaubert and Mallarmé. A Spaniard, Gómez Carrillo (1902), who knew Wilde at the time that *Salomé* was written, has stated that Wilde insisted on the death of Salomé and indeed had intended to entitle the play *The Double Beheading*. Herod's final cry, "Kill that woman!" suggests another of Wilde's ritualistic attempts at expiation, such as occurs in *The Picture of Dorian Gray,* a wish perhaps to destroy the feminine part of his psyche. As Moers (1960, p. 309) has stated, the English Decadents of the 1890s feared the "decay of one sex beside the looming dominance of the other."

By 1894, the relationship between Wilde and Bosie had reached a critical stage. Despite the fact that Wilde's friends were quietly warning him of the consequences of such an open relationship, Bosie made little attempt to conceal their homosexual affair. When going to dine with Wilde at the Savoy Hotel, Bosie once insisted that they use the front door: "I want everyone to say, 'There goes Oscar Wilde and his boy' " (Ellmann, 1977, p. 10). In regarding Wilde as his ideal father, Bosie was intent on rejecting John Sholto Douglas, the eighth Marquess of Queensberry, his "bad" father.

Richard Ellmann (1977) has given us a sympathetic view of Queensberry, whom Bosie regarded merely as a mad brute. In 1887, Queensberry's wife had divorced him on the grounds of adultery. His eldest son had taken the position of private secretary to Lord Rosebery, the Foreign Minister, whom Queensberry suspected of being a homosexual. And his younger son, Percy, had married the daughter of an impoverished clergyman. In 1893, Queensberry remarried, but shortly thereafter, his wife left him and obtained an annulment on the grounds of impotence, which he vehemently denied. He now regarded Bosie as still another source of worry. In April, 1894, he saw Bosie with Wilde in the Café Royal and afterward wrote to his son: "With my own eyes I saw you both in the most loathsome and disgusting relationship as expressed by your manner and expression. Never in my experience have I seen such a sight as that in your horrible features." Replied Bosie by telegram: "What a funny little man you are." Queensbury continued to warn Bosie of the consequences of his relationship with Wilde. By October, 1894, his eldest son, who had been Lord Rosebery's secretary, shot and killed himself. Despite the official explanation that it was a hunting accident, rumors persisted that the son feared exposure as a homosexual.

Queensberry was now determined not only to save Bosie—a noble but misguided mission—but also to expose Wilde's homosexuality. Despite the fact that Queensberry, a good amateur boxer, had persuaded England and America to adopt certain regulations governing boxing, now known as the Marquess of Queensberry rules, he did not hesitate to hit Wilde, at least metaphorically, below the belt. He planned to mount the stage on the opening night of Wilde's play, *The Importance of Being Earnest,* in February, 1895, to lecture the audience, presumably on Wilde's sexuality. On that night, he appeared with a prize fighter as a bodyguard and a bouquet of what was believed to be of carrots and turnips, an emblem of Wilde's sexual preference. However, Wilde having heard of this plan, had already called the police, and Queensberry was prevented from entering the theater. As Wilde described Queensberry's behavior to Bosie, "He prowled about for three hours, then left chattering like a monstrous ape." (Hart-Davis, 1962, p. 383). Before leaving, however, Queensberry left the offensive vegetables at the stage door. His obsession concerning Wilde's homosexuality raises questions about his own unconscious sexual preference. The image of Queensberry walking through the London streets clutching a sexual bouquet to be used aggressively against Wilde certainly seems to have the force of a public announcement.

Queensbury's final gesture eventually brought about Wilde's disaster. In February, he left a card for Wilde at his club with the message: "For Oscar Wilde, posing as sodomite." However, Queensberry misspelled the word as "somdomite," an interesting slip that reduces the word to nonsense but which raises the intriguing question of its cause. The ensuing events once again reveal Wilde's self-destructive course, for Bosie, insisting that here was an opportunity to make his father suffer for this outrage, urged Wilde to sue for libel. As a result, instead of ignoring the card, Wilde lied to his solicitor, claiming total innocence of any homosexual activity.

However, lying, in life as well as art, had a different meaning for Wilde from the conventional conception. In his essay, "The Decay of Lying," Wilde (1889, p. 320) states that "Lying, the telling of beautiful untrue things, is the proper aim of Art." By "lying," he meant the creation of an imaginative world divorced from and superior to the world of fact and conventional morality—a characteristic splitting into "good" and "bad" worlds inhabited by Dandies and Philistines, respectively. In his controlled imaginative world, lying, deception, secrecy, and the double life are central elements of many of his works, including his comic masterpiece, *The Importance of Being Earnest.* At the trial, Wilde apparently believed that these same elements that he had so brilliantly controlled in art could also be controlled in life by an act of individual will. Indeed, like other Aesthetes of the late nineteenth century, he was convinced that Life should be transformed into Art, for Art existed as transcendent order and beauty. As a dandy, the living embodiment of that order, he was determined to exhibit perfect control in order to magically destroy the threatening Queensberry, the "bad" father in the chaotic "bad" world of fact.

On the witness stand, Wilde gave an extraordinary performance. For one who was an overt homosexual pretending to be innocent of merely *posing* as a sodomite, Wilde exhibited a mask of grandiose invulnerability, reinforced, undoubtedly, by the successes of his two comedies, *An Ideal Husband* and *The Importance of Being Earnest,* both playing at the time to packed houses. The grandiose self had indeed found confirmation of its power in the approval of London audiences. At the trial, he could not, apparently, grasp the disparity between his dandaical composure and his obvious guilt, of the potential danger that might at any moment destroy him. As Kernberg (1976, p. 46) has stated, this kind of splitting may be accompanied by consciousness of "severe contradiction" in one's behavior, but such a person "can alternate between opposite strivings with a bland denial of this contradiction and with what is, seen from the outside, a striking lack of concern over it."

In being questioned about his relationships with various renters and others, Wilde responded with wit and banter until a crucial moment when Queensberry's attorney, Edward Carson, asked Wilde whether he had ever kissed a young male servant; for an unguarded moment, the truth broke through: "Oh no," Wilde responded, "He was a peculiarly plain boy. He was, unfortunately, extremely ugly. I pitied him for it." Carson responded instantly: "Was that the reason why you did not kiss him?" (Hyde, 1975, p. 219). This damaging exchange and the fact that Queensberry had been searching for and finding, with the help of private detectives and bribes, the renters who had had relations with Wilde were sufficient reasons to drop the suit against Queensberry on the morning of April 5. Wilde had now placed himself in jeopardy.

He spent the day with Bosie, first lunching at a nearby hotel, while Queensberry's solicitor sent the Director of Public Prosecutions copies of the witnesses' statements that constituted evidence of Wilde's criminal activity. This set in motion a series of events that have led to considerable conjecture. For example, the magistrate at Bow Street police station who examined the evidence did not immediately grant a request for an arrest warrant but adjourned the court for more than an hour and a half. A story that has persisted in biographies of Wilde is that the magistrate inquired of his clerk when the boat-train to the coast was scheduled to leave London. The magistrate did not issue the warrant until after five o'clock, by which time the train had already departed. No evidence exists to suggest this action was officially sanctioned.

During this time, Wilde was at the Cadogan Hotel, where Bosie was staying. Various friends who stopped by urged Wilde to flee to France. His wife, Constance, when she heard the news that he had dropped his suit, said to a friend: "I hope Oscar is going away abroad" (Hyde 1975, p. 225). At the hotel, Wilde remained indecisive, lamenting at five o'clock that the train had gone. At six-thirty, two Scotland Yard detectives arrested him in the hotel room.

Why was Wilde unable to save himself? Was his masochistic need for self-surrender and self-punishment so strong that public disgrace and imprisonment were for him the other side of the narcissistic coin? Did he perceive his doom as a glorious Christ-like martyrdom and that, despite his feasting with panthers or perhaps because of it, he was being elevated to a transcendent plane of existence, to a higher redeeming innocence? To reject such elevation and expiation would, to be sure, be folly, for masochistic-narcissistic fantasies of debasement and elevation are, after all, confirmation of one's extraordinary worth when confronted by an archaic, punitive superego. To flee in abject fear would be too threatening to his grandiose image of self. To flee from Bosie—and thus desert him—would be tantamount to the ideal father rejecting the ideal son, his narcissistic reflection, ironically unworthy of such devotion but essential to the maintenance of Wilde's self-stability. In an unpublished paper, "The Masochistic-Narcissistic Character," Arnold Cooper provides a striking passage that illuminates Wilde's psychic dilemma:

> The frustrations and discomforts of separation-individuation, necessary events in turning us towards the world, are perceived as narcissistic injuries—i.e., they damage the sense of magical omnipotent control, and threaten intolerable passivity and helplessness in the face of a perceived external danger. This is the prototype of narcissistic humiliation.

In his long prison letter to Bosie in 1897 (Hart-Davis, 1962, p. 430), Wilde recalled the events leading to his disaster, and compared himself to the traditional sacrificial animal, the ox, which the early Church fathers had associated with the crucified Christ:

> Between you both [i.e., Bosie and Queensberry] I lost my head [indeed, like Jokanaan!]. My judgment forsook me. Terror took its place. I saw no possible escape, I may say frankly, from either of you. Blindly I staggered as an ox into the shambles [i.e., a slaughterhouse]. I had made a gigantic psychological error. I had always thought that my giving up to you in small things meant nothing: that when a great moment arrived I could reassert my will-power in its natural superiority. It was not so. At the great moment my will-power completely failed me.

Indeed, perhaps what failed him is related to the fact that, according to Pliny, the source of the name Narcissus is the Greek word *narke,* meaning "paralysis."

When the jury could not reach a decision on Wilde's guilt or innocence, a second trial was ordered. Out on bail, he was once again urged by his friends to go abroad. Indeed, a private yacht was waiting for him in the Thames. But he would not betray those who had stood bail for him, and he had reportedly given his word to his mother that he would act like a gentleman. (Later, [Hart-Davis, 1962, p. 478] he wrote that "one of the most wonderful things in the whole of recorded time" was the crucifixion of the "Innocent One before the eyes of his mother....") In a gesture of self-delusion, he insisted that he "had a good chance of being acquitted." Yet he appeared progressively less flamboyant and witty, more filled with anxiety as the two trials revealed increasingly damaging evidence. Though subjected to injury, Wilde was able to maintain his stability. He later wrote that when he heard the prosecutor's "appalling denunciation" of him and "being sickened with horror" at what he heard, it suddenly occurred to him (Hart-Davis, 1962, p. 502): "*How splendid it would be, if I was saying all this about myself!* [Wilde's italics.] I saw then at once that what is said of a man is nothing. The point is, who says it."

Wilde's lengthy prison letter to Bosie (written in the final months of his sentence and later published under the title *De Profundis*) reveals an intense, compensatory identification with Christ, who, Wilde said, had the imagination of the Romantic artist. Indeed, after his release in 1897, he signed one of his letters to Bosie (Hart-Davis, 1962, p. 613): "Ever yours (rather maimed and mutilated)," and he used the pseudonym of "Sebastian Melmoth" when he went into exile in France, the Christian name "Sebastian" referring to the third-century martyr who was slain by arrows (providing additional fantasies of mutilation and sexual penetration); "Melmoth" was taken from the doomed figure in the Gothic novel *Melmoth the Wanderer,* written by Charles Maturin, Wilde's great-uncle.

Except for his final work, *The Ballad of Reading Gaol,* Wilde's career as a writer came to an end. Having completed the poem in 1897, he found himself unable to write, for, he told his friends, he had lost the joy of life. He could no longer don the creative mask of ironic detachment, for his presumed lofty innocence had been exposed and brutally punished. Narcissistic injury had been too devastating for a significant recovery of his creative power.

In *De Profundis,* Wilde (Hart-Davis, 1962, pp. 309–310) quotes from the prophetic song of Isaiah, who foresaw the suffering Christ: "He is despised and rejected of men, a man of sorrows and acquainted with grief"—a prophecy fulfilled by Wilde himself in his final years. In his poem "The Sphinx," which Wilde worked on sporadically for many years and finally published a year before his imprisonment, the Sphinx, emblem of the half-woman, half-animal that was the riddle and the secret of his own life, sits in a corner of the room watching the speaker, who concludes his address to the silent creature as though he were another maimed Oedipus:

> Hideous animal, get hence!
> You wake in me each bestial sense, you make
> me what I would not be.
> . . . .
> False Sphinx! False Sphinx! By reedy Styx old
> Charon, leaning on his oar,
> Waits for my coin. Go thou before, and
> leave me to my crucifix.

Wilde died in November, 1900, at the age of forty-six, of an intracranial complication of otitis media. Shortly before his death, he had an operation, the details of which are unknown, but it may well have been an incision to drain an absess from the mastoid, precisely the same procedure introduced by his father.

BIBLIOGRAPHY

BERGLER, E. (1956). Salomé, the Turning Point in the Life of Oscar Wilde. *Psychoanalytic Review,* 43:97–103.

EKSTEIN, R. & CARUTH, E. (1972). Keeping Secrets. In *Tactics and Techniques in Psychoanalytic Therapy,* P. L. Giovacchini (ed.). New York: Science House, Inc., pp. 200–215.

ELLMANN, R. (1977). "A late Victorian love affair. In *Oscar Wilde: Two Approaches.* Los Angeles: William Andrews Clark Memorial Library, University of California, pp. 3–21.

FREUD, S. (1917). Introductory lectures on psychoanalysis. *S.E.,* 16:358–377. London: Hogarth Press, 1963.

GÓMEZ CARRILLO, A. (1902). Comment Oscar Wilde rêva Salomé. *La Plume* (Paris), pp. 1149-52.

GRINSTEIN, A. (1970). On Oscar Wilde. *Bulletin of the Philadelphia Association for Psychoanalysis,* 20:246-49.

HART-DAVIS, R., ed. (1962). *The Letters of Oscar Wilde.* New York: Harcourt Brace and World.

HOLLAND, V. (1960). *Oscar Wilde: A Pictorial Biography.* London: Thomas & Hudson.

HYDE, H. M. (1975). *Oscar Wilde: A Biography.* New York: Farrar, Straus & Giroux.

KERNBERG, O. (1976). *Object-Relations Theory and Clinical Psychoanalysis.* New York: Jason Aronson.

KOHUT, H. (1971). *The Analysis of Self.* New York: International Universities Press.

KRIS, E. (1956). The personal myth: a problem in psychoanalytic technique. In *Selected Papers of Ernst Kris.* New Haven and London: Yale University Press, pp. 252-271.

LAMBERT, E. (1967). *Mad with Much Heart: A Life of the Parents of Oscar Wilde.* London: Muller.

MOERS, E. (1960). *The Dandy: Brummell to Beerbohm.* London: Secker & Warburg.

SCHAFER, R. (1967). Ideals, the ego ideal, and the ideal self. *Psychological Issues: Motives and Thought,* 5:131-76.

SOCARIDES, C. W. (1978). *Homosexuality.* New York and London: Jason Aronson.

SPOTNITZ, H. & RESNIKOFF, P. (1954). The myths of Narcissus. *Psychoanalytic Review,* 41:173-81.

STOLOROW, R. (1975). Toward a functional definition of Narcissism. *International Journal of Psycho-Analysis,* 56:441-448.

WEILL, E. (1958). The origin and vicissitudes of the self-image. *Psychoanalysis,* 6:3-19.

WHITE, T. de V. (1967). *The Parents of Oscar Wilde: Sir William and Lady Wilde.* London: Hodder & Stoughton.

WILDE, O. (1881a). Ballade de Marguerite. In *Poems, The First Collected Edition of the Works of Oscar Wilde,* R. Ross (ed.). London: Dawsons of Pall Mall, 1969. (A reprint of fourteen volumes, unnumbered, originally published in 1908 by Methuen & Co.), pp. 160-162.

_____ (1881b). Requiescat. In *Poems, The First Collected Edition.*

_____ (1889a). The birthday of the Infanta. In *A House of Pomegranates and Other Tales, The First Collected Edition.*

_____ (1889b). The decay of lying. In *The Critic as Artist: The Critical Writings of Oscar Wilde,* R. Ellmann (ed.). New York: Random House, 1968, pp. 290-320.

_____ (1891). *The Picture of Dorian Gray. The First Collected Edition.*

_____ (1894a). Salomé. In *The Portable Oscar Wilde,* R. Aldington (ed.). New York: Viking Press, 1946.

_____ (1894b). The sphinx. In *Poems, The First Collected Edition.*

_____ (1895). An ideal husband. *The First Collected Edition.*

WILDE, W. (1853). *Practical Observations on Aural Surgery and the Nature and Treatment of Diseases of the Ear.* London: J. Churchill; Philadelphia: Blanchard & Lea.

WYNDHAM, H. (1951). *Speranza: A Biography of Lady Wilde.* London: T. V. Boardman.

8

The Passion of Lucretius

CHARLES P. DUCEY*

Intriguing paradoxes confront the student of Lucretius. This foremost advocate of Epicurean tranquility composed the most passionate philosophical poetry of ancient times. His profound antipathy to religion is enshrined in his worshipful devotion to Epicurus' rationalistic system. His avowedly impersonal and mechanistic exposition of the processes of the universe, the *De Rerum Natura (On the Nature of the Universe),* resonates with the vitality of the personal experience that engendered it. Although almost nothing factual is known of his life, a surprisingly vivid picture of Lucretius' personality emerges from this work. The intensity and vehemence of his poetry, with its purported aim to penetrate "behind the scenes" (*De Rerum Natura,* IV. 1186) into "all the hiding places and drag truth out of there" (I.408–409),[1] challenge the reader to respond in kind by seeking to know the psychology of this remarkable poet-philosopher.

This inquiry is designed to transcend the purely diagnostic, ever fertile, *cul-de-sac* issue of whether, as the only extant biographical note has it, Lucretius was intermittently insane and committed suicide. The potentially more fruitful psychoanalytic and structural approaches should elucidate the reasons for recurrent and distinctive themes and images in

*Director of Psychological Training, Department of Psychiatry, The Cambridge Hospital, Harvard Medical School. I am grateful to Dr. Bennett Simon for his penetrating critique and to Andra Ducey for her extensive help in preparing earlier drafts.

1. The best English editions of the poem are those of Leonard and Smith (1942), which I employ here, and Bailey (1947). Translations in this paper are mine, aided by consultation of two published sources: Latham (1951), an outstanding *tour de force,* by far the best modern translation available and closest to the language and spirit of the original, and Mantinband (1965), a highly readable and generally accurate verse translation. The critical work in English on the poem do not approach the extent and quality of the many French works, from Martha (1869) through Logre (1946), Boyancé (1963, containing a thorough multilingual bibliography), and Schrijvers (1970); but Leonard's introduction to his edition is excellent, and Minadeo's (1969) demonstration of the careful and purposeful construction of the poem is clear and convincing.

the poem, and illustrate the Protean manifestations of unconscious motivation in a work of genius.

LUCRETIUS AND EPICUREAN PHILOSOPHY

Titus Lucretius Carus (99?-55? B.C.) came from an ancient but not politically illustrious noble Roman clan. Born into an era of marked social upheaval, he shunned the customary life course of military service and political ambition. Instead, he devoted himself to the study of Greek philosophy and undertook to set forth the logical and ethical principles of the philosophy of Epicurus (341-270 B.C.) in the *De Rerum Natura.* His originality consists not so much in substantive philosophical contribution as in his unique poetic treatment of the fundamental causes of natural phenomena and human behavior. The grandeur, perceptiveness, and beauty of this poetry is virtually unequalled in Latin literature. The acuteness of his perception, the striking vividness of his descriptions, his sensitivity to his natural and cultural environment and in particular to the psychological subtleties of human experience, the passion and forcefulness of his persuasive passages—it is these qualities that make Lucretius not only a great poet but the most insightful psychologist (by modern standards) that Roman culture produced as well. They also provide the solid foundation necessary for a psychological study of the poet himself.

The primary aim of the *De Rerum Natura,* as of Epicurean philosophy in general, is to dispel the fear of death that lays a heavy burden of anguish and depression on human beings and makes them engage in destructive and self-destructive (neurotic) behavior. In order to accomplish this aim, Epicurus employed and modified the materialist physics of Democritus: according to the atomic theory the universe is composed of atoms and void, and the atoms of different shapes and sizes combine in different arrangements and structural forms to produce everything that can be perceived or whose effects can be sensed or inferred, although the atoms themselves and often their compounds remain below the threshold of human perception. If only a person could rationally comprehend this scheme and all its ramifications, the Epicurean argument ran, then he could be released from his anxiety in the face of death, for he would then realize that there is no afterlife in which punishments must be eternally endured; death is nothing more than the dispersal of atoms that had been bonded together. Nor is it rational to fear the gods, since they never meddle in human affairs. Composed of very fine atoms, they dwell in the spaces between the worlds that make up the universe, and their perfect tranquility is undisturbed by passions, anxieties, and unfulfilled wishes (such as, for example, the desire to help or hurt human beings). These gods in fact serve as ideal models of what the good Epicurean always strives for: the ultimate pleasure of perfect peace of mind or tranquility, defined as freedom from all superfluous passions and anxieties and secured only through the dispassionate (i.e., Epicurean) examination of the workings of the universe.[2] On the basis of this ethic Lucretius can launch perhaps the most vitriolic attacks ever composed on both the fear of death and the passion of love, whose similarity consists in their excessiveness and disruption of tranquility.

From our limited knowledge of Epicurus it is apparent that Lucretius' version of his philosophy is distinctive and based on his own personal psychology. Lucretius' intense poetry, complicated arguments, and, most of all, the passion that animates the poem are original. He also makes subtle modifications of Epicurus' system by emphasizing certain elements, ignoring others, offering new examples and justifications, and especially by emotionally coloring the material to suit his own needs and anxieties. Fortunately, some writings of Epicurus himself have been salvaged, admittedly a tiny proportion of his vast output, but a sufficient amount so as to permit a judgment on this matter (Epicurus, in Geer, 1964). These writings are cool, dispassionate, didactic, and stuffy, full of homilies and handy guides to behavior and thought, sometimes similar to Lucretius' more technical scientific passages, but far less detailed and virtually unillustrated. More strikingly, there is nothing in the work of Epicurus that remotely resembles the passionate, vehement, arm-twisting poet of the "purple passages" that constitute the more beautiful and clearly more interesting (to Lucretius as well as to us) core of Lucretius' work. Indeed, Epicurus and his other followers openly disapproved of the composition of poetry itself, because it was one of those passionate activities that interfered with the attainment of tranquility. (How ironic it is that his philosophy has been preserved primarily in the poetry of a disciple who stays awake at night [I.142] composing enthusiastic and passionate verse in order to win a hesitant pupil over to the serenity of Epicureanism!)

A couple of specific examples show clearly Lucretius' alteration of Epicurean ideas to fit his own outlook. His well-known pessimism, the tragic view of life and death that permeates his poetry, is diametrically

---

2. The similarity of this system to Freud's implicit philosophy is too striking to overlook: "true" pleasure defined as complete tension reduction, as opposed to "false" stimulatory pleasure, are shared by both systems (cf. Ducey and Galinsky, 1973), as well as a rationalist ethic of cure (despite the emphasis on the overwhelming role of irrational forces in human experience). Even more strikingly, both systems were grossly misinterpreted as justifying sheer hedonism as soon as they passed into the public sphere. Lucretius' attack on the passion of love bears a distant resemblance to Freud's (1921) theory of love.

opposed to Epicurus' calm and unshaken optimism; while the philo-sophical system had been designed to provide comfort in times of stress, Lucretius frequently stands it on its head and employs it to prove how miserable and doomed the world really is, an approach that belies his conscious and explicit intention of providing relief from anxiety. After the vivid descriptions, tinged with grotesque delight, of the terrible physical and mental anguish that the dying person must endure (in the at-tack on the fear of death in Book III) or the nightmarish account of the plague at Athens which dramatically terminates the poem (VI.1090-1286), the reader may be forgiven if he has not been entirely persuaded to give up his fear of death. Again, while the idea that love is a disruptive and dangerous emotion can be found in Epicurus, the violence and extensiveness of Lucretius' attack show what a fertile soil for the sowing of this abstract Epicurean principle he provides. Hence, even when the content of the philosophical ideas is employed to demonstrate a point, our conclusions apply only to Lucretius, in the context of his life and work.

It is the striking contrast between the intensity of Lucretius' passion and his profound wish for tranquility (i.e., passionlessness) that fascinates students of his work. Dread of his own "passionate intensity" is a plausible explanation for his emphasis on Epicurean tranquility as an aim or even as a *fait accompli* (II.1 ff.). The extensive evidence of inner conflict in the poem appears to reinforce the hypothesis of some form of insanity first found in Jerome's *Chronicle,* written four centuries after Lucretius' poem (but possibly copied from Suetonius, an early second-century source); Jerome claims that the poet was driven mad by a love potion, composed his great poem in "lucid intervals" between attacks of madness, and killed himself. This romantic and bizarre tale has often been rejected for the simplistic (and pre-Freudian) reason that a "mad-man" could not compose such a careful, powerful, and complexly reasoned work. Several elements of the poem do, however, suggest the possibility of serious mental disturbance: his preoccupation with death, suicide, and destruction of the universe; the simultaneous presence of ex-uberant exultation and brooding melancholy in the same passages; his fascination with madness, depicted with meticulous clinical accuracy; and the ever-shifting balance between anguished agitation and wishes for death-like tranquility. He enshrines in his system itself the eternal war-fare between the *genitales auctificique motus,* "generative and ag-gregatory motions" of the atoms, and their *motus exitiales,* "destructive motions" (II.569–580), a warfare that sounds to modern ears like a transcription of personal subjective experience.

Despite the extensive evidence of internal conflict often associated with mental or emotional disorder, the remarkable adaptation

represented by the composition of the *De Rerum Natura* must be emphasized. Not only does Lucretius experience intense conflicts, but he
presses them into service for the achievement of highly adaptive goals: to
understand the incomprehensible universe (his scientific goal), to
duplicate its beauty, order, and grandeur in his poetry (his aesthetic
goal), and to communicate his own understanding and the emotional
calm that accompanies it to other people (his didactic and therapeutic
goal). This strong capacity for sublimation does not of course rule out
the possibility of a diagnosable mental disturbance, but it does perhaps
help to show that mere diagnosis is the least important aspect of any
psychological study.[3] We are far more interested in the psychodynamics
of the poet, as he attempts to resolve fundamental, potentially universal
conflicts symbolically, i.e., within the context of his philosophy of the
universe and his poetry. The similarity of Lucretius' solutions, in terms
of both latent content and its symbolic reworking, to a previously analyzed shamanistic legend from aboriginal Siberia (Ducey, 1979) illustrates the profound continuities across disparate cultures of both the
issues at stake in becoming human, and the mind's manifold ways of
reducing or resolving inevitable inner conflicts. In both cases, two
modern, complementary systems of thought, psychoanalysis and struc-
turalism, help to bring these continuities to light.

THE TORMENT OF INSATIABLE PASSIONS

The central theme of *De Rerum Natura* can be identified as the torment of insatiable passions. In Lucretius' view, people make their lives
wretched by always desiring what they do not and cannot have, for all
they desire are illusions or fantasies, inessential for either the
maintenance of or "true" satisfaction in life. They pursue such illusions
as wealth, prestige, political power, warfare, and love because they unconsciously fear death; they try madly to avoid this fear by indulging in
all the complicated and unnecessary pleasures available in life, but, like
Freud's return of the repressed, the anguish inevitably returns to haunt

---

3. In the end, the point is *not* which view is correct, since we can never know, but what
   types of arguments manage to advance our understanding. Logre's pro-madness arguments and evidence (1946) are as thorough and impressive from a psychological perspective as some "anti-madness" arguments (e.g., Kinsey, 1964) are marred by psychological naiveté and special pleading, even when they manifest clear sensitivity and
   sophistication otherwise (e.g., Wormell, 1960, 1965). Such a contrast would almost by
   itself justify concurrence with Jerome's story, far-fetched and exotic as it sounds. But
   classicists have been just as perspicacious in identifying flaws in allegedly simplistic
   psychological presentations (e.g., Clay, 1971).

them. Even the desire to continue living in the face of death is interpreted within the Lucretian framwork of the torment of insatiable passions:

> As long as what we crave is out of reach, it seems to surpass everything else in importance; once it is ours, we crave something else, and an unquenchable thirst for life keeps us forever gaping in frustration [*hiantis,* "with mouth open wide"]. (III.1082-1084)

The remedy Lucretius proposes is akin to the psychoanalytic "tragic point of view" (Schafer, 1970): people must learn to distinguish between what is essential for life and what is superfluous, what is actually needed and what is merely desired. This distinction may be facilitated by a dispassionate study of the physical principles of the universe, which should help people to distinguish between the *coniuncta,* necessary properties built into the very structure of the universe, and the *eventa,* mere accidents. Death is no more than the dispersal of atoms, with no continuing *post mortem* tortures, such as those of insatiable desires in Hades (III.978-1023); indeed, the very termination of life is comforting, in that a limit is thereby set on suffering and unfulfillable desires. Lucretius' descriptions and explanations of neurotic, self-defeating, self-destructive behavior rank among the most compelling and perspicacious in literature and deserve extensive treatment in their own right. But here we are concerned with their implications for the rest of his own work and possible applications of these findings to the meaning of the "torment of insatiable passions" in present-day neurosis and character problems.

Lucretius' famous attack on the passion of love employs the prototype of all insatiable passions. Love is "the only thing, the more of which we have, the more fiercely the heart burns with horrible craving" (IV.1089-1090). His metaphors of sexual intercourse between lovers (as opposed to mere passionless sex) show its intriguing and terrifying aspects:

> The body makes for the object by which the mind was wounded with love, for people generally fall in the direction of their wound; the blood spurts into that region from which we are stricken with the blow, and, if the fighting is hand to hand, the red stream covers the enemy. (IV.1048-1051)

> They squeeze the object they have sought tightly and inflict pain on the body, and often dash teeth against lips and smite the mouth, because the pleasure is not pure, and there are underlying impulses that stimulate them to hurt the very source, whatever it may be, from which these germs of madness arise. (IV.1081-1083)

They glue their bodies together greedily, mingle the saliva of their mouths, and breathe into them, mashing mouths with teeth—all in vain, since they are unable to rub off anything or to penetrate and disappear completely into the other's body with their own. After all, this is what they sometimes seem to want and strive to do. . . . Then the same madness returns, the frenzy comes again, when they ask themselves what they desire to attain and are unable to find the device that would overcome this bane; in such a state of confusion they waste away from a hidden wound. (IV.1108-1112; 1117-1120)

Haven't you ever seen lovers often so enchained by mutual bliss that they are tormented in their common bondage? How often dogs on the streetcorners, craving to pull apart, strain avidly in opposite directions with all their might, when meanwhile they stick together through the powerful bonds of Venus? (IV.1201-1205)

These passages, excerpted from his longer diatribe, leave no question of his view of sexual intercourse: it arouses unmanageable excitement, passionate unfulfillable longing, incomprehension and the subjective sense of being controlled by alien forces, intense anxiety over regression and possible loss of identity, and sadomasochistic fantasies. All these elements involve the continuing sense of being plagued by uncontrollable desires and anxieties. It is not difficult to identify the fantasy that is directly represented in these remarkable passages: the primal scene, the child's fantastic interpretation and reconstruction of his parents' sexual intercourse, in accordance with his own early level of psychosexual functioning and the relative immaturity of his sense of separate identity, due to incomplete differentiation between his own and his parents' excitement and experience (Freud, 1918; Esman, 1973; Ducey, 1979). In Lucretius' view, which appears to be based on this primitive conception, sex is an alien and overwhelming experience, motivated by unconscious (*stimuli subsunt,* "there are underlying impulses") aggressive desires that causes suffering and permanent invisible damage ("hidden wound"). As is regularly true of Lucretius, he is describing with sharp-sighted clinical accuracy a frequently found perversion of the sexual act; but he claims general applicability of his ideas, whereas we would be more inclined to see their direct personal relevance to his own view and experience of sex.

Clinical experience traces three somewhat independent sources for the child's aggressive interpretation of sexuality. First, sexual and aggressive drives and fantasies are not clearly distinguished from one another in the preoedipal phase of development, and both types of drives are represented in primitive and extreme ways. Second, the child may accurately understand that the parents' actual relationship is filled with violence and murderous rage, and may represent these feelings in sadomasochistic sexual terms. Finally, his own rage and despair at being excluded from the parents' sexual life may contribute its share to his own violent view of the scene. It is this last aspect that most clearly has relevance to Lucretius' experience of the primal scene. He attacks the passion of love because it is based on fantasies and arouses desires that can never be fulfilled. Unlike hunger or mere sex, the passion of love cannot be satiated by the ingestion of any concrete substance or by taking any definite action, since it feeds only on *simulacra tenuia*, "insubstantial images" ("fantasies," as we know them), or, in his atomic scheme, a combination of very fine atoms that can satisfy desire to only the same degree that dreams of water can satisfy a thirsty man (IV.1091 ff.).[4] A close examination of the poem will show that the prototype of the betrayal intrinsic to the passion of love, as Lucretius views it, is the realization that the primal scene fantasy, which so intensifies and escalates desire for participation and fusion, will remain forever only a fantasy, that is, that the child can never possess the mother. Yet there is also the dread that this fantasy will plague him forever, that even after death he must endure this torture of insatiable desire. It is not surprising that Epicurean philosophy should appeal to him so much, with its pervasive emphasis on the need for tranquility of mind, the despising of the fear of death (and dread of the notion of a life after death), and the elimination of all superfluous desires. In order to demonstrate the profound interconnection of the poem's themes and their ultimate association with the primal scene fantasy, I shall trace the more subtle representations and the structural transformations of this unconscious fantasy throughout the poem. I shall first show that the primal scene participants are indeed disguised versions of the parents.

THE UNIVERSE'S MOTHERS

A striking characteristic of Lucretius' poem is that it is filled with and indeed built around maternal figures, words, symbols, and themes, a fact all the more striking for the poem's purportedly objective, impersonal nature. In a work whose avowed purpose is to provide humankind with a sense of security in the face of a harsh external world and inner dissatis-

---

4. This analogy is peculiarly reminiscent of one of Freud's great metaphors for the ultimate inadequacy of thought or fantasy in counteracting human dissatisfaction: mere intellectual "knowledge about the unconscious . . . have as much influence on the symptoms of nervous illness as a distribution of menu-cards in a time of famine has upon hunger" (1910, p. 225).

faction, this pervasiveness of the mother is understandable; throughout life the mother remains the unconscious prototype of the sense of security, even when she is represented in the poem metonymically (as womb or breast) or metaphorically (as earth, Nature, or Venus). But to treat the concrete reality of the mother as a pale reflection of the abstract idea of security is to make the same error as the dwellers in Plato's cave, who believe they see living figures in the insubstantial shadows on the wall (*Republic,* 514A ff.). These themes are inextricably connected: the ubiquitous maternal figures derive their significance from the poet's preoccupation with security, and also this preoccupation reflects his continuing unresolved entanglement in his relationship with his mother. An examination of the mother's many masks in the poem should lead us closer to an understanding of the reasons for this entanglement and its influence on the content and structure of his philosophy.

Two maternal figures (not always easy to distinguish) and their allegorical representatives dominate Lucretius' view of the dynamics of living things and the universe itself: Nature, with her divine counterpart Venus, and the earth, with her divine representative, the Magna Mater, the Great Mother of the Oriental religions. The widespread perplexity over the presence of these animistic forces in the work of a rationalistic and violently anti-religious poet is removed when we realize that Lucretius' psychological investment in these figures supersedes and makes irrelevant his much vaunted rationalism. Moreover, it is striking and significant that these animistic figures share the unusual characteristic of maternity: male and non-maternal female deities hold no interest and do not appear in the poem (except as occasional foils for the maternal figures, like Mars below). This distinction could hardly be accidental.

The poem opens with the grand invocation to Venus, a celebration of the sexual and reproductive drives of the animate beings in the universe, and of the divine mother who sets the whole process in motion.

Mother of Aeneas' race, delight of men and gods, bounteous Venus, who under the wheeling constellations make the ship-filled sea and the fruit-laden earth teem with life, through you every living creature is conceived and emerges to look upon the sunlight. Before you, goddess, the winds flee, and at your coming the clouds in the sky vanish. For you the skillful earth makes sweet flowers spring; for you the ocean levels laugh, and the sky, grown calm, glows with diffused radiance. When the day assumes the look of spring and the fertilizing breath of the west wind is unleashed in all its vigor, the birds of the air are the first to herald your arrival, goddess, their hearts resounding with your force; next the beasts run wild, leap through the fertile pastures and swim the swift streams. Spellbound [*capta*] by your charm, every one follows you wherever you lead with fierce desire. So throughout seas and mountains, raging torrents, the leafy homes of birds, and verdant meadows, you strike alluring love into the hearts of all and make them procreate their breeds, each after its kind, with passionate longing. You alone steer the course of the universe, and without you nothing emerges into the shining shores of light, nothing joyous or lovely comes into being. (I.1-23)

This beautiful passage, in which nearly every third word, either by meaning or by etymology, alludes to sex or birth, is a joyous celebration of the sexual and generative power of the mother. In the first line and a half the poet applies three "loaded" terms to Venus that define the three fundamental functions of the mother: she gives birth (*genetrix,* poetic for "mother," from that prolific Indo-European sexual root *gn*-[Bunker and Lewin, 1951]), makes love (*voluptas,* "delight, sexual pleasure"), and nurses (*alma,* "bounteous," literally "nourishing, nursing, nurturant"). Venus' creatures are not only her offspring but her sexual slaves as well (*capta,* "captive, captured"): controlled by forces greater than themselves (cf. Freud's id or "it"), they go mad (*ferae,* "wild") with desire, only to continue the never-ending process of birth (and death, a reality the poet chooses to suppress here). As we shall see, the constant overlapping and confusion, in Lucretius' mind, of the mother's sexual, reproductive, and nurturant functions simultaneously generate his philosophy and strike its death knell.

Venus, the poem's first maternal figure, makes occasional "personal" appearances hereafter (always as a mother; e.g., I.227-228) but is employed primarily as a poetic symbol of sexual desire (IV.1030-1287), thus reinforcing the oedipal interpretation of the invocation. Her place is taken by Nature, the personification and teleological representative of Lucretius' scientific world view. Nature is represented throughout the poem as a mother: she gives birth to everything in the universe (I.56, 199, 263-264, 322-328, 629-630; II.167-174, 224, 880, 1116-1117; V.225, 234, 1361-1366). She is also represented as feeding all her creatures and creations (I.56; II.706, 879-880; III.23; V.220) and is explicitly compared to a woman nursing her infant (II.367-370; V.811-815). Even the atoms, out of which Nature builds and fashions all the objects of the universe, have a maternal connotation. The commonest term applied collectively to the atoms is *materies* ("matter, material"), whose etymological connection with *mater* ("mother") the poet recognized clearly, long before Freud rediscovered it (1900, p. 355). In his proof (I.159 ff.) of the specificity of generation (the anti-religious proposition that a creature can never be created out of nothing, but only by a creature of its own species), Lucretius launches an extended word-play between the two concepts, *mater certa* ("species-specific mother") and *materies certa* ("species-specific matter"). As we shall see, the sexual activity of Nature and her atoms is ubiquitous in the poem and reinforces the primal scene interpretation.

The earth is employed most explicitly and frequently as a maternal figure, by virtue both of giving birth and of feeding all her creatures (I.3, 7-8, 178-179, 228-229, 250-264, 1032-1034; II.594-599, 658-660, 991-1001, 1150-1160; V.783-836, etc.). This is not mere poetic convention, but scientific fact for Lucretius; in a famous description of the evolution of life, he visualizes the whole process:

Then the earth brought forth the mortal races. For heat and moisture was abundant in the fields. So, wherever a suitable place was available, there grew up wombs, clinging to the earth by roots. These, when the time was ripe, were burst open by the maturation of the infants, as they fled the moisture and struggled for air. Then Nature directed to that spot the pores of the earth and made a juice similar to milk flow from its open veins, just as every woman now, when she has given birth, is filled with sweet milk, because the whole forceful flow of nourishment is directed into her breasts. Earth offered food to the young, warmth clothed them, and the grass, rich in soft down, gave them a bed....So I say again and again, the earth has acquired and deserves to hold the name of Mother, since she herself created the human race and brought forth in due season every animal that runs wild all over the mighty mountains and similarly the birds of the air in all their rich variety. (V.805-817, 821-825)

STRUCTURAL TRANSFORMATIONS OF THE PRIMAL SCENE FANTASY

The confusion of the mother's different functions noted in the invocation of the poem suggests some difficulty in detaching sexual fantasies from the mother and transferring them to other women. This difficulty, as Freud (1912) has suggested, lies at the root of the inability to unite affectionate and sexual wishes toward the same love object. Sex is seen as demeaning the object of one's idealized love. Such appears to be the case for Lucretius, whose exquisitely sensitive and painful description of the lover's state of mind and behavior (cf. Freud, 1921) could have been composed only by a man who has fallen desperately in love and has suf-

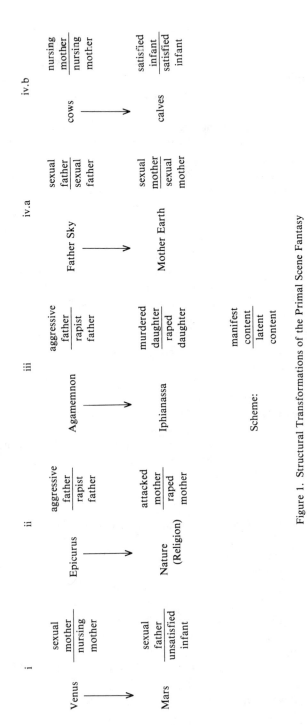

Figure 1. Structural Transformations of the Primal Scene Fantasy

fered for it. Now he renounces idealized illusions and sees only the unconscious wish to hurt the beloved in a futile attempt to penetrate completely into her body; the outcome of such reasoning, for Lucretius as for modern men trapped in this oedipal dilemma, is the advice to seek out prostitutes (IV.1058-1120).

Here we can trace a direct link between these oedipal issues and the ascendancy of the primal scene fantasy. After the invocation, four sequential scenes are depicted. They appear to have little to do with each other on a manifest level but make sense on a latent level as structurally transformed variants of the primal scene fantasy: the encounters between Venus and Mars, Nature and Epicurus, Iphianassa and Agamemnon, and Father Sky and Mother Earth. A movement toward the resolution of endopsychic conflict may be traced through these scenes, from the confusion of parent-child and husband-wife relationships to their disentanglement and differentiation. Hence, the way the poet's mind works to resolve conflict through a dialectical process may be traced directly, and compared with a similar process involving the same fantasy in a Siberian shamanistic legend (Ducey, 1979).

The confusion is strikingly portrayed in the first scene, in which the manifest content is sexual, while the latent is maternal (see Fig. 1, i). The poet pleads with Venus, the creative mother of the Roman people, to use her sexual wiles to conquer Mars, the god of war and the Romans' destructive father, and thereby to "bring it about that the brutal works of war . . . may be lulled to sleep and grow quiet" (I.29-30). This striking image of a mother coaxing an infant to sleep is reinforced by a visual representation of Venus holding Mars, "vanquished by the wound of love" (I.34), in her lap. Although the "manifest content" is sexual, the latent message, as Logre (1946, pp. 55-59) has astutely noted, is that Mars is Venus' helpless infant:

> He feasts his eyes, ravenous with love, upon you with an open-mouthed gaze, and his breath hangs suspended from your lips as he lies on his back. May you, O glorious goddess, envelop him from above with your holy body as he reclines, and pour sweet babbling sounds from your lips, beseeching tranquil peace for the Romans. (I.36-40)

The glut—as one is tempted to say—of oral imagery of the first two lines (almost every word) indicates the utter helplessness and dependence of an infant on his mother: *pascit,* "feeds, feasts"; *avidos,* "greedy, ravenous"; *inhians,* "gaping with an open mouth"; *pendet,* "hangs suspended," whence the word "dependent" itself; *resupini,* "lying on the back"; *spiritus,* "breath"; *ore,* "mouth." Venus' maternity, as well as her passion, is suggested by her "enveloping him from above" *(cir-cumfusa super,* literally, "poured all around from above," almost like amniotic fluid), by her "pouring" of words out of her mouth *(ex ore...funde)* as though she were nursing him, and by the baby talk *(lo-quellas)* that serves as communication for both lovers and mother-infant dyads.[5]

This passage conveys not only Venus' maternal quality, but also the absolute and insurmountable frustration that an infant separated from his mother must endure. The metaphor employed to communicate this state of frustration combines oral and visual imagery: mouth and eyes gape open hungrily but remain unsatisfied, as they can never appropriate and possess the mother. The poet here represents the mouth-eye unit, the mode of sensory experience characteristic of earliest infancy (Fliess, 1956, pp. 55-60). Yet according to Lucretius this mode generalizes to the later experience of the inevitable frustration engendered by the passion of love: try as they may, lovers can never penetrate and be entirely absorbed into each other's body (IV.1111). The word *inhians* ("gaping") alludes also to the gaping frustration *(hiantis)* engendered by the "unquenchable thirst for life" (III.1084). As Logre points out, the Venus-Mars passage beautifully conveys the "infinite aspiration, and exasperation, of desire" (1946, pp. 55, 59) that so fascinated and dismayed Lucretius.

What causes this insatiable craving? The poet's own acute dissection of the passion of love has already supplied the answer: love feeds on fantasies that can never be fulfilled.[6] This apparently satisfactory answer leads, none the less, to a further question: where does this idealized fantasy come from? Here again it is Lucretius who has already supplied the answer, without consciously recognizing its significance: desire is doomed to "infinite exasperation" to the extent that one confuses his relationship with his beloved with his relationship with his mother. The recognition of this fact surely explains why the passage of Venus' sexual conquest of Mars so beautifully illustrates the "infinite exasperation of desire": Mars is simultaneously Venus' lover and her infant. This condensed image depicts the inevitable disappointment inherent in love for the man who maintains a too deep attachment to fantasy images *(simulacra)* of his mother. It is freedom from this passion that Lucretius desires when he prays so fervently for peace and tranquility.

---

5. This term is not really a diminutive, but Leonard (1942, p. 203) and Logre (1946, p. 55) support my treating it as one. Lucretius later uses this term explicitly for "baby talk," modified, it is true, by *infracta* ("broken"; V.230).

6. In connecting the atomic *simulacra* with unfulfillable fantasies of love, the poet cleverly meshes remarkable psychological insight with the requirements of adhering to Epicurus' materialist physics. He also employs this theory to explain the unusual images in dreams (IV.818 ff., 962 ff.), consistent with his treatment of love as a fantasy.

Thus, the sexual encounter of the mythological father and mother of the Roman people, Mars and Venus, is implicitly transformed into a scene of eternal oral-erotic yearning for the mother. As Edelheit (1972) has shown, representation of the mother-child dyad is one version of the "primal scene schema." This unusually clear condensation of Mars as both mother's lover and her fascinated infant—who gapes with hungry eyes, just as the child gapes for the mother's breast and gapes at parental lovemaking—is repeated in other forms in the poem: for instance, the "impossible" hybrid creatures (II.700-706; V.878-924), of which Lucretius is so fond but whose existence he denies, is, as Róheim (1934), Edelheit (1972), and others have shown, a common secondary version of the primal scene (Shakespeare's "making the beast with two backs," *Othello,* I.i.117), as are the comparison of the horse in its prime (a common symbol of the parent; Fliess, 1973) with a suckling child (V.883-885; cf. Venus and Mars) and the unusual dream image that Lucretius mentions of a woman changing into a man (IV.818 ff.). Such condensations as these can regularly be traced to the confusions, shifting identifications, and unstable boundaries of the self- and object images associated with the primal scene fantasy (cf. Ducey, 1979).

The structure of this scene of Mars lying in Venus' arms, if not its emotional tone, is repeated at once in the image of human life lying beneath the personified—or rather demonized—and feminized figure Religion, but this time the primal scene gains direct representation in Epicurus' counter-attack on the secrets of Nature:

When human life lay prostrate on the ground for all to see, foully crushed under the oppressive weight [*gravi*] of Religion, who reared her head from the four quarters of the sky, her dreadful features louring upon mortals from above, a man of Greece was the first to dare to raise mortal eyes to meet her, the first to take a stand against her. Neither fables of the gods nor lightning flashes nor the sky's menacing rumble crushed his spirit; rather they spurred on his eager manhood [*virtutem*] all the more, that he might be the first to long to burst open the close-barred bolts of the gates of Nature. (I.62-71)

It is as though the hungry and eternally unfulfillable yearning of infant for mother, as depicted in the Mars-Venus scene, came to be experienced as an intolerable oppression, just as "the festering sore" of romantic love "grows in strength and becomes chronic by being fed" by continued unfulfillable fantasies (*simulacra*), "and day by day the madness swells and the grief becomes oppressive [*gravescit*]" (IV.1068-1069). This oppression, represented in both passages as a crushing weight, can be ended only by Epicurus' decisive and explicitly sexual action: those threats which should render him impotent only "stimulate his *virtus*" (the quality of being a hero, a "real man," *vir*) all the more, and he longs figuratively to rape the mother, Nature, by bursting open (*ecfringere,* "derived from breaking into a closely barred house and carrying off a reluctant mistress," Leonard and Smith, 1942, p. 307) her well-protected gates. Since Lucretius explicitly addresses Epicurus as "father" (III.9-10) and, as we have shown, treats Nature as mother, he is clearly representing a cosmic version of the primal scene (Fig. 1, ii).[7] This view is reinforced by the passage that immediately follows Epicurus' assault, in which the poet gives a concrete example of the evils to which men are led by Religion: the sacrifice of Iphianassa (Iphigenia) at the hands of her own father, Agamemnon (Fig. 1, iii). Lucretius makes abundantly clear that he is actually representing incestuous rape behind the ironically less threatening content of murder, by his remarkable use of word play and double entendres.[8] She had been summoned to Aulis on the pretext of marrying Achilles, and the sacrificial ceremony is in fact a mock marital ceremony: her "virgin locks" are bound by a fillet and braided like a bride's, and, just as in a Roman wedding,

> she is lifted up by the men's hands and escorted [*deductast*] trembling to the altar, *not,* however, so that at the completion of the solemn ritual of marriage she could be accompanied by the clear-ringing hymn of Hymen, but rather so that she might die, a wretched victim at the blow of her father, a chaste virgin incestuously [*inceste*] tampered with at the very hour of her marriage. (I.95-99)

The passage is riddled with double entendres: her being lifted (as a bride is lifted over the threshold of the groom's house) and escorted (as in the *deductio,* the wedding procession), the ritual trembling (sexual passion and mock terror of the bride), the simultaneous denial and affirmation of marriage,[9] the violated virginity, and, most significantly, the

---

7. The replacement of Venus by Nature is apparent from the application of the same or similar terms to both (I.1, 629; II.1117; V.1362; I.21; V.77), best exemplified in the striking similarity of the invocation to Venus and a later passage on Nature's maternity (II.167-174). As Nature is almost always personified, I follow Leonard and Smith in capitalizing the word.

8. Such verbal games appeal to explorers of latent meaning like Freud and Lucretius: elsewhere, the latter plays on *ignis-lignum* ("fire-wood," I.912-914), *amor-umor* ("love-fluid," IV.1054-1056), and *Mavors-mors* ("Mars [god of war]-death"; cf. Wormell, 1960).

9. Here again Lucretius uncannily anticipates Freud. His careful and extensive disclaimer that he is referring to marriage serves only to call attention to its crucial significance for the whole passage. This technique of elaborate negation is the precondition of bringing unconscious meanings to consciousness: "'this person in the dream . . . is *not* my mother.' We amend this to: 'so it *is* his mother'" (Freud, 1925, p. 235).

qualification of the father's act by a term that means both "unchastely" and "incestuously" (*inceste,* whence "incest"). Thus, this passage is the exact reverse of the Venus-Mars passage: in that one the sexual element is manifest and the parent-child latent, while in the Agamemnon-Iphianassa scene the parent-child relationship is manifest and the sexual content latent (see Fig. 1, iii).

The very same confusion of sexual intercourse and the parent-child interaction is repeated in yet another nearby section. It opens with an explicit, though symbolic, representation of the primal scene: "Father Sky" pours down his showers "into the lap of Mother Earth," where "they die" (*pereunt*: commonly used in Roman love poetry [Catullus], as well as in English poetry [Donne] as a reference to orgasm) (Fig. 1, iv.a). The liquid flow fertilizes her and makes life grow. But this scene passes imperceptibly into a picture of a mother nursing her infant, as in the Venus-Mars encounter (Fig. 1, iv.b):

> Throughout the lush pastures cattle, wearied by their fatness, fling their bodies down, and the white milky liquid flows from their swollen udders; the new offspring frolic friskily on wobbly legs through the soft grasses, their brand new minds inebriated on undiluted milk. (I.257-261)

Thus it is apparent that the three contiguous passages (Venus-Mars, Nature-Epicurus, Iphianassa-Agamemnon), along with the nearby subsequent one (Father Sky-Mother Earth), that follow the invocation to Venus are unrelated only on the surface: when analyzed they turn out to represent different versions of the same underlying fantasy, the primal scene. But the apparent confusion of generations and shifts of perspective reflect more than the perpetual repetition of an unconscious fantasy: they show the dynamic forces of intrapsychic conflict and ambivalence arising from oedipal wishes and anxieties. It is noteworthy, for instance, that the participants in the primal scene struggle are depicted as unequal in strength and power. Thus, Mars, nominally Venus' lover, is actually her dependent infant. This image is continued in the picture of human beings under the weight of Religion and is then shifted to place Epicurus in a superior position over Nature and Religion; this latter image is then continued as Agamemnon holds absolute power over his daughter. The portrait of Father Sky covering Mother Earth and pouring his flow into her lap, which has its structural source in Agamemnon's power over Iphianassa, becomes a depiction of a mother pouring her flow into her offspring, making it drunk with pleasure. In other words, a similar structure underlies these four scenes despite the apparent changes in content, a common finding in the analysis of myth, literature, and even society (Lévi-Strauss, 1958, 1964; Barthes, 1964). A further noteworthy characteristic of these passages is the constant shift in the poet's emotional perspective on and evaluation of these relationships: no final solution, no homeostasis or equilibrium is reached. Thus, Mars' utter dependency on and fascination with Venus becomes the "foul" oppression of human beings under the domination of the threat of Religion; this intolerable dependency is counteracted by Epicurus' glorious and audacious attack on the secrets of Mother Nature. But this glorious attack by the idealized father figure becomes, in the next panel, a cruel and hideous perversion, the rape-murder of a daughter by a father who justifies his action by an appeal to Religion! This violence is soon transformed back into its original elements, sexual intercourse and nursing. The reason for these "*per*versions of the primal scene," as we might call these alternative versions, is that they are under the spell of oedipal desires and anxieties: the Oedipus complex exerts a fatal attraction on the primal scene fantasy, so that the sexual intercourse of mother and father becomes continually confused in Lucretius' mind with his own regressive incestuous (mother-son and father-daughter) and sadistic (dependency-oppression, sex-murder) conceptions of love. It is no wonder that this is the poet who identified sexual intercourse as both a wish to return to the womb (no matter how strong his wish, a lover cannot "penetrate into and bury himself inside the [other's] body entirely with his own body," IV.1111; cf. Ferenczi, 1924) and a manifestation of unconscious sadistic impulses ("the pleasure is not pure, and there are unconscious impulses [*stimuli subsunt*] that stimulate them to hurt the very source, whatever it may be, from which these germs of madness arise," IV.1081-1083).

The constant shift of emotional perspective provides the motive force for the dynamic transformations of these structurally similar scenes. In scene (i), the role of lover to the mother is confused with the role of son; manifest and latent desires are at variance, and it is this discrepancy or conflict that makes this scene so appropriate for illustrating the "infinite exasperation of desire." This frustration, perhaps representative of the emotional experience of the exclusion and helpless longing, augments the child's own aggressive wishes and thus his sadomasochistic conception of the parents' sexual life: therefore, scene (ii) depicts another confusion or conflict, this time between sexual and aggressive aims. Incestuous desires reemerge in scene (iii), where the poet appears conscious of the two levels of discourse: sexual-incestuous wishes shine through the filicidal surface.

The intervening lines, between scenes (iii) and (iv) involve important elaborations of the filicidal theme. The shadowy images (*simulacra*) of hell and the concern with death show the continuing primal scene themes: in terms of atmosphere, the theme of darkness and obscurity illustrates the usual setting of the fantasy, while in terms of psychodynamics, death is simultaneously a punishment for incestuous wishes (as with Iphianassa, scene [iii]), a release from their torment, and a disguised fulfillment of them. This condensation appears most vividly in the one dream Lucretius cites, of being terrified, while "buried in sleep," by seeing dead men whose bones "[mother] earth embraces" (I.132-135). This unusually clear primal scene fantasy is followed at once by his promise to throw light on this "dread and darkness of the mind" by his reasoning. He then proceeds to convince himself rationally that his aggressive fantasies of scenes (ii), (iii), and the section that follows them can never actually come true: Mother Nature (Venus, etc.) can never create something out of nothing nor annihilate any living thing. After all, infants do not suddenly spring up into men (I.186), nor do objects fall to pieces at a mere touch. But if the poet can thus convince himself that his aggressive fantasies cannot be fulfilled merely by wishing them, he must also come to accept that his incestuous fantasies are doomed to failure as well. It is this bridge of reasoning that leads him from scene (iii) to scene (iv). In the latter he finally discovers the secrets of the primal scene that he knew all along, but of which he seemed willfully, if unconsciously, ignorant: that father's sexual relationship with mother (iv.a) is qualitatively different from the son's dependent one (iv.b); that the parents' intercourse is not a battle, but the aggressive aspects of the fantasy derive largely from the child's non-participation; that this act leads, in fact, to the generation of children; and that the mother's nursing of the child excludes the father. Here at last manifest and latent content coincide: that is, unconscious truths have become conscious ones.

His power of dialectical reasoning leads him to realize and avow that the sexual relationship between mother and father (Fig. 1, iv.a) is different from the dependent one between mother and child (iv.b). Furthermore, when these relationships can be recognized as separate, the satisfactions intrinsic to both can be acknowledged: scene (iv.) depicts the gratifications of each form and contains traces neither of the "infinite aspiration, and exasperation, of desire" characteristic of scene (i), nor of the sex-aggression confusion of scenes (ii) and (iii). But frustrated desire, strong ambivalence, terrifying anxiety, and sadomasochistic associations are dynamic forces that will always make demands on the psyche and will have to be mastered repeatedly through translation into language and evocative imagery. In the very line after his disentanglement of these motives, he claims that Nature can create nothing new without the death of another, as though the child's life led to the father's demise.

DARKNESS, IMMOBILITY, WORLD CATASTROPHE

Primal scene imagery recurs in one of the most important metaphors of the poem: the dispelling, by the light of Epicurean rationalism, of the illusions perpetuated by religion and the dark shadows of fear that arise from the ignorance of the processes of Nature. For instance, in the passage that follows his illustration of the dangers of religion, Lucretius attacks the *somnia* ("dreams, phantoms, figments of the imagination") conjured up by seers that ruin human happiness by making people dread eternal punishment after death in the darkness of hell (*tenebras Orci,* I.115) among its "shadowy images [*simulacra*], ghastly pale" (I.123; Latham). He then promises to explain, among other things, hallucinations and dreams, as when a man "buried in sleep" (I.133) sees someone whose bones lie in "the earth's embrace" (I.135). Finally, he claims that he will try to "throw light upon the veiled [*obscura*] secrets discovered by the Greeks" (I.136-137) by

> staying awake through clear and tranquil [*serenas*] nights, so that I may be able to hold up before your mind such clear torches as will enable you to gaze deeply into hidden realms. This dread and darkness of mind must therefore be dispelled, not by sunbeams, the shining shafts of daylight, but by an understanding of Nature's outward form and inner law. (I.144-148)

Lucretius has not selected the metaphors of darkness and light, of illusion and clarity, by chance: these images are regularly found in representations of the primal scene, since the child constructs his fantasy of parental intercourse out of the visual fragments available to him in the obscurity of night, and then employs his imagination to supply the details. Both components appear clearly in this passage that follows on the heels of several primal scene representations (Venus-Mars, Nature-Epicurus, Iphianassa-Agamemnon) and anticipates another (Father Sky-Mother Earth). The seers' images of fear are termed *somnia,* "dreams," a word that at once indicates the presence of autistic fantasy and the phantasms of the imagination. These *somnia* depict eternal punishment in the darkness of hell, the abode of *simulacra,* the ghosts of the dead. As in previous passages, where oedipal wishes and anxieties were interchangeable or even condensed into a single image, so here Lucretius' ambivalence about the primal scene fantasy transforms desire into its own punishment. The unusual use of *simulacra* for the shades of the dead confirms this interpretation strikingly, because the only other *simulacra* in the poem are the phantasms and illusions of love, which, as we have seen, draw their uncanny power from their association with that taboo form of love, the oedipal wish for the mother. Lucretius himself, in his next "free association," supports this point: in promising to explain hallucinations and dreams, he refers to the dreamer as though he were dead ("buried in sleep," equivalent to both castration, the unconscious representation of death [Freud, 1926], and return to the womb) and uses as his sole example a dream of the deceased, whose bones are "embraced" by Mother Earth. This is no thoughtless or "cheap" metaphor, as Lucretius informs us explicitly that the earth is "the mother of all things, and also their common tomb" (V.259). Hence, the earth's embrace of the dead repeats Venus' embrace of Mars and signifies both sexual intercourse and the return in fantasy to the womb. It is relevant in this connection that Lucretius regards death as the deep dreamless sleep in which a person is no longer tormented by plaguing fantasies and insatiable desires (Book III), in other words, as castration. Here the significance of Freud's (1920) theory of the death drive and its connection with castration (Laplanche and Leclaire, 1966) are given direct expression by Lucretius.

The contrast of light and dark that permeates this passage also closes it with a proliferation of images more appropriate for the relevation of arcane religious mysteries than for a scientific exposition. Lucretius' promise to his pupil to allow him to "gaze deeply into hidden realms" calls to mind Mephistopheles' pact with Faust; this imagery of intense gazing is also a regular feature of the child's visual fascination with his parents' lovemaking (Freud, 1918). Indeed, we have already encountered this fascination in Mars' open-mouthed intrigue with Venus' face. This image also recalls the famous metaphor of the search for truth: like dogs tracking wild beasts to their lairs, we must "penetrate into all the hiding places and drag truth out of there" (I.408-409). This metaphor includes not only the light-dark contrast, but an explicit allusion to sexuality as well (the term *insinuare,* "penetrate," literally "to thrust into the bosom or lap"). The final line of the passage quoted also alludes to the primal scene fantasy: darkness elicits dread of the unknown by calling to mind the unassimilated spectacle of parental intercourse, whose shadowy spectre Lucretius' philosophy is designed to illuminate, by dragging truth out into the light.[10] The poet himself again supplies the relevant connection by alluding to his own insomnia in undertaking this task, a symptom regularly traceable to continuing conflict concerning the primal scene (which includes both the fear of what goes on when one falls asleep, in the outside world and in one's own dreams, and the wish to see it happen). It is no surprise that Lucretius' later scientific explanation of sleep and dreams should lead, via the topic of wet dreams, directly into his disquisition on sex and love (IV.907-1057), considering how closely

---

10. To judge from Simon's (1972–1973) independent demonstration of the relevance of the primal scene experience for Plato's philosophy, it is conceivable that philosophical speculation in general may have as one of its fundamental motivations the need to assimilate this experience by intellectual means.

associated these topics are in his mind. The sleepless nights that he claims to experience are called *serenas,* a word that conveys several levels of meaning: "clear, cloudless," as the sky appears at the appearance of the mother, Venus (I.6-7); "clear" in the intellectual sense of rationality, as opposed to the shadow phantoms of hell and the veiled (*obscura*) secrets of the Greeks; "calm, stormless"; and "calm, peaceful, tranquil," in the technical Epicurean sense of attaining emotional tranquility by the rational elimination of unnecessary desires (like the *simulacra* of love). The high ethical value that the poet places on tranquility, defined as freedom from tormenting desires, itself reflects the important compromises and sacrifices of instinctual pleasure that are required in his struggle for *serenitas*; and, as will be demonstrated for another passage, this is an affirmation by negation of his emotional turmoil over the primal scene, just as he himself affirmed Iphianassa's marriage to her father by repeatedly denying it (cf. Freud, 1925).

The programmatic sentence at the end of the above quoted passage ("This dread and darkness...") punctuates another section of the poem that makes the connection between the play of light and dark and the child's dread of the primal scene even more explicit. It follows his incisive demonstration—which, for its contemporary relevance and psychological insight, could have been written today—that the insane struggle for wealth and political and military power arises directly out of the fear of death:

> All life is a struggle in the dark. For just as children in sightless [*caecis,* "blind"] darkness tremble and start at everything, so we in broad daylight are at times afraid of things that should inspire no more fear than those that children in the dark dread and imagine are about to happen. (II.54–58)

"All life is a struggle in the dark": here Lucretius evokes the atmosphere of Matthew Arnold's "Dover Beach," which portrays a terrifying world "where ignorant armies clash by night." These metaphors are direct descendants of the child's dread of darkness, a major clinical indicator of ambivalent anticipation and violent reconstruction of parental intercourse. For Lucretius, the child's dread is perpetuated in the adult's waking fantasy life. As he says, even when we are awake, we are still snoring and dreaming, "drifting in a drunken stupor upon a wavering tide of fantasy" (III.1046-1052; Latham).

The passage that most forcefully conveys the poet's continued enslavement to the primal scene fantasy, and includes all its themes as well, opens the book (III) on the fear of death; it is an expansion of Epicurus' attack on Nature, rendered in almost mystical poetry.

Out of the depths of darkness you were the first to lift up a radiant light, illuminating the blessings of life. It is you I follow, O glory of the Grecian race, and in your well-marked footprints now I firmly plant my steps, *not* so much from a desire to rival you as from my longing out of love to imitate you. After all, how can the swallow contend with the swan, or the kid with its rickety legs compete in a race with a strong-limbed steed? You are my father, glorious discoverer of truth, and give me fatherly guidance. From your pages, just as bees in flowery glades sip every blossom, so I too feed upon all your golden sayings: golden, as they are forever most worthy of everlasting life. (III.1-13)

The familiar theme of light penetrating the dark sets the stage for the primal scene, with a new element appended: the poet's recognition, again anticipating Freud in detail, of the ultimate hopelessness of the oedipal project, reflected in the rivalry—simultaneously negated (Freud, 1925) and admitted to be doomed to fail—and subsequent identification with the father, an inevitable sequence in every male's development (Freud, 1923). (The hostile element is repressed here, but finds attenuated expression in the immediately preceding passage, at the close of Book II, where a farmer, cursing that "Mother Earth," unlike before, now yields up her fruits only grudgingly, "frequently praises his father's good fortune" [II.1167].) Then the primal scene takes place, in all its grandeur and violence:

As soon as your philosophy, sprung from your godlike mind, lifts up its voice to proclaim the nature of the universe [*naturam rerum*], the terrors of the soul take flight, the walls of the world part asunder, and I behold the procession of events [*geri res*] throughout the whole of space [*inane*]. The majesty of the gods stands revealed and their peaceful abodes, that winds never lash [*concutiunt*] nor rainclouds [*nubila*] drench [*aspergunt*] nor snow congealed by bitter frost violates [*violat*] with its white blanket; always a cloudless [*innubilis*] sky envelops [*integit*] them and smiles with lavishly diffused radiance. Now Nature supplies all their wants, and nothing at any time mars their peace of mind. But nowhere do the realms of Hell come into view, though earth is no barrier to my observing everything that goes on [*geruntur*] underneath my feet throughout space [*inane*] below. At these events I am seized with a kind of divine delight [*voluptas*] and trembling awe [*horror*], that Nature, by your assault [*vi*], lies wide open [*patens*], so unveiled [*retecta*] and exposed [*manifesta*] in every part. (III.14-30)

The portrayal of the primal scene in this passage is apparent both in its visual representation and in its language. Just as previously Epicurus' mind had broken open the barred gates of the mother, Nature, so here again his mind "bellows" (*vociferari,* an unexpectedly violent word, as Leonard points out) the "Nature of things," causing the walls of the world to part like the Red Sea, and Lucretius beholds "things being done" (*geri res*) in the "void" (*inane*). This phrase, *res gerere,* "to do things," has a clear sexual connotation in Latin, where *res* signifies *res Veneris* ("acts of Venus," i.e., "sexual affairs," as in II.173, 437; IV.1058 ff.; etc.). As if to reinforce this meaning, Lucretius repeats it a few lines later (III.27: "all those things that are being done through the void below"). In both places the word *inane* appears, whose everyday meaning ("empty, void, without substance") has become both a technical philosophical term (*"the* void"), used to indicate the im-material area where atoms (matter) move, and a general term, that refers to what we call "space," the site of cosmic processes. In the context of the unconscious significance of this passage, however, it is probable that *inane* sustains yet another meaning, that void or space into which the penis penetrates, the vagina (cf. Erikson's "creative inner space," 1968). Words of double meaning inserted in Latin accumulate in the passage and serve to remind us constantly of the latent sexual theme, even when these words are—as we have become accustomed to expect from the am-bivalent Lucretius—negated: *concutiunt* and *violat* allude to rape, while snow has been identified as a symbol of blood (Fliess, 1973); the drenching rain and the sky that covers or envelops the gods' abode calls to mind the vivid description of the fertilization of Mother Earth by Father Sky, that gives rise to all life (I.250-264); the "cloudless sky" recalls the poet's sleepless "clear nights" as well as the sky swept cloudless at the coming of the sexually stimulating mother Venus (I.6-7); moreover, the words for "cloud" resemble and share a common root (*nub-*) with words that signify marriage (or, more exactly, "mar-riageability"). The culminating sentence of the passage is so pure that it may be read either for its manifest meaning or for its latent meaning and still make complete sense either way. The peculiar characteristic of the primal scene, that it is simultaneously sexually exciting and terrifying, gains literal expression here: Lucretius beholds both heaven and hell (the latter in negated form) and then claims that he is seized with "divine delight" (*voluptas*: "sexual pleasure," as in the first line of the poem as an epithet of Venus) and "trembling awe" (*horror*), emotions that clear-ly convey his utter fascination with this nearly hallucinatory vision. He then reveals the reason: Epicurus' violence has denuded Mother Nature of all her protective covering, and she "lies wide open and exposed" to his assault. It is no wonder that Lucretius believes he can behold "everything that is being done in the space."

Our analysis of this passage can even be carried beyond this linguistic dissection and description of its visual effect. Although the simple meanings of the words for the most part can be rendered in translation, their resonances and emotional tone, that ride on the power and vehemence of the Latin, cannot be easily conveyed. Lucretius' extraordinarily acute capacity for visualization takes on an auxiliary element here, which can only be called kinesthetic: in other words, his own bodily participation in the very texture of this passage is palpable, and he conveys its full impact to the reader by appealing directly to the analogy of bodily experience, in order to encourage an identification that compels conviction. This kinesthetic quality of the poetry has occurred in other quoted passages, such as the invocation to Venus, where her sexual animation of all creatures is communicated kinesthetically to the reader by carrying him away on a sea of poetry just as forcefully as Venus' creatures are carried away on a sea of passion. This level of poetic discourse can be understood by reference to the Rorschach Inkblot Technique (Rorschach, 1921; Klopfer et al., 1954; Schachtel, 1966). A human movement response that reflects the influence of a kinesthetic impulse in the subject that hs been inhibited and thus gains expression through the medium of the perception of the inkblot itself; in his self-inhibition, the subject has animated or vivified an otherwise motionless percept. This process may underlie the composition of all forceful poetry, insofar as it conveys its meaning spontaneously to the reader by bringing the poet's world to life for him (cf. Ducey, 1979).

This passage has another intriguing attribute. The human movement in it is gradually transformed into two seemingly opposite forms of expression: immobility (the static realm of the gods and the paralysis of the beholder) and violent inanimate movement (the workings of the abstract forces of the cosmos). The immobility calls to mind directly the source of the discovery of the primal scene fantasy, the famous wolf dream of Freud's (1918) patient, the Wolf-Man. The sensitive patient himself arrived at the interpretation that the static wolves of his dream alluded to violent movement, later recognized as his parents' sexual intercourse that he observed as an infant. Considering the context of the static quality of the gods' abode, and the liberal use of negatives here (winds never strike them, etc.), it is highly probable that by the opposite (Freud, 1900, 1925) the immobility represents parental intercourse. The poet's own paralyzed observation signifies directly another regular feature of a primal scene representation, the infant's fascination with the scene, and calls to mind the many instances of gaping and gazing in the poem. At the same time the immobility suggests again the ideal that Lucretius hopes to attain by Epicurean contemplation: release from his torturing vision and the unfulfillable desires it arouses, which, as he himself demonstrates, are the real tortures that the punishments of hell symbolize (cf. III.978 ff.; VI.9 ff.).

It is clear from these considerations that the violent inanimate movement of this passage, like the immobility, refers to the primal scene. The shift from human movement to the movement of abstract, inanimate forces (through Lucretius often personifies them) can be understood by further examination of Rorschach theory. Klopfer hypothesized, and clinical experience confirms, that "inanimate movement" responses indicate an "awareness of forces outside the control of the subject, which threaten the integrity of his personality organization" (1954, p. 266); they reflect the tension and conflict engendered by instinctual forces whose disruptive, explosive potential derives from the rigidity of defensive efforts against their emergence. Such responses are found particularly in those for whom unacceptable infantile fantasies are pressing for conscious recognition and explicit expression. This description derived from psychodiagnostic theory is tailor-made for Lucretius' poetry (and shamanistic legend; cf. Ducey, 1979).

The above passage (III.14-30) is not the only one in which control by external, non-human forces has appeared. The invocation to Venus shows all living creatures in the grip of "drives" against which they are powerless; the oppression of man by Religion and the fertilization of Mother Earth by Father Sky further illustrate this theme. It may be objected that these are, after all, "merely" poetic personifications, designed to give vividness to the processes described. This may well be true, but it is no prima facie justification for rejecting the extensive evidence of the influence of psychological factors here, particularly when the most technical and least poetic passages still depict a world controlled by powerful forces outside human control. Furthermore, the poem is filled with similar descriptions of the power of truly inanimate (not personified) forces, all the way from the atoms, the building blocks of Epicurean theory, to the cosmic processes. As for the atoms, it has been pointed out the *materies*, "matter," which alludes etymologically to the mother, is one of several terms used to refer to the atoms: other terms are almost invariably sexual (*genitalia corpora*, "genital bodies"; *genitalis materies*, "genital matter"; *semina rerum*, "seeds of things"; *semen*, "seed, semen"; *corpora prima*, "first bodies"), and their activities are represented in directly sexual language (*concilium, coitus, concursus,* "sexual intercourse"). The sexual nature of the cosmic processes reaches clearest expression in Lucretius' scientific aphorism, *corporibus caecis igitur Natura gerit res* (I.328), literally, "with blind bodies therefore

Nature does things." The manifest meaning is that Nature carries on cosmic process with invisible atoms; but, as we have seen, the phrase "Nature does things" may also have a sexual significance, while the phrase "blind bodies" calls to mind the bodies of loves writhing in passion (IV.1112 ff.), an activity that arises from a "blind [i.e., unseen] wound" (IV.1120), as well as the lover's blindness to faults in the beloved (IV.1153) and even the children "in blind [= sightless] darkness," trembling at the primal scene. The sexual behavior of the atoms is clearly a miniature representation of the primal scene. But even on this level, Lucretius cannot portray sex without violent movement, conflict, and aggression: the atoms are engaged in eternal war, striking and jostling each other, coming together and coming apart, in perceptual motion (II.95-141). Moreover, these seemingly impotent atoms are the ultimate foundation of all natural and cosmic processes and can therefore cause hurricanes, torrential floods, and all the other inanimate forces and natural disasters that Lucretius takes such delight in describing (I.269 ff.). He devotes two-thirds of the last book (VI) to a depiction of natural disasters and then climaxes the poem with a minutely detailed and devastating description of the ravages of plague. This ending, like his vivid and terrifying description of death (III), is scarcely likely to provide comfort to an audience whose fear of death Lucretius is trying to dispel, but his avowed purposes are continually subverted by his drive-powered fantasies. The paradigmatic portrayal of the drives out of control in his bizarre and grotesque depiction of the use of wild animals in war (V.1308-1349), where the animals, "enflamed by promiscuous carnage" (Latham), run wild and tear to shreds foe and master alike, heedless of attempts to restrain them with chains. Even the world itself is seen as going out of control, in the vivid descriptions (cf. V.95 ff.; VI.565-567, 603-607) of the inevitable destruction of the world: almost as in Epicurus' attack,

> with the speed of flame the walls of the world will suddenly dissolve and fly into the boundless void, and the rest will follow in just the same fashion: the thundering regions of the sky will rush down from aloft, the earth will tear itself away violently from beneath our feet, its particles dissolved amid the mingled debris of objects and sky. The whole world will vanish into the abyss, so that in an instant nothing will be left but empty space and invisible atoms. (I.1102-1110)

Such passages, dispersed throughout the poem, demonstrate Lucretius' fascination with overwhelming inanimate forces, which both Rorschach theory and our analysis of his fantasy life would interpret as overwhelming but inadmissible instinctual impulses.

Behind this theme of world destruction lies the final element that completes any portrayal of the influence of primal scene and oedipal fantasies: intense castration or body destruction anxiety. As Freud (1926, pp. 129–130) has shown, the concept of death gains no concrete representation in the unconscious, since no one can conceive of his own death; therefore, the dread of death may serve as a vehicle for the expression of intense castration anxiety arising from oedipal wishes. Hence, it is not surprising that in his attempt to dispel the dread of death (Book III) Lucretius employs extensive castration imagery to convey his idea of death. In his representations of large parts of the body cut off, eyes torn out, atoms dispersed, the body split in half, or snakes chopped into many pieces (III.117-120, 396-416, 558-579, 634-669), he is always concerned about whether life continues or not. Indeed, in his account of the plague he states that some castrated themselves, cut off limbs, or put out their eyes in order to remain alive (IV.1205-1212). This portrayal is the obverse of another peculiar phenomenon that he identifies: at times a person comes to despise life so much, because of unrelenting death anxiety, that he commits suicide (III.79-86).[11]

Lucretius himself identifies the ultimate source of his dread of castration in his long digression on the worship of the Magna Mater, the Great Mother of gods, men, and beasts, the deified Mother Earth (II.600-660). In spite of every sort of denial and disclaimer of her importance, he cannot restrain himself from including this extended portrait, not, however, as some critics of his virtual atheism have it, because he was "unconsciously religious," but rather, as I have shown, because he was fascinated with maternal figures. But this description arouses oedipal fantasies that make him anxious. For instance, he claims that her attendant priests in her cult are eunuchs because "they have violated their Mother's divine will and have been judged to be ungrateful to their fathers" (II.614-615). Lucretius' explanation is suspiciously incomplete in that he offers no direct indication of their actual sin, but his language makes it clear enough: they have "violated" (*violarint,* with its usual sexual significance) the Mother, thereby displeasing the father and calling forth their own castration. A few lines later Lucretius commits a parapraxis, as he is still under the influence of unconscious fantasy: he mistakenly calls the Corybantes (the Great Mother's attendant band of ecstatic musicians, dancers, and warriors; Leonard [1942], p. 372;

---

11. This theory too is echoed in modern psychodynamic thought: in order to maintain the illusion of complete control over one's own fate, a person may castrate himself, literally or figuratively, or commit suicide to alleviate intense castration anxiety. This appears to be related to the tendency for a child to master a passively experienced trauma by active repetition in play (Freud, 1920).

(Dodds [1951, pp. 77-79]) the "Curetes," a Cretan group involved in the worship of Jupiter. These "Curetes," he tells us, protected the infant Jupiter from his father's devouring him (regressive version of castration; cf. Ducey [1979], which would "deal his mother's heart an everlasting wound" (II.633 ff.). Though Lucretius himself does not mention it, the myth goes on to show Jupiter's conquest of his father Saturn, which, as Grant (1962, p. 116) points out, is a duplication of Saturn's castration of his own father. Thus, to one castration story (the Great Mother's eunuch priests) Lucretius associates another (Jupiter and Saturn), without regard for the facts (that Curetes and Corybantes are distinct and separate groups of worshipers). But a subtle shift will be noted here: the castration of the son for violating the mother has been transformed into the protection of the son from father's attempt to castrate him, the siding of mother with son against father, and, implicitly, the eventual murder of father by son. In other words, Lucretius has successfully turned castration anxiety into patricidal impulse. His next association shows, however, that he cannot allow himself to indulge in his wish-fulfilling fantasy for long without succumbing to his characteristic guilt and ambivalence.

> The goddess commands that men be willing to defend their fatherland [*patriam terram,* "father's earth"] by courage in battle and be ready [*parent*] to be a source of protection and pride to their parents [*parentibus*]. (II.641-643)

As the extensive word-play on parents on this passage demonstrates, Lucretius arrives finally at the only realistic solution to the problem of oedipal wishes and castration anxiety: he yields up mother to father (Mother Earth, *terram,* is really father's, *patriam*) at mother's command (the goddess, Great Mother Earth), and by that inevitable mixture of sublimation and hypocrisy that appeared previously in his renunciation of competition with his father, Epicurus, he depicts men as undertaking to protect the parental relationship and making their parents proud by directing oedipal hatred outward toward those who would harm the parents or destroy their relationship.

This renunciation of the mother, painful and difficult as it is, must occur for the individual to grow beyond the desires and fears of childhood; and while Lucretius recognizes this fact, the accumulated evidence suggests that he was unable or unwilling to effect this renunciation. Therefore, he remains enslaved to his unconscious infantile fantasies, in pursuit of mere illusions (*simulacra*) that are poor substitutes for what he really wants but is unconscious of; he remains trapped in an eternal, dynamically maintained structure that never changes but only appears under different guises. Yet for all his haranguing, which is really self-haranguing, he can only acknowledge but cannot renounce them. Surely it was personal experience that made Lucretius such a great psychologist, such a brilliant diagnostician of his own and the world's woes (Ducey and Simon, 1974), that he divined the connection between humanity's eternal frustration (*hiantis* in this passage) and the frustration of the infant at the breast (*inhians* in the Mars-Venus passage):

> As long as what we crave is out of reach, it seems to surpass everything else in importance; once it is ours, we crave something else, and an unquenchable thirst for life keeps us forever gaping in frustration [*hiantis*]. (III.1082-1084)

SUMMARY

Lucretius' impassioned indictment of passion, the *De Rerum Natura,* is not only a scientific discourse on the Epicurean theory of the universe, but also a sublimated transcription and attempted resolution of the poet's unconscious conflicts. The conflicts which animate the work appear to derive from a continuing investment in the primal scene fantasy, the distorted, infantile representation of the parents' sexual intercourse. This experience leads explicitly to a sadistic interpretation of love and sex, and implicitly to the gnawing sense of frustration, the constant anticipation of impending catastrophe, and the torment of insatiable passions that permeate the poem. Extensive structural and psychoanalytic interpretations of style and imagery show the symbolic transformations that the primal scene fantasy undergoes in its mental representation and "working through," with the result that parental and sexual relationships are temporarily distinguished from one another and disentangled. Thus, incestuous desires and anxieties are symbolically overcome, and the torment of insatiable passions subsides to Epicurean tranquility. Yet, for Lucretius as well as for his tormented lovers,

> the same madness returns, the frenzy comes again, when they ask themselves what they desire to attain and are unable to find the device that would overcome this bane; in such a state of confusion they waste away from a hidden wound. (IV.1117-1120)

BIBLIOGRAPHY

BAILEY, C., ed. (1947). *T. Lucreti Cari De Rerum Natura.* 3 vols. Oxford: Clarendon Press.
BARTHES, R. (1964). *On Racine.* New York: Hill and Wang.
BOYANCÉ, P. (1963). *Lucrèce et L'épicurisme.* Paris: Presses Universitaires de France.

BUNKER, H. A. & LEWIN, B. D. (1951). A psychoanalytic notation on the root, GN, KN, CN. In *Psychoanalysis and Culture: Essays in Honor of Géza Róheim*, G. B. Wilbur & W. Muensterberger (eds.). New York: International Universities Press, pp. 363-367.

CLAY, D. (1971). Review of L. Perelli, *Lucrezio, poeta dell'angoscia*. *Amer. J. Philol.*, 92:119-121.

DODDS, E. R. (1951). *The Greeks and the Irrational*. Berkeley: University of California Press, 1966.

DUCEY, C. (1979). The shaman's dream journey: Psychoanalytic and structural complementarity in myth interpretation. In *The Psychoanalytic Study of Society*, Vol. 8, W. Muensterberger & L. B. Boyer (eds.). New Haven: Yale University Press, pp. 71-117.

_____ & GALINSKY, M. D. (1973). The metapsychology of pleasure. *J. Amer. Psychoanal. Assn.*, 21:495-525.

_____ & SIMON, B. (1974). Ancient Greece and Rome. In *World History of Psychiatry*, J. G. Howells (ed.). New York: Brunner-Mazel, pp. 1-38.

EDELHEIT, H. (1972). Mythopoiesis and the primal scene. In *The Psychoanalytic Study of Society*, Vol. 5, W. Muensterberger & A. Esman (eds.). New York: International Universities Press, pp. 212-233.

ERIKSON, E. (1968). *Identity: Youth and Crisis*. New York: Norton.

ESMAN, A. (1973). The primal scene. *Psychoanal. Stud. Child*, 28:49-81. New Haven: Yale University Press.

FERENCZI, S. (1924). *Thalassa: A Theory of Genitality*. New York: Norton, 1968.

FLIESS, R. (1956). *Erogeneity and Libido. Psychoanalytic Series, I*. New York: International Universities Press.

_____ (1973). *Symbol, Dream, and Psychosis. Psychoanalytic Series, III*. New York: International Universities Press.

FREUD, S. (1900). The interpretation of dreams. *S.E.*, 4 & 5. London: Hogarth Press, 1953.

_____ (1910). "Wild" psychoanalysis. *S.E.*, 11:221-227. London: Hogarth Press, 1957.

_____ (1912). On the universal tendency to debasement in the sphere of love: Contributions to the psychology of love II. *S.E.*, 11:179-190. London: Hogarth Press, 1957.

_____ (1918). From the history of an infantile neurosis. *S.E.*, 17:7-122. London: Hogarth Press, 1955.

_____ (1920). Beyond the pleasure principle. *S.E.*, 18:7-64. London: Hogarth Press, 1955.

_____ (1921). Group psychology and the analysis of the ego. *S.E.*, 18:69-143. London: Hogarth Press, 1955.

_____ (1923). The ego and the id. *S.E.*, 19:12-66. London: Hogarth Press, 1961.

_____ (1925). Negation. *S.E.*, 19:235-239. London: Hogarth Press, 1961.

_____ (1926). Inhibitions, symptoms, and anxiety. *S.E.*, 20:87-172. London: Hogarth Press, 1959.

GEER, R. M., ed., trans. (1964). *Epicurus: Letters, Principle Doctrines, and Vatican Sayings*. Indianapolis, Ind.: Bobbs-Merrill.

GRANT, M. (1962). *Myths of the Greeks and Romans*. Cleveland: World Publishing Company.

KINSEY, T. E. (1964). The melancholy of Lucretius. *Arion*, 3:115-130.

KLOPFER, B., AINSWORTH, M. D., KLOPFER, W. G., & HOLT, R. R. (1954). *Developments in the Rorschach Technique. I: Technique and Theory*. New York: Harcourt, Brace, & World.

LAPLANCHE, J. & LECLAIRE, S. (1966). The unconscious: A psychoanalytic study. In *French Freud: Structural Studies in Psychoanalysis*, J. Mehlman (ed.). *Yale French Studies*, 48:118-178.

LATHAM, R. E., trans. (1951). *Lucretius: On the Nature of the Universe.* Baltimore: Penguin Books.

LEONARD, W. E. & SMITH, S. B., eds. (1942). *T. Lucreti Cari De Rerum Natura Libri Sex.* Madison, Wisc.: University of Wisconsin Press.

LÉVI-STRAUSS, C. (1958). *Structural Anthropology.* New York: Basic Books, 1963.

———— (1962). *The Savage Mind.* Chicago: University of Chicago Press, 1966.

———— (1964). *The Raw and the Cooked (Mythologiques I).* New York: Harper and Row, 1969.

LOGRE, D. (1946). *L'anxiété de Lucrèce.* Paris: J. B. Janin.

MANTINBAND, J. H., trans. (1965). *Lucretius: On the Nature of the Universe.* New York: Frederick Ungar.

MARTHA, C. (1869). *Le Poème de Lucrèce.* Paris: Hachette.

MINADEO, R. (1969). *The Lyre of Science: Form and Meaning in Lucretius' De Rerum Natura.* Detroit: Wayne State University Press, 1969.

RÓHEIM, G. (1934). *The Riddle of the Sphinx.* London: Hogarth Press.

RORSCHACH, H. (1921). *Psychodiagnostics.* Berne: Hans Huber, 1942.

SCHACHTEL, E. (1966). *Experiential Foundations of Rorschach's Test.* New York: Basic Books.

SCHAFER, R. (1970). The psychoanalytic vision of reality. *Internat. J. Psycho-Anal.,* 51:279–297.

SCHRIJVERS, P. H. (1970). *Horror ac Divina Voluptas. Études sur la Poétique et la Poésie de Lucrèce.* Amsterdam.

SIMON, B. (1972–1973). Models of mind and mental illness in ancient Greece: II. The Platonic model. *J. Hist. Behav. Sciences,* 8:389–404, & 9:3–17.

WORMELL, D. E. W. (1960). Lucretius: The personality of the poet. *Greece and Rome,* 2nd ser., 7:54–65.

———— (1965). The personal world of Lucretius. In *Lucretius,* D. R. Dudley (ed.). London: Routledge and Kegan Paul.

9

The Author and His Audience:
Jean Genet's Early Work

STANLEY J. COEN

This essay was stimulated by Khan (1965) and Bach and Schwartz (1972) who suggested the existence of a writing perversion which certain gifted authors can substitute for perverse sexual behavior. The implicit hypothesis maintained that the relationship between a perverse writer and his audience may approximate a perverse sexual experience. Unfortunately, the relationship between artist and audience has been relatively neglected in psychoanalytic studies of art. In order to investigate Genet's relationship with his audience, I decided to observe my own emotional responses to his writings, using myself as reader, audience, and psychoanalyst. This approach to applied psychoanalysis quickly led me into the complications and concerns about methodology and aims that exist in contemporary psychoanalytic literary criticism.

I will refrain from speculation about the actual Jean Genet. The relationship between narrator/author and reader is examined by a study of "the reading experience" of the works and the fantasies of the narrator/author I have constructed. For Fish (1980) "the structure of the reading experience" refers to what is happening to the reader as he reads and for what purposes. Fish (1970) has turned the affective fallacy around to argue that what the poem does is precisely what it means. Wimsatt and Beardsley (1954) have warned ("the affective fallacy") that the psychological effects of a poem should not be confused with what the poem itself is. My construct of the narrator/author is congruent with Wayne Booth's (1979) distinction between the "implied author" and the "flesh-and-blood author." The former refers to the creating person who is implied by the choices made in crafting the work precisely as it has been done. Following Cooper (1981), I now disagree with Booth's further opinion that our picture of the "implied author" should be compatible with established biographical facts about the author. At issue here are reasonable standards for interpretation, such as those offered by Kris and Kaplan (1948) of correspondence, intent, and coherence rather than biographical reconstruction or consistency between our fantasied construct of the "implied author" and any real life person. I do agree with Bleich (1978, p. 263) that "every reader's conception of an author is his own construction."

My material is based on the early works of Genet: *Our Lady of the Flowers* (*Notre-Dame-des-Fleurs,* 1943, to be abbreviated here as OLF), his first novel, written entirely in prison; *The Maids* (1947), his second play; and *The Thief's Journal* (1948, here designated as TTJ), an autobiography. I have chosen three different literary forms: novel, drama, and autobiography, in order to explore several forms of relationship between narrator/author and reader or audience. I will argue that the relationship between narrator/author and reader is central to these works, more important than any specific content or fantasy elaboration. My fantasied construct of the narrator/author of these works is one in which he seeks to engage and force his reader into an intensely responsive relationship, representative of loving parent and child, whose task is to provide him with affirmation, admiration, and acceptance. It will be necessary to argue that such psychological meaning can be reasonably attributed to the narrative point of view of these works.

Review Of The Literature

Although much has been written about the multiple functions art serves for creative integration and adaptation of inner and outer reality (e.g. Waelder, 1965; Rose, 1978, 1980; Roland, 1978; Rothenberg, 1978; Noy, 1979), the author's attitudes and relation to his text and audience have been insufficiently investigated. There have been a few notable exceptions. Sachs (1942), and later Myers (1979) pointed out that the artist seeks relief from guilt and the undoing of narcissistic mortification from his audience. Kris (1952) noted that the creative artist must have some "idea of a public," real or imaginary. According to Kris, the approval of an audience, alleviates guilt, confirms the artist's belief in his work, and restores a balance which may have been disturbed by the creative process. Communication within the aesthetic experience "lies not so much in the prior intent of the artist as in the consequent re-creation by the audience of his work of art" (p. 254). Kris believed that ambiguity in poetry does not serve to convey a pre-existing poetic content; rather, ambiguity functions as "the instrument by which a content is made poetic through the process of re-creation." Greenacre (1957, p. 490) concurred that the artist always has "some fantasy of a collective audience or recipient"; the artistic creation is regarded as a love gift which aims to approach perfection. Rose (1972, 1973) emphasized the artist's pull toward rapprochement with the early mother and his subsequent detachment from her as an essential narcissistic motivation in creativity. More recently (1980), Rose considers several psychological functions served by the relationship between audience and work of art. He discusses tension regulation, and temporary experiences of fusion and regression which lead to the potential for separateness and redefinition, reorientation, new synthesis, and enhanced self-esteem. Rose emphasizes a dialectic during the aesthetic experience between the polarities of ambiguity—control, feeling—thought, and fusion—separation.

In 1976, Niederland had stressed defense against narcissistic injury as motivation for creative work. This involves a pathological body image and the fantasy of perfect "autoreconstruction," as well as the restitution of a lost or destroyed object. Niederland noted (p. 209) three ways that the artistic product provides "affirmation of the artist's own and often fragile self": the creation of something new gratifies the male's unconscious wish for pregnancy and birth; the artist proves, to himself, and if successful, to others, that he is the creator of the product; by identification with the artistic product, he demonstrates his ability to "recreate himself in a perfect, no longer incomplete or deficient form." Noy (1979) specifies the need for the communication and sharing of personal experiences as one function of art; other needs are for self-definition in relation to the object and adaptation between self and reality. Noy also emphasizes the search for forms through which meanings and experiences can be transmitted from artist to audience as a central problem of the creative artist.

Significant connections between writing and perversion have already been suggested. Khan (1965) noted that confession is a function of perverse behavior. He referred to the "extravagant sincerity" of writers like Oscar Wilde, Andre Gide, Henry Miller, and Jean Genet. Khan suggested that such confession, whether through sexual contact or writing, approximated dreaming or hallucinating more than organized ego activity. Bach and Schwartz (1972) speculated that one goal of the Marquis de Sade's writing *The 120 Days of Sodom* in prison was its effect on imaginary readers. Following Kohut they interpreted this as de Sade's wish to so devastate his readers with "horror, disgust and outrage" that they would have to affirm his grandiose self as it appears in the exercise of his sadistic power. Imaginary readers are "both his mirroring audience and his victims" (p. 470). They suggested that the "brilliance, intensity and sensation" of de Sade's fantasies were the means by which he evoked such vivid reactions in his characters and in his readers. Bach & Schwartz's major emphasis, however, was on de Sade's delusional attempt within the text to validate grandiose self-images and idealized object-images as defenses against psychotic fragmentation. Writing about Oscar Wilde's narcissism, Kavka (1975) regarded the creative process as an attempt at self-cure which involved the re-establishment of self-cohesion. Kavka also cited E.S. Wolf's idea that Wilde treated his artistic creations as self-objects used for reconstituting a cohesive self.

Reader-response criticism (e.g., Rosenblatt, Fish, Iser, Gadamer, Poulet) has strongly influenced certain psychoanalytically influenced critics (e.g., Holland, Schwartz, Bleich). Then philosophical approaches to the phenomenology of reading have been stressed in efforts to move criticism away from limited efforts to determine the objective meanings hidden within a text, which need to be extricated by the reader. The subjective experience of the reader, the interaction between reader and text (and, at times, even with the author), and the values and premises with which the reader approaches interpretation of the text have all been emphasized. According to Schwartz (1978), the literary relationship, occurs between people; the reader seeks an experience, not with a text, but with his own "embodiment" of the author. Schwartz (1978, p. 150) maintains that "the author I seek is actually always a fiction I recreate through his fictions." Bleich (1978, p. 161) suggested that the more unfamiliar a reader is with an author or "his language system," the greater will be his need to "invent an author as part of the normal activity of response and interpretation." Such reader concentration on a construct of the author may serve a variety of psychological functions.

Winnicott (1971) has influenced two psychoanalytic commentators on the relationship between author and reader. Green (1978) describes writing as "communication with the absent" (p. 282); the absence as well as the illusory re-presentation of the reader are both intensely felt and "fashioned" by the writer. The reader's experience of the writer mirrors the writer's experience of the reader. The author's and reader's doubles, "ghosts which never reveal themselves—communicate through the writing" in "this no-man's land . . . . this site of a transnarcissistic communication" (Green, 1978, p. 283). Green hints that one motivation of Proust's (or at least of the literary Marcel's) writing was a search for contact with a mother who desired literary more than live objects.

Gorney (1980) describes a dialectic of co-authorship, an imaginary relationship between reader and writer when a reader interprets a text. "It is within the field of illusion provided by the text," Gorney writes "that a discourse between author and reader is established, interpretation occurs and meaning is freshly created" (p. 14). Gorney (1979), p. 4) argues that language and literary creation, with the role of illusion, aims at a "wished-for recognition of a real or fantasied other" or at least the illusory re-creation of an absent other. He agrees with Poulet (1970) that the author attempts to render "himself present through his re-creation within the reader" (p. 14); this is related to themes of immortality and identity.

The Real-Life Genet: Some Background

Jean Genet wrote *Our Lady of the Flowers* in Fresnes Prison at the age of thirty-two. He was awaiting trial for theft for which he feared he would receive a ten year sentence. Prior to this novel he had written only a few poems which have been regarded by critics as crude. Considering his extreme emotional deprivation and the fact that he received little formal education, Genet's literary accomplishment is remarkable. Born illegitimately in the public maternity hospital of Paris, he was abandoned at birth by his mother; his father was unknown. Raised in an orphanage by the French Public Assistance until he was seven, he was then placed with a peasant foster family in the Morvan, a rural region of France. There is suggestive evidence (TTJ, p. 224) that Genet may have been accepted as a replacement for the foster parents' dead daughter; this may have interfered with the care he received and added to an identification he made with the dead and the feminine. At age ten, Genet was branded a thief by his foster parents which concretely labeled him an outcast, no doubt intensifying his feeling of being a bastard. His writings and the meager factual information available about Genet suggest that he never felt loved and accepted. At fifteen he was sent to Mettray Reformatory, most likely as punishment for theft. Unfortunately, as with the rest of Genet's biography, there is little reliable information about this incident. Genet's self-revelations are contradictory; however, in *Miracle of the Rose* (1946) Genet says (p. 225) that what led him to Mettray was the unprovoked gouging out of a child's eye. Is this fact or fantasy? Although Genet's works abound with sadistic, destructive images, there is no evidence that he actually engaged in such acts.

After Mettray, he briefly joined the Foreign Legion, then lived as a vagabond, beggar, homosexual prostitute, smuggler and thief, and was often in and out of prison. Sartre (1952) says that at the age of sixteen Genet had an opportunity to learn from a professional songwriter. Actually it is not known how he gained his impressive knowledge of language, art, and literature. Genet jokingly says he learned the art of browsing in bookstores by pilfering valuable books. He claims to have written *Our Lady of the Flowers* on the brown paper convicts were given to make paper bags. When his manuscript was confiscated, he rewrote it from memory on notebooks purchased at the prison canteen. How he smuggled the novel out of prison and had it printed is unclear. After publication of his first novel Genet was adopted by a group of French writers. In 1948, a number of them, including Sartre, Cocteau, Mauriac, Gide, Mondor, and Claudel, successfully petitioned the French President, Auriol, to pardon Genet who faced life imprisonment for his tenth criminal offense. Genet, the petty criminal was transformed into Genet, the poet.

THE READING EXPERIENCE OF GENET'S EARLY WORK:
SOME EXAMPLES

Our Lady of the Flowers is dedicated to the memory of Maurice
Pilorge, who, as we are told on the very first page, "killed his lover,
Escudero, to rob him of something under a thousand francs, then for his
twentieth birthday, they cut off his head, while *you* will recall, he
thumbed his nose at the enraged executioner." (Emphasis added.) On
this first page, we are also told the author is writing this book in honor of
the crimes of three murderers and one traitor. The very first sentence
contains a substitution of the reader for the narrator, representative of
many similar shifts to follow: "Weidman appeared before *you* in a five
o'clock edition, his head swathed in white bands, a nun and yet a
wounded pilot fallen into the rye one September day. . ." (Emphasis
added.) The tension between narrator and audience is kept taut by
repeatedly calling attention to the fact that he is the writer and that
"you" are the reader. The reader feels shocked by the suggestion that he,
like the narrator, spends his time idealizing murderers. This engages the
reader in the narrative, connects reader and narrator more intimately
while making the reader want to protest and disclaim the identity with
the narrator which has been conferred upon him. Without doubt, the
author/narrator is also evoking his own personal version of the prevalent
contemporary critical principles of subjectivism, uncertainty, relativism,
and indeterminacy.

On the fourth page "you" become part of the narrator's masturbatory
fantasies, as he offers to caress the reader's prick, and even boasts and
recalls that this has already happened. The reader is startled, confused,
wants to protest, perhaps is even titillated with such offers of phallic
worship. But just as you feel this, the narrator jostles you again. Perhaps
this is all make-believe, perhaps he is only playing with you. The final
orgasmic image of this scene evokes religious adoration, sainthood, confusing the reader about the level of illusion to which the narrator has now
moved. Then again, as narrator and reader are ascending heavenward,
the narrator again shakes you, reminding you in the next paragraph that
he is telling you practical and important details of his prison life.

The narrator becomes the barker for a carnival sideshow, seductively
offering to gratify the reader's most perverse fantasies, once you enter
into his world. These asides put the reader in his place and emphasize his
dependence on the narrator. The arrival of Darling Daintyfoot, a pimp,
is grandiloquently announced; the narrator interrupts the description to
interject (OLF, p. 70), "which *you* can only imagine" (Emphasis added).
He rhapsodizes, "I was his at once, as if" and again interrupts, "who
said that?" before completing the thought, "he had discharged through

my mouth straight to my heart." The narrator again invites the reader into his bed, encouraging the reader's jealousy and lust; simultaneously the narrator is ramming your perverse curiosity down your throat.

The narrator of *Our Lady of the Flowers* describes his writing as an interlude between masturbating and says that he is reporting his masturbation fantasies. However, the narrator drives home to the reader that he is unable to cope with his severe depression, fears of madness, isolation, loneliness, and vulnerability when he is alone with his fantasies and with his masturbation. He needs the reader's enthusiastic participation; at this point it is still ambiguous whether the narrator longs for imaginary readers or believes he is soon to acquire actual readers. He tells us that he knows that his imagination is lovely but he feels insubstantial, inconsequential and remote, lost in his daydreaming. His fantasies lack credibility for him, even when he tries to vitalize them by masturbation; alone, he is unable to feel better about himself. The reader is being invited to draw nearer as friend, lover, and healer. Genet writes (OLF, p. 132): "My mind continues to produce lovely chimeras, but so far none of them has taken on flesh. Never. Not once. If I now try to indulge in a daydream, my throat goes dry, despair burns my eyes, shame makes me bow my head, my reverie breaks up . . . The despondency that follows makes me feel somewhat like a shipwrecked man who spies a sail, sees himself saved, and suddenly remembers that the lens of his spyglass has a flaw, a blurred spot—the sail he has seen." He adds (p. 138): ". . . in the evening the preliminaries of sleep denude the environs of my self, destroy objects and episodes, leaving me at the edge of sleep as solitary as I was one night in the middle of a stormy and barren heath. Darling, Divine, and Our Lady [his characters] flee from me at top speed, taking with them the consolation of their existence, which has its being only in me, for they are not content with fleeing; they do away with themselves, dilute themselves in the *appalling insubstantiality of my dreams.*" (Emphasis added.) In writing he seeks experiences in which the word (OLF, p. 178) "ceased to be word and became flesh."

The mood of *Our Lady of the Flowers* is one of depression. The narrator talks about suicide. All this is frightening and convincing to the reader; so are the images of madness. Village, the handsome black murderer, has been painting tiny lead soldiers in his cell—they take over: "One morning, after waking up, he sat down on his bed, looked around the room, and saw it full of stupid-looking figurines that were lying about everywhere, as mindless and mocking as a race of fetuses, as Chinese torturers. The troops rose up in sickening waves to attack the giant. He felt himself capsizing. He was sinking into an absurd sea, and the eddies of his despair were sucking *me* into the shipwreck. *I* grabbed hold of a soldier. They were all over the floor, everywhere, a thousand,

308   STANLEY J. COEN

ten thousand, a hundred thousand! And though I was holding the one I had picked up in the warm hollow of my palm, it remained icy, without breath . . . The little soldiers whipped up a swell that made the room pitch'' (p. 189). (Emphasis added.) The change of pronoun plays with uncertainty between object and subject and allows the reader to identify more closely; but it is experienced as if the narrator were losing his grasp on reality, alarming us. The narrator then immediately transforms this image of impending madness into one of sexual dizziness, orgasm. Perhaps he was only being carried away by passion rather than madness. It is characteristic of each of these three works that negative, dangerous images of self and object are transformed by sexual seduction and poetry into exciting and beautiful counterparts. Sexual feelings are used to still pain, to make unpleasant reality illusory, and to dominate and control others.

The narrator is anxious about his forthcoming trial. As he reveals this (p. 189), he quickly shifts to describing himself masturbating, as if that will change what is real for him. The trial scene at the conclusion of *Our Lady of the Flowers* seems to lessen the narrator's anxiety by the mastery involved in writing about it. The psychiatrist's report about the defendant reads "unbalanced . . . psychopathy . . . schizophrenia . . . unbalanced . . . equilibrist" (p. 295). "Equilibrist" is then defined as "one who balances himself in unnatural positions and hazardous movements, as in rope dancing." This describes well how the narrator attempts to master his frightening feelings within the text by going right to the edge of the abyss, looking down, then reminding himself and the reader, that this is all illusory and under the former's full control.

The narrator continuously proclaims the importance for him of his audience. He writes (OLF, p. 212): "I feel such a need to complain and to try to win a reader's love!" (TTJ, p. 207): "By the gravity of the means and the splendor of the materials which the poet used to draw near to men, I measure the distance that separated him from them . . . By the gravity of the means I require to thrust you from me, measure the tenderness I feel for you. Judge to what degree I love you from the barricades I erect in my life and work . . . so that your breath—I am corruptible to an extreme—may not rot me. My tenderness is of fragile stuff." (TTJ, p. 268): "I aspire to your recognition, your consecration."

That the narrator "thrusts" his reader away while craving his presence seems apparent from almost any page of Genet's writing. Images of the ugly and despicable represented as beautiful shock and confuse us. The reader is dazzled and surprised by the narrator's sudden turns and the unexpected and unusual transformations in his images. The reader continually loses his footing, not knowing what to believe, what is real and what is illusory, what is evil and mean and what is good and valuable. Just as one feels this, the narrator introduces a dialogue with the reader warning the latter how treacherous he can be while offering to rescue the reader. The narrator reminds the reader of the latter's dependence on him, his helplessness in the narrator's world, and protectively offers to sit close beside the reader and guide him.

When the narrator has revealed tender feelings, when he seems to become more gentle and caring, and the reader relaxes his guard and enjoys himself, then he pulls himself and you up short. The reader continually feels manipulated as he is invited into the narrator's finely crafted poetic images, only to be frustrated ultimately. For example, the aging Divine, the drag queen who is losing her charm and lovers, meets the "Archangel Gabriel," who is supportive and accepting. Divine "swooned with love like a nymph in a tree" (OLF, p. 160) at Gabriel's potency and passion with her; "Divine's eyes became brilliant and her skin suppler." Then Gabriel's role is reduced to "fucker," whereupon we are told: "Then he died in the war" (p. 161).

The narrator reminds the reader, that he, not you, is creating the poetry. This is his world, not yours. You are an invited guest and if you want to find your way in it, you need him to direct you; otherwise you will become lost in a labyrinth. One is reminded of Stilitano (TTJ, p. 265), humiliated and trapped in the "crystal prison" of the Palace of Mirrors, unable to find his way out of this game of glass, some of it transparent and some mirroring; occasionally he would see his own reflection, sometimes he'd see others beyond the glass. Since the narrator keeps inventing and changing the images, there is no way for the reader to find his own way. Yet the narrator keeps taunting the reader with possibilities of sharing in the creation of the poetry only to then emphasize his own central role as author. He writes (OLF, p. 109): "Here are some 'Divinariana' gathered expressly for you. Since I wish to show the reader a few candid shots of her, it is up to him to provide a sense of duration, of passing time, and to assume that during this first chapter she will be between twenty and thirty years of age." It is emphasized that this is an impossible task for the reader. Or again, the narrator introduces Darling and Our Lady and tells the reader: "I leave you free to imagine any dialogue you please. Choose whatever may charm you. Have it, if you like, that they hear the voice of the blood, or that they fall in love at first sight, or that Darling, by indisputable signs invisible to the vulgar eye, betrays the fact that he is a thief . . . Conceive the wildest improbabilities. Have it that the depths of their being are thrilled at accosting each other in slang. Tangle them suddenly in a swift embrace or a brotherly kiss. Do whatever you like" (p. 134). The reader becomes an-

noyed wishing that the narrator would proceed without so many interruptions and by the teasing implication that the reader also is homosex-
ually aroused by the characters and by the narrator himself.

A character in these works always remains intermediary between self
and not-self, never clearly becoming another separate three-dimensional
(literary) person, with his own destiny, nor yet fully the author. Unlike
Our Lady of the Flowers, in *The Thief's Journal* and *The Maids,* the narrator no longer reminds us that the characters are figments, representing
himself; but they still are. They are depicted more realistically but they
never take on their own literary life. A number of critics (see especially
McMahon, 1963) have commented on the increased confidence and
audacity that lead Genet to greater objectivity of the characters in his
later works. This is only partly true. Characters may have the external
trappings of real people, but inside they are hollow, or one finds an image of the author himself mocking the reader. Even Armand, in *The
Thief's Journal,* with his tolerant acceptance of others whom some
would treat with contempt, seems to be only a wish, the embodiment of
an ideal. The reader too is denied his independent existence; the narrator
repeatedly demonstrates this. The technique, whereby the narrator
threatens to turn the novel into a drama which can be replayed or
directed further into a number of different versions, elevates the narrator
to off-stage omnipotent master. Reader and characters are reminded
(OLF, p. 136): ". . . however rigorous the destiny I plot for you, it will
never cease to be—oh, in the very faintest way—tormented by what it
might also have been but will not be because of me." When the reader is
cautioned not to believe the authenticity of the characters or the narrator's self-revelation, this too is double-edged; the narrator imposes on
the reader the latter's experience of not knowing what to believe.

The narrator emphasizes his difficulty tolerating the independent existence of others. When another can make his own autonomous
responses and movements, the images the narrator superimposes on him
are destroyed and he feels himself crumbling. For example, he writes
(OLF, pp. 302-303): "In each child I see—but I see so few—I try to find
the child I was, to love him for what I was . . . I saw myself in his face,
especially in his forehead and eyes, and I was about to recognize myself
completely when, bang, he smiled. It was no longer I, for in my
childhood I could no more laugh, or even smile, than in any other period
of my life. When the child laughed, I crumbled, so to speak, before my
very eyes." Other people should exist as the author's creations, born
from his rib or his feces, as living characters of his imagination. He
writes (OLF, p. 238): "Solange had become like one of those chilled ex-
crements which Culafroy [representing the author most directly] used to
deposit at the foot of the garden wall among the current bushes. When

they were still warm, he took a tender delight in their odor, but he spurned them with indifference—at times with horror—when they had too long since ceased to be part of himself . . . Solange was no longer the chaste little girl taken from his rib. . ." The narrator describes his search for a smile in the eyes of others that he himself has evoked; he becomes affronted and outraged that responses in the eyes of others are not under his control. The description in *Miracle of the Rose* (p. 255) of the narrator/author gouging out the eye of a child, fits this theme.

Words become things, metaphors become reality with the narrator/author's incantations and transformations. He says he is trying to turn the word into flesh and to gain our assent for this. His words come alive by their brilliance and intensity as do his images by their unusual, abrupt, and startling turns; the vile and loathsome become poetry. This engages the audience and leads us to concentrate on the narrator/author's poetic gift for magical transformations. For example, the narrator greets the reader, at the beginning of *The Thief's Journal,* by announcing that "convicts garb is striped pink and white," (p. 10). He tells us there is a close relationship between flowers and convicts, and then proclaims: "The fragility and delicacy of the former are of the same nature as the brutal insensitivity of the latter." He will portray a convict by "so bedecking him with flowers that, as he disappears beneath them, he will himself *become* a flower, a gigantic and new one." (Emphasis added.) He turns convicts and flowers, word and image, into each other. He forces us to acknowledge his skill in making us believe in his images which are contrary to our values and expectations. Our values are turned upside down; gold becomes shit and shit becomes gold.

In the trial scene at the end of *Our Lady of the Flowers,* the made-up names of the drag-queens and pimps are stripped away. He writes: ". . . the little faggots from Pigalle to Place Blanche lost their loveliest adornment, their names lost their corolla, like the paper flower that the dancer holds at his finger tips and which, when the ballet is over, is a mere wire stem. Would it not have been better to have danced the entire dance with a simple wire?" (p. 291). The writer convinces us that indeed it was these characters' names which made them sparkle. He presents us with contradictions which we find jarring; at the same time there is an underlying synthesis within the contradictions that converts the nonsense and parody into poetic truth. To a degree, this is true for the "aesthetic plasticity" of all poetry; but here the striking contradictions which can be synthesized call attention directly to their creator. Genet writes (OLF, p. 228): "It is customary to come in drag, dressed as ourselves." Or there is Sartre's favorite example of such whirligigs (Sartre, 1952, pp. 508-510): "The gardener is the loveliest rose in his garden."

Stilitano, the one-armed pimp in *The Thief's Journal* is often pictured with a gob of spit at the corner of his mouth. The narrator rhapsodizes over the loveliness of the image. Is he really trying, as he claims, to turn spit into pearls? After a while, the reader too is able to picture Stilitano with his gob of spit, to feel that the image fits very well: that's Stilitano, that's how one remembers him. Grudgingly, the reader acknowledges the aptness of the narrator/author's idiosyncratic and repelling images.

DISCUSSION

My reading of these three early texts of Genet's is that the narrator/author's vigorous efforts, conscious and unconscious, to engage the reader, should not be dismissed merely as an aspect of contemporary literary technique and style. Nor would I say that Genet primarily sought to identify with other contemporary authors. In reading these works the relationship between narrator and reader is actively in the foreground rather than the background upon which a story is told. This has been documented by the above excerpts from the texts. What is at issue here is the interpretation of this aspect of the narrative point of view.

Scholes and Kellogg (1966) have argued that the narrative point of view of the novel is not an aesthetic or psychological issue but relates to a shared perception of reality between author and readers. They stress cognitive and epistemological factors in the determination of narrative point of view. Rose's (1980) psychological aesthetics also emphasize "a theory of reality and perception rather than one primarily related to motivation" (p. 10). I think that Rose here restricts motivation to drive discharge, whereas his actual aim is to discuss the role of motivation within perception and the relation of the self to external reality. Rose argues that the aesthetic experience assists the audience with newly creative integrations between subjective and objective. We could claim with little difficulty that Genet attempts to guide himself and his readers through internal and external chaos and to help himself and his readers to feel less depressed, vulnerable, and insecure. Or we could argue that Genet tries to create his own dilemmas within the audience as if to infect us with what he hates and fears most in himself. To some degree these motivations are present within all of us and will contribute to every author's unconscious needs from his audience. My argument is that in these early texts of Genet's, the pattern of relationship between narrator/author and reader must be considered in detail rather than taken for granted as the vehicle for the work, i.e., possessed of meanings common to contemporary (experimental) literature.

The concept of "implied author" allows me to organize the strategies I have encountered during my readings of these texts into a coherent whole, which I have then symbolized and personalized as "the implied author" of these works. He is preoccupied with the closeness and responsiveness of his audience. He seeks to establish a controlling relationship with his audience that is deprived of its own independent responses, unable to make a move without him. The audience must be near at hand but not close enough to restrict his control and domination. He attempts to seduce and arouse his audience, alternately repelling and shocking us, carefully manipulating our feelings to just the optimum pitch. It is in Genet's dramas that this becomes clearest: the audience is attacked, forced into submission, with the demand that even in the face of this aggression, we admire and applaud, love and forgive the author, even feel guilty ourselves and make expiation for his sins. Affirmation and acceptance must be forced out of an audience against its will. He turns our world upside down, exposing the illusion in our reality, the blindness in our vision, the evil in our goodness, the hatred in our love. My fantasied construct of "the implied author" here attacks the reader for having neglected him. In his literary creations he externalizes and concretizes an aggressive struggle between himself and the other, symbolically represented as mother. We are repeatedly confronted with the angry, aggressive demand that we celebrate the author's creativity to compensate for past neglect. "A child is being murdered" is a central theme and complaint in these works of Genet's as in de Sade's (see Bach and Schwartz, 1972). Ernestine, the mother in *Our Lady of the Flowers* had tried to murder her child (who most directly represents the author in the novel) as her child does later to another young victim. Child murder here refers to abandonment and neglect, to the murder in childhood of what are potentially the most valuable aspects of oneself. The murder is associated with intense helplessness, rage, and an inability to communicate his need to others, as illustrated by another scene of eye gouging. Alberto lay prostrate (OLF, p. 284) "with a dagger stuck into his eye . . . as he could not make it visible to people's eyes, he had to transport it into himself . . . [The country people] did not understand the meaning of the slowness of his walk, the bowing of his forehead, and the emptiness of his gaze."

To resume his development, our implied author must turn death into life, give birth to himself anew, become his own creator with the audience-mother as midwife. For him, creativity and self-recreation proceed hand-in-hand. *Our Lady of the Flowers,* the beginning of Genet's creativity, opens with the death of Divine (Genet), whereupon her struggle for life begins. Turning death into life is a major theme. In this respect, the magical transformations in the images represent rebirth, while the audience provides its own validity for this myth.

Paradoxically, these writings contain no female characters who are appealing as mothers or women. Rather, the world of the imagination is portrayed as a man's world in which women are irrelevant or can be replaced by men, as demonstrated by the author's fascination with female impersonation. Deleuze' (1971) formulation that the sexual sadist attempts an "active negation" of the mother applies to this work. The sexual sadist must convince himself that he is the creator and omnipotent director of his own world in order to hide his helpless dependency on a dangerous maternal imago (Socarides, 1974). The characters in these works may turn to men for nurturance but, unable to really trust and need others, they remain hungry and discontent. The reader is touched by the narrator when he notes twice as an aside in *Our Lady of the Flowers* that two of the characters, Darling and Our Lady, are father and son, without knowing so; they become lovers.

With repulsion or admiration, the audience is forced to respond to "the implied author" of these works, demonstrating his ability to elicit response from those who are potentially unloving and unresponsive. That the audience is awed by his magic with words and images confirms his grandeur and his ability for omnipotent manipulation. The audience is to provide him with affirmation of his existence and value, to admire and encourage him, to support his self-esteem, which he had been unable to do alone. Genet has told us seductively that his fantasy constructions, being only words and not flesh, had lacked credibility for him. They missed the warm breath of a loving parent—the task to which the audience has been elevated. He needs tangible, concrete ways and experiences for restoring faith and belief in himself; he must grab hold of the other's intense response in order to trust and believe in its authenticity so he can nourish himself. The audience's response must reassure our implied author that he is not vile, loathsome, destructive and deserving the contempt of his conscience and of others; he has shown us the worst qualities in himself and convinced us it is all poetry. He is worthy of being loved. He, like everyone else, wants to be loved and accepted, as he tells us, but he judges himself unacceptable, fears being so to others, and is afraid to allow himself genuine needs for other human beings.

The narrator (OLF, p. 293) tells his audience that he wants them to confer a new destiny upon him, to "elect him" to greatness. He says (TTJ, p. 99) that in writing his "secret history, in details as precious as the history of the great conquerors . . . it was therefore necessary that these details make me out to be the rarest and most singular of characters." His "secret glory," "a poem written only for himself, hermetic to whoever did not have the key to it" (OLF, p. 294), becomes the public acknowledgment of greatness when the author becomes famous. The narrator makes this connection (OLF, p. 294) when he moves from describing his self-created secret glory to telling about the augury that "ennobles" him: a fortune teller in a fair-booth assured him that one day he would be famous. He uses this as others would use family ties, traditions, or a mother's love. This will provide more substantial roots than the connection he plays with, that his name means broomplant which is native to French soil (TTJ, p. 45).

By his constant preoccupation with destruction and murder, the implied author reveals his fearfulness of his own destructiveness towards others and himself. I suggest that he needs to idealize destructiveness, to enact it as theatrical ritual and ceremony, obscured by illusion and imposture, to reassure himself against the danger of self-destruction, physically or actually. Nobody has been destroyed if it can be affirmed that death is the precondition for life, and that evil is virtue and the material for poetry. Hatred and destructiveness can be transformed into (recreated as) sexual arousal and passion or the poetry of drama. On stage, before a large audience our implied author gains concrete reassurance when murder does not destroy self or object. It is only a ritual! Moreover, it is one that affirms his greatness and creativity rather than his evil. The implied author's connection of the divine magic of creativity with the miracle of rebirth also affirms that destruction is never final.

To counter depression, lack of vitality, and fears of his own destructiveness, our implied author seeks concrete representation for himself and the characters of his imagination in order to demonstrate their continued existence. This he seeks in the written word, in black and white, from the audience's intense responses, and from the impersonation by living people of his characters. If he can establish, once and for all, his creative omnipotence, then he is beyond the terror of destruction, the danger of his own or his characters "crumbling." He gives himself a concrete form via his works; by creating them he has actually given birth to something indestructible. He ends *Ours Lady of the Flowers* playfully by leaving us with the image of the outline of his penis on the paper. *The Thief's Journal* concludes with the narrator's regarding his book as his "Genesis" and his "commandments." Each, together with the collusion of his audience, imaginary and real, provides indestructible, irrefutable testimony that their author is a poet and creator rather than a devil and a destroyer. If he can create beauty from inner evil, he cannot be all bad; there must be redeeming goodness within him which the audience must acknowledge. We are to reassure him (as he tries to reassure himself) that his shit, piss, semen, sweat, snot, as well as his selfishness, greed, hunger, exploitation, murderous hatred, and aggression are not only not bad, but are the very stuff from which beauty and virtue are created.

Baudry (1979) suggested, somewhat like Sartre, that Genet may have been despairing and "given up the possibility of attaining any meaningful positive relationships in the real world." Then, Genet's books may have represented for him a substitute object, or at least an affirmation that some part of himself was alive. I think that Baudry's point is too much an "either/or" formulation. My fantasied construct of the implied author of these works does treat his book as the only living part of himself, his penis. But that is just his dilemma; he is forced to make himself feel more alive and authentic, less depressed and insubstantial. He will do this however he can, including a relationship with an audience, which is to some degree despairing and dangerous. He does not feel lovable nor can he take for granted that the audience will respond lovingly. He must force them under his own control, or at least the illusion of such control, to respond to him; however, of this he is confident.

It may be that different authors in different texts allow the reader to participate in varying degrees of collaborative co-authorship. All interpretation involves a subjective reformulation or re-creation of the author's text. I have been arguing that the implied author of the texts under discussion attempts to impose on the reader certain feelings, states of mind and ideas which allow for little flexibility in the reader's experience. It may be that the enjoyment of such works requires that the reader allow himself to submit to the author's manipulations without too much distress or protest. In this type of writing, the implied author seems unwilling and unable to allow the reader, or the characters for that matter, to truly participate on their own as collaborators. The reader (as well as the characters) is denied his own independent existence, because of the limited range of response to the narrator's offerings. Like de Sade, our implied author revels in the total domination of his characters, showing us that they are creations of *his imagination,* so that he can mistreat them if he so chooses.

In contrast to the position I have taken, Baudry (1979) has argued that biographical data about the author can be used to support the critic's reading of the text. Rosenblatt (1938) claims that "to derive an interpretation of a text from the author's life or stated intentions is . . . critically indefensible." Iser (1978) and Fish (1980) especially point out that stated intentions establish expectations in the reader, draw responses, are part of the reading experience, and are neither to be believed nor used as the basis of interpretation. Thus the fact that the narrator/author tells us something about himself does not by itself directly reveal something about him. This is certainly the case with an author like Genet who is so deceptive and contradictory. Scholes and Kellogg (1966) point out that one function of an unreliable or semi-reliable narrator in modern fiction is to have the reader participate in the artistic creation. The reader must struggle to understand what the narrator cannot fully grasp. Scholes and Kellogg emphasize that this device is in keeping with a contemporary epistemology of relativism and uncertainty. Nevertheless, how does my fantasied construct of the implied author of these works correspond with his stated intentions and available biographical data?

My thesis is at variance with Sartre's (1952) claim that Genet's early writing was often meant only for Genet as pleasurable masturbatory fantasies, autistic reveries or as a self-focused attempt at rehabilitation. My construct does fit Genet's statements about himself, which Sartre (1952) affirms, that Genet has difficulty tolerating the independent existence of others. Sartre has argued in support of the thesis of an essential, intended relationship between Genet and his audience. My fantasied construct of the implied author of the works under discussion has seductive, controlling, and possibly sadistic qualities similar to what is found in structured perversion. Nevertheless, I must remind you that I have sought a cogent reading of these texts rather than psychoanalytic understanding of the real-life author. Whatever similarities there may be between our implied author and the flesh-and-blood author are fortuitous.

Thus, I conclude that the implicit hypothesis of Khan (1965) and Bach and Schwartz (1972), that the relationship between a perverse writer and his audience may approximate a perverse sexual experience, can guide us towards a useful reading of the author's texts but that it should not be taken literally. Eschewing biographical reconstruction, where the relationship between narrator and reader is so obviously central to a work, and overshadows plot, themes, and characters, we must understand this and determine its psychological component and functions during our reading experience. The narrator-reader relationship should never be reduced to psychological factors no matter how prominently it appears. A fantasied construct of the implied author of a work is an organizing strategy for interpretation of the work, not of the real-life author, however similar they may seem.

By his writing, Jean Genet succeeded in transforming himself from an outcast petty criminal into a celebrated poet, adopted as an object of veneration by a distinguished group of writers as well as by the general public. Genet and Sartre both remarked on the therapeutic efficacy of Genet's writing. Genet's autobiographical work (TTJ, 1948) surprisingly reveals little about Genet that we have not already learned from his earlier work. The tone has become more intellectual, abstract, argumentative, explanatory. He claims that by giving song to his life he is providing it with an order it never had, i.e., he is rewriting his past. He says, and Sartre concurs, that he is struggling to understand himself. Genet stresses that he has ceased idealizing others, including criminals, and has begun work at changing himself and setting his own values. *The Thief's Journal* often reads like Sartre's study of Genet even though the latter was published subsequently; still Genet and Sartre had spent much time together before the autobiography was published in 1948. The narrator has become less seductive with the reader and, at times, less appealing. By this time Genet had already become well known in French literary circles and regarded himself as a poet. His narrator seems less profoundly depressed, more confident of his own creativity and of his ability to engage the audience. With the production of his plays (*Deathwatch* and *The Maids*) in 1947, Genet quite literally had accomplished his avowed goal of turning the word into flesh: living people play the roles he invents in the scenes he creates while an audience watches, responds and, at times, is even part of the drama. Genet wrote (1963): "The actors' function is thus to don the gestures and costumes which will enable them to show me to myself, and to show me naked, alone and in the joyfulness of solitude."

BIBLIOGRAPHY

BACH, S. & SCHWARTZ, L. (1972). A dream of the Marquis de Sade: Psychoanalytic reflections on narcissistic trauma, decompensation and the reconstitution of a delusional self. *J. Am. Psycho-anal. Assn.,* 20:451–475.

BAUDRY, F. (1979). Discussion of "The perverse author and his audience: A psychoanalytic essay based on Jean Genet's early work" by S. J. Coen. Unpublished. Presented to The Amer. Psan. Assn., Dec., 1979, New York, N.Y.

BLEICH, D. (1978). *Subjective Criticism.* Baltimore & London: The Johns Hopkins Univ. Press.

BOOTH, W. (1979). *Critical Understanding: The Powers and Limits of Pluralism.* Chicago & London: Univ. of Chicago Press.

COOPER, A. (1981). Contribution to the Panel: The Relationship of Author and Reader: Transference Implications for Psychoanalytic Literary Criticism. Assn. Psan. Medicine Symposium on Current Concepts of Transference and Countertransference, New York, N.Y., March, 1981.

DELEUZE, G. (1971). *Sacher-Masoch, an interpretation, together with the entire text of "Venus in Furs."* London: Faber & Faber.

FISH, S. (1970). Literature in the reader: Affective stylistics. In *Is There a Text in This Class?: The Authority of Interpretive Communities.* Cambridge & London: Harvard Univ. Press.

_____ (1980). *Is There a Text in This Class? The Authority of Interpretive Communities.* Cambridge & London: Harvard Univ. Press.

GENET, J. (1943). *Our Lady of the Flowers.* Trans. by B. Frechtman. New York: Grove Press, 1963.

_____ (1946). *Miracle of the Rose.* Trans. by B. Frechtman. New York: Grove Press, 1966.

_____ (1947). *The Maids.* In *The Maids and Deathwatch, two plays by Jean Genet.* Trans. by B. Frechtman. New York: Grove Press, 1961.

_____ (1947). *Deathwatch.* In *The Maids and Deathwatch, two plays by Jean Genet.* Trans. by B. Frechtman. New York: Grove Press, 1961.

_____ (1948). *The Thief's Journal.* Trans. by B. Frechtman. New York: Grove Press, 1964.

_____ (1963). As quoted in P. Thody, *Jean Genet, A Study of His Novels and Plays.* New York: Stein and Day, 1968, p. 175. Original source is Genet's preface to the

1963 French edition of The Maids: Les Bonnes. Preceded by "Comment jouer *Les Bonnes.*" Barbezat.

GORNEY, J. (1979). The field of illusion in literature and the psychoanalytic situation. *Psychoanal. and Contemporary Thought,* 2:527-550.

GREEN, A. (1978). The double and the absent. In *Psychoanalysis, Creativity, and Literature:A French-American Inquiry,* A. Roland (ed.). New York: Columbia Univ. Press.

GREENACRE, P. (1957). The childhood of the artist: libidinal phase development and giftedness. In *Emotional Growth,* Vol. 2. New York: Int. Univ. Press, 1971.

ISER, W. (1978). *The Act of Reading: A Theory of Aesthetic Response.* Baltimore & London: The Johns Hopkins Univ. Press.

KAVKA, J. (1975). Oscar Wilde's narcissism. *The Annual of Psychoanalysis,* 3:397-408.

KHAN, M. M. R. (1965). The function of intimacy and acting out in perversions. In *Sexual Behavior and the Law,* R. Slovenko (ed.). Springfield, Ill.: Thomas.

KRIS, E. (1952). Approaches to art. In *Psychoanalytic Explorations in Art.* New York: Int. Univ. Press.

_____ & KAPLAN, A. (1948). Aesthetic ambiguity. In *Psychoanalytic Explorations in Art,* E. Kris. (ed.). New York: Int. Univ. Press.

McMAHON, J. (1963). *The Imagination of Jean Genet.* New Haven & London: Yale Univ. Press.

MYERS, W. A. (1979). Imaginary companions in childhood and adult creativity. *Psychoanal. Q.,* 48:292-307.

NIEDERLAND, W. (1976). Psychoanalytic approaches to artistic creativity. *Psychoanal. Q.,* 45:185-212.

NOY, P. (1979). Form creation in art: An ego-psychological approach to creativity. *Psan. Quart.,* 48:229-256.

POULET, G. (1970). Criticism and the experience of interiority. In *The Structuralist Controversy. The Language of Criticism and the Sciences of Man,* R. Macksey & E. Donato (eds.). Baltimore: The Johns Hopkins University Press.

ROLAND, A. (1978). Towards a reorientation of psychoanalytic literary criticism. In *Psychoanalysis, Creativity, and Literature: A French-American Inquiry* A. Roland (ed.). New York: Columbia Univ. Press.

ROSE, G. J. (1972). The French Lieutenant's Woman: The unconscious meaning of any novel to its author. *American Imago,* 29:165-176.

_____ (1973). On the shores of the self: irredentism and the creative impulse. *Psychoanalytic Review,* 60:587-604.

_____ (1978). The creativity of everyday life. In *Between Reality and Fantasy: Transitional Objects and Phenomena,* S. A. Grolnick & L. Barkin (eds.), in collab. with W. Muensterberger. New York & London: Jason Aronson.

_____ (1980). *The Power of Form: A Psychoanalytic Approach to Aesthetic Form. Psychological Issues Mono. 49.* New York: Int. Univ. Press.

ROSENBLATT, L. (1938). *Literature as Exploration.* New York: Noble and Noble.

ROTHENBERG, A. (1978). The unconscious and creativity. In *Psychoanalysis, Creativity, and Literature: A French-American Inquiry,* A. Roland (ed.). New York: Columbia Univ. Press.

SACHS, H. (1942). The community of daydreams. In *The Creative Unconscious. Studies in the Psychoanalysis of Art.* Cambridge, Mass.: Sci.-Art Publishers, pp. 11-54.

SARTRE, J. P. (1952). *Saint Genet: Actor and Martyr.* New York, Toronto & London: New American Library, 1963.

SCHOLES, R. & KELLOGG, R. (1966). *The Nature of Narrative.* London, Oxford, New York: Oxford Univ. Press.

SCHWARTZ, M. (1978). Critic: Define thyself. In *Psychoanalysis and the Question of the Text*, G. Hartman (ed.). Baltimore & London: The Johns Hopkins Univ. Press.

SOCARIDES, C. (1974). The demonified mother: A study of voycurism and sexual sadism. *Int. Rev. Psycho-Anal.,* 1:187–195.

WAELDER, R. (1965). *Psychoanalytic Avenues to Art.* New York: Int. Univ. Press.

WIMSATT, W. & BEARDSLEY, M. (1954). *The Verbal Icon.* Lexington: Univ. of Kentucky Press.

WINNICOTT, D. W. (1971). *Playing and Reality.* New York: Basic Books.

PART V

MUSIC

10

Charles Ives and the Unanswered Question

STUART FEDER

(1)

(2) "The light which puts out our eyes is darkness to us. Only that day dawns to which we are awake. There is more day to dawn. The sun is but a morning star."

Thoreau, Conclusion of *Walden*

In January of 1918, in his forty-fourth year, Charles Ives sketched out a short piece for chamber orchestra similar in style to a number of works he had written during and after 1906. This particular piece, *Premonitions,* was to be the third of a group, two of which Ives had already completed, and he took this occasion to assemble them into what he was to call *Set Number Three.* Like many other of Ives' works, *Premonitions* was associated with a text and was to appear as a song in Ives' *114 Songs* (1922, #24) four years later. The text was a poem by a favorite of Ives, Robert Underwood Johnson, who had been the source of other texts, including that associated with one of Ives' best-known works, *Three Places in New England (The Housatonic at Stockbridge).*

Premonitions

There's a shadow on the grass that was never there before; and the ripples as they pass whisper of an unseen oar; And the song we knew by rote, seems to falter in the throat, a footfall, scarcely noted, lingers near the open door. Omens that were once but jest, Now are messengers of Fate; and the blessings held the best cometh not or comes too late. Yet whatever life may lack, not a blown leaf beckons back, Forward! Forward! is the summons. Forward! Wherever new horizons wait.

Before the year was over Ives sustained a severe heart attack, occurring at the beginning of October within weeks of his forty-fifth birthday. The following January of 1919 found him recovering in Asheville, N.C., where, nursed by his wife Harmony, he began to experience the final brief burst of creative activity which would produce the trilogy which became Ives' love-gift to the world: The *Second Piano Sonata* (The "Concord"), its accompanying prose *Essays Before A Sonata,* and The *114 Songs.* He had been working on all three over the course of some time. The *Sonata,* for example, had been written essentially between 1909-15, and required only final revision and editing. The songs of *114* harked back to Ives' very first composition and included pieces from every phase of his life. He now added a few new songs and hastened to adapt other earlier works, casting them in the form of songs in order to include them in this volume. The entire endeavor was a summing-up.

Ives' creative pace as composer was a singular one (Feder, 1980, 1981). He wrote his first composition at the age of twelve, and subsequently composed as a matter of course while pursuing his musical activities with his father during the latter's lifetime and, following that, during his student days at Yale. Afterward, embarking on his well-known double life, he began a business career which ultimately made him independently wealthy while he concurrently composed nights and weekends. With day-to-day regularity, mostly in artistic isolation, Ives continued to compose from his college years onward. This pace persisted, even more intensely following his marriage at 34 in 1908. His productivity promised to flourish well into his fourth decade when it rapidly began to flag. As Ives (1972) experienced it, he composed his major work during the two decades between 1896 and 1916, wrote little music "in 1917, as the War came on," and, after his illness during October of 1918, could not "get going 'good' music" (p. 112). His final burst of activity, which required considerable organization and rewriting, had yielded, in addition to The "Concord" Sonata, the *114 Songs,* a collection which was fundamentally autobiographical. The latter (1922) included a valedictory prose postface. Ives compared its preparation to housecleaning—spring cleaning to be exact—stating, "In fact, gentle borrower, I have not written a book at all—I have merely cleaned house. All that is left is out on the clothes line . . . (Postface, unnumbered). Ives paid scant attention to his few minor later works and, writing retrospectively he omitted mention of the preparation of his "trilogy" and dated his decline to the time of *Premonitions*: "As I look back, I find that I did almost no composing after the *beginning* of 1918" (1972, p. 112, italics mine). By his early fifties the impetus was totally extinguished, documented by Harmony's poignant description of Ives' descending the stairs with tears in his eyes, saying he could no longer compose (p. 279). His last songs, which doubtless merit a higher evaluation than their composer gave them, were written between 1923 and 1926, when he was a year or two on either side of age fifty. *Sunrise,* his very last song was written when he was 52, and set to his own text. It marked the end of the terminal trickle of creativity which followed publication of the last three major works. Ives scrawled a "memo" on one of its manuscript pages: "Taken from chords and parts of an II S.Q. [second string quartet] + put into the song Aug. 1926—but not a good job—The words are N.G. but better than the music" (Kirkpatrick, 1960, p. 212). As we shall see later, both words and music embodied a characteristic Ivesian idea.

Prior to Ives' heart attack in 1918 he experienced a cardiac episode which was to exert a strong psychological effect. This occurred in 1906 when he was halfway into his most productive period. Just before, he had entered into the business relationship with Julian Myrick which was to make his fortune and had begun the love relationship which was to lead to marriage in 1908. We will consider some of these details later as well as certain music associated with this earlier period, in particular *The Pond* and *The Unanswered Question.*

I have drawn attention elsewhere to the almost uncanny parallel between Charles Ives' creative lifetime and the biological lifetime of the most influential person in his life, his father George Edward Ives (Feder, 1980, 1981) (see Fig. 1). George had died in his forty-ninth year just as Charles was entering his first year at Yale. Earlier, as I have suggested, in anticipation of educating Charles and his only sibling, the younger brother Moss, George had gradually given up his own rather thankless career in music and entered the business world on a menial level in order to earn a steadier income. Perhaps too he had belatedly sought to bring his own life into alignment with family tradition, certainly the lives of his boys; for George himself had been a maverick and became the black sheep of the family when he pursued the life of a nineteenth century village musician. This had been the story of his own forties. He was forty-four when he accepted the part-time job as a clerk in a business owned by his nephew; later, at forty-seven, just two years before his death, he began a regular job with the Danbury Bank. Although no doubt he remained active in Danbury musical life, that, like everything else in the industrial town, was rapidly changing as it moved into the twentieth century. Thus, George began to yield his identity as professional musician. Earlier it had provided him with visibility, esteem, and leadership. Now, as he approached his fiftieth year, by becoming a mere clerk in the bank founded by his own family, he virtually renounced all that his life as a musician had meant to him.

To Charles, however, George remained the hero of his boyhood. Pursuing an insight by the first of Ives' biographers, Sidney Cowell (with Cowell, H., 1955), that "...the son has written his father's music for him" (p. 12), I have shown how for Ives the activity of composition became an intrapsychic collaboration, a "secret sharing," and a facet of a protracted process of mourning. That the waning of this endeavor paralleled George's biological lifetime is a phenomenon which is richly overdetermined. Physical illness should be taken into account as well as the psychological effect of World War I (which has probably been uncritically overestimated, critics failing to look beyond the manifest). Emphasized here is the complex nature of identification, with guilt and mourning but two of the elements.

Although Charles idealized the relationship between father and son, there is some evidence that it was not without its external strife and tensions, as well as intrapsychic conflict. In many respects adolescence appears to have been a difficult and critical period (Rossiter, 1975, pp. 48-49). The consequent ambivalence this would necessarily engender clearly affected the later course of this idealized relationship, in particular the mourning process. The work of mourning progressed with music serving both as its medium and its product. The process of mourning, its artistic parallel in composition and its musical precipitate in a body of work—under such circumstances all may be flawed in some sense. To a degree, this may be no more than an exaggerated instance of what frequently, even usually, occurs in mourning. (One hesitates to say "normally," since this implies an ideal of the process, which was certainly not achieved in this case.) In any event, what follows in this study tends to adhere closely to Charles' idealized version of the father-son relationship, with emphasis on their strong mutual love. This view hews most closely to the available material. Moreover, in connection with Charles' strong, conscious feeling of longing for his father and nostalgia for past times together, this view would tend to foster the fantasies of afterlife, immortality, reunion, and manipulations of time which are the focus of the present study. However, since ambivalence inevitably takes its toll, at some point it must receive proper consideration. Although this ambivalence will not be fully discussed here, certain aspects should be highlighted. From a defensive point of view it seems likely that affects other than love buttressed the close attachment. Its result, for example, may be seen in a kind of identification which was essentially a compromise: As much as Charles was like his father, he was also in many ways his opposite. Charles led a double life—one of the intimate continued sharing of music; the other, a successful career in business such as his father could not have shared in life or death. It was the sharing of music that was intimately involved in the mourning process.

As I have suggested elsewhere, the presence of aggression and guilt may dictate a limit to productivity. One may not survive the person who made the sacrifice and evoked aggression and guilt. From the point of view of the superego, "collaboration" may well be a duty but its continuation, a transgression (Feder, 1981). To the degree that this obtained, a strong natural gift which might have been capable of further unfolding in a relatively conflict-free atmosphere may have been impeded. This would constitute the background contribution of conflict to events which are greatly overdetermined. As for the mourning process in such a case, it might approach completion—however, at a price.

When Charles offered his three final fruits, sans copyright and free to whomever requested it, they become father *and* son's gift to the world. In the Postface to the *114 Songs* (1922), he had written about the "freedom" of a song ("...a song has a *few* rights, the same as any ordinary citizen"). The music was free; so too was Charles, free of the task of mourning, redeemed. This then was the background of Ives' mental state in his fourth decade of life, a decade that had become his father's last. Even under ordinary circumstances, it would not be unusual for a man to harbor a fantasy of dying at his father's age; all the more so in this instance where the father, as internalized creative collaborator, would finally come to rest in Charles' own creative death. The first time around, as it were, George's physical death had coincided with Charles' creative birth as the latter departed for Yale. When Charles was forty-one, he had belatedly become a father himself, albeit an adoptive parent; the circle would be complete. Now, three years later, at the beginning of 1918, the time to which he retrospectively dated the sense of his own failing creative impetus, Charles wrote the piece called *Premonitions*. Before the year was over, he sustained a life-threatening heart attack, and, by the same time the next year, like the good insurance man he was, he endeavored to put his musical estate in order. As it turned out he actually lived to be nearly eighty, surviving the composer in him by more than thirty years!

But is there more to the writing of *Premonitions* than the kind of coincidence which may become astonishing in its elaborated context? Did he in an arcane way—in fantasy, in creative life—experience something approaching a premonition? Then, what is "premonition" when translated into psychoanalytic terms? Is premonition the representation of an expectation, of a wish itself? How is it related to the mental representation of time? Let us pursue these questions within the mode of thinking in which they arose in Charles Ives, namely, the musical work itself.

First, a few comments on the text of *Premonitions*. What portends manifestly is obvious: death. The very terms of the poem, "premonition," "omen," and "Fate" relate to the future just as the affects elicited by the imagery are related to fear. A line that is striking in its coincidental biographical significance is: "And the song we knew by rote, seems to falter in the throat..."—the threat of the composer's flourishing creativity coming to a halt as in fact it shortly would. Finally, one perceives a massive denial manifested by vigorous optimism, the fervent optimism of faith. Past, present, and future are accounted for in the line, "Yet whatever life may lack, not a blown leaf beckons back, Forward!" This is of particular interest in view of Ives' veneration of the past and the nostalgia that he experienced his entire life. Despite the symmetry imposed by rhyme, in a different sense the form the poem assumes is in two simple sections, asymmetrical in length. The first is portentous and vague, the second optimistic and certain. Fundamentally, these constitute a question and an answer which underlie the formal structure of the song qua music.

In this instance, however, Ives had not written the words as he did for so many of the *114 Songs* (1922); he observed carefully in the notes of *Premonitions*, "Where no author is indicated the words are by Harmony Twitchell Ives or her husband" (following p. 259). Here only the music was his, although clearly he was drawn to the poem.[1] A description follows:

The brief piece is unbarred (except for the final two measures) but seems to fall into three asymmetrical sections. The first (Ex. 1) in a

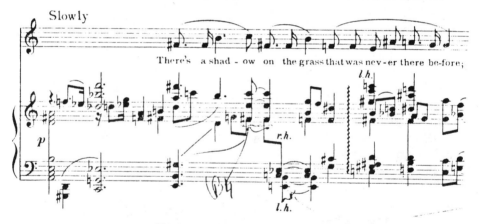

EX. 1   IVES, *Premonitions,* beginning

whispery texture of harmony, is carefully annotated in dynamics among the fine distinctions of *piano* (p,pp,ppp,mf,mp,pp) and serves as setting for the poem through "...lingers near the open

---

1. For our purposes, we will consider the version of *Premonitions* in the *114 Songs* be-
    cause of its ready availability. The version for chamber orchestra is not identical. In
    at least one recorded performance it is realized with variant dynamics and relatively
    little prominence to the leading voice, thus creating a somewhat different impression.
    This pattern occurs with many of Ives' compositions because of his own variations of
    material as well as the freedom and alternatives he wished to allow performers.

door." The brief second portion (through "...comes too late") introduces a ponderous figure in parallel chords reminiscent of the tolling of bells and marked "heavily" at the words "... messengers of fate..." (Ex. 2). These two musical sections correspond to the

EX. 2   IVES, *Premonitions*

first of the poem's two-part form noted above, the "question" part. The "answer" follows: It consists of a musical idea which is essentially an extended, simultaneous crescendo and accelerando. Yet there is more to it, although it only occupies a period of time equivalent to eighteen quarter-note beats. The tempo quickens (the score marked "faster" then "accel.") and the volume increases from a mezzo-forte to a triple-forte. But at the same time the harmonic foundation expands both in quality of dissonance and literally, in musical space—two sets of chords proceeding in contrary motion to the final dissonant polychord (essentially a combination of the F major chord in the treble and the E-flat major in the bass) (Ex. 3). At this point the solo line has reached its apogee

EX. 3   IVES, *Premonitions,* ending

(high f), and it is revealed that this has been its goal since its inception on middle F-sharp throughout its meanderings and gradual ascent. A motif which seems to dominate the lead (or vocal) line appears to be a quotation of *Taps* with its rising fourth (Ex. 1). (Kirkpatrick [1960] does not include this in his catalogue of Ives quotations and questions whether this is the case—personal communication.) The *Taps* motif appears five times in the first section and from a formal point of view underscores the contour of the gradually rising line.

As for its appearance in the *114 Songs,* from an aesthetic point of view, it would be hard to call this song appealing; perhaps Ives himself would have numbered it among those that "cannot be sung—and if they could perhaps might prefer, if they had a say, to remain as they are—that is, 'in the leaf'..." (1922, Postface).[2] However, while it may not have immediate appeal, there can be no question of its expressiveness, and what it may reveal concerning the musical realization of an idea deserves our interest. The poem is, of course, about death, more specifically, the shuddering awareness of death's insinuation into life. It is this sense that is conveyed in the musical idea,—even *Taps* is subordinated to it, that is, incorporated in a manner not obvious to the listener. Some may experience this as an unpleasant, even frightening music. (It is similar in this regard to certain late works of Schoenberg such as his *String Trio* and *A Survivor from Warsaw,* which are manifestly, even consciously, related by the composer to death.) In this sense, *Premonitions* may be a successful rendering of a text in musical idea. The final line serves as if it is an answer to the question raised by the "unseen" of the first part. The answer is the precise opposite of death. The poem makes clear that the movement is not backward but forward; one is not "beckoned" to the past but *"summoned"* to the future; one is not recalled (as in the Shakespearian, "...we owe God a death") but *reborn*; more precisely, as the text indicates, a *"new"* birth. Ives attempts a tonal symbolic respresentation of this idea in the quickening and burgeoning of the final two measures (Ex. 3). To the listener it may sound no less awesome than the earlier portion relating to death, for the "answer" is yet another unknown, but one which is eagerly anticipated.

In the context of Ives' biography then, a consideration of a text he selected, and, more importantly, his realization of it in music, have led us to a certain group of ideas and particular formal features of both a

---

2. Perhaps that is why until very recently, no recording of the song had been made and even now the single performance is not readily available. (*Selected Songs By Charles Ives,* Peter Del Grande, Orion Records, CST-106). The chamber orchestra version of 1918 may be found as the third movement of *Set No. 3.* (in *Charles Ives Calcium Night Light,* Gunther Schuller, conductor, Columbia MS 7318.)

literary and auditory (musical) nature. The ideas referring to the ominous presence of death in life and its unknown aftermath ramify to considerations of time, past and future. Fantasies are implied, particularly fantasies of what lies ahead. So too are affects, most prominently anxiety and an excited anticipation tinged with enthusiasm, even optimism. All are embodied, encoded perhaps, in text and in music. I have suggested already that the fundamental formal unit in both consists of two elements, the first of which is associated with uncertainty and death, the second with confidence and the future. The transition between the two is both direct and unidirectional. I have termed this formal configuration in its simplest state "question and answer."

This basic "two-part" form recurs repeatedly in the *114 Songs,* as well as in others of Ives' songs. It should be made clear that we are not speaking of any traditional two-part song form. Indeed, the variety of realizations and solutions to the possibilities of this particular formal principal which Ives achieves is characteristically rich. However, I suggest that where Ives works with these *forms* in both music and text (many of which he himself wrote), he concerns himself with variations and transformations of particular ideas and (literary) themes. Fundamentally, these themes are death, rebirth, and immortality.

A further example may be sought in a song which is in fact entitled, *Immortality* (1922, #5), both words and music written by Ives. Its text questions: "Who dares to say the spring is dead in Autumn's radiant glow! Who dares to say the rose is dead in winter's sunset snow! Who dares to say our child is dead! Who dares to say our child is dead!"—and answers: "If God had meant she were to die, she would not have been."

Immortality was written in February or March of 1921 as the forty-seven year old Ives was preparing the *114 Songs* for publication, revising and adapting older pieces and adding new ones. Immortality was among the last added to the collection. According to Harmony Ives, its composition was prompted by "an alarming illness of Edie," their adopted daughter, then seven years old, a "badly infected ear" (Kirkpatrick, 1960, p. 207). The entire song is based upon the hymn-tune, *St. Peter* (Ex. 4A), which appears undisguised following a dissonant climax in the reassuring setting of the last line, the "answer," where it is accompanied by rich organ-like chords. The score is marked "quietly and firmly."

Interestingly, *St. Peter* is quoted again in *Two Little Flowers* (1922, #104), the text of which was written by Charles and Harmony together and set by him after the child's recovery later that spring. *Two Little Flowers* commemorates a sunny day with Edie playing in the backyard with a friend. While not in the question-and-answer form, it seems to serve as the expanded answer itself in relation to *Immortality*. As in *Immortality, St. Peter* is quoted in a benignly lyrical way (Ex. 4B), here in its first and last phrases. In most of Ives' musical quotations, rich per-

EX. 4   St. Peter
A. IVES, *Immortality*
B. IVES, *Two Little Flowers*
Reinagle/Hosmer

sonal associations and cultural allusions may be sought; this is no exception. St. Peter, of course, was the disciple of Christ to whom the keys of the Kingdom of Heaven had been given and who in popular mythology is the keeper of the doors of Heaven.

Two Little Flowers, with harp-like accompaniment, musically depicts a moment of heaven on earth in a backyard Garden of Eden. While the hymn-tune (by Alexander Reinagle, 1799-1877) is used for several Protestant hymns, all of which would have been known to Ives as a church organist, because of the similarity of word and idea, one would wonder whether Ives' associations extended to a particular contemporary setting (by Frederick Hosmer, 1840-1929): "I cannot think of them as dead/Who walk with me no more; ..." Ives' irate, "Who dares to say the spring is dead . . . ." would sound inadvertently satirical were it not so dead serious. But the gentle "immortality" of hymn verses is of the kind that characterized his lifelong relationship with his father: "There lives are made forever mine/What they to me have been/Hath left henceforth its seal and sign/Engraven deep within/Mine are they by an ownership/Nor time nor death can free/For God hath given to Love to keep/Its own eternally" (Tweedy, 1939, #666). And, of course, it had been Ives' own daughter whose life had been threatened earlier that winter.

It seems more than likely that, in view of Ives' relationship with his father and his intense, ongoing involvement with his father's memory, he would have wished to have children in order to achieve the everyday, homespun immortality characterized in the hymn. His involvement with his own family and his later closeness to Harmony's support this. No doubt his marriage on June 9, 1908 involved the expectation of children.

Ten months later Harmony was in the hospital for nearly a month, probably for a hysterectomy necessitated by the complications of pregnancy.[3]
The couple was a devoted one which perhaps made the fact that they
could not have children both more, and less, bearable. At this time
Charles wrote another of his "question-and-answer" songs.

Like A Sick Eagle (1922, #26), its text a fragment from Keats, was
probably written on April 29, 1909. It was certainly associated with that
day, since Ives, characteristically using the manuscrift as if a page of
diary, made the note "H. T. I. in Hospital—Sally singing, 70 W. 11,
April 29, '09" (Kirkpatrick, 1960, p. 48). In a brief phrase, time, place,
event, persons were all captured, commemorated as if in a snapshot.
(Sally, Harmony's sister came to keep house for Charles.) This "memo"
might serve as some arcane illustration for a story told in the music, for
the text may be misleading in its manifest form: "The spirit is too weak;
mortality weighs heavily on me like unwilling sleep, and each imagined
pinnacle and steep of God-like hardship tells me I must die, I like a sick
eagle looking towards the sky."

Only in the last image is some redeeming relief offered from the grind-
ing weariness and inexorable fate of the previous portion; only here is
some faint and not very hopeful "answer" suggested for the overwhelming "question" of mortality. The music, a miniature, tightly written
masterpiece, merits interest from several points of view. On paper it appears to be a study in chromatics in the form of short phrases with weary,
sigh-like pauses between. It is marked, "very slowly, in a weak and dragging way," and each phrase arches downward at the same time that a
climax is aimed for at "God-like." From here, a single long phrase slowly drifts down chromatically with only the final five notes detached
from it—the five that bear the faint hope, "...looking towards the sky"
(Ex. 5).

Other than the usual markings no indication concerning performance
is given in the published version of the *114 Songs*. In a later version, Ives
(1933, #22) makes it clear that this was also intended to be an exercise in
quarter tones and other unusual intervals. He noted: "...a slide was
made down or up through a 1/4 tone, in a semitone interval and through
2 or 3 tones in a whole tone interval, except between the last 5 notes." He
also provides the history of the brief work, stipulating that the original
version of 1909 was meant to be "an Intonation for Voice or English

---

3. Biographical sources close to the Ives family fail to mention this; one did not speak
    freely then about such things, nor were the Iveses the kind of people who would do so
    in any event. Wooldridge (1974) notes an emergency operation at St. Luke's Hospital
    for cholecystectomy, adding, "There were complications that suggest the termination
    of pregnancy" (p. 144). However, he fails to provide a source. Sidney Cowell agrees
    with my impression (personal communication).

*) This part in the score was played by violin and a slide was made down or up through a ¼ tone, in a semitone interval and through 2 or 3 lesser tones in a whole tone interval, except between the last 5 notes. The voice may do similarly.

EX. 5   IVES, *Like A Sick Eagle,* ending

Horn with Flute, Strings and Piano'' and that later it had been arranged for voice in 1920 in preparation for the *114 Songs.* Ives' interest in such innovations relates strongly to his identification with George Ives who had been an avid experimenter in music. In the course of one of his rare theoretical writings, *Some Quarter-Tone Impressions* (1961), Charles Ives wrote, ''This idea may be due to a kind of family prejudice, for my father had a weakness for quarter-tones—in fact he didn't even stop with them. He rigged up a contrivance to stretch 24 or more violin strings and tuned them up to suit the dictates of his own curiosity. He would pick out quarter-tone tunes and try to get the family to sing them...'' (p. 110).

But none of the above serves to convey the expressive impact of *Like A Sick Eagle,* which is unique in the vocal literature. The sounds are those of crushing weariness and animal despair. Subtly, a faint inflection of aspiration sounds briefly in the ''answer'' of the last five tones which are sung normally. Here the piano accompaniment participates with the kind of contrary motion ''opening'' figure observed in *Premonitions* and a final single rising note of weak resolution (Ex. 5). After Harmony's surgery that spring, whatever hopes Ives may have had for that genetic immortality provided by fatherhood were dashed.

Other ''question-and-answer'' songs are found frequently in Ives' work. Among the ''114'' there are songs in which sunset (or winter) and dawn (spring) are juxtaposed (*Disclosure #7, Spring Song #65, Berceuse #93, Allegro #95*); an optimistic future anticipated (*Resolution #13*) or resolve asserted (*Duty #9a*); or some redeeming quality perceived in nature; some aspect of life in death (*Evidence #58, Evening #2*). Of these, all the texts are by Ives except for the last (by Milton), *Duty* (Emerson), and *Spring Song* which was written by Harmony during their courtship in the summer of 1907. *Spring Song* is so strikingly congruent with themes that preoccupied Ives that it attests to the similarity of mind which served as a basis for their strong relationship: ''...Now all the dry brown things are ans'wring, with here a leaf and there a fair blown flow'r, I only heard her (spring) not and wait—and wait." Later that fall Harmony wrote to him, "our Spring Song is a good one." In a few days they "asked her father's blessing."

The year after Harmony's hospitalization, her mother died. Ives wrote another poem in the same category which he set to music and later included in *114 Songs, Mists* (#131): "...The grey skies weep with us who bid farewell. But happier days through memory weaves a spell, and brings new hope to hearts who bid farewell." Ives' setting is a small jewel. Like many of his other songs, it is of special musical interest, for at the same time it is a fine study in the use of the augmented triad. It is also an unusually symmetrical Ives song, beautifully balanced, with an aspiringly rising line at the climax at "happier days." It was characteristics of Ives that in this domestic, even sentimental, context he would be stimulated to invent music which was expressive and innovative while remaining deeply personal in content and style.

In a few settings, notably those connected with actual hymn tunes, a glimpse of the heavenly life is offered (*Watchman* #93, *At The River* #94). In one, the humorously dramatic cowboy song, *Charlie Rutlage* (#19, from a ballad collected by John Lomax), there is a scene of reunion after death: "...But I hope he'll meet his loved ones beyond in eternity, in eternity, I hope he'll meet his parents, will meet them face to face, And that they'll grasp him by the right hand at the shining throne, the shining throne, the shining throne of grace." Here, a steadfastness of faith and simple sincerity magically transforms the final measure of this tragicomic song (Charlie died during the spring roundup when his horse fell on him (into a moving, religious moment. At the close, a quiet plagal ("amen") cadence at the "throne of grace" unexpectedly ends the piece. It is a style of "answer" similar to that observed earlier in *Two Little Flowers* (1922, 104) in which the peaceful rendition of the hymn, *St. Peter,* occurred in a scene of heaven-on-earth.

The prototype of this scene is elaborated in what is often thought to be Ives' greatest song, *General William Booth Enters Heaven.* It was written on September 26, 1914 following the "Guns of August" outbreak of World War I, when Ives was about to turn forty. Ives' creative decline has sometimes been attributed to his disillusionment concerning the war; there can be no question that it had a profound effect upon him in several important ways. But the sweep of his life history, in particular the significance of this fourth decade, should be considered. "General Booth" will not be discussed in any detail at this time, but several observations should be made. The text, excerpted from the Vachel Lindsay poem, depicts Booth leading the poor, unwashed legions ("with the ways of Death"), the leprous and crippled, and the martyred saints and degraded sinners alike into heaven. There, Jesus himself ("...from the courthouse door...") blesses them, and they "...Marched on spotless, clad in raiment new./The lame were straightened, withered limbs un-curled,/And blind eyes opened on a sweet new world." Here again Ives grasps the opportunity to construct a musical image of an afterlife. It is an "American primitive" view of the resurrection, and Ives proves equal to it with his characteristic use of American hymn tunes and the subtle transformation of what is essentially a march. In its musical proportions, "Saint Peter" is writ large while at the same time remaining folk-like: It is Jesus himself who holds forth, not at the pearly gates, but in any New England town's courthouse square. The music is full of the band figures familiar to Ives from his childhood, including the "piano-drum" writing he associated with his father's Danbury Band, and even glimmers of the band's "roll-off" introduction as the motley mass, renewed, gets under way. *Reveille* is quoted in the voice line at the climax of a fervent prayer meeting superimposed musically on the Lindsay text, and the work closes with a somewhat asymmetric setting of the words to the hymn tune, *Cleansing Fountain*. Ives evidently considered General Booth to be in a class by itself and it was not included in the *114 Songs* which has con-cerned us so far.

At this point, a word about the general form of the volume of *114 Songs* is in order. Taken as a whole, it is work which is essentially autobiographical. It is chronological, but it starts with the end and ends with the beginning. The above mentioned *Evening* (#2) was to have been the first song in the collection and, having been among those specifically prepared for this volume and dated 1921, it would have been among the last written. Perhaps Ives meant it to be the very last, as it ends on a somewhat recondite quotation of Beethoven's "Les adieux" theme (from Opus 81). Thus the volume would have *begun* with the valedictory theme which characterizes one group of songs. Several of these songs were written in 1921, and were characterized by the fervently, often religiously optimistic "answer" noted earlier. Years later Ives regretted that, against his "better judgment", he had felt provoked to change this intent. He was so angry at the "stupid or unfair" judgments of his music by the "old ladies" that he felt "just mean enough to want to give the 'old girls' another ride—and then, after they saw the first page of *The Masses* as No. 1 in the book, it would keep them from turning any more pages and finding something 'just too awful for words, Lily'..." (1972, p. 127). And, indeed, the volume opens with the massive tone clusters of *The Majority* (#1) which has a shocking and aggressive appearance on the page itself!

Were Ives to have carried out his original intent, however, the collec-tion would have opened with the recent *Evening* and ended with one of his earliest songs, the *Slow March* (#114), quite literally a funeral march written when he was 13 or 14 following the death of the family dog. It already reveals some of Ives' stylistic characteristics: quotation, (here, the *Dead March* from Handel's *Saul*), the use of various types of marches, and the use of music to express memorialization. The dignified elegance of Milton's *Evening* contrasts curiously with the homespun sentimentality of the boy, Charles Ives.

Milton: "Now came still evening on, and Twilight gray had in her sober livery all things clad; Silence accompanied; for the beast and bird—They to their grassy couch, these to their nests were slunk . . . ."

Ives: "One evening just at sunset we laid him in the grave; Although a humble animal his heart was true and brave. All the family joined us, in solemn march and slow, from the garden place beneath the trees and where the sunflowers grow."

This earliest piece also reflected Charles' lifelong collaboration with his father, George, into whose notebook it was copied (Kirkpatrick, 1960, p. 157). That Ives would have started his collection with a late piece and ended with his first is similarly characteristic, reminiscent of his hero Thoreau, who wrote of the "true husbandman" finishing the day's labor and ". . . relinquishing all claim to the produce of his fields, and sacrificing in his mind not only his first but his last fruits also." In addition, in the overall form of this important, culminating work, Ives performs a major manipulation of time. In effect, he reverses the clock.

There are three other important Ives works in which questions and answers assumed prominence in subtle ways. Two are for theater or chamber orchestra (a flexible combination and a favorite of Ives), *The Pond* (Ives, no date, a) and *The Unanswered Question* (Ives, no date, b); and one a movement of the *Fourth Violin Sonata* (Ives, 1942), an earlier version of which had been called, *Children's Day at the Camp Meeting* (which subsequently served as subtitle). Interestingly, these three works were all composed around 1906; as we shall see, this may be meaningful.

The "question" in *Children's Day* is as apparent as it is in the songs; in fact, the third movement is a treatment of a song, a hymn by Robert Lowry called *Beautiful River* (1942, p. 19). It was one of several musical quotations in this sonata evocative of the tender memories Ives had of the boyhood camp meetings in which his father played such an important role as village musician and leader. Ives concludes this movement (thus the entire *Sonata*) with a *repeat* of the first phrase of the song corresponding to the question of the text, "Shall we gather by the river?" Thus, in the straightforward rhetoric of the question-and-answer form that the musical phrase implies, there follows no answer at all—no resolution, no ending; silence prevails (Ex. 6). Implied, however, *is* an answer, latent in the silence of the unresolved phrase and in the song's unsung words of affirmation: "Shall we gather at the river/Where bright

EX. 6   IVES, Sonata No. 4, Violin and Piano, ending

angel feet have trod/With its crystal tide forever flowing by, the throne of God./Yes, we'll gather at the river/The beautiful, the beautiful river/Yes, we'll gather at the river that flows by the throne of God."

Here we may observe an expectable counterpart of Ives' continuous relationship with his internalized father; namely, the question of what is the fate of the relationship *after* life. If, in intrapsychic life, the object is immortal, a portion of its mental representation must include its post-life potential. Reunion is prominent among the various fantasies which this mechanism may engender. At odds with the accomplishment of mourning in which, for Charles Ives, musical composition played so large a role, was his persistent conscious longing for his father. The natural consequence of this longing was the psychological "loophole" provided by unconscious fantasies of immortality and reunion, derivatives of which inevitably found representation in his music.

In *The Pond,* another chamber piece of 1906, related references are both richer and subtler. Here, in its original form—it is a "song without words"—in which the actual words are written in below the lead line. The latter (which *may* be sung, however) is scored for trumpet or basset horn, two of George's instruments. There is manifest reference to his father in Charles' words, "A sound of a distant horn, O'er shadowed lake is borne—my father's song." *The Pond* is also to be found as one of the *114 Songs,* retitled in the Index as *Remembrance* (#12). Here it is dated 1921, the original chamber version having been 1906. In lieu of a title, on the printed page a couplet by Wordsworth appears: "The music in my heart I bore/long after it was heard no more." (Ex. 7.)

Ex. 7   IVES, *Remembrance*

There are remarkable features in this brief work. (It occupies only 11 measures in printed full scores; reproduced here as Ex. 7.) For one, the "sound of the distant horn" is rendered literally with the spatial features emphasized in an echo. Distance is represented not only in space but in time, as the melody played by the trumpet (or basset horn; or vocalized) is repeated in canon a measure later by the echoing flute. Distance is emphasized in the instructions provided on the orchestral score: "PPPP (as in distance)." Similarly, on an earlier sketch (crossed out by Ives, characteristically using the same piece of manuscript paper, now upside down, for a sketch of something else) Ives scribbled: "cornet (in distance) taps etc." (Kirkpatrick, 1960, p. 24). Indeed, at the close of the piece the first notes of *Taps* are heard in the distance.

The tune itself is a rendition of a melody slowed beyond recognition. *Kathleen Mavourneen* is an Irish love song about parting and death: "Kathleen Mavourneen, the grey dawn is breaking. The horn of the hunter is heard on the hill (beginning) . . . It may be for years, and it may be forever; Then why art thou silent, thou voice of my heart? (ending)."

This Irish song had achieved extraordinary popularity after its composer (an Englishman, F. N. Crouch) came to the United States in 1849. It was published by thirty different music houses and sung widely during that fine period when George Ives was village musician and Charles the admiring youth. It had even captured the imagination of James Whitcomb Riley who wrote an imitative poem which served both as a tribute and a sequel. ["Kathleen Mavourneen! thy song is still ringing." It ends with the ". . . yearning refrain: The old vision dims, and the old heart is breaking—Kathleen Mavourneen, inspire us again" (Fitzgerald, 1901, p. 160–165).]

The foregoing gives an impression not only of the quality of affect characteristic of a particular time and place (mid-nineteenth century America) but of the association of idea and affect with music. The music may then represent both by encoding affect and idea within its nonverbal medium. This musical sealing of affects associated with time and place may assume greater significance by its association with persons. I would suggest that in the above instance a tune is associated with Charles' earliest experience with his father. In this sense, music may be said to incorporate a memory.

The memorializing function of music has received scant attention (Feder, 1980; Pollock, 1975). The above considerations raise the twin questions of whether art in general and music in particular are human endeavors that are highly adaptable for purposes of memorialization. The general thesis has been well demonstrated in its relationship to object loss (Meyer, 1972; Neiderland, 1975, pp. 2467ff.). With regard to the special instance of music, I believe it is *uniquely* related to object loss as well as a unique way of expressing and serving as a memorialization. A full discussion is beyond the scope of this study, but one important feature should be noted: the singular relationship of music to time. Music is the form of art most immediately concerned with the process and organization of virtual time. As such, it may relate to all dimensions: past, present, and future.

The examples we have found in Ives' music so far, as well as those to follow, are particularly good instances of what I believe may be encountered often in music. In *The Pond,* within the condensed scale of time afforded by music, present and past are intimately juxtaposed. Thus, as suggested above, objects may be represented in terms of memory and at other times, in concrete, symbolic terms. For example, in the context of Ives' manifest references to his father in *The Pond* plus those derived from interpretation, might the tune itself with its purely auditory presentation rendered by his father's instrument represent his father? If so, the canon, the imitation, may be said to represent himself, the pair progressing through time in parallel, but generational, fashion. On the crossed-out manuscript sketch mentioned earlier, Ives had written, "Echo piece!!" The echo, as if a mirror in time, relates not merely objects but, more specifically, objects in time. Moreover, future is involved as well as expectation being aroused. Thus, in a skillful organization and manipulation of time, the composer fuses past and future within a highly condensed immediacy of the present. As such, the piece looks chiefly to the past and to the reconciliation of the present with the pain of object loss. Insofar as it is a reproducible, hence enduring, artistic object, there inheres a potential future. This kind of memorialization involves then a more realistic future than the images of afterlife we have found side by side in the music of Ives that involves the "question and answer" form.

It is of interest that in the echo of *The Pond* we have a highly concrete representation of question and answer. Its most abstract and highly developed form may be seen in Ives' most epigrammatic question-and-answer piece, *The Unanswered Question*. The two pieces, written around the same time and sharing certain stylistic features, contrast sharply in certain aspects. Both create an "other-wordly" impression. However, *The Pond* contains mundane, domestic, references which are either manifest or yield readily to analysis. The other world of *The Unanswered Question* is remote, austere, and abstract. While instruments are personified in Ives' program (e.g., "The Fighting Answers" below), they lack the warm human qualities of *The Pond* in word and tone. If the first is the other world of the wishful believer, existing somewhere, perhaps just within reach, the second is the world of the cool agnostic.

The Unanswered Question was probably written in the summer of 1906 (Kirkpatrick, 1960, p. 44). The stylistic features it shares with *The Pond* are similar to those of the *Premonitions* of 1918 with which this essay began. These are for small chamber orchestra, and in all a typical Ivesian style prevails, one characterized by a reflective mood and epigrammatic musical statement. Clusters of polytonal harmony or, alternatively, diatonic chords may be deployed as if they were "washes" in a painting. A sense of timelessness is induced through various rhythmic devices, and the spatial features of the musical idea receive particular emphasis. As already noted, in two of these three there is an associated text; but there is no text in the most enigmatic of all, *The Unanswered Question*. However, in a postface Ives did provide detailed directions for its performance, virtual program notes and a philosophy as well (no date, B). The essential musical ideas are condensed within the first line of Ives' sketch. (The chief motif appears as musical epigraph to this study.)

A description of the piece by Henry Cowell (1955) merits quotation. It incorporates the above (the language mostly Ives') as well as Cowell's own listener's response. (Cowell had been Ives' late-life friend and musical executor and, along with his wife Sidney Robertson Cowell, Ives' first biographer.)

> One of Ives's most spectacular achievements is the invention of a form which logically uses consonance and dissonance in a single piece; this occurs in the music for small orchestra called *The Unanswered Question*. The orchestra is divided, the strings playing very softly throughout offstage, representing the silence of the seers who, even if they have an answer, cannot reply; the wind group, on stage, is dominated by the trumpet, which asks the Perennial Question of Existence over and over in the same way, while "the Fighting Answers (flutes and other people)" run about trying in vain to discover the invisible, unattainable reply to the trumpet. When they finally surrender the search they mock the trumpet's reiteration and depart. The Question is then asked again, for the last time, and the "silence" sounds from a distance undisturbed.

> Silence is represented by soft slow-moving concordant tones widely spaced in the strings; they move through the whole piece with uninterrupted placidity. After they have gone on long enough to establish their mood, loud wind instruments cut through the texture with a dissonant raucous melody that ends with the upturned inflection of the Question. At first the Question is asked briefly and infrequently, the quiet strings emerging in between; but the Question soon becomes more insistent, louder, longer, oftener heard; and it arouses more and more dissonance in the other wind instruments each time. When the dissonant voices disappear, the faint consonant chords continue to hum softly in the distance, like the eternal music of the spheres.

Probably this is Ives' most frequently performed orchestral work. It should be noted that the "orchestra" for which this composition and those discussed earlier (*Premonitions, The Pond*) was what Ives called a "theatre orchestra" the makeup of which depends "on what players and instruments happened to be around." He was fond of these combinations of "smaller towns and cities" and noted warmly that the "pianist usually led—his head or any unemployed limb acting as a kind of Ictusorgan" (Ives, 1972). Actually *The Unanswered Question* is one of a pair of complementary 1906 chamber pieces which were first titled as follows (Kirkpatrick, 1960, p. 45).

> I   "A Contemplation of a Serious Matter"
> or "The Unanswered Question"

II   "A Contemplation of Nothing Serious"
      or "Central Park in the Dark in 'The Good Old
      Summer Time.'"

Ives, at 32, approaching an earlier turning point in his life than that of
1918, shared an apartment dubbed "Poverty Flat" at 65 Central Park
West with several friends. This pair of "Contemplations" constitute a
kind of antithesis, the "Question" other-worldly in program and in
sound; "Central Park," although similar in sound, in program firmly
temporal—in Ives' words, a "picture in sounds of . . . happenings that
men would hear some thirty or so years ago (before the combustion
engine and radio monopolized the earth and air), when sitting on a bench
in Central Park on a hot summer night."

An appreciation by Hitchcock (1977) designates these works as important precursors of the "stereophonic and collage techniques" as well as
other advances of more recent composers. In particular, he notes the
handling of the time elements in music: " . . . 'time' in the usual musical
sense [rhythm, meter, pulse, etc.] does not exist; the only time-sense is of
the chronological continuum, and the music simply unrolls in it—like a
scroll in space, at once plastic and concrete" (p. 81).

The trumpet theme itself (quoted as musical epigraph to this paper)
identified by Ives as "the Perennial Question of existence," incorporates
question *and* answer in the detail of musical motif—cosmos in musical
microcosmos. Following the entrance of the trumpet on B-flat, the rising
musical inflection of the motif C-sharp—E, is "answered" in the higher
octave with another but comparable interval, E-flat—B-flat, in inversion
and mirror image. The phonetic inflection of a question may be dis-
cerned in the disposition of the notes of this motif. At the same time it is
as close a graphic representation of a question mark as could be notated
on music paper. The disposition of off-stage strings as well as the "layering" of discrete musical groups constitute spatial effects in this counter-
temporal context which were characteristic of Ives.

A relationship between 1906, the year of the "Contemplations," and
1918, the year of *Premonitions,* may be sought in the mundane facts of
Ives' medical history. In 1906, when Ives was 32 and a decade into what
he considered to be his most productive period, he developed a severe
cardiac illness. Retrospective diagnosis is difficult, and medical records
have thus far been unavailable. However, his business partner, Julian
Myrick, relates: "Ives had something like a heart attack as early as 1906,
I believe. Apparently he had had something there for a long time, and I
think it was diagnosed then. We had a medical department in Mutual
Life, and he used to go to them. They recommended that he go for a
rest..." (in Perlis, 1974, p. 36). Myrick accompanied Ives to Old Point

Comfort, Virginia, where they spent the Christmas holidays of 1906. It was a year prior to a partnership in the insurance business which was to make Ives financially secure. In the course of that year, Ives resolved to marry Harmony. Also it was the year of the season of their *Spring Song* (discussed earlier) which led to their marriage in June, 1908. A creative period ensued in both business and music (especially from 1910 on) which the Cowells assert was his most energetic time. It continued until his heart attack in 1918. Harmony actually felt that this creative phase had already started in 1906. In any event, the dozen years between 1906 and 1918 were of the greatest importance in Ives' creative life. At its boundaries were the two cardiac episodes preceded by the composition of the mysterious and unique *Unanswered Question* in the first episode and by *Premonitions* in the second.

Although thoughts related to the perennial question of life and death cluster around these two events—these "omens," with creative activity their issue—Ives was not death-haunted as were other artists, for example his European contemporary, Gustav Mahler. There are two interesting parallels between Ives and Mahler which, in turn, point to an important contrast. First, both resolved to marry following a life-threatening illness. I have discussed elsewhere (Feder, 1978) how Mahler's precipitous decision to do so was related to his bid for "the common immortality of man," the desire to have children. One may reasonably surmise that this theme played a role in Ives' life, considering his deep attachment to his father and the importance of family throughout his life. A second parallel was the enduring involvement each had with his own childhood. In contrast, however, Mahler was preoccupied with death or, at very least, concerned with death in a different manner. Mahler, more conflict-ridden and symptomatic, suffered from anxiety, while Ives was concerned less with anxiety than with affects associated with mourning. His father, George Ives, was at the center of this, and, *pari passu,* a time and a place closely associated with him: post-Civil War Danbury and Charles' boyhood with his father. Thus his work has the mark of the celebration of life and a nostalgia for the past which engenders a certain faith and optimism. Within such a context and in the face of a growing awareness of and resignation to the inevitable, wishes for a future life may flourish in the form of fantasies of immortality and reunion.

DISCUSSION

Ives, in his own comments "In Re:...'The Unanswered Question'" (no date, B), writes that the "Perennial Question of Existence" is stated "in the same tone of voice each time, But the hunt for the 'Invisible Answer' undertaken by the flutes and other human beings, gradually more active, faster and louder...The 'Fighting Answerers,' as time goes on...seem to realize a futility, and begin to mock 'The Question'—the strife is over for the moment. After they disappear, 'The Question' is asked for the last time, and the 'Silences' are heard beyond in 'Undisturbed solitude.'" The program to its more temporal companion-piece, *Central Park in the Dark,* ends similarly: ". . .—again the darkness is heard—an echo over the pond—And we walk home."

The "question," specified as "perennial," is apt, for it introduces the element of the continuing, the enduring, the recurrent, and the cyclical. At its center are the twin mysteries of birth and death, first experienced by the child and later persisting in conscious fears and unconscious fantasies which become modified by life's experiences. With the loss of objects and object love, insult is added to injury by the threat of one's own death. Psychic representation of this state of affairs is reflected in all forms of ideation and human activity, often most prominently in the arts. Music, however, by virtue of its overt, non-representational nature tends to elude interpretation.

The life and work of Charles Ives serve us handsomely to attempt this kind of interpretation at the same time as we try to interpret through his work the content of his inner life. With Ives, there was great consistency in the character of his work, his music, and his love relationships. While this should not seem surprising in many individuals, a certain openness and lack of guile tends to make this consistency more apparent in Ives than it might be in many other artists. This also corresponds to the autobiographical nature of his work and is fostered by a particular style which is rationalized perhaps in a Transcendental philosophy of unity. "The fabric of existence," Ives wrote, "weaves itself whole" (Cowell, 1955, p. 97). All of these trends are made manifest in a typical Ives "artifact" which may be at once a page of musical manuscript (hence a guide to the performance of those acoustic forms we call music) and, at the same time, a diary, a reminiscence, a document of personal history, a secret collaboration with past objects (or a conscious one with current objects), and, finally, the representation of fantasy in word and tone.

In certain of Ives' works, a cluster of ideational elements emerge which center on a "question" most epigrammatically, if mystically, put in *The Unanswered Question,* but identifiable in other configurations. The content of this complex includes the sense of mystery itself, general notions relating to death and birth, and more organized fantasies of rebirth, reunion, and immortality. Representation is achieved extramusically in verbal, literary, even spatial terms, and, musically, through those normal, non-objective means characteristic of music. Thus the "question and answer" form itself, as developed above, may serve to represent one or another aspect of this cluster—an idea, an affect, a fantasy, even a memory. A brief reconsideration of some of the works discussed may bring this into focus.

Among the songs: 1) In *Premonitions* (text Johnson) the spectre of death threatens and denial serves to mobilize a fantasy of rebirth tonally elaborated with forward motion and an opening gesture beckoning a future life. 2) In *Immortality* (text Ives) outrage at the reality of death and faith in the essential immutability of God's creations is expressed and annotated musically with associations related to St. Peter. 3) In *Disclosure* (text Ives) and 4) *Spring Song* (text Harmony Ives) respectively, evening awaits sunrise, and winter, the spring—each with appropriately detailed musical devices. Similarly, 5) *Evidence* (text Ives), in which we are assured of an everlasting sun which can penetrate the shadows. The "still" and "but" of the text is reflected in the handling of musical motive. In *Evening* (text Milton), the wakeful nightingale perseveres through the night in the text, while in the music his song is superimposed upon the reference to "Les Adieux."

In the chamber music, these ideas are elaborated more subtly. In the *Fourth Violin Sonata,* a childhood memory of children's day at the camp meeting is evoked in the song *Beautiful River.* There is no traditional cadence and the piece ends with a question, an unresolved silence which invites the listener to participate in closure by inwardly providing the missing phrase which affirms, "Yes," we'll gather by the River!" The alternative is silence.

Silence is also brought into the foreground in various ways in *The Pond* and the two "Contemplations." At the end of the latter, in "Central Park", after all the night-sounds subside, Ives writes in the program, "—again the darkness is heard—an echo over the pond...." As in Freud's *Theme of the Three Caskets* (1913), silence may represent death but not necessarily a death without compassion: in one example, Cordelia who "remains dumb...loves and is silent" (p. 294). At the close of *The Unanswered Question,* the trumpet intones the question a final time and the "silences," writes Ives, "are heard beyond in 'Undisturbed Solitude.'" In the carefully contrived silence in which *The Pond* ends, the tiny voice of a piccolo plays the opening of *Taps.*

There are significant spatial features in all of these chamber pieces. In the most literal sense, Ives was endowed with an acute sense of place. The spaces of his boyhood had a magical and tender quality for him, and he wrote and spoke of them with reverence: Main Street, the Village Square, the Camp Meeting. His musical references to these places range from honorable mention in the songs to entire movements; such as the *Three Places in New England.* Nostalgic feelings for past places tend to foster wishes for future places in the form of heavens and utopias. Involved here is a cyclical view of time which facilitates fantasies of rebirth. The "perennial question" may be answered in fantasy. In its most naive form, there is a "place," a heaven, a gathering at the Beautiful River by the throne of God. As indicated such wishes are to be found represented in the music, but Ives also expressed them in other ways. (He was deeply interested in utopias of various kinds, and it would be difficult to say whether this was the result or the cause of his interest in the New England Transcendentalists.) His longest single essay, *The Majority* (1961), was written during the same period of time (1919–1920) he wrote what I have called his final trilogy. It is best left unsummarized in few words except to stress its utopian content and tone. On a practical level, Ives strove constantly for a "better world" with efforts which ranged from letters to leading political figures such as President Wilson and Governor Coolidge (regarding a twentieth amendment), to generous financial support for the quarterly *New Music,* to everyday charities such as the Fresh Air Fund. (His generosity in this charity ultimately led him to Edith's adoption.) It may seem that we have drifted from a discussion of the spatial features in music with reference to boyhood places, heavens, utopias, politics, and charity—but only if one fails to take into account the mind that conceived the music.

In *The Pond* the prominent spatial features are of a different nature. Ives' "stage directions" indicate sections to be played off-stage to give the effect of distance and, in particular, "the echo over a pond." This sort of effect is not only associated with George Ives' musical-spatial experiments but in another, more literal sense, with Ives' father: In the text Charles writes of "my father's song". It is indeed rendered by his father's instrument, for the trumpet takes the "vocal" lead as George might have in camp meetings. In what is probably the earliest sketch, written on a half-page scrap of music paper, the instrument is made even more specific: the "Cornet in A" (Ex. 7). If the musical reference to *Kathleen Mavourneen* has overtones which seem too erotic, it can be noted that in the field manual for military trumpet and drums the words for *Taps* are given as follows: "Love, good night,/Must thou go, When the day/And the night/Need thee so?/All is well./Speedeth all/to their rest" (Safranek, 1916, p. 131). Across the pond there is a sense of someone there by the use of an echo. The projection of one's voice results in its audible return. Ives himself was the "echo" of his father, whose presence in this piece and in his life is acknowledged with unabashed sentiment. As I have suggested, it was Ives' internalized collaboration with George which enhanced his musical creativity. Transformed into a song, *The Pond* appears in the *114 Songs* as *Remembrance;* indeed it is a small masterpiece of mourning, and the transformations and limitations of mourning.

Spatial features also prevail in the pair of "Contemplations" in the second of which, *Central Park in the Dark,* one again hears the sound of music across the pond among the sounds of the past. However, it is in the companion-piece, *The Unanswered Question,* that we find the most abstract spatial expression and, in contrast to "General Booth" and "Children's Day," the least literal and naive pictorial (not musical) representation. Here, the very motif uncurls a musical question mark in which there is already a musical question and answer. In *The Unanswered Question* the statements are metaphysical, and, once again, the coexistence of other places and other states is acknowledged. Finally, time itself is obliterated. In this sense, *The Unanswered Question* stands in contrast to the musical idea of time elaborated in *Premonitions* with which we began these considerations. In that piece, a pause in the normal progress of time is occasioned by the shadow of death in life. Portentous chords follow first, marking time and then creating a quickening forward thrust into the future. Thus an image of time is rendered in *musical* time. In *The Unanswered Question,* the image of time lacks both impetus and direction. A *timeless* state prevails in which neither life nor death has significance; a fantasy of peaceful eternity prevails.

*   *   *   *   *

In these considerations of word, music, form, space, and time, we encounter man attempting to come to terms with universal human conditions. Object love and loss and one's own life and death are continuous challenges. In essence, these constituted the unanswered question for Ives.

As experienced the "question" defies articulation: "What is life; what is death?" does it no justice; Similarly, with issues of the boundaries of life and the contemplation of fantasied states before or after death. Of such experiences, the question, "What is existence" may be a pale translation. Attempts at objectifying such states may contribute to cultural or personal eschatologies; for example, naive notions of heaven or more sophisticated transcendental solution. Ives' personal philosophy incorporated both.

Perhaps the limitations of wording such "questions" stem from the same source that led Freud to his oft-cited dictum that "...it is indeed impossible to imagine our own death; and whenever we attempt to do so we can perceive that we are in fact still present as spectators...or, to put the same thing in another way, that in the unconscious every one of us is convinced of his own immortality" (1915, p. 289). Whether or not this is strictly the case I would suggest that, to say the least, secondary process *verbal* articulation of such states fall far short of effective definition and representation. Indeed, it is "dumbness" itself that "is a common representation of death in dreams" (Freud, 1913, p. 295).

Accordingly, that medium of communication which can best incorporate elements of silence and time may well provide the most appropriate and effective means of representation of fantasies of death, afterlife, and the progress in time of life itself. These questions, profound yet vague, which may even sound sophomoric in their verbal form, achieve a more gripping significance and compelling immediacy in their 'translation' to auditory representation through musical form. I believe this is Charles Ives' achievement in *The Unanswered Question.*

That Ives was extraordinarily endowed as an artist and that his gift was further enriched through his identification with his father made it only natural that his very human concerns would emerge in music—in text and context and, above all, in its forms *sui generis.* As Ives wrote in some notes about a *Universe Symphony,* "...yet these elements as man can touch them with hand and microscope . . . They are not single and exclusive strains, but incessant myriads, for ages ever and always changing growing, . . . of life and death, and future life—the only known is the unknown . . . " (Kirkpatrick, 1960, p. 28). The "question" is, of course, fundamentally unanswerable. What may be more significant is the fullest appreciation of the question. It may serve as a stimulus for many of life's endeavors. Whether from the points of view of anxiety or grief, trauma or mourning, it exacts a working through which is manifest in the way a life is led. Inevitably it influences the quality of the products of a life, artistic products in particular. In this sense, we may say that Ives' "answer," for all its human limitations, was a very effective one indeed.

EPILOGUE: SUNRISE

The "song we knew by rote," which faltered in the *Premonitions* of 1918, was stilled completely within the next few years. The *Sunrise* of 1926, written when he was 52, was Ives' last statement in music. Ives was to survive until he was nearly eighty. There were illnesses to cope with but also an honorable retirement from business (in 1930) and continued involvement in what the Cowells call "the career of the music," that is, in its dissemination and performance. In spite of the self-criticism of both the words and music of *Sunrise,* they show a remarkable consistency with the ideas which had so occupied him throughout his creative life. The words alone convey this: the vague doubts of a "question" yielding to a hope dimly viewed at first but then bursting into hopeful anticipation:

A light low in the East,—as I lie there!—it shows but does not move—, a light—, a light—as a thought forgotten comes again. Later on as I rise it shows through the trees and lights the dark grey

rock and something in the mind, and brings the quiet day. And
tomorrow a light as a thought forgotten comes again, and with it
ever the hope of a new day. (Ives, 1926)

EX. 8   IVES, *Sunrise,* ending

A burgeoning figure (Ex. 8) which characterized *Premonitions* (Ex. 3),
a musical idea characterized earlier as the representation of "a new
birth"is found for the last time in *Sunrise*. The persona of the text,
recumbent at first, rises hopefully to meet the future. At the same time
the sound and sense of the poem reflect that "faith in a resurrection and
immortality" of the final passage of Thoreau's *Walden* (1962, p. 266).
Ives had written in the *Essays,* "...my Thoreau—that reassuring and true
friend, who stood by me one 'low' day, when the sun had gone down,
long, long before sunset" (1961, p. 67). The day was Sunday, November
4, 1894, when George Ives died suddenly in Danbury. The comfort Ives
found in Thoreau that day is reflected in *Sunrise* where the sense and
cadence suggest the closing words of *Walden* (which serve as an epigraph
to this essay).

BIBLIOGRAPHY

COWELL, H. & COWELL, S. (1955). *Charles Ives and His Music.* London, Oxford, New
York: Oxford University Press.
FEDER, S. (1978). Gustav Mahler, dying. *Internat. Rev. Psycho-Anal.,* 5, Part 2:125–148.
_____ (1980). Decoration Day: A boyhood memory of Charles Ives. *The Musical Quar-
terly,* LXVI, No. 2:234–261. New York/London: G. Schirmer.
_____ (1981). Charles and George Ives: The veneration of boyhood. *The Annual of
Psychoanalysis,* Vol. IX. New York: International Universities Press.
FITZGERALD, S. S. A. (1901). *Stories of Famous Songs.* Vol. 1, Philadelphia and Lon-
don: Lippincott.
FREUD, S. (1913). The theme of the three caskets. *S.E.,* 12:29–301. London: Hogarth
Press, 1955.

_____ (1915). Thoughts for the times on war and death. *S.E.,* 14:273–300. London: Hogarth Press, 1955.

HITCHCOCK, H. W. (1977). Ives. *Oxford Studies of Composers,* 14. London: Oxford University Press.

IVES, C. E. (1922). *114 Songs,* Redding, Conn. Reprinted 1935, Merion Music, Bryn Mawr, Pa.

_____ (1926). *Sunrise.* Pencil sketch, 4 pgs. (as described by Kirkpatrick, 1960, p. 212), Yale University Library.

_____ (1933). *34 Songs.* New Music, Vol. 7, No. 1, San Francisco.

_____ (1942). Sonata No. 4 for Violin and Piano, "Children's Day at the Camp Meeting." New York/London: Associated Music Publishers.

_____ (1961). *Essays Before A Sonata, the Majority and Other Writings by Charles Ives.* Selected and edited by H. Boatwright. New York: Norton.

_____ (1972). *Charles E. Ives—Memos,* J. Kirkpatrick, ed. New York: W. W. Norton.

_____ (no date, a). *The Pond.* Photostat of Full Score; 5 pages with Postface (as described in Kirkpatrick, 1960, p. 44), Yale University Library.

_____ (no date, b). *The Unanswered Question* for Flute Quartet, Trumpet and String Quartet (or String Orchestra). Photostat copy of Full Score; 5 pages with Postface (as described in Kirkpatrick, 1960, p. 51), Yale University Library.

KIRKPATRICK, J. (1960). *A Temporary Mimeographed Catalogue of the Music Manuscripts and Related Materials for Charles Edward Ives 1874–1954.* New Haven: Library of the Yale School of Music.

MEYER, B. C. (1972). Some reflections on the contribution of psychoanalysis to biography. In *Psychoanalysis and Contemporary Science,* R. Holt and E. Peterfreund (eds.). Vol. 1, New York: MacMillan, pp. 373–391.

NEIDERLAND, W. G. (1975). Psychiatry and the creative process. In *Comprehensive Textbook on Psychiatry/*II, A. M. Freedman et al. (eds.). New York: Williams and Wilkins, pp. 2462–2471.

PERLIS, V. (1974). *Charles Ives Remembered, An Oral History.* New Haven and London: Yale University Press.

POLLOCK, G. H. (1975). Mourning and memorialization through music. *The Annual of Psychoanalysis* 3:423–436. New York: International Universities Press.

ROSSITER, F. R. (1975). *Charles Ives and His America.* New York: Liverright.

SAFRANEK, V. F. (1916). *Complete Instructive Manual for Field Trumpet and Drum.* New York: Carl Fischer.

THOREAU, H. D. (1962). *The Variorum Walden.* Annot. W. Harding. New York: Twayne.

TWEEDY, H. H., (ed.) (1939). *Christian Worship and Praise.* New York, London: Harper.

WOOLDRIDGE, D. (1974). *From the Steeples and Mountains—A Study of Charles Ives.* New York: Knopf.

ACKNOWLEDGMENTS

Examples 1, 2, 3, 4, and 5 used by permission of Theodore Presser Company. *Thirty Four Songs* by Charles Ives. Copyright 1933 Mercury Music Corporation. Also, courtesy Yale University Music Library.

Examples 6 and 7 used by permission of Assocciated Music Publishers, and Yale University Music Library.

Example 8 used by permission of C. F. Peters Corporation.

Example for musical epigraph used by permission of Yale University Musical Library.

Figure 10.1   *Chromological biography of Charles and George Ives*

Charles (1874–1954)		George (1845–1894)	
		b. 1845,	Danbury, Connecticut
		Age	
		15	Serious musical study
		17	Youngest Union band-master
		20	Ill, discharged from Army Study in New York City
		23	Return to Danbury as vil-lage musician
		29- 30	Start of creative musical experimentation Marriage
b. 1874,	Danbury, Connecticut		Birth of Charles
Age			
16 mos.	Birth of Moss	30- 31	Birth of Moss
12-13	First compositions; *Slow March*	40	Part-time work as account-ing clerk in hat factory Decreasing musical activity
14-15	First musical jobs, or-ganist Earliest performances of works		
17	Danbury Academy		
19-20	Hopkins Academy (preparation for Yale) Tension with George	47	Full time—Danbury Bank Gives up professional music
20 (1894)	Matriculation at Yale Organist, Centre Church, New Haven Death of George	48- 49 (1894) 49	Tension with Charles d. November 4, 1894 Danbury
24 (1892)	Graduates Yale "Poverty Flat" (until age 34) Starts work, Mutual Life Insurance Co.		

25	Starts parallel part-time composition—First creative decade To Raymond & Co. (insurance); Meets Myrick
27-28	Organist, Central Church, New York City (Last paid work in music)
32 (1906)	First cardiac episode *The Pond* (later *Remembrance)* *The Unanswered Question* (one of two "Contemplations") *Children's Day* (later, *Fourth Violin Sonata*) Courting Harmony Twitchell Start of second creative period: "Experimental" (H.T.I.)
33 (1907)	*Spring Song,* words by Harmony
34 (1908)	Marriage Start of second creative decade (C.E.I.)—to 1918
35	Establishment of Ives and Myrick Harmony Ives miscarries *Like a Sick Eagle*
38	Buys property at Redding (nr. Danbury)
40 (1914)	Outbreak of W.W.I Fortieth birthday *General William Booth Enters Heaven*
42 (1916)	Adopts child, Edith (age 2)
43 (1917)	U.S. enters war

(Charles, *continued*)

44 (1918)	*Premonitions* Heart attack Start of final creative period Preparing "Concord" sonata and essays
45-46 (1919-1920)	Work on *114 Songs* Publication of *Concord Sonata* (written between 1909-15) and *Essays Before A Sonata* (completed, edited)
47 (1921)	*Immortality* *Two Little Flowers* *Evening* (last of *114* composed)
48 (1922)	*114 Songs* published
49-51 (1923-1925)	(a few songs)
52 (1926)	*Sunrise,* final composition Told Harmony "...couldn't seem to compose any more...'
53 (1927)	First contact with Henry Cowell and start of interest in *New Music* quarterly and the "career" of his own music
79 (1954)	d. New York City

11

In Pursuit of Slow Time:
A Psychoanalytic Approach to
Contemporary Music

GILBERT J. ROSE

The experience of time has become drastically different from what it was previously. As during other disturbed periods in history, there is pervasive, random violence, meaningless death, and bankrupt faith. Man has long known dread of total destruction, of course, but never its actual feasibility. What is further unprecedented about the contemporary dread of extinction is the speed, range, and scope of the instruments of destruction. While previous ages had a wider margin of time to buffer the unpredictability of life, and powerful religious ideologies to rationalize the seemingly senseless, our own age is largely lacking in both.

It would be impossible to prove that such a profound change in our temporal experience is reflected in contemporary music. On the other hand, music being the art of time, as well as in the avant garde of cultural sensibility, it is plausible to assume it. As Susanne Langer wrote (1942), music is subjective time made audible. Utterly unlike clock-time with its tremendous useful advantages, musical time has volume, complexity, and variability. It is a representation of the emotional quality of lived time.

We might expect that the change in our experience of time should also be reflected in clinical practice, which is a mirror of subjective experience. May we learn something about music or clinical practice by putting them side by side? More specifically, can contemporary music help sensitize us to clinical nuance? Can psychoanalysis throw light on contemporary music?

There are many difficulties that stand in the way of trying to explore these matters. First is Freud's attitude towards non-literary art. While he admired creative writers, he had little use for non-representational painting, dismissing the German expressionists, for example (in a letter to Otto Pfister), as "lunatics." After an evening in an artist's company, he wrote to Jones (1957, p. 412): "Meaning is little to these men; all they care for is line, shape, agreement of contours. They are given up to the *Lustprinzip*."

As for music, his indifference to it to the point of aversion was perhaps as heretical, in a city like Vienna, as his calling attention to infantile sexuality. He told James J. Putnam that he had no ear for it. According to Jones (ibid), with few exceptions (which ones he does not mention), music afforded him hardly any pleasure at all. It is said that as a youngster he insisted that his sister's piano be removed because her practice interfered with his study. His son Martin relates that none of Freud's children ever studied a musical instrument.

The question has been raised whether in his indifference to music and non-representational art, and his opposition to certain cultural forms such as religion, Freud may have been manifesting not only his commitment to "science" and rationality but also his *denial* of significant areas of experience, such as the mother-child relationship (Fuller, 1980, p. 166). Be that as it may, his tastes in art may well have had something to do with projecting such matters beyond the scope of psychoanalytic research and indirectly setting the reductionist tone of much subsequent applied psychoanalysis.

At the beginning of his paper, "The Moses of Michelangelo," Freud (1914, p. 211) states that the reason he is "..almost incapable of obtaining any pleasure..." from music is that he is unable to "explain" to himself the effect music had upon him. Aside from the defensive, clinical implications of this remark, such need to explain the effect music has on one before allowing oneself any pleasure from music may go to the heart of a basic problem of dealing psychoanalytically with art: the relationship of language to non-verbal experience. Nietzsche remarked (in *The Birth of Tragedy*) that art must be seen as the necessary complement of rational discourse. This is quite different from "understanding," let alone "explaining," in discursive language the aesthetic experience of non-verbal art. In my opinion, to depend on language as the key to open the lock of non-verbal experience breaks the key off in the lock, destroying both.

Though he knew from the outset that the relationship was a complex one, Freud tended to link art with the primary process and neurosis, on the one hand, and verbalization with the secondary process and health, on the other. Perhaps his epochal discovery that the pictorial aspects making up the manifest dream could be "read" like a rebus to unlock the meaning of the latent content led him to assume that painters, too, painted scenes that could just as well be expressed in words. This is not true. Delacroix is said to have remarked that a painting that can be thus "explained" is not worth painting. More recent thinking about the continuum between the primary and secondary processes, the ubiquity of the primary process and its capacity to undergo development into advanced thought (metaphor, music) bears out the complexity of the inter-relationships that Freud always insisted upon (Rose, 1980).

Two works that bear directly on the difficult area of the relationship of language to non-verbal art are artist-analyst Marion Milner's (1957), *On Not Being Able To Paint,* and music philosopher, Victor Zuckerkandl's (published posthumously, 1973), *Man The Musician.* Both make a clear distinction between formal, logical thinking, on the one hand, and creative or aesthetic thinking on the other. According to formal logic, all thought which does not make the total separation between what a thing is and what it is not is irrational. Thus, according to formal logic, the whole area of symbolic expression is irrational, since the point about a symbol is that it is both itself and something else. Formal logic, then, gives a false picture in aesthetics; this false picture is only avoided, Milner writes, "...if we think about art in terms of its capacity for fusing...subject and object, seer and seen and then making a new division of these..." (p. 161).

Similarly, Zuckerkandl spells out the differences between objective hearing, on the one hand, and musical hearing, on the other. He writes that the "I" that hears music is different from the "I" who is the subject of a sentence, who is going to attend to outside signals in order to react to them one way or another. The "I" who listens to music is more like the swimmer who allows himself to be carried by the water as he swims. Language, being firmly tied to subject-object-predicate structure, fails us here. The "I" that listens to music is no longer something that "does," that is, hears and now "has" the results of what it has done, namely the sensations of tones. Hearing music involves not only hearing tones but also their direction, tension, motion, organic structure. It is the kind of hearing that moves with the tones and draws the hearer into their motion. Thus, it involves an interpenetration of subject and object, within rationality, drawn into the experience of the movement of felt time (Zuckerkandl, 1973, pp. 160–162). (The similarity to psycho-analytic listening is so striking as to require no comment.)

Both Milner and Zuckerkandl make clear that aesthetic hearing or viewing is more like creative, non-logical thinking; also, that they both are quite different from objective perception and cognitive, logical thinking. The difference lies in the opposition between subject and object—their separateness—in the case of cognitive, logical thinking, and the togetherness of thinker and thought—their mutually influential motion—in aesthetic, creative thinking.

Milner summarizes the problem neatly: "Clearly the great difficulty in thinking logically about this problem is due to the fact that we are trying to talk about a process which stops being that process as soon as we talk about it, trying to talk about a state in which the 'me-not me' distinction is not important, but to do so at all we have to make the distinction" (p. 161).[1]

The justification for such a lengthy introduction to a brief contribution is to try to clear a little space in two ways: (1) by frankly pointing to the effects of Freud's limitations in the area of non-verbal art, and (2) by acknowledging the limitations of language in this field—in order to begin to approach it with language, of course, but hopefully with renewed sensibility.

As representatives of modern music I have somewhat arbitrarily selected Charlie Parker's bebop jazz and Arnold Schoenberg's twelve-tone atonal music. What they both have in common is that, as they reflected a new experience of time, they also contributed significantly to altering the musical experience of time. The clinical vignette which I hope may throw some light on the psychological meaning of this has to do with a woman who mistook her appointment, thinking it was one hour before, at 3:00 P.M. instead of actually at 4. She then came fifteen minutes late for the imagined appointment, slept in the waiting room, and left fifteen minutes before the actual appointment was ready to begin. As I hope to show, she was uprooting time from its usual matrix in a way somewhat analogous to certain aspects of modern music. First to Charlie Parker and Arnold Schoenberg.

Bebop style of the '40s and early '50s represents a startling break from preceding jazz styles, and one which still causes consternation among today's jazz listeners. Ron Rose, in an unpublished ethnomusicological paper on bebop jazz, maintains that the musical changes brought about by the bebop movement strongly reflected the changing black self-image in America. I am indebted to him for what follows on bebop.

> Dixieland had its childhood in New Orleans. It became refined into the smoother and more "literate" styles in the years to follow, reaching its height of polish under the rule of the big band style, where improvisation (the original tenet of jazz) became the exception rather than the rule . . . Bebop . . . appears to be a clear and

---

1. Any verbal separation of the world leads to some truth, some falsehood. The essence of Zen Buddhist enlightenment refers to the overcoming of perceptual and conceptual division of the world into categories. It struggles against the reliance on words through the use of koans which abuse words and set the mind a-reeling. Cf. also, the opening of the *Tao Te Ching*: "The Tao of which we speak is not the real Tao."

unsubtle black rebellion against the white dominated swing scene, as well as the historically established caricature of the black entertainer as mindless and officiously amusing . . . The bebop musicians were intent upon creating a music which would allow a complete break from its "iliterate" black predecessor, and their white competitors. The music itself . . . with its difficult chord changes and rhythmic bridges, often executed at breakneck speeds, helped keep the movement "pure" of musicians not entirely competent, as well as create a new standard for the white establishment.

The leader of the bebop movement was Charlie Parker. Most contemporary jazz musicians consider him one of the major innovative forces in the history of jazz. Perhaps his major contribution was his conception of the musical phrase as both tied to, yet, at the same time, free from the limitations of meter. Specifically, while the musical phrase had previously been restricted to the bar-lines, he extended it through the bar-lines. This means that, as soloist, he would sometimes speed up, sometimes slow down, to bring the melodic line "out of sink" with the underlying metric foundation. This was all the while being provided reliably by the other instruments. The relationship between the melodic line and the rhythmic pulse was thus rendered much more ambiguous; it was no longer bound to the down-beat. Instead of classic syncopation with its stress on up or down beats, melodic emphasis could now be placed on any division of the beat on a sixteenth and thirty-second note level. This led other jazz musicians to experiment with unorthodox meters, fragment the beat until the meter became indiscernible, or blur the distinction of the downbeat much as a twelve-tonist avoids the concept of a tonic.
    In short, Parker's restructuring of pulse into what might be called a fluid meter superimposed upon a metric foundation turned the rhythmic conventions of Western popular music on end. One far-reaching effect was the shifting of functions of the other instruments. The beat could now be displaced to the lighter cymbals, freeing the drum to become a most articulate instrument on its own. The same might be said of freeing the pianist's left hand.
    Just as Parker's rhythmic innovations loosened the relationship between the melodic line and the underlying beat, Arnold Schoenberg's twelve-tone scale had already freed musical harmonics from the concept of the tonic. This also had far-reaching effects on the musical experience of time. A brief excursion into elementary musical theory is necessary to show how.
    A musical scale describes the relationship among the tones making up the musical organization of a culture. It is a system of order among tones. In Western culture the scales are based on the physical phe-

nomenon of overtones making up the harmonic series. The starting
point or tonic tone in the key of C is C; the tonic tone in the key of G is
G, etc. The main overtone of the tonic is five tones away, and is called
the fifth, or dominant. The main overtone or dominant of C in the key of
C is G. One may move from the key of C to its main overtone, G, and
then take that as the starting point, or tonic, of the key of G. One may
move on in the key of G to its main overtone or dominant, D, and the
key of D; thence to its main overtone or dominant, A, and the key of A;
thus on to the keys of E, B, F#, and ultimately back to C, completing the
circle. This moving from one key to another from tonic to dominant
makes possible a circle of fifths. It is based on the underlying organization of the scale, namely, a stable relationship of tonics and dominant
which is based on the universal *physical* phenomenon of the harmonic
series of overtones.

A second point: because of the tonal organization of the Western
scale, the tones strive in certain directions. They have driving qualities.
These driving qualities of the tones of a scale account for one of the main
ways in which music sets up a current of motion, a system of expectancies. For example, the tonic tone of any key is the one of ultimate rest
and stability towards which all other tones tend to move. Thus, tones
that come before lead one to expect that certain tones will come after;
this is so even though, in order to build up tension, this motion or expec-
tancy may be delayed in various musical ways. Listening to tonal music
feels like the natural experience of time flow to Westerners because it is
learned so early, but it is far from universal. (The conception of time is
quite different among certain peoples of Asia, Africa, and our own
Southwest.)

Now, if one could set up a series of tones which was lifted out of the
gravitational pull of tonics and dominants, the overtones of the harmonic series, we would no longer be in a secure circle of fifths, going
from one key to another in an orderly way. Any single tone would no
longer carry implications for where it came from or where it was going.
In other words, we would be taken out of the ordinary flow of time—
from past to expected future.

Essentially, this was what Schoenberg did with his twelve-tone scale. It
represents a whole system based on rootlessness from the harmonic
series. The twelve tones and their sequence are selected in such a way that
no tone has any implications for what tone preceded it or what tone may
follow it; much of the directedness of tones has been rendered in-
operative. Each of the tones can be played forward, backward, in
mirror-image, or backward and mirrored. Since there are twelve tones in
the Schoenberg system, we now have 48 possible sequences. All of them
alter the ordinary experience of time as we know it in the West—not, it

must be stressed, by tampering with time directly, i.e., through rhythmic changes, for example, but through changes in the tonal system, setting up ambiguous expectancies.

In addition to these changes in tonality which modify our expectancies of what will follow what musically, in much of the music of the twentieth century there is a deliberate dissolution of the ordinary sequential flow of musical events as we have come to know it. Instead of a musical event in a composition depending on at least one previous musical event in order to build up to a climax or resolve tension, each musical event arises independently. For example, the sections of a piece of music may be put together in any possible sequence from one performance to the next with no set beginning or ending. Instead of development and recapitulation as we used to know it in sonata form, for instance, a piece of music in so-called "vertical time" does not purposefully set up expectations or fulfill any that might arise accidentally. The listener is forced to give up any expectation, any implication of cause, effect, antecedents or consequents. Young listeners who have learned to enter "vertical time" revel in the sounds unhampered by referential meaning. It has been compared to looking at a piece of sculpture: each viewer is free to walk around it, view it from any angle, in any possible sequence and linger as long or as briefly with each, leave, return, whatever. In "vertical time" there is nothing to direct the way time passes (Kramer, 1981).

In other words, in the new temporalities in music, past and future have been collapsed into a present moment which floats in uncertainty. There being no impulsion from the past, the over-arching present leads to no-future. More than this: the bond tying cause and consequence together has been loosened and meanings are cast adrift.[2]

Not only music, but art and literature have been foretelling and mirroring such a picture of the world for decades. Take art: if discontinuity is the key to the new temporalities in music, fragmentation describes much of art history after the turn of the century and before World War II. Cezanne fragmented the image; the cubists fragmented shape; the impressionists and pointillists, light and color; the surrealists, reality itself.

After World War II, abstract expressionism and then minimalist painting rejected three-dimensionality as well as all imagery or symbolism which might permit any conventional meaning to be read into these

---

2. Having stated this boldly for the sake of clarity, it is now necessary to add that experienced listeners to contemporary music insist that while at first it may sound random, expectancies inevitably emerge and order the musical experience—even that of John Cage. Thus has it ever been with innovation. What is at first disturbingly new becomes even comfortably familiar. The dialectic between new and strange, on the one hand, and good old familiar, is inherent in any organically evolving process.

paintings. Instead, oversize canvases and large expanses of color draw the viewer "inside" the canvas, "enclosing" him. With some painting one is drawn through the skin of paint between successive gauze-like veils of color so that the viewer feels suspended within some interior, timeless space. The sense of enclosure and oneness is the visual counterpart of the auditory immersion into the "vertical time" of some contemporary music. Just as in the painting there are layers of color and light which draw one into a timeless space, in some "vertical time" music there are layers of dense sound; relationships take place between the layers of simultaneous sound, rather than between the successive events which take place in conventional linear music. "The result is a single present stretched out into an enormous duration . . . that nonetheless feels like an instant." (Kramer, 1981, p. 549).

When it comes to contemporary literature, one finds analogous discontinuities and fragmentations, resulting in a similar prolongation of the present moment lifted out of the flow of past-to-future. In the six years since her work first began to appear in *The New Yorker,* Ann Beattie has become for many readers the representative young American writer. Here are some of the things she said in an interview with *The New York Times* (with Joyce Maynard, May 11, 1980):

Beattie: I don't know how to write a novel . . I would like to take a course on that sometime, if I ever take another course . . . It's very hard for me to work on Monday and Tuesday, and on Wednesday I wonder what I said on Tuesday, let alone what I'm moving toward . . . That's why all the chapters jump around. I can't think how somebody would move from one to the next, so I have to take a breather and hope that I come up with something . . . I certainly listen to records a lot. But if I write a story I tend to put on what my husband is playing on the stereo at that moment . . . just what's on the turntable . . . I really love the notion of found art. Warhol soup cans—that kind of stuff. When I write something, I like to look out the window the night I'm typing and see what kind of moon it was on July the 15th and put it in . . .

Interviewer: "Do you write about the relationships between men and women?"

Beattie: I just assume that there are going to be moments. But when I start to write it isn't with the thought

that I want to communicate about the relationship between men and women. I think, "I'd really like to work that interesting ashtray I just
bought into a story about men and women . . ." I
read a lot—mostly modern fiction, nothing before 1960 if I can help it. I'm a great time waster.
See what a shiny coat my dog has? I go buy him
vitamins. I rap with him. I brush him.

Interviewer: And did you actually know somebody who did
what the two lovers in "Falling In Place" did,
during the early days of their relationship—hold
hands uninterruptedly for two days?

Beattie: Yes—four days. They've split up now.

Alienated adolescents and their middle-aged followers, in their addiction to the present timeless moment, "freed" from past history and
future plans, whether or not enhanced by the use of drugs, are current
clinical manifestations of a pervasive cultural phenomenon: the experience of time is radically different from what it has been.

Does our clinical perspective give us an inkling as to the significance of
this change? Let us return to the woman who came late for an appointment she did not have, slept, and left before her actual appointment was
due to start. While not "removed" from the flow of time from past to
future, this was surely a slippage—whether one thinks of it as backward
or foreward—a slippage in the ratcheting of the cogs of time. Let me tell
you more about her and the clinical situation.

I had seen her years before in analysis. She was now 47, and had asked
to come in for a few sessions. We greeted each other warmly. She sat
down and smiled. I asked how she had been. She struggled with her
features and said, "Since Nancy was killed it hasn't been the same," and
burst into sobs. Shocked, I blurted, "What!?" Nancy was her daughter,
and she would now be about 22. The manner of her breaking the news
was not incidental, as we shall see. The story now unfolded.

Indeed, her 22-year-old daughter had been killed instantly in a car accident one year before. The patient had managed to continue all her activities but experienced a numbing disconnection from her feelings. Not
mourning her daughter, she felt, was like holding onto her, not letting
her go. She had only recently begun to weep, and this brought some relief
from her own sense of deadness.

She had entered analysis originally saying that she rarely knew what
she was feeling; whenever she was under stress she would disconnect
herself from her feelings and hide inside. In this way she could fight off
depression and "keep moving and smiling." Convent upbringing had

taught her it was more important to maintain a prayerful attitude than seek to understand many things. She had cultivated a vague fogginess as a defense against sexual and aggressive impulses. This was modelled partly on her mother. Mother was remembered mostly for her bland smilingness and the way she cultivated stereotyped dialogues to handle any situation. Father was a powerful political figure whose family life was characterized by towering rages and emotional withdrawal. Neither parent ever exchanged a single word with her after she had married outside the Church. She had been temporarily expelled from the family in adolescence for always getting into "trouble" though she was not sure what it was. She of course knew there was a past but the quality of herself in it was not available to her, and when it was it was like remembering the feeling of having had a nightmare but not knowing what it was about. She had married a driving man who became very successful. She married him to get herself "organized" by him and play out the roles he assigned her. She did this very well and was known as a sophisticated hostess, responsive friend, generous volunteer worker for good causes, and a natural athlete. A few close friends also knew that she was very bright and had a discerning literary and musical taste and had graduated with high honors at a top college. She experienced modified analytic treatment as the only calm relationship she had ever known and the first time she had allowed herself to feel she was taking something for herself instead of being selfless.

The clinical vignette relevant to our discussion has already been related. It was easy to imagine that it represented a conventional resistance of ambivalence to talking about painful matters, but the form it took seemed unusual.

At the next session when we discussed what had happened I asked, on the basis of what I knew about her from the past, whether having come late for an imagined appointment and having left before a real one was a way of expressing something about wanting to reverse what was real and unreal. Whether this was wrong or irrelevant, her answer in any event led elsewhere. She said that repeatedly when she met someone she had not seen for some time, the other person would "surprise" her by asking innocently and casually about her daughter, that the patient would then have to say her daughter had died, that this would always come as a shock to the other person and the patient would have to soothe *her* down. I said it seemed surprising that it always came as a surprise to her that someone should ask innocently about her daughter and how come she did not anticipate this and somehow try to cushion the news and shield both of them from the shock. She replied that everything seemed to come as a surprise to *her* nowadays, *she* was just never ready for anything. For example, although she had been an excellent tennis player, now every time the ball came to her it seemed to come from the blue; because she did not keep her eye on her opponent's movements she could not anticipate where the ball would come to her and as a result her return would always be late.

I wondered if she might be turning every moment into a kind of shock and a surprise, ripping each moment out of its context in the flow of time, and in this way perhaps continuously repeating, actively, the traumatic moment when she was informed of Nancy's death. As for coming early and leaving early before her appointment was due to start, we might speculate that it was a way of dislocating time—in order to correct and master it—of saying, "If only it had been an hour earlier, or later, Nancy would be alive now."

One might wish for more data regarding this vignette, particularly the role of transference. But since the episode of the missed appointment arose out of a brief contact many years following the termination of treatment it is not possible to comment on the role of unresolved transference. Before dismissing the matter for insufficient data (as one might if this were in the context of an ongoing psychoanalysis), we might ask whether, in the context of an interdisciplinary communication, there may not even be some advantage notwithstanding.

I refer to the role of reality. The unavoidable omission of transference in this vignette necessarily directs our attention to that earliest of psychoanalytic problems, the question of trauma and one's reaction to it. We know that random, meaningless violence can destroy both the sense of self and reality. Somewhat less drastically, reality may be denied and disavowed. Interrupting the flow of time from past to future is another means of altering the impact of reality—uprooting the connection between cause and consequence.

What mechanisms, however, help to master and defend against a reality which, while well recognized, flies in the face of common sense and logic? The patient of course understood very well that a head-on collision led to her daughter's death, but this bears so little relation to sense that the mind recoils from such "meaning" as absurd. If it cannot totally sever cause from consequence, past from future, it can at least defensively *modify the experience of time flow*—slowing it down, speeding it up. Is this what the patient was doing in coming late for an appointment she did not have and leaving early for one she did? Or in being too slow in meeting her tennis opponent's return, too slow in preparing the ground for breaking the news of her daughter's death, too quick in always blurting out the news as she did?

If this seems tenable, we might ask whether such temporal manipulation to deal with past and anticipated trauma is more widespread than usually recognized. Is the fragmentation, discontinuity, and "timelessness" which characterizes so much contemporary art a defensive cultural response to the fear of sudden death which, though largely disavowed, pervades our age?

As previously discussed, some of the new temporalities of music represent even more drastic attempts to cool the flow of time—actually to separate each moment from its historical context, deal with each like rootless tones, without implications, in the discontinuous Now. Thus, in the words of the folk ballad: "We'll make a space in the lives we've planned/And here we'll stay,/Until it's time for you to go./Don't ask why,/Don't ask forever,/Love me now." (Buffy St. Marie)

If we were to accept the hypothesis that it was the sudden shocking death of her daughter that led the patient to defensively modify her experience of time flow, could we make a parallel hypothesis about some contemporary music? In short, the question is: should some aspects of modern music and of current clinical phenomena be bracketed together as defensive alterations in the experience of time—attempts to modify and thus "master" its inexorable passage?

The immediate musicological answer might be: "No. The new temporalities in music represent (1) experimentation, (2) reflecting the gradual absorption of music of different cultures (for instance, the Javanese gamelan), (3) making use of technological innovations like radio, records, electronics and tape-splicing." (Kramer, 1981, pp. 543–544)

Yet, all this being true would not negate one possible meaning of this musical experimentation: like the patient's reaction to sudden, random death, the new temporalities in music may still represent a deeply felt need to suspend time, to deal with the possibility that any succeeding moment might fracture conventional sense and flood the self. In other words, just as my patient experienced a defensive alteration in her sense of time in response to the life-threatening unpredictability of daily life, some contemporary music (and art), perhaps in similar response to shared anxieties of the age, dissolve familiar frames of reference—temporal (and spatial).

Whatever the cause, it would be misleading to dismiss such apparent dissolutions of familiar structures as simply regressive. It is a frequent analytic finding that a temporary dissolution of structure may be a prerequisite for further development. Thus, in the case of my patient, if what she went through were to lead to further growth, or in the case of music or art, it is to be an aesthetic experience, such partial dissolution is regularly followed by a redifferentiation of the self (Rose, 1980).

This two-phase process—partial dissolution and reconstruction—occurring in rapid oscillation, appears to be central to the aesthetic experience. Much slowed down, it also describes the process of growth. We observe it, too, in that particular form of growth we call psychoanalysis, and refer to it there as an alternating movement of therapeutic regression and working through, losing and refinding the self, emotional reliving and thoughtful reflection. We might conclude, in agreement with John Dewey (1934), that the aesthetic experience is continuous with the normal processes of living; more specifically, that there is a *biological* component to the aesthetic experience, and an "aesthetic" dimension accompanying growth.

It may well be objected that neither clinical nor cultural data warrant sweeping conclusions and that alternative interpretations are possible. With this I agree, but respond that the thrust of my remarks is directed elsewhere: to noting some parallels in form between contemporary music and psychoanalytic practice. Just as psychoanalysis can deepen our responsiveness to non-literary contemporary art, the latter can sensitize us as practitioners to myriad aspects of form, including, as I have tried to show, temporal form. At least one thing seems certain: there is much to be learned from either side as equals, without reverence or reductionism.

BIBLIOGRAPHY

FREUD, S. (1914). The Moses of Michelangelo. *S.E.,* 13:211–238. London: The Hogarth Press, 1955.

FULLER, P. (1980). *Art and Psychoanalysis.* London: Writers and Readers Publishing Cooperative.

DEWEY, J. (1934). *Art As Experience.* New York: Minton, Balch.

JONES, E. (1957). *The Life and Work of Sigmund Freud,* Volume III. New York: Basic Books.

KRAMER, J. (1981). New temporalities in music. *Critical Inquiry,* University of Chicago, Spring 1981:539–556.

LANGER, S. (1942). *Philosophy In A New Key.* New York: New American Library, 1948.

MILNER, M. (1957). *On Not Being Able To Paint.* New York: International Universities Press.

ROSE, G. J. (1980). *The Power of Form. A Psychoanalytic Approach to Aesthetic Form.* New York: International Universities Press.

ROSE, R. D. (1980). An ethnomusicological look at Bebop Jazz. Unpublished.

ZUCKERKANDL, V. (1973). *Man The Musician. Sound and Symbol.* Volume II. Princeton: Princeton University Press.

Author Index

Subject Index

A

Access Samadhi, 203, 204–205, 206
Acting-out, 11, 12n, 30, 32
Adaptation
  to flow of internal experience, 200–201
  in Freud's religious view, 129–130
Adoption, in Eskimo society, 64–65
Advanced Insight Group in meditation,
    Rorschachs of, 189–197
  classic psychological changes in, 209–217
Affective fallacy, 301
Aggression
  control of, 70
  limiting effect of, 324
  socialization against, 66–68
Ahistoricism of Freud's religious view,
    127–130, 132–133
Animism, 118
Anxiety
  castration, 12, 19–21, 22, 49
  paranoid, 9
  uncontrollable development of, 31
Anyi
  marriage customs, 45
  mother-child relationship of, 31, 32, 33,
    48–49
Art, non-literary, Freud's attitude toward,
    353–355
Art, non-verbal. See Music, contemporary
Artist-audience relationship in Genet's
    works, 301–320
  analysis, 312–318
  examples of, 306–312
Associative elaborations, 180, 181, 184–187
  styles of, 185–186

Atoms, 294–295
Attention
  bare, 170
  deployment, 165, 167
Attentional training, 201
Attitudes
  culture-specific, 12n
  toward law, 54, 71–72
  projective-animistic, 20
Author-audience relationship. See Artist-
    audience relationship in Genet's works
Authoritarianism, in religious movements,
    94–95
Authoritarian personality, 95
Authority
  figures, 9, 35
  outside, 78–79, 80
  repressive, 48
Automaton, concept of, 240–241
Awareness
  "choiceless," 170
  on different levels, 212
  in Enlightenment, 209–214
  in stages of insight, 205–208
  in stages of samadhi, 203–205
  training, 167

B

Bare attention, 170
Barefoot, B., 106–107, 108
Beginners Group in meditation
  criteria for, 176
  Rorschachs of, 179–180
    classic psychological changes in,
      199–202